CHINA'S ECONOMY

WHAT EVERYONE NEEDS TO KNOW®

CHINA'S ECONOMY

WHAT EVERYONE NEEDS TO KNOW®

Second Edition

ARTHUR R. KROEBER

OXFORD
UNIVERSITY PRESS

OXFORD
UNIVERSITY PRESS

Oxford University Press is a department of the University of Oxford. It furthers the University's objective of excellence in research, scholarship, and education by publishing worldwide. Oxford is a registered trade mark of Oxford University Press in the UK and certain other countries.

"What Everyone Needs to Know" is a registered trademark of Oxford University Press.

Published in the United States of America by Oxford University Press 198 Madison Avenue, New York, NY 10016, United States of America.

Library of Congress Cataloging-in-Publication Data
Names: Kroeber, Arthur R., author.
Title: China's economy : what everyone needs to know /
Arthur R. Kroeber. Description: [Second edition]. |
New York, NY : Oxford University Press, [2020] |
Series: What everyone needs to know |
Includes bibliographical references and index.
Identifiers: LCCN 2020007946 (print) | LCCN 2020007947 (ebook) |
ISBN 9780190946470 (hardback) | ISBN 9780190946463 (paperback) |
ISBN 9780190946494 (epub)
Subjects: LCSH: Economic development—China. | China—Economic
policy—2000– | China—Economic conditions—2000–
Classification: LCC HC427.95 .K76 2020 (print) |
LCC HC427.95 (ebook) | DDC 330.951—dc23
LC record available at https://lccn.loc.gov/2020007946
LC ebook record available at https://lccn.loc.gov/2020007947

1 3 5 7 9 8 6 4 2

Paperback printed by LSC Communications, United States of America
Hardback printed by Bridgeport National Bindery, Inc., United States of America

CONTENTS

PREFACE

Why This Book?

This book is an effort to explain how China's economy got to where it is today, where it might be headed in the coming years, and what China's rise means for the rest of the world. It is intended to be useful to the general reader who has an intelligent interest in China and its global impact but not necessarily a specialized background in either China or economics. Since the first edition was published in 2016, China's relevance to the world has increased dramatically, thanks to the assertive foreign policy of President Xi Jinping and the move by the United States under the Trump Administration to treat China as a geopolitical rival. Because of its sheer size, the growing tensions with the United States, and the gulf in basic values between China and the international system, it increasingly seeks to expand its influence, understanding modern China's origins and trajectory is more important than ever.

An economy is a complicated organism that does not easily lend itself to description by narrative, as one might tell the story of a person's life. It is more like a jigsaw puzzle—to be precise, a three-dimensional jigsaw puzzle in which the shapes of the pieces keep changing. Rather than a fixed structure like a molecule, a skyscraper, or a mathematical equation, an economy is a set of fairly solid institutions and fairly fluid arrangements created by people to enable them to get the goods and services they want. The nature of these institutions and arrangements is largely determined by the political bargains made among the important groups in a society. As the composition, relative power, and interests of these groups change over time, so do the economic arrangements. In other words, considerations of political practicality usually trump those of economic efficiency. For economic policymakers, this means that they must make do with second- or third-best versions of their ideal recipes. For analysts, it means that describing an economy is more of a historical art than a natural science. To the extent it is a science, it is more physiology than physics.

China is also a complicated organism. It is arguably the oldest state in the world, whose geographic core has been governed almost continuously by a rationalist bureaucracy since the late sixth century c.e., when the famous examination system was established. The centuries of accumulated knowledge about the craft of running an enormous, nominally centralized but practically quite fragmented polity doubtless continue to play an important role in the country's political and economic governance. Any outside observer should start with a measure of respect for the durability and resourcefulness of this governing ethos. At the same time, the nation of China as we know it today is quite young, dating from the establishment of Communist Party rule in 1949, and both its political organization and economic development strategy were based on extensive borrowings from abroad. Knowledge of the parallels and precedents of Soviet Russia and the neighboring "developmental states" in East Asia are essential to understanding how China got to where it is.

Proceeding from these biases, I have organized this book to touch on all of the major topics needed to gain a comprehensive understanding of how China's economy works and why it is built the way it is. At the same time, I will sketch out the main currents of its evolution since 1979, when Deng

Xiaoping inaugurated the period of what he called "reform and opening" and what I and most other analysts loosely refer to as the "reform era."

The first three chapters set the context by summarizing why China's development is important for the world today and laying out the country's key historical, geographical, and political economy features. Chapters 4 through 6 describe the sectors of economic activity—agriculture, industry, and the construction of cities and infrastructure—that were successively most crucial to China's economic development story between 1980 and 2020. Chapters 7 through 10 analyze what one might call the "nervous system" of the economy: the organization of business enterprises and the financial, fiscal, and energy systems. Chapters 11 through 13 attempt to bring the discussion down to a more human level by describing changes in demographics and the labor market; the emerging consumer economy; and the social problems most likely to upset the central political bargains, namely, inequality and corruption.

The last two chapters return to the stratosphere and take on the two large questions that dominate current public debates about China. Chapter 14 examines China's chances of making a successful transition from the "resource mobilization" type of growth it has enjoyed since 1979 to the "resource efficiency" type of growth that is now required. The final chapter assesses what China's rise to economic power means for the rest of the world.

To fit all this material into the confines of a book succinct enough to enlighten readers without burying them under a hail of data and qualifications, I have naturally had to simplify a great deal, although I hope not in a way that will cause specialists to cringe. A particular peril of this sort of work is that it can leave the impression that China's economic development has been the working out of a master plan designed in advance and supervised at every point by wise officials with exact knowledge of the consequences of all their actions. This is of course absurd: China's economic story was created by fierce battles between rival groups, decisions taken under emergency conditions with imperfect information, the belated and partial rectification of past errors, and the constant swirl of a billion people seeking personal advantage. Readers hungry for this sort of detail should consult the For Further Reading section at the end of the book.

ACKNOWLEDGMENTS

This book is the result of nearly three decades spent in and around China immersed in questions about China's economy and society. It could not have come to life without the help of many people, to whom I expressed my gratitude in the first edition. Once again, the principal thanks go to my past and present colleagues at the *China Economic Quarterly* and Gavekal Dragonomics, who have done much of the research that has guided my thinking and provided continuous intellectual stimulation over many years. Successive editors at Oxford University Press—Scott Parris, David Pervin, and James Cook—initiated and nurtured this project and provided superb editorial guidance. My children Susannah and Sylva have provided continuous inspiration and delight, and their fearless questioning of me (and everything else) at every turn has made me a better thinker, and a better person. Without the tireless support and good cheer of Elizabeth Knup, neither the first nor the second edition would have seen the light of day. Many other friends and colleagues have contributed knowledge and insight; any mistakes are all my own.

1

WHY CHINA MATTERS

Why should I care about China's economy?

In 1991, the Soviet Union collapsed and the Cold War ended. Until then, the single biggest force affecting global economics and geopolitics had been the rivalry between the United States and the USSR. Since then, a period spanning over three decades, the biggest global forces have been the rise of China and the technological revolution driven by personal computers and the Internet. Today those two forces have converged to create a new strategic rivalry: one between the United States and China, both vying for geopolitical and technological leadership. To understand this rivalry and the massive economic changes that led to it, it is crucial to know why China has been so successful, what position it occupies in the world economy today, and where it is headed.

China's economic rise is also a story about people—and not just Chinese people. China's long economic boom has raised the living standards of nearly a quarter of the world's population and has brought hundreds of millions of people out of poverty. And its ripple effects—positive and negative—have been felt in virtually every other country in the world.

Consumers have enjoyed the benefits of low prices of China's many mass-produced goods, ranging from the smartphones that people in wealthy countries use to run their lives to the motor scooters that people in developing countries use to get to work. Companies have found it hard to compete against low-cost Chinese firms and have had to adopt new product lines, move their production to China, or go out of business. China's hunger for commodities has pushed up the prices of oil, coal, iron ore, and copper. In addition, its huge amount of savings has helped keep interest rates low, enabling households, companies, and governments in many countries to take on more debt to fuel consumption and investment. Wherever you look in the world economy, it is almost impossible to figure out what is going on without understanding China's role.

How much has China's economy grown, and what does that mean for ordinary people?

China has an enviable growth record. From 1979 through 2011, its economy grew at an average real (inflation-adjusted) rate of 10 percent a year—easily the longest period of double-digit growth ever recorded. Since then, its economy has slowed a bit, but it still grew at an average rate of around 7 percent from 2012 through 2018, the fastest rate of any major economy during that period.

These numbers are impressive but a bit abstract. Their meaning is easier to understand if they are put in individual terms. Since 1979, China's GDP per person has grown at an average rate of about 8.5 percent a year. At that rate, income doubles every 9 years. The income of the average Chinese person is thus more than 30 times higher today than it was in 1979.

Put another way, in 1979, China's national income per person was under $200. This was less than one-tenth of the world average. China was by any reasonable definition a very poor country. Living standards for the average Chinese were not that much different than those in Afghanistan, Bangladesh, or many African nations. In 2018, however—just 40 years later—national income per person was about $9,400, or about 84 percent of the world average. China is now considered an "upper-middle-income country," with an average standard of living not much different from that in Brazil, Mexico, Russia, and most of eastern Europe.

In 1979, the vast majority of China's population—at least 800 million people—lived in what the World Bank calls "extreme poverty," meaning that they were able to spend no more than $1.90 per day in today's money. Today the number of those living in dire poverty is less than 10 million, with virtually all the reduction in the numbers of the extremely poor coming since 1990. At the same time, the number of Chinese people meeting an international definition of a "middle-class" lifestyle has risen from virtually zero to around 300 million. The number of middle-class Chinese now exceeds the *total population* of every other country in the world, except India and the United States.

And of course because these average income figures apply to China's enormous population of 1.4 billion people, the total size of its economy—and hence its international economic power—is much greater than that of countries with a similar standard of living. In 1979, China's total economic output was just 7 percent of that of the United States, even though China had about four times as many people. Today it is about two-thirds the size of the U.S. economy, and two and half times bigger than the next-largest economy in the world, Japan. Although projections are perilous, many economists expect that China could surpass the United States as the world's biggest economy around 2030.

How did China grow so fast and for so long?

We used 1979 as the starting date for analysis of China's growth because that was the year when China's leaders made a decisive pivot in its economic policy. Until then, the ruling Chinese Communist Party (CCP) had governed a socialist, planned-economy system in which the state owned virtually all assets and set prices for virtually all goods. This system, imposed by Mao Zedong and his colleagues in the 1950s and in part patterned on the Soviet Union model, achieved some successes, notably in spreading basic literacy and hygiene, and in establishing a good foundation for basic industries such as steel, coal, and petrochemicals. But it failed miserably in raising living standards for average Chinese people, and it left China far behind not just the United States and Europe, but also neighbors such as Japan, South Korea, and Taiwan, which had all grown rapidly after World War II and were well on their way to becoming solidly middle-class countries.

In December 1978, however, at a key meeting of the CCP's central committee, Deng Xiaoping emerged as China's top leader, ending a 2-year succession struggle after the death of Mao. Deng, then 73, had been one of Mao's comrades, going back to the 1930s. Deng was a general during the civil war that brought the CCP to power in 1949 and a senior leader for 16 years until he was purged during the 1966–1976 Cultural Revolution.

Over the next year, determined to break the pattern of isolation and backwardness of the Mao era, Deng launched a strategy known as "reform and opening" (in Chinese, *gaige kaifang*). The general aim was that China would *reform* its domestic economy by gradually reducing the role of the state and increasing the role of markets; and it would *open* to the outside world, welcoming ideas from other countries and inviting companies to invest in China and export China-made products to the world.[1] This was not so much a master plan for development as an announcement that the country was open to new ideas, experimentation, and business. At the beginning there was no detailed strategy: Deng and other leaders often described reform and opening as a process of "crossing the river by feeling the stones."[2] In retrospect, we can identify five main contributors to China's unusual success.

1. Successful application of the East Asian developmental state model

When China went looking for models of rapid industrial and technological development, it did not need to go far. By 1979, Japan had already vaulted past West Germany to become the world's second-biggest economy, and its companies were conquering global markets for steel, cars, cameras, consumer electronics, and many other goods. Following in its wake were South Korea, Taiwan, Hong Kong, and Singapore, all of which were rapidly industrializing and growing rich. All these countries had adopted some variant of what scholars later called the East Asian developmental state model in which strong governments channeled investment into infrastructure and export manufacturing, although private companies did most of the production. In many respects, China's post–1979 growth was simply the largest scale application of this time-tested recipe.

2. Successful post-communist transition

In 1962, development economist Alexander Gerschenkron introduced the concept of "the advantage of backwardness."[3] His idea was that a poor country could grow very fast for a long time simply by marrying the technology already developed in rich countries with its low-cost labor force. This kind of growth—which does not require much innovation—is called "catch-up" growth. Like the other East Asian success stories, China's involved a lot of this catch-up growth thanks to its large supply of rural workers who were willing to work in modern factories for relatively low wages. But China in 1979 also had another "advantage of backwardness": its economy was organized around the socialist principles of government ownership of assets and control of prices. Simply by gradually letting go of these state controls, China enjoyed a productivity boom as economic decision making shifted from crusty state bureaucrats to private and public actors who, driven by increasing market forces, tried to squeeze more productivity and profit out of the assets they controlled.

3. A unique political structure: both centralized and decentralized

Economic activity cannot be separated from—and in fact is substantially determined by—a country's political arrangements. China's political system is unusual, perhaps unique, in combining a high degree of formal centralization and actual decentralization. In theory, the central government in Beijing, controlled by the CCP, sets all policy, controls tax rates and revenues, and guides the economic ship. In practice, local governments at the provincial level and below have enjoyed great latitude in adapting (or even ignoring) central policies, setting local development priorities, and encouraging local businesses. This *de facto* decentralization enabled bottom-up local entrepreneurship to thrive and saved China from the rigidity and inability to adapt that doom centrally planned economies. But the central government's effective control over key economic levers, through the financial system and nationally organized state-owned enterprises (SOEs), meant it could build out critical national infrastructure far more rapidly than is usual in really decentralized countries. (Details on these first three factors can be found in Chapter 3.)

4. Favorable demographics

Contrary to a popular saying, demographics is not destiny— but it is important. Generally speaking, economies tend to grow faster when the population is relatively young and in particular when there are a large number of people of working age (15–64 as defined by demographers) relative to the number of "dependents": young people in school (ages 0–14) and older people of retirement age (65 and up). Growth tends to be especially fast when the ratio of dependents to working-age people falls. A period during which this "dependency ratio" falls is called a "demographic dividend"—a boost to economic growth that a country gets solely because of a favorable change in its population age structure. Between 1975 and 2010, China enjoyed an unusually large demographic dividend, as its dependency ratio fell by more than half. The abundance of productive workers, along with relatively modest requirements to fund the pension and health care costs of old people, did not cause China's fast growth. But it created fertile conditions for an economic boom. (A deeper explanation of the demographic dividend is given in Chapter 11.)

5. Being in the right place at the right time

Geography and historical circumstance have great impact on a country's ability to grow. China had at least three pieces of good luck in this respect. First, it was in a neighborhood—East Asia—which by the late 1970s was already very dynamic. Proximity to rich neighbors is a key determinant of economic growth, and in this regard China won the lottery.[4] Many nearby countries with successful companies were eager to invest in China to take advantage of its lower costs and gain access to its potentially huge market. Second, China chose to open up just at the moment when logistics technologies such as containerized shipping made it cost-effective for companies to split up production chains so that high-cost components produced in one country could be shipped to a second (low labor-cost) country for final assembly and then shipped to consumers in a third and often very distant country. In other words, China opened up right when economic globalization was beginning to go into high gear, and it was perfectly placed to become the final assembly hub for Asian production chains. (For details, see Chapter 5.)

Finally, China benefited from a cooperative relationship with the United States, even though it was nominally a communist country and the United States had a strong anticommunist stance. This was because, starting with President Nixon's visit to Beijing in 1972, the two countries decided that they should bury their differences in order to counter a common adversary, the Soviet Union. China continued to benefit from its special relationship with the United States for many years after the end of the Cold War. This relationship has now soured and is turning into an intense strategic rivalry (see Chapter 15).

What are the impacts of China's growth? Are they positive or negative?

China's economic growth has produced enormous effects both at home and abroad. In the most general terms, the net effect has been strongly positive: enormous wealth has been created, average Chinese people live far better lives than they did a few decades ago, and the rest of the world has benefited economically from China's increased demand for their goods and services.

When we look below the surface, however, the picture gets muddier. Within China, some groups and regions have prospered far more than others, and breakneck growth has generated many problems: inequality of income and wealth, corruption, and severe environmental damage. Society has also shifted massively: from a mainly agrarian one in which incomes were low but the state provided cheap access to basic services such as health care and education to a densely urban one in which the pressure to compete is intense, access to services is determined mainly by money, and traditional family and cultural ties have frayed. On balance, China's leaders have responded successfully to the social tensions wrought by rapid development (in part through political repression). But these tensions continue to proliferate and, if not managed carefully, could lead to political unrest or economic slowdown.

Turning to China's global impact, it is useful to divide the reform era into two periods. During the first period, from 1979 until the Asian financial crisis of 1997, China's growth was impressive but had little effect outside its own borders. This was partly because China's starting point was so low that it could grow fast for a long time before it accumulated enough purchasing power to start making its presence felt in big international markets. Another reason was that the most important reforms of the 1980s and 1990s had to do with reorganizing China's internal markets and gradually allowing the market to determine prices for a host of goods and services that had previously been tightly rationed, under prices set by the state. This meant that Chinese people were able to buy many products that had been unavailable before, so their standard of living rose. But neither Chinese people nor Chinese companies had much extra money to buy imported products or to spend or invest outside of China.

After 1997, this changed, dramatically. Some analysts would put the inflection point a few years later: in 2001, when China joined the World Trade Organization (WTO). While China's entry into the WTO was an important event, the foundations of China's world-shaking growth were actually laid earlier, and it is misleading to attribute all of what followed to the WTO export boost. In 1997, China teetered on the edge of an economic precipice, as a financial crisis engulfed its neighbors from Indonesia to South Korea, and its own state enterprises were virtually bankrupt, with debts to the state banks of over $200 billion that they could not repay. Beijing responded with massive reforms to its enterprises and banks, its first big national infrastructure program (an interstate highway system), and a privatization of urban housing that set the stage for the biggest real estate boom in world history.

All of these factors, plus the increased export competitiveness that came with WTO entry, transformed China's growth from something of purely local interest to a phenomenon whose effect was felt in almost every corner of the world. The impacts are illustrated by Figure 1.1.

This table tells a simple story. In 1997, China punched well below its weight. Even after nearly 20 years of rapid growth, its share of most indices of global economic activity was still far below its share of global population. But by 2017, its share

China share of global total of various indicators, 1997–2017			
	1997	**2017**	**China share of global increase 1997–2017**
Population	21.3%	18.7%	**9%**
Urban population	*15.4%*	*19.9%*	*28%*
Economic indicators			
GDP	3.1%	15.4%	**23%**
Investment	4.2%	26.5%	**41%**
Manufacturing value added	5.5%	23.6%	**40%**
Exports	3.2%	13.1%	**18%**
Manufactured exports	*3.9%*	*17.9%*	*26%*
Imports	2.5%	9.8%	**14%**
Official military expenditures	2.2%	12.9%	**21%**
Energy and environment indicators			
Primary energy consumption	10.5%	23.0%	**49%**
Oil imports	3.0%	14.1%	**34%**
Electricity production	8.1%	24.8%	**47%**
CO_2 emissions	13.7%	27.3%	**57%**
Financial indicators			
Foreign exchange reserves	9.0%	27.9%	**31%**
Stock market capitalization*	0.8%	12.0%	**15%**
Foreign direct investment flows (inbound)	9.4%	7.7%	**7%**
Foreign direct investment flows (outbound)	0.4%	4.9%	**6%**
Portfolio investment stock (inbound)	0.0%	1.5%	**2%**
Portfolio investment stock (outbound)	0.0%	0.8%	**1%**

* Includes Chinese companies listed in all global stock markets

Sources: World Bank World Development Indicators; BP Statistical Review of World Energy 2017; World Trade Organization; IMF International Financial Statistics; UN World Population Prospects 2017; UNCTAD; WIND; Gavekal Dragonomics calculations

Figure 1.1 Measuring the China shock.
China's share of the global total of various indicators, 1997–2017.

of many of these economic indicators was at least as high as its population share. And its share of the 20-year *increase* in many of these indices was enormous—especially in those indicators relating to physical production. Over the two decades from 1997 to 2017, China accounted for 40 percent or more of the global increase in manufacturing, fixed investment, electricity production, total energy consumption, and emissions of greenhouse gases (especially carbon dioxide) that cause global climate change. (A notable exception to this pattern is in finance, where China's influence is still modest except in infrastructure-related projects in developing countries. The reasons for China's relative financial isolation will be explored in Chapter 9.)

By the early 2000s, China was such a huge buyer of commodities, such as iron ore, copper, oil, and soybeans, that it pushed up their prices to new highs. At the same time, it had become such a big exporter of low-cost consumer goods that it pushed *down* their prices. It began to run big trade surpluses, and it recycled those surpluses into purchases of U.S. Treasury notes and other safe bonds. This huge inflow of capital pushed interest rates down.

These trends produced a combination of positive and negative impacts. Countries that produced a lot of commodities (many of them in the developing world) benefited from the higher prices China was willing to pay for their output. But rising surpluses from the commodity trade pushed up the value of their currencies, making it harder for their manufacturers to stay in business—especially if they were competing with low-priced Chinese imports.

Conversely, consumers in the United States and other rich countries benefited from the lower prices on the many goods made in China. But many rich-country companies found that to compete, they had to shut down high-cost factories at home and move production to China. This caused job losses and social dislocation. Lower interest rates had similarly mixed effects. A lower cost of money meant it was cheaper for companies to invest and for households to borrow money for expensive purchases, such as homes. Up to a point, this was good—but it also contributed to the housing bubble and subsequent financial crisis in 2008 in the United States.

All these impacts will be discussed in detail in later chapters. Throughout that discussion, though, we should remember that, while China was an important force driving global change, it was by no means the only one. Other technological and social shifts played major roles. The shift of manufacturing from the rich world to China and other developing countries was driven in part by technological changes that enabled wealthy countries to focus more on high-value services. Lower interest rates were driven in part by demographic changes throughout the world that increased the supply of saving. Thus, while it is crucial to understand China's role in global change, it is just as crucial to understand the complexity of these changes and not assign exclusive praise or blame to China.

How has China's rise affected geopolitics?

Even if you don't care that much about economics, China is important. Its rise is not just economic; it is also geopolitical. This became obvious in the 2017 and 2018 news headlines, which chronicled a "trade war" or "technology war" between the United States and China. These frictions are not just short-term irritations prompted by China's large trade surplus with the United States. They are evidence of tectonic shifts in the world's economic and political arrangements. China has the ability to change the global geopolitical order because it is:

- A durably successful economy large enough to eventually displace the United States as the world's biggest;
- An economy with a far higher degree of state ownership and state intervention than any other major country;

- An independent geopolitical actor with no alliance or security partnership with the United States; and
- An authoritarian, illiberal, nondemocratic state that is becoming more authoritarian and illiberal rather than less.

Let's look at each of these assertions in more detail. First, China is not just a successful economy; it's one whose success has been sustained over a very long period of time and under a wide range of conditions. Time and again it has defied predictions that it would go off the rails because of a unresolvable contradiction between its capitalist economy and its Leninist political system, excessive levels of debt, unproductive state enterprises, or some other reason. China's growth rate will almost certainly slow in the coming years. But given its 40-year track record, it is probable that China will continue to grow substantially faster than the United States for an extended time, and there is a good chance (though not a certainty) that it will overtake the United States as the world's biggest economy. This would constitute a material shift in global power relations: the United States has been the world's undisputed leader in economic output and technological development since the 1870s.

Next, the nature of China's economy is important. After World War II, the United States and its allies built a global economic order designed to generate sustained economic growth and contain the spread of communism. The countries that participated in this order had a wide range of political and economic arrangements. But the basic presumptions of this system were that market forces would play a much larger role than state direction; that most assets would be owned privately, with the state mainly focusing on market regulation; and that barriers to trade, investment, and capital flows between countries would gradually fall.

After 1979, China integrated into this system and enjoyed many of the benefits of membership, notably unfettered access to global markets and big inflows of capital and technology from the developed world. And for a long time it appeared that it was converging toward an economic structure that was fairly compatible with the global system's norms: market forces played an ever greater role, more and more assets moved from state to private ownership, and the state assumed more of a regulatory role; and China's market became gradually more open to international companies and investors.

But over the past decade—and especially since Xi Jinping became China's leader in late 2012—these trends have slowed or ground to a halt. Instead of "crossing the river by feeling for the stones" and steadily increasing the role of the market, officials now stress the need for "top-level design" and a high degree of state ownership. The Communist Party increasingly tries to influence private firms through party committees embedded in companies. Access to China's market for foreign firms remains far more tightly restricted than in most advanced economies. An industrial policy initiative launched in 2015, "Made in China 2025," includes specific targets for the amount of market share Chinese companies should take from their foreign rivals in technology-intensive industries. This initiative is backed by hundreds of billions of dollars of state subsidies. Finally, China's rapidly growing international investments—notably through the "Belt and Road" global infrastructure program announced in 2013—are spearheaded by state-owned construction firms and banks.

Chinese leaders, understandably, justify these practices on the grounds that each country is entitled to choose its own path to economic development and that China's approach has been demonstrably successful. But for the United States and the other countries that built the postwar economic and political order, the emergence of China not just as a large but a very different kind of economy is troubling. They fear a deeply unfair outcome in which heavily subsidized Chinese national champion companies make huge gains in international markets, while international firms are blocked from opportunities in China.

On a deeper level, many fear that China will use its new-found economic might to challenge the United States for global political and military supremacy—because, unlike earlier postwar economic rivals like Germany and Japan, China lies outside the American security network. They also worry that an authoritarian China will try to change global rules in ways that strengthen dictatorial regimes and under-mine democratic norms. In the words of Elizabeth Economy, a scholar at the Council on Foreign Relations, China is increasingly "an illiberal state seeking leadership in a liberal world order."[5] Whether managed well or poorly, the frictions caused by China's global impact are likely to become ever more acute in the coming years.

2

POPULATION, GEOGRAPHY, AND HISTORY

How does China's size and population affect its economy?

It is an obvious fact, but it bears repeating: China is the world's largest nation by population (1.4 billion) and its fourth largest by area, with a geographic size almost identical to that of the United States. Its size presents China with an unusual set of constraints and possibilities. These are summed up in a motto frequently cited by one of China's most famous economists, Justin Lin, who attributes it to former Premier Wen Jiabao: "When you multiply any problem by China's population, it is a very big problem. But when you *divide* it by China's population, it becomes very small." The point is simple, though easy to miss: China's size means that any challenge it faces—unemployment, environmental degradation, social unrest, you name it—exists on an almost unimaginably large scale. But it also means that the resources available to tackle the problem are gigantic. The difficulty lies in marshaling all those resources and deploying them effectively.

This observation illuminates a common feature of China's economy in both the Maoist and reform eras: the main goal throughout has been to *mobilize* resources. Maximizing the *efficiency* with which those resources are used has always been a secondary concern. This often distresses economists from rich countries, where virtually all economic growth and improvement in living standards come from improvements in efficiency. Visitors to China observe the waste and inefficiency visible everywhere and often conclude that the economy will soon hit a crisis. These predictions have always been wrong, not because observers are wrong about the degree of waste, but because they fail to realize that in a country of China's size, such waste can be irrelevant as long as it is a by-product of an effective process of meeting basic needs.

To cite a simple example: in each year of the decade 2000–2010, just to meet the basic employment and shelter needs of its population, China had to create over 20 million new jobs (nearly equivalent to the entire population of Australia), and build 8 million new urban housing units—six times as many as the average in the United States during that period and four times the peak rate during the U.S. housing bubble. It is hardly surprising that during this scramble many fairly useless jobs were created and many housing units were built that had to wait months or years for buyers.

This is not to argue that China's growth had to be wasteful and inefficient, or that this level of waste can go on forever. Other, more efficient (and probably slower) growth paths were certainly viable. The point is simply that China's enormous size gave its leaders the option of a high-speed growth model that emphasized quantity over quality. There is growing evidence that this phase of "extensive" growth is drawing to a close and that China must shift to a growth model that emphasizes efficiency rather than scale.

A second implication of China's size is that it had much more latitude to conduct large-scale trials of policies before rolling them out nationwide. The country has thirty-one province-level jurisdictions,[1] of which the smallest (Tibet) has a population of 3 million and the largest (Guangdong) 104 million—about the same as Mexico. The average province has a population of around 45 million, roughly that of Spain. In many respects, it is thus appropriate to think of China as a continent-sized assemblage of countries. The formal structure in which these provinces operate is a centralized polity run from Beijing, not a federal system like the United States or Germany. But in practice, provincial officials have a lot of leeway to run things as they see fit. Since the late 1970s, national leaders have consciously exploited the advantages of this local autonomy by either tolerating or explicitly authorizing policy experiments in particular cities or provinces. As a result, China has the luxury—unavailable to smaller countries—of testing out new ideas on a relatively large scale. Successes can be replicated elsewhere, but failures—even big ones—do not damage the country as a whole. This makes a trial-and-error style of policy formulation more viable.

How does China's geography affect its economy?

Three features of China's geography have a particular impact on its patterns of economic development:

- The "Hu Line," running diagonally from the far northeast to the far southwest, bisecting China into a well-watered, densely populated half and an arid, sparsely populated one.
- The division between the long coastline where most export-oriented activity clusters and the vast landlocked hinterland.
- The two main rivers, the Yellow and the Yangtze, which influence crop patterns and provide channels for inland development.

The Hu Line (Figure 2.1) is an imaginary line, drawn by 1930s Chinese geographer Hu Huanyong, that runs from the city of Heihe on the Chinese-Russian border to the city of Tengchong on the border with Myanmar. The line divides China's land area roughly in half, but the two halves are starkly different. The half east and south of the line contains

Figure 2.1. Map of China.
Shaded area: coastal provinces.
Source: Gavekal Dragonomics.

94 percent of China's population and most of the country's available water, with annual precipitation ranging from 500 to 2,000 millimeters. The half west and north of the line contains just 6 percent of the population (many of them ethnic minorities such as Mongolians, Tibetans, and Uighurs) and is very dry, with most regions receiving no more than 400 millimeters of precipitation a year.[2] This area does, however, contain large deposits of oil, gas, and minerals, so it is an important part of China's natural resource endowment.

The division indicated by the Hu Line is similar to the division in the United States between the relatively wet, densely populated area east of the Mississippi River and the relatively dry, lightly populated area to the west. There is, however, one big difference: the western United States also has a seacoast, whereas China's western half is landlocked. This is important because economic development is highly correlated with access to ports. Countries or regions without port access tend to grow much more slowly, because they are unable to develop export sectors and so they benefit less from the flows of technology and ideas associated with active trade.

China's two main river systems are also important both as dividers and as vectors of development. The silt-heavy Yellow River, running through northern China, was the cradle of China's earliest civilizations and was also the driver of China's traditional water engineering techniques, thanks to its frequent floods and changes of course. The Yangtze, which flows from the Tibetan plateau through central China, roughly divides the rice-growing south from the wheat- and millet-growing north, and has long been the crucial inland waterway connecting China's coastal ports with the country's deep hinterland. Many cities along the Yangtze, such as Nanjing, Wuhan, and Chongqing, became import transport hubs and commercial and industrial centers. The famous Three Gorges Dam, the world's biggest generator of hydropower when it was completed in 2012, is on the Yangtze River.

The most persistent effect of these geographical constraints on economic decision making is the tendency of high-powered economic activity to cluster on the coast. In order to foster equitable development, the government must continuously create ways to enable the landlocked interior to catch up. State-owned enterprises (SOEs) generally account for a larger share of the economy in the interior than along the coast because they can afford to skimp on profits to perform their social mission of spearheading employment and economic growth. A series of huge regional development plans (such as "Develop the Great West" from 2001 and "Revitalize the Northeast" beginning in 2005) directly aim at raising living standards in the interior, and in fiscal terms they amount to a large wealth transfer from the coast to the hinterland. On a grander scale, the Belt and Road Initiative (begun in 2013) was conceived in part as a way to link the landlocked parts of southern and western China to international markets. And a host of smaller-scale programs link individual cities in rich (usually coastal) provinces to cities in poor (usually interior) regions, and compel the richer cities to pay directly for economic or social development programs in the poorer ones.

How does China's long historical experience affect its economy?

China is one of the world's oldest continuous civilizations, and modern Chinese are acutely aware of being the inheritors of millennia of culture and history. These traditions mold society, government, and daily life in ways far too complex to recount here. For our purposes, however, it is useful to highlight three elements of China's long history that are very relevant to the country's recent economic development.

First, China is not just an old civilization (like India) but, more importantly one of the world's oldest *states*. Although dynasties rose and fell, we can trace the Chinese state back at least to the late sixth century c.e., when examinations were first held to select members of the imperial civil service. Since then, despite the changes in ruling house, there has been a steady history of bureaucratic rule of the core regions of what is now China, with only relatively minor breaks. This legacy of centuries of systematic, generally competent bureaucratic rule set China apart from virtually all other developing countries (including India) in that the level of state capacity is quite high. "State capacity" means broadly the ability of a government to organize itself and its finances and to perform its key functions, such as building infrastructure, providing social services, and managing an economic development strategy. A key reason why China's modern economic growth has been so fast for so long—and why the country has so far avoided the kind of crippling financial or economic crisis that has derailed so many developing countries—is this high level of state capacity.

Second, for about a thousand years until the Industrial Revolution in Europe, China was the largest, most sophisticated and technologically advanced economy in the world. Economic historians have estimated that, as late as the 1820s, China probably accounted for about one-third of world gross domestic product (GDP), roughly in line with its share of world population (Figure 2.2). It had market-based systems of domestic manufacturing and trade at least as sophisticated as those in Europe, and dominated global trade in premodern manufactures such as silk, textiles, and ceramics.[3]

Taking a very long view, one might argue that China's resurgence since 1979 simply represents a "return to normal." During the nineteenth and early twentieth centuries, Europe and North America fully industrialized, but China failed to do so. Once it started to industrialize and adopted an open trading system in the early 1980s, the advantages that led

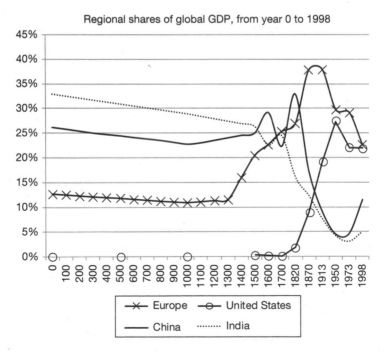

Figure 2.2. China's economy in the long run.

Source. Adopted from Maddison (1998).

to its pre-nineteenth-century eminence—a large, relatively well-educated population and well-established traditions of manufacturing and commerce—kicked in once more. After four decades of high-speed growth, China is once again punching its weight in the global economy. By 2017, China's share of global economic output (15 percent), manufacturing value (25 percent), and manufactured exports (18 percent) were all roughly around China's share of global population (19 percent).

Finally, a historical narrative surrounding this fall from eminence and recent recovery is an essential part of the mythology of the ruling Chinese Communist Party and a carefully cultivated part of its strategy for legitimating its monopoly on political power. China's fall from its position as the world's greatest economy was sealed by the Opium War of 1840–1842, which ended in a humiliating defeat by Great Britain and ushered in what modern Chinese historians call a "century of humiliation."[4] Over the next hundred years, China suffered a catastrophic civil war in which at least 20 million people died (the Taiping Rebellion of 1850–1864), a continuous erosion of its sovereignty at the hands of European colonial powers, the collapse of its 2,000-year-old imperial system of government in 1912, and another quarter-century of civil war that overlapped with a savage war with Japan that was conducted entirely on Chinese soil. The communist victory of 1949 put an end to this chaos.

The early years of communist rule under Mao Zedong (1949–1976) had their own elements of political and economic turmoil, including the brutal privatization of industry and collectivization of agriculture in the 1950s, the disastrous forced-march industrialization of the Great Leap Forward (1956–1958), which led straight to a famine in which upwards of 30 million people starved to death, and then the near civil war and constant ideological battling of the Cultural Revolution (1966–1976).[5] But even through these calamities, the new communist state held together and achieved some notable gains: spreading basic literacy to virtually the whole population, imposing basic standards of hygiene and health care that helped life expectancy rise from about 48 years to around 75, and putting in place some of the basic infrastructure for a modern industrial economy.

Under Deng Xiaoping (China's paramount leader from 1979 to 1993) and his successors, communist ideology was shelved in favor of pragmatic, more market-oriented policies that delivered fast economic growth and a steady rise in living standards for most Chinese. A basic premise has been that only the Communist Party is capable of ensuring this sustained growth and, furthermore, that only because of CCP rule was China able to overcome its "century of humiliation" and return to greatness. Dispassionate historians may find much to argue with in this account; but the narrative is powerful and has become an indispensable part of the CCP's strategy for legitimating its authoritarian rule.

3

CHINA'S POLITICAL ECONOMY

What is China's political system?

Understanding China's unique and resilient governance system is essential for making sense of the country's economic past, present, and future. We may briefly describe it as follows: China is (1) a *one-party state* that (2) governs in a *bureaucratic-authoritarian* style and (3) is in principle *highly centralized* but in practice *substantially decentralized*. We will examine each of these three main features in turn.

What kind of a one-party state is China?

The important thing is not the obvious fact that the Communist Party is in effect the sole legal party[1] but rather the *nature* of the party. Rather than a tiny cabal of secretive leaders, it is a vast organization of some ninety million members (more than 5 percent of the nation's population) that reaches into every organized sector of life, including the government, courts, the media, companies (both state-owned and private), universities, and religious organizations. Top officials in all these organizations are appointed by the party's powerful Organization Department.

"A similar department in the US," writes journalist Richard McGregor in his book *The Party*, "would oversee the appointment of the entire US cabinet, state governors and their deputies, the mayors of major cities, the heads of all federal regulatory agencies, the chief executives of GE, Exxon-Mobil, Wal-Mart and about fifty of the remaining largest U.S. companies, the justices on the Supreme Court, the editors of the *New York Times*, the *Wall Street Journal* and the *Washington Post*, the bosses of the TV networks and cable stations, the presidents of Yale and Harvard and other big universities, and the head of think-tanks like the Brookings Institution and the Heritage Foundation."[2] The party no longer tries to control the minutiae of every individual's life, as it did during the Maoist era, but it does seek to directly control or heavily influence every sphere of *organized* activity. In recent decades, the party has exercised its control in a flexible, not a dogmatic, way. This flexibility helps explain its resilience amid the rapid changes in China's economy and society.

Another source of resilience is the encouragement and management of large flows of information between local governments and the central authorities in Beijing, and the conversion of that information into policies that address problems on the ground. Much foreign commentary focuses on the ways in which the party censors and controls the Internet and other media; this censorship is real, pervasive, and in many respects harmful. Yet the party has tolerated an explosion of conventional and online media and has invested heavily in Internet infrastructure because it finds media reports helpful in gaining information on problems that local officials would prefer to conceal.

Beyond this, both the party and the central government commission enormous amounts of research, including ground-level surveys, via state-controlled think-tanks and universities. This information feeds into a sophisticated policy-formation process in Beijing. The most visible manifestation of this process is the Five-Year Plan, which has evolved far beyond its original purpose of setting production targets in a command economy into an ongoing procedure for converting information from the grassroots into policy and adjusting policies as conditions change.[3]

Why is China different from other authoritarian states?

China's governance style is best described as *bureaucratic-authoritarian*. It is not a democracy like the United States and most other high-income developed countries. But since 1979 (at least until a crucial shift in early 2018, which we discuss below) it has not been a dictatorship— that is, a country ruled by a single person or small group of persons in which the personal authority of the dictator or junta supersedes that of all bureaucratic institutions. Dictatorial states include the purely personal dictatorships in many African countries; military juntas such as those that ruled Brazil and other Latin American nations in the 1960s and 1970s, or Myanmar until recently; and hereditary quasi-monarchies within communist states, of which the main examples are the Castro family in Cuba since 1959 and the Kim family in North Korea since 1946.

Under communist rule, China has experienced several different governance styles. Mao Zedong ran China essentially as a personal dictatorship from 1949 to 1959 and again during the Cultural Revolution of 1966–1976; in between, power was held by a bureaucratic elite that tried to govern in a more collective way. Deng Xiaoping was a key figure in this bureaucratic elite; after he became the country's paramount leader in 1978, he designed a bureaucratic-authoritarian system of "collective leadership" specifically to prevent the reemergence of a dictator such as Mao. This system endured at least until 2018, when Xi Jinping changed the constitution to abolish term limits for state president, enabling him to serve indefinitely as China's top leader. Along with Xi's other moves to concentrate virtually all decision making in his hands and to establish a cult of personality around himself, this suggests that China is moving back toward dictatorship.

However, party institutions are far more complex and entrenched than they were during Mao's rule, and constraints on personal power are greater for Xi than they were for Mao. Because of these institutional complexities and the uncertainty over whether Xi will succeed in establishing a personal autocracy, it is arguably still fair to describe China's governance style as bureaucratic-authoritarian—but with a strong caveat that it is heading in a dictatorial direction.

In Deng's bureaucratic-authoritarian system, ultimate authority lies not in the individual leader but in the Communist Party, which sits atop the political system; directs the operations of the government and military; and selects leaders who are subject to term limits, mandatory retirement ages, and more or less formal requirements to obtain consensus from the rest of the senior leadership group on major policy decisions. This senior leadership group could include retired officials. For instance, President Jiang Zemin continued to play an important behind-the-scenes role for at least a decade after his formal retirement in 2003. These constraints on the power of any one individual were never fully institutionalized but operated fairly consistently until Xi's 2018 constitutional change.[4]

Along with this conscious system of collective leadership, a key difference between reform-era China and most other authoritarian regimes was its method of leadership succession. In dictatorships, leadership transitions are tricky. The simplest solution is to have power go from one family member to another, as in a traditional monarchy. Or it can be transferred from one member of a small ruling oligarchy to another, as in some military dictatorships. Often it is necessary to wait for the death of the old ruler before the new one can be installed. Sometimes succession occurs earlier, not through a formal process but by coup d'état.

China, almost uniquely among modern authoritarian regimes, achieved three successive transfers of power from one living leader to another unrelated one. (Only Vietnam has done better, with four leadership transitions since 1991.) These transitions are complex because the top Chinese leader holds three concurrent positions: General Secretary of the Communist Party, Chairman of the Central Military Commission (which controls the army), and State President (a mainly ceremonial role that confers ultimate control of the government). A leader must hold all three positions—but especially the first two—in order to exercise full control of the state.

Since 1992, leadership transitions have come at alternate Party Congresses. At the Fourteenth Congress in 1992, Deng Xiaoping retired and transferred control of the party, military, and government to Jiang Zemin. At the Sixteenth Congress in 2002, Jiang ceded control of the party and government to Hu Jintao; but he did not give up chairmanship of the Central Military Commission until 2 years later. At the Eighteenth Congress in 2012, Hu gave way to Xi Jinping, who assumed control of the party, government, and military.[5] Xi, though, used the Nineteenth Congress to lay the groundwork for his constitutional change, and it is likely that he will remain the country's top leader even after the Twentieth Congress in 2022.

This record of leadership transitions distinguishes China from most other modern authoritarian states and especially from the former Soviet Union. All leadership transitions in the Soviet Union's 74-year history occurred only after the death of the old leader or by coup d'état. China's mechanism for leadership transition has meant that the Chinese state is more stable and resilient than other authoritarian states. Along with other institutional procedures—notably the mandatory retirement rules that force top leaders to step down around the age of 70 and other officials to retire by the age of 65—it also ensures that there is a constant circulation of new personalities and ideas in government and that the system is not captured by old leaders resistant to change. Again, Xi has cast doubt on the durability of these virtues by his power play, although he has not tampered significantly with the mandatory retirement rules.[6]

What is the balance of power between central and local governments?

China is *formally centralized but in practice highly decentralized.* The formal centralization is easy to see. Unlike a federal system such as the United States, there is no division of powers between the central and provincial governments. The same party controls the bureaucratic apparatus at all levels of government (center, province, prefecture, county, and township). The party's central Organization Department in Beijing appoints the senior leadership of all provinces and many cities. Many crucial laws or policies, notably the famous "one-child" population control policy,[7] have been enforced with a high degree of consistency across the whole country.

In reality, though, local governments enjoy a high level of discretion and autonomy. One measure of decentralization is the share of government expenditure that takes place at the subnational level. A 2004 International Monetary Fund (IMF) study found that, in the period 1972–2000, this figure averaged 25 percent for democracies and 18 percent for nondemocracies. For China, the average figure for 1958–2002 was 54 percent; and by 2014 it had risen to a staggering 85 percent.[8] China's level of fiscal decentralization is unusually high by any standard and extraordinary for an authoritarian country.

This pattern is deeply embedded: even when China was a Soviet-style "centrally planned" economy, it was far more decentralized than its model, the Soviet Union.[9] This decentralization means that China, unlike most authoritarian states, benefits from the economic dynamism and entrepreneurship enabled by local experimentation. On the ôther hand, formal centralization means that when Beijing decides on a major national infrastructure project—such as an interstate highway system or high-speed rail network—it has the ability to mobilize resources on a large scale to achieve its aims.

This leads us to the apparent paradox of Chinese governance: an apparently centralized, one-party authoritarian state presiding over a dynamic, decentralized economy. In the modern era, no such combination has lasted very long. Authoritarian regimes that depended on centralized control, such as the Soviet Union, succumbed to economic stagnation and ultimately to political collapse. Regimes that prioritized market-based economic growth were forced to open up their political systems, as South Korea did in 1988 after 27 years of military dictatorship. No wonder foreign observers have predicted for decades that China's mix of authoritarian politics and economic dynamism could not possibly last.[10] So far, these predictions have been wrong. Why?

What did China learn from the failures of other communist countries?

The first key to understanding why China has not lapsed into economic stagnation or evolved into a democracy is to examine the lessons its leaders learned from the failure of other communist states, notably from the traumatic collapse of the Soviet Union in 1991.

Economists sometimes describe China as a "transitional" postcommunist economy. This means it is making a transition from a centrally planned economy to a more market-driven one. It does not necessarily mean that the Communist Party gives up political power. Most eastern European countries are examples of nations that combined an economic transition from plan to market with a political transition from communist authoritarianism to multiparty democracy. China and Vietnam are examples of countries trying to make an economic transition while maintaining the Communist Party's monopoly on political power.

In the early 1990s, China's political position seemed very shaky. Protests in Beijing's Tiananmen Square in the spring of 1989 swelled at their height to over a million demonstrators, who denounced official corruption, runaway inflation, and the lack of political freedoms. The Communist Party under

Deng Xiaoping restored order at the cost of a bloody crackdown and the house arrest of Zhao Ziyang, who until late May that year had been the party's top official and had spearheaded many of the economic reforms of the 1980s. In the next 2 years, China suffered economic sanctions by the United States and other Western countries, and its economic growth rate sagged to an average rate of 4 percent in 1989–1990—a recession compared to the 10 percent average growth rate in the prior decade. Conservative officials, led by Deng's rival Chen Yun and Premier Li Peng, blamed the political unrest on Deng's reformist economic policies. The country was diplomatically isolated and in economic and political lockdown.

Meanwhile, the rest of the communist bloc was crumbling with a speed unimaginable just a few years earlier. Communist regimes in the USSR's satellite states in Eastern Europe all disintegrated by early 1990, and by Christmas 1991 the Soviet Union itself had fallen apart: the Communist Party lost power after a failed coup against Mikhail Gorbachev, fourteen republics from Lithuania to Kazakhstan declared independence, and Boris Yeltsin installed himself as the noncommunist president of a reduced Russian Federation.

In such circumstances, it was easy to imagine either that China would be the next domino to fall or that the party would tighten its grip on power by crushing dissent and reining in the economic reforms that had proved so politically disruptive. In fact, it did neither. By 1991, the economy was picking up steam again, and in early 1992, Deng launched a master stroke with his celebrated "Southern Tour." Accompanied by senior military leaders, he visited the hot spots of economic reform in south China, beginning with the special economic zone of Shenzhen, right next to Hong Kong, which had been the laboratory for his boldest experiments. On the trip he held a meeting with senior military leaders and the head of the national security services, in which he bluntly declared, "Whoever is opposed to reform must leave office."[11]

This message was intended for Jiang Zemin, whom Deng had appointed head of the party after the Tiananmen uprising and who was sitting on the fence between Deng's reformers and the conservative camp. Jiang got the message and launched a new round of reforms. Over the next 5 years, economic growth surged by an average of more than 12 percent a year.[12]

An old revolutionary, Deng was as committed as anyone to preservation of the party's monopoly on power. But he gambled that the best way to preserve that monopoly was to run a dynamic economy that boosted living standards at home and raised China's international prestige and leverage. He reasoned that a better-fed population, proud to live in a China that was once again "standing tall" in the world, would in the long run be more supportive of Communist Party rule than people living in a stagnant economic backwater. Economic reform must come first, and political reform—if ever—a distant second. Or in his own words, plastered prominently on billboards throughout China in the 1990s: "Development is the only iron law."[13] In this respect, he differed diametrically, and self-consciously, from Gorbachev, who began with political reforms in the hope that they would help unblock bureaucratic resistance to economic reforms. Deng, long before Tiananmen, declared Gorbachev to be "an idiot" for putting political reforms ahead of economic ones.[14]

Deng's judgment about the importance of strong economic growth was later validated by a series of studies of the collapse of the USSR conducted by party scholars in the 1990s. These scholars concluded that the Communist Party of the Soviet Union (CPSU) fell for four main reasons:

- The economy did not grow fast enough, leading to frustration and resentment, and this failure resulted from insufficient use of market mechanisms.
- The CPSU's propaganda and information systems were too closed and ideologically rigid, preventing officials

from getting accurate and timely knowledge about conditions both inside and outside the Soviet Union.

- Decision making was far too centralized and hence far
  too slow.
- Once reforms started under Gorbachev, they undermined
  the core principle of the party's absolute monopoly on
  political power.[15]

These findings have continued to inform Chinese policymaking over the past two decades. Unlike Western analysts,
who see a fatal contradiction between a dynamic economy
and a tightly controlled political structure, Chinese leaders see
the two as complementary. Tight political control provides the
stability within which economic activity can be decentralized;
and the resulting rapid economic growth in turn enhances the
party's legitimacy for having "delivered the goods" of higher
living standards. ("Higher living standards" means not just
higher incomes, but also public goods such as health and
education services, a social safety net, a clean environment,
and safe food and drugs.) With strengthened legitimacy, the
party's grip on power becomes more secure, and most people
find the risk of switching to another, untried system to be un-
acceptably high.[16]

The ideas that economic growth is the key to sustained political power and that a government's legitimacy can just as well
spring from economic growth as from democratic elections are
not uniquely Chinese creations. They are also common among
China's successful East Asian neighbors, whose experiences
Chinese leaders have studied closely since the beginning of
the reform era.

What did China learn from the success of its East Asian neighbors?

When China came out from its period of Maoist isolation in
1979, government officials and scholars began to travel around

the world. They quickly found that, in economic and techno-logical terms, China had fallen far behind not only the estab-lished Western powers but also several of its smaller neighbors in East Asia: Japan, South Korea, and Taiwan. All three had experienced sustained economic booms since emerging from the wreckage of World War II, the Korean War, and the Chinese civil war, respectively, in the early 1950s.

By 1979, Japan was already the world's second-biggest economy and seemed poised to wrest global technological leadership away from the United States. South Korea, under the inspired, Draconian, and occasionally manic leadership of President Park Chung-hee (1961–1979), had risen from being the poorest country in all Asia to a nascent industrial pow-erhouse. Most embarrassingly, Taiwan, a poor agricultural province in 1949 when the defeated Nationalist government of Chiang Kai-shek took refuge there after losing the civil war to the communists, was now a thriving middle-income country on the verge of becoming an important exporter of electronic goods.

East Asia's economic achievement is a rare feat. Few coun-tries manage to grow fast enough for long enough to close the gap between their living standards and those of the richest countries. Between 1970 and 2010, only fourteen countries in-creased their per capita income relative to that of the United States by 10 percentage points or more. Eight were peripheral countries in Europe, plus Israel, which presumably benefited from spillover effects from the great postwar European eco-nomic boom. The other six were all in East Asia, and by far the biggest gains in relative income were in Taiwan, South Korea, and Japan. During this period, the only countries in the entire world to jump from "poor" (defined as 10 percent or less of U.S. per capita GDP) to "rich" (50 percent of U.S. per capita GDP) were Taiwan and South Korea (Figure 3.1).[17]

The best explanation for this success is that Japan, Taiwan, and South Korea all adopted varieties of a model called the *developmental state*, a term coined by economist Robert Wade

Per capita GDP at PPP, percent of US level			
Country	Pre-1970 low (%)	2008–2010 Average (%)	Increase in percentage points
Asian exporters			
Taiwan	9%	68%	59
Japan	21%	72%	51
South Korea	10%	58%	48
Malaysia	9%	29%	20
China	**2%**	**18%**	**16**
Thailand	5%	19%	14
Peripheral Europe			
Austria	44%	99%	55
Spain	29%	68%	39
Greece	29%	65%	36
Finland	45%	79%	34
Portugal	19%	48%	29
Italy	40%	69%	29
Israel	34%	60%	26
Romania	10%	25%	15

Figure 3.1   Successful catch-up growth countries.

in 1988. Subsequent research has suggested that the successful East Asian developmental state economic-growth model has three pillars: land reform, export manufacturing, and financial repression.[18]

"Land to the Tiller" Agricultural Reform. This reform generally means breaking up big estates or plantations and creating a class of rural smallholders. In populous countries with an unconstrained supply of rural labor, per-acre yields are much higher on small owner-cultivated farms than on plantations tilled by tenant farmers or wage labor. These higher yields create a significant agricultural surplus, and since farm

ownership is fragmented, it is much easier for the state to capture a large share of this surplus than it would if it were dealing
with politically powerful big landowners. The resources thus
captured provide the seed capital for state-led investment in
basic industry and infrastructure.

Export-Oriented Manufacturing. Poor countries are poor
mainly because they lack the technological capital of rich countries, which makes output per worker dramatically higher. To
get rich, poor countries must undertake a process of "technological catch-up" in which they acquire technology from rich
countries and use it to boost the productivity of their own
workforce. Exports help this catch-up process in two ways.
When a country is poor, foreign technology is expensive and
must be paid for in scarce hard currency. Exports (initially of
agricultural products, handicrafts, and cheap manufactures)
can earn the foreign exchange needed to buy the capital equipment that enables higher-value production.

Later, when the country has an established industrial base,
exports provide a handy, and much cheaper, way of ensuring
that the country's production techniques keep pace with improvements in global technology. If you are selling your goods
on world markets, you must compete with producers from
all around the world and cannot benefit from market rules
rigged in your favor. The only way to keep up is to make sure
that your technology (which includes not just machines but
also management techniques, supply-chain control, and other
"soft" technologies) is reasonably close to the global standard.
Export manufacturers engage in a constant process of upgrading their technology—through purchases, licensing agreements, reverse engineering, or outright theft of intellectual
property—in order to stay competitive and gain market share.
Producers who rely mainly on the domestic market often have
less incentive to invest in technology, since they may find it
cheaper to use political influence to have the local market
rigged in their favor.

Financial Repression. This term refers to a set of practices designed to control financial markets so that the state can direct capital to the sectors favored by its development strategy. These practices typically include:

- Regulated low interest rates, so that the cash flows from economic growth are not captured by "rentiers" living off interest income, but instead subsidize borrowing to fund state investments in infrastructure and corporate investments in industry.
- A tightly managed and typically undervalued exchange rate to make the country's exports cheaper on global markets.
- Capital controls to prevent companies and rich individuals from siphoning off national wealth into investments abroad and instead to compel profits to be reinvested in the domestic economy.

With many variations driven by local political institutions, Japan, South Korea, and Taiwan implemented these core elements with rigor. (Southeast Asian neighbors such as Thailand, Malaysia, and the Philippines followed the script halfheartedly, which helps explain their less impressive results.) This often required them to resist intense lobbying by advanced countries such as the United States, and multilateral institutions like the World Bank and the International Monetary Fund, which pressed for freer exchange rates and more open financial markets.

These three East Asian nations generated the fastest economic growth of the second half of the twentieth century: each saw average real GDP growth of 8 to 10 percent a year for three decades before slowing down. Scholars of economic history were not surprised. The "East Asian development model" is in essence an adaptation of the strategy advocated by German economist Friedrich List (1789–1846), which in turn drew inspiration from the "American System" created in the early

United States by Alexander Hamilton and Henry Clay. The United States and Bismarck's Germany (which adopted much of List's program) were the two most successful "catch-up" economies of the nineteenth century. Japan's first modernization drive, which turned it from an agrarian feudal state to Asia's first industrial power in the decades after 1870, more or less copied the German model.[19]

As we will see in our subsequent discussions of agriculture (Chapter 4), industry (Chapter 5), and finance (Chapter 9), China adopted this program by breaking up the Mao-era communes into small owner-tilled plots, aggressively promoting export manufacturing, and repressing its financial system in order to finance large-scale investments in infrastructure and basic industry. But China's development strategy also differed from the usual East Asian recipe in two respects.

First, China has relied far more heavily on state-owned enterprises (SOEs). In postwar Japan, the state set the rules and controlled the resource flows, but most of the companies and banks were privately owned. South Korea's banks were mainly owned by the state, but most of its large companies were private conglomerates. Taiwan had a much larger stable of companies owned either by the state or by the ruling Kuomintang Party; all the big banks were (and still are) state-owned. But there was also a very large body of private small- and medium-sized enterprises (SMEs) that spearheaded the island's drive into export markets. Many of the state- and party-owned enterprises were privatized in the 1980s and early 1990s.

Because of its communist heritage, China began its high-growth era in 1979 with virtually all assets in state hands; 40 years later, China still has by a wide margin the biggest state sector of any major economy. As noted earlier, China's political system hinges on the Communist Party having an outsized influence on all organized activity, and corporations are no exception. A secondary factor is that economic officials of the reform era inherited a country virtually without legal or regulatory systems. They therefore found it convenient to regulate via the enterprises they controlled, rather than through the impotent regulatory agencies. The implications of China's unusually high and persistent degree of state ownership will be explored further in Chapter 7.

The second big difference between China and its East Asian models lay in the extensive use of foreign direct investment (FDI). FDI played virtually no role in the postwar development of Japan, South Korea, or Taiwan; in China, it was central. One of the groundbreaking economic reforms of the early 1980s, the establishment of special economic zones (SEZs), was specifically designed to lure foreign companies to set up export manufacturing factories. FDI became virtually a mania after Deng's 1992 Southern Tour, and annual inflows surged from an average of $2 billion in the preceding decade to $37 billion in 1992–2001.

Another surge after China's 2001 entry into the World Trade Organization (WTO) carried annual inflows of greenfield investment up to over $100 billion a year by 2010; the numbers are even higher if one includes reinvestment of profits. From 1993 to 2002, new FDI inflows accounted for about 10 percent of all fixed investment in China, although this figure has since fallen to under 3 percent. One of the enduring impacts of this is that, even today, over 40 percent of all Chinese exports are produced by foreign firms. This state of affairs is utterly different from that of the other East Asian countries, whose exports are virtually all recorded by domestic firms.

What accounts for this extraordinary surrender of economic sovereignty, which has led many Chinese critics to complain that China was simply renting out its vast army of cheap workers to foreign capitalists, who grew rich on the proceeds?[20] One reason is that, in the aftermath of the Mao era and the chaos of the Cultural Revolution (1966–1976), China found itself in a position of extreme technological backwardness. It therefore required a strategy for rapid import of foreign technology. The first approach was a massive program of plant imports, initiated in 1977 and carried out in fits and starts for another decade or more. This had some successes, but the nation's ability to import plants was constrained by the availability of foreign exchange to buy them. Moreover, the import of plants on a turnkey basis is intrinsically self-limiting because only physical technology is imported. To gain access to the intangible technologies of management and engineering techniques and supply chain management, direct investment by foreign firms was needed.

Another explanation for China's FDI reliance is political. Japan, South Korea, and Taiwan were part of the United States' alliance structure in East Asia. They therefore benefited from technical assistance, educational exchanges, and essentially unfettered access to America's gigantic market. This gave them the financial and intellectual resources to continuously upgrade their technological base, without the need to invite foreign investment. China, on the other hand, lay outside the U.S. alliance structure, although there was an alignment of convenience with the United States from the late 1970s until 1989, driven by a shared strategic desire to contain the Soviet Union. China would never enjoy the kind of privileges that its East Asian neighbors extracted from the United States. Moreover, after the collapse of the communist bloc in 1989 and of the USSR itself in 1991, the logic of strategic alignment with the United States evaporated. To keep up the flow of technology, a more liberal FDI policy was required.

A third factor is simply timing and luck. Japan, South Korea, and Taiwan all began their industrial takeoff in the period 1950–1980, when production chains were essentially national and international trade consisted either of raw commodities or of finished goods. After 1980, advances in transport and logistics technology made possible the internationalization of production chains. China, with its abundant low-cost labor force, proximity to the existing production chains of East Asia, and access to one of the world's greatest ports in Hong Kong, was thus perfectly placed in both time and space to become a major location for outsourced manufacturing. There is no evidence—and it is barely conceivable—that this outcome was the strategy of Chinese reformers in the 1980s. It was more in the nature of a lucrative opportunity that presented itself and that policymakers decided to accept, along with all its various consequences.

Who runs economic policy?

Our discussion of China's economic strategy inevitably invites the question "Who are the strategists?" We can address this issue from two angles: personalities and bureaucratic structures. As noted earlier, China is a bureaucratic-authoritarian state, and the role of institutions in shaping economic policy directions is large. But the personal authority of the leaders is also large. So let us start with a brief review of the key economic decision makers since the beginning of the reform era in 1979.

A popular view is that from December 1978, when Deng Xiaoping became China's paramount leader, until October 1992, when he retired from the Politburo, Deng was the sole architect of economic policy. This is not really true. Throughout his leadership, Deng had to contend with a powerful rival, Chen Yun, who had broad support among conservative officials and in the state planning system, which he had created in the 1950s and continued to oversee in the 1980s. Although Deng had overall management of national affairs, in economic matters he and Chen had almost equal influence, and they were referred to as "two tigers on one mountaintop." Chen was an important counterweight to Deng, who often favored bold reforms without calculating their long-run impact. The development of economic reforms during the Deng years is best seen as a balancing act between the adventurous Deng and the look-before-you-leap Chen.

Deng also left most of the details of execution to lieutenants. The most important was Zhao Ziyang, who vaulted from a position as the party secretary of Sichuan Province (1975–1980) to that of prime minister (1980–1987) and finally to general secretary of the Communist Party (1987–1989), before being put under house arrest in the wake of the Tiananmen Square protests. Throughout his tenure, Zhao was an influential advocate of market-oriented reforms.

After Deng retired, leadership of the country passed into the hands of President Jiang Zemin. Continuing the precedent set by Deng, Jiang left the management of the economy mainly to his prime ministers: Li Peng (through 1997) and Zhu Rongji (1998–2003). The conservative Li Peng generally put political stability ahead of economic growth, but his influence gradually waned as it became clear that Zhu, his first vice premier, was a more innovative policymaker and a very tough politician.

Zhu, who had been handpicked by Deng, was vice premier and head of the central bank from 1993 through 1997 and tamed the inflation that had frequently exceeded 20 percent in the preceding decade. In his one term as premier, he masterminded the reorganization and downsizing of the SOEs, recapitalization and reform of the banking system, privatization of the housing market, and China's long-delayed entry into the World Trade Organization. Zhu is widely considered the most effective economic leader in the history of the People's Republic.

The practice of leaving economic management mainly in the hands of the prime minister continued during the two terms of the next leadership team, President Hu Jintao and Premier Wen Jiabao (2003–2012). Although the economy experienced rapid growth during this period (an average of 10.5 percent a year, compared to 9.9 percent in the prior decade), Wen was widely criticized as a weak premier who was ineffective in pushing through key economic reforms, tolerated bloat in the SOEs and rampant official corruption, and left the nation saddled with enormous debts after two rounds of economic stimulus following the 2008 global financial crisis. He did, however, oversee important agricultural reforms and the creation of a modern social welfare system.

Partly in response to this perception of weak leadership, the next president, Xi Jinping, made clear that he, not his premier Li Keqiang, would be the main architect of economic policy for the next 10 years. The reform blueprint published after the Communist Party's November 2013 plenary meeting appears to have been written under Xi's close personal supervision. Xi has also appointed himself the head of most of the "leading small groups" that the party uses to coordinate top-level policy decisions, including the finance and economics group.

Xi's highly centralized approach to policymaking is a noteworthy departure from the usual practice over the prior three decades of the top leader delegating much of this authority to lower-level leaders. But it also comes in the context of a much more complex, developed, and powerful bureaucracy than existed in the early reform era. So we must now consider policymaking from an institutional perspective.

At the top of the pyramid of Chinese power sits the standing committee of the party's Politburo (Figure 3.2) This group, which at present consists of seven members, is the nation's core leadership, and the most important decisions require consensus within this group—although of course the views of the top leader carry a lot of weight. The standing committee sits inside the broader, twenty-five-member Politburo, which meets several times a year and ratifies many major decisions.

Next in line below the Politburo are the "leading small groups" (LSGs), which the party and government organize to coordinate policy on major issues. Membership in these groups typically includes a range of officials holding government or party posts in a variety of agencies. They may also have a permanent office staff whose job is to manage the paper flow and distill the group's discussions into specific policy recommendations for the party leadership. There are at present over eighty LSGs, and their number has increased significantly under Xi Jinping, who personally chairs many of the most important ones.[21]

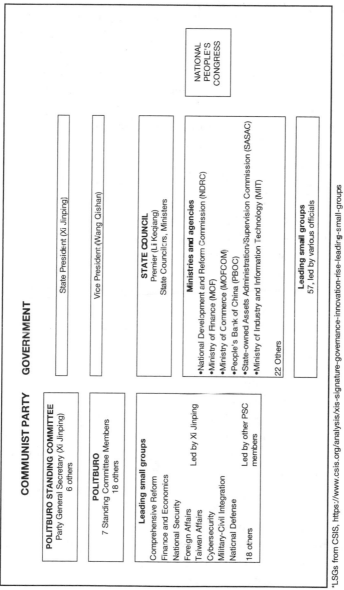

Figure 3.2 Organization chart of party and government.

*LSGs from CSIS, https://www.csis.org/analysis/xis-signature-governance-innovation-rise-leading-small-groups

Lower still is the State Council, chaired by the premier, which is the highest organ of the government and roughly equates to the cabinet in other countries. But its structure is different: in addition to the heads of all the government ministries and agencies, it has several State Councilors—senior officials who outrank ministers, some of whom carry the additional distinction of vice-premier rank. The full State Council meets just twice a year; most of the time the council's standing committee (the premier and the State Councilors) act on their own, in consultation with the Politburo.

Below the State Council are the ministry-level bodies, of which the most important for the economy are the National Development and Reform Commission (NDRC), a descendant of the old State Planning Commission; the Ministry of Industry and Information Technology; the Ministry of Finance (MOF); the Ministry of Commerce (MOFCOM, which also handles foreign trade issues); and the People's Bank of China (PBOC), the central bank. As this quick sketch suggests, a key difference between China and other countries is that officials like the minister of finance or central bank governor are less powerful than elsewhere because they are in fact relatively low-ranking. As in all systems, of course, politically savvy individuals can punch above their bureaucratic rank.

Finally, significant economic decision-making power lies in the hands of officials outside the central government: those who run important provinces such as Guangdong or cities such as Shanghai, or manage big SOEs. The ability of these leaders to act independently of central dictates, and in response to local needs, has contributed to China's resilience and dynamism. Again, however, we must note that Xi Jinping has made strong efforts to curtail the independence of local officials. At the same time that he amended the constitution to abolish term limits for the president, he pushed through another amendment that extended the reach of the party's disciplinary agency, the Central Commission for Discipline Inspection (CCDI). Previously, CCDI's main job was to investigate officials for corruption.

Now it can also probe and punish them for failing to carry out central policies. The positive element of this change is that the central government may find it easier to enforce necessary but locally unpopular policies (for instance, on environmental protection). The negative is that it may stifle the local-government innovation that has been a key part of China's growth model.

How do leaders manage the trade-off between economic growth and political control?

As we have seen, China's leaders generally view a dynamic economy and authoritarian political control as complementary rather than contradictory. Even so, the liberal-democratic critique of the Chinese system is hard to dismiss.

Liberal analysts both in the rich democracies and inside China observe that virtually all of the world's richest countries have democratic, or at least relatively open, political systems. They also observe that authoritarian regimes eventually tend to put their own survival ahead of the economic welfare of their citizens. Regimes as diverse as the Soviet Union, Francisco Franco's Spain, and Hosni Mubarak's Egypt, not to mention more extreme examples like North Korea, all chose economic stagnation or worse rather than risk fostering the economic freedoms that might lead to demands for political ones. Meanwhile, authoritarian regimes that did put a premium on broad-based economic growth, such as Park Chung-hee's South Korea or Augusto Pinochet's Chile, tended to shift to democracy once the original strongman was out of the way. Many conclude that China's leaders will ultimately be forced to choose between opening up their political system or keeping a grip on power and letting the economy wither.

Chinese leaders continue to reject this choice, so far with success. Xi Jinping tightened political control, while still achieving average annual GDP growth of 7 percent in 2013–2018. But of course many individual economic reforms require the state to give up some power. Streamlining the SOEs means a big reduction in the state's ownership of assets. Financial liberalization means cutting the government's ability to direct capital to its favored projects. Enabling a dynamic Internet risks giving citizens new channels to criticize the government. The enduring dilemma of party-driven economic policy is *how much* and *what kind* of power are Chinese leaders willing to sacrifice in exchange for *how much* and *what kind* of economic growth?

There is no one-size-fits-all answer. On several occasions, the leaders have accepted some erosion of state power in order to keep the economy humming. This willingness was visible in the original reform decisions in the late 1970s and early 1980s, as well as in the reforms of the 1990s and early 2000s that involved eliminating most state-controlled prices, opening up to foreign investment, and privatizing many SOEs. The one major instance when economic growth was sacrificed for political control was in the crisis of 1989, and as we have seen, once political control was reestablished, the focus quickly returned to economic reform. As China tries to move to become a more consumer- and innovation-driven economy in the 2020s, further erosion of state controls may be required.

Yet rather than signaling more openness, Xi Jinping has moved in the opposite direction: he has strengthened the central state's control over localities and moved China closer to a personal dictatorship. These moves put at risk the flexibility that has made the Chinese system more resilient and successful than other authoritarian states. Over the past 40 years, China's leaders have done an impressive job of striking the balance between economic dynamism and political control. Whether this success will continue in the coming years is very much an open question.

4

AGRICULTURE, LAND, AND THE RURAL ECONOMY

Why does agriculture matter?

It may seem odd to begin our discussion of a great industrial economy with agriculture. In China today, agriculture accounts for only 8 percent of GDP. But about 40 percent of the population still lives in rural areas, and more than a quarter of the national workforce—about 200 million people—till the fields. Maintaining rural livelihoods and stability for this large group of people is always an important aim of national policy. So is "food security"—ensuring that China can grow enough key crops to feed itself, without relying on imports.

We start with agriculture mainly because that is where economic reforms began in the late 1970s. This was no accident. Agriculture was then the biggest sector of the economy, accounting for 37 percent of GDP and nearly three-quarters of all employment.[1] And as we saw in our discussion of the East Asian development model, getting agriculture right has proved to be the essential first step for successful industrialization.

How did agriculture jump-start China's growth in the 1980s?

On the eve of the reform era, in 1978, China's countryside was overpopulated and impoverished thanks to two decades of bad policy. Beginning in the mid-1950s, private ownership of farmland was abolished, and agriculture was organized under communes, which in turn were divided into smaller collective units called "brigades" and "work teams." These communes were instructed to produce as much grain as possible, with little scope permitted for vegetables and other cash crops, and the state procured this grain at low prices designed to minimize the cost of staple foods for people living in cities. Stringent internal passport controls made migration from the countryside to the city virtually impossible, except for soldiers who were recruited from the countryside and later demobilized to cities.

The consequences of these policies were uniformly bad. Rural income growth was glacial: only 1 percent a year in real terms from 1957 to 1978. Per capita production of grain, at about 300 kilograms, was no higher in 1978 than it was in 1955, and output of oil seeds (an essential product since virtually all cooking in China involves frying in oil) fell by about a third during that period. And because of restrictions on mobility, the rural share of the national population, at 82 percent, was actually higher in 1978 than it had been in 1958.[2]

Between 1978 and 1983, the agricultural economy was revolutionized by the "household responsibility system." It started in a village in Anhui province, where a group of farmers got together in secret and signed an agreement to dissolve their collective and divide up their farmland into individual plots. This innovation rapidly spread, and the province's party secretary, Wan Li, realized he was facing a powerful popular revolt against an immiserating system. Rather than crush it, he decided to promote this land-to-the-tiller reform. The party secretary of Sichuan Province, Zhao Ziyang, made a similar decision.

The national government took a while to catch up. The December 1978 Party plenum that launched the reform era raised agricultural prices and endorsed experiments in land management by rural collectives, but it still condemned private farming. By 1980, however, Zhao Ziyang had become premier and Wan Li was vice premier in charge of agriculture policy. Together they rammed through a national policy to disband the communes and return to family farming. By the end of 1982, virtually all agricultural collectives were gone, and family farmers had been assigned rights to cultivate individual plots of land.

The effect on agricultural output and farm incomes was spectacular. By 1984, grain output was over 400 million tons, a third higher than 6 years before; production of oilseeds and cottons sustained annual growth rates of 15 percent; and meat production was growing by 10 percent a year. Rural per capita income more than doubled between 1979 and 1984. Per capita cash savings by rural families rose from essentially zero in 1979 to 300 renminbi (Rmb) by 1989. Rapid gains in agricultural output and incomes continued throughout the 1980s, as farmers continued to diversify their crops and apply new technologies that increased yields. Use of chemical fertilizer, which had risen gradually in the 1970s, tripled between 1978 and 1990. So did the use of farm machinery, notably pumps, small tractors, and food processing equipment.[3]

The benefits of agricultural reform soon cascaded into the rest of the economy. Because they had more incentive to invest, farmers became important sources of demand for basic industrial sectors such as fertilizer and farm equipment. As their cash incomes rose, their bank savings also grew, funding loans to nascent manufacturing enterprises. And as farmers could now determine the value of their labor, more began to seek off-farm wage labor to supplement their incomes. All this triggered China's first wave of entrepreneurial industry, the township and village enterprises.

What role did township and village enterprises play in China's economic development in the 1980s and early 1990s?

Township and village enterprises (TVEs) are business enterprises formally owned, or informally sponsored, by local "collectives," that is, by township and village governments. They are not considered SOEs, which are formally owned by central, provincial, and city governments.

The TVEs took off in the 1980s for two reasons. First, there was rising demand from newly well-off farm households for a wide range of goods, and a growing supply of willing workers for factories producing these goods. Second, TVEs offered a convenient structure for combining private entrepreneurial energy with government patronage, which was essential to ensure access to capital. TVEs were thus spared the common fate of small private firms in other postcommunist "transition" economies, where lack of access to capital was a severe constraint on growth.[4]

By 1985, employment in collectively owned TVEs had hit 40 million, and employment in all forms of rural enterprises was about 70 million. A decade later, rural enterprises of all kinds employed 18 percent of the national labor force and produced one-quarter of GDP. Collective TVEs accounted for about half these figures. This represented the peak of the collectively owned TVE model. Over the next several years TVEs faced intense competition from more efficient, reformed SOEs and from private enterprises in urban areas. By 2004, most collectively owned TVEs had been privatized, mainly through buyouts by firm managers. Although statistics continue to refer to TVEs, most of these are better considered to be private firms that are simply based in rural or semirural areas.[5]

TVEs played key roles in industrial development. They laid the foundations for the extensive production of consumer goods, since they rapidly expanded beyond producing goods for farm households into a broader range of consumer products, including fans, bicycles, and kitchen appliances. TVEs also created space for what was effectively private enterprise in a transitional period when private firms were formally discouraged. And they provided the first large-scale mechanism for the transfer of excess agricultural labor into the modern industrial economy. They declined in relative importance after the mid-1990s because urban private-sector firms were finally large enough and enjoyed enough regulatory support to take over these roles.

Why did rural–urban inequality grow after 1989?

The reforms of the 1980s started in the countryside, and disproportionately benefited the rural population. Prices for agricultural products rose quickly, as did opportunities for off-farm wage employment in TVEs. Rural incomes grew faster than urban incomes. This was a welcome corrective to the prior decades of urban bias, but it did not last. Among the varied reasons for the shift from rural-focused reforms in the 1980s to urban-focused reforms in the 1990s, the political disturbances of 1989 were a crucial hinge.

The demonstrations in Beijing's Tiananmen Square and in other Chinese cities in the spring of 1989 had several causes. A background condition was that the 1980s were a period of great intellectual ferment during which discussion of alternative political systems was widespread and, to a surprising degree, tolerated by the government. (The central government even had its own office for studying political reform.) For the first time since the 1949 revolution, Chinese students and scholars began to travel abroad in large numbers, and they were attracted by the much higher living standards and greater political openness that they found not only in the United States and Europe but also closer to home in places like Japan and Hong Kong.

Against this backdrop, a number of specific grievances caused discontent. The rapid rise in food prices translated into inflation that routinely hit double digits; in late 1988 and early 1989, it was running at 20 to 30 percent. Urban incomes were also rising fast, and the urban standard of living had improved noticeably since 1980, but many urban households felt that rising prices made their gains precarious. Students coming out of urban high schools and universities faced poor employment prospects, as the SOEs struggled to create enough jobs and private companies labored under heavy restrictions. The most common form of private firm was the *getihu* or household enterprise, which by law could have no more than seven employees. And there was widespread anger over corruption by government officials, in particular the practice of buying up goods at low state-plan prices and reselling them for a big profit on the free market. All these resentments boiled over into the demonstrations, which the government finally crushed on June 4, 1989, as the army dispersed protesters, killing thousands.

As reformers in the Communist Party and government regrouped over the next few years, they coalesced around a strategy that shifted the center of reform energy back into the urban arena. Unlike the situation in 1978–1980, when the party made a series of explicit decisions to favor rural areas by raising farm prices and permitting private farming, this was not an overt move to raise urban incomes relative to rural ones. But party leaders clearly drew from 1989 the lesson that the greatest threat to the regime's hold on power came from the cities, so they needed to concentrate on raising urban living standards.

The background of key personnel also shaped this decision. Major reformers of the 1980s, notably Wan Li and Zhao Ziyang (who was premier from 1980 to 1987 and then party secretary in 1987–1989 before being deposed as a result of the Tiananmen disturbance), had cut their teeth in the provinces, addressing rural problems. The central figures of the 1990s, President Jiang Zemin and Zhu Rongji (who was vice premier and financial czar from 1993 to 1997 and then premier until 2003) were both former leaders of Shanghai and had mainly dealt with urban issues.

Throughout the 1990s, reforms in the cities accelerated, while the countryside entered a period of relative stagnation. The government restructured SOEs and the financial system and promoted private enterprise. Rules on internal migration were relaxed to make it easier for workers to move to the cities for wage labor; but their families were prohibited from moving, so the burden of providing social services for these migrant families remained in the countryside. Prices for manufactured goods (produced mainly in cities) were liberalized; government procurement prices for grain and some other agricultural goods remained capped. At the same time, provinces were ordered to maximize production of grain, at the expense of cash crops that farmers could sell at higher prices on free markets.

Most consequentially, beginning in 1998, the urban housing stock controlled by SOEs was privatized, ultimately delivering gigantic windfall gains to the urban households that bought housing at well below its market value. By 2003, urban households had won unrestricted rights to own, buy, sell, and mortgage real property. To this day, rural families enjoy no such property rights. (See Chapter 6 for a discussion of housing privatization.) Taken together, these policies created a widening chasm of inequality between rural and urban households. The average urban income rose from 2.2 times the average rural level in 1990 to 3.2 times in 2003 (Figure 4.1).[6]

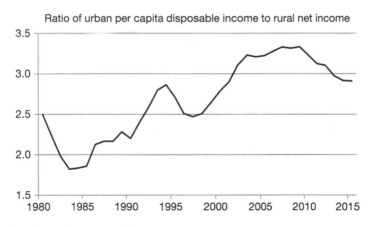

Ratio of urban per capita disposable income to rural net income

Figure 4.1. Urban versus rural incomes.
Source: NBS/CEIC.

How did the government address rural–urban inequality in the 2000s?

The administration of Hu Jintao and Wen Jiabao, which took power in late 2002, sought to correct the urban bias in policy and boost rural incomes. It launched a broad range of policies to address the problems of farmers, agriculture, and rural areas. Grain procurement prices were hiked, and taxes on agricultural produce were abolished in 2006. The government promoted large investments in rural roads and infrastructure as well as in food-processing plants that could provide off-farm employment. Beginning in 2006, it began to rebuild rural social service networks, which had disintegrated in the previous two decades of reform. The 9 years of compulsory education were made free for rural residents in 2006. In 2007, a new Rural Cooperative Medical System (RCMS) was launched, providing basic health insurance, and the minimum income guarantee was expanded from urban to rural areas. In 2009, a rural pension scheme for the first time in Chinese history guaranteed farmers a cash income after they were too old to do farm labor.

These policies had a large and beneficial impact on both rural incomes and agricultural production. The gap between urban and rural incomes stabilized at 3.3 times in 2007 and then began to fall. By 2013, virtually all rural residents had some kind of health insurance, up from 13 percent in 2000. In the same year, about 40 percent of the rural population (240 million people) was covered by pensions, a figure that has since probably risen to over half.[7] Total grain output, which fell from over 500 million tons in 1999 to just 430 million tons in 2003, steadily climbed, and in 2012 it exceeded 600 million tons for the first time. Real growth in agricultural value added, which grew at less than 3 percent a year in 1997–2003, accelerated to nearly 5 percent a year in the subsequent decade.

This improvement in agricultural fortunes prompts a few observations. First, it belies the common judgment that the Hu Jintao/Wen Jiabao years were a "wasted decade" without progress on reforms. These criticisms come from urban elites, who ignore rural issues. The reversal of the decline in agricultural production, and the establishment of a comprehensive, albeit basic, social safety net in both urban and rural areas, were both major achievements.

Second, rural reforms played an important role in reducing poverty. Between 1981 and 2015, the number of people in China living in what the World Bank defines as extreme poverty sank from 840 million to 10 million—from 84 percent of the population to 1 percent (Figure 4.2). Some of this decline came from moving people into higher-wage occupations in the city, but given that about half the population still lives in the countryside, improving rural livelihoods was also crucial.[8]

Finally, the history of the reform era shows that it is hard for policy to maintain a perfect balance between urban and rural interests. The first decade of reform delivered disproportionate gains to the countryside; the reforms of 1989–2003

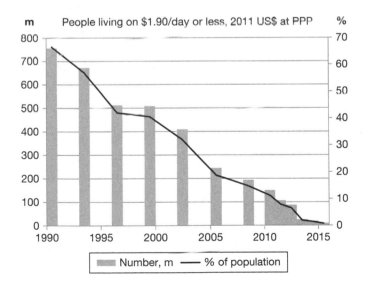

Figure 4.2. Poverty reduction.
Source: World Bank.

skewed heavily in favor of the cities. The Hu/Wen decade was more balanced, but the renewed emphasis on rural concerns prompted pushback from urban lobby groups, who have succeeded in framing China's development challenge over the next two decades as one of urbanization. Yet even under an optimistic urbanization scenario, China in 2040, about 20 years from now, will still have 400 million people, or nearly 30 percent of its population, living in the countryside. Tension between urban and rural interests will continue to be a headache for Chinese policymakers for many years to come.

Do Chinese farmers own their land?

Chinese farmers do not own their land, but they do generally have long-term contractual rights to use it. The issue of rural land tenure is one of China's most intractable policy problems, and the chasm between rural and urban property rights is one of the most important sources of inequality in wealth and income.

When farms were first decollectivized in 1978–1983, farm households typically got the right to farm a specified plot of land for 1 to 3 years. By the mid 1980s, household farm assignments were generally extended to 15 years. But these rights were insecure. The land was still owned by "the collective" (i.e., by the village as a whole), and it was common for the village authorities to reassign plots of land within the contract period. Sometimes reassignments were made for good reasons, such as changes in family size. But the power of reassignment also meant that if you got on the wrong side of the village party secretary, you could suddenly find yourself farming a new and inferior plot. This uncertainty over how long they would have the right to farm a particular piece of land meant that farmers were reluctant to make large capital investments.

The government has steadily strengthened farmers' land-use rights. The standard contract term for agricultural land was extended to 30 years in 1993, and this term was written into the Land Management Law of 1998. The Rural Land Contracting Law of 2004 specified that use rights had to be set down in a formal contract and that the village authorities could not arbitrarily reassign land before the end of the contract period. Reassignments are permitted with a two-thirds vote of the village assembly. The 2007 Property Law established that farmers' land-use rights are private property rights.

These laws have been implemented with varying degrees of rigor. According to a 2010 survey by the land-use rights organization Landesa, a bit over 60 percent of farm families had land-rights certificates, and about half have formal contracts. Stronger ownership rights have increased the incentives for farmers to make productivity-enhancing investments, such as putting in permanent greenhouses or advanced irrigation systems. They have also made it possible for agribusinesses to take out long-term subleases on groups of neighboring plots and begin to develop large-scale mechanized agriculture.[9]

Yet even as the government bolstered farmers' land rights, it also worked hard to ensure that the monetary value of those rights stayed as low as possible. For one thing, it continued to insist that ownership of the land itself resided in the collective, which meant that individual farmers had no right to sell or mortgage their land. For another, it tolerated the practice of city governments acquiring large swaths of nearby rural land for a modest sum, then reselling it to property developers for a large markup. This meant that virtually all the profit from converting low-value agricultural land to high-value urban land went not to rural families, but to city governments and urban property developers (who also reaped huge gains from the housing and offices they built).

The sums involved were staggering. The World Bank estimated that in 1990–2010, local governments expropriated land from farmers for a total of Rmb 2 trillion less than its market value (around $300 billion at the present exchange rate). If farmers had received the full market value of their land and enjoyed normal investment returns, by 2013 they would have had an additional Rmb 5 trillion (roughly $650 billion, or 8 per-cent of GDP) in household wealth.[10]

One motive for this "cheap land" policy was to enable the growth of cities, since by the early 2000s the government had decided that the way to maximize economic growth was to move as many people as possible, as quickly as possible, off the farm and into higher-productivity urban jobs. Another, some-what contradictory concern was that if farmers were free to sell their land, they might be cheated by sharp-eyed speculators. In other words, it was perfectly fine for farmers to be cheated out of the fair value of their land by government buyers but not by private buyers.

To appreciate the full impact of this policy on wealth and income distribution, one must understand the great discrep-ancy between rural and urban rights to real property. Urban land is all owned by the state, in the same way that rural land is owned by collectives. When an urban family buys a house, it is really buying a long-term leasehold, typically for 70 years.[11] Other than the length of the term, this may not sound much different from a farmer with a 30-year use right on his farm-land. But in practice the difference is enormous. The farmer has no right to sell his land to someone willing to pay a high price in order to convert it to a more valuable use. All he can do is sublease his cultivation rights. An urban homeowner can sell her property to anyone, for whatever price the market will bear. As more and more people move into the cities, the value of a given piece of urban real estate almost invariably rises, and the urban homeowner is perfectly free to realize that in-creased value. A farmer can own the rights to only one piece of land for personal cultivation; an urban resident can buy as many houses as she can afford, generating rental income or using the property as security for a mortgage to finance a small business.

Finally, as we will explain in Chapter 6, millions of urban households were allowed to buy formerly state-owned housing units, at far below their market value, during a 1998–2003 housing privatization program. They were later allowed to re-sell these houses at market prices. The aggregate value of the capital gain they were allowed to harvest was about Rmb 4.5 trillion—more than twice as much as the already large amount farmers lost due to local government expropriation in 1990–2010. In sum, the property rights of rural and urban residents followed exactly opposite paths. Farmers were forced to *sell* their land for far less than it is worth; while city dwellers (some of them anyway) were allowed to *buy* property for less than it was worth and to pocket most of the resulting gains. This inequity in property rights may be the single biggest cause of the huge wealth and income inequality between urban and rural areas.

What is being done to improve rural land rights?

Chinese scholars have long recognized the injustices imposed by the rural land tenure system, and the government has begun to undertake reforms to correct them. These efforts have been aided by the belated recognition that urbanization must be made more orderly and that city governments must find other ways to finance themselves than by buying up farmland cheap and selling it at a dear price.

Rural land tenure reform faces two major constraints. First, the collective ownership of rural land remains sacrosanct. Thus, the simplest and best solution to the rural land problem—giving farmers the same kind of strong private property rights that urban homeowners enjoy and that farmers in most of the rest of East Asia have had for decades—is off the table.

The second constraint is the "red line" on arable land: a policy that has been in place since 2006, which states that the total amount of cultivated land in the country may not fall below 120 million hectares. The rapid conversion of rural land to urban use over the past two decades means that arable land is only just above this red line. In practice this means that any future increase in urban land area must be offset by conversion of wasteland or rural construction land back into land for cultivation.[12]

Within these strictures, the central government is pursuing several reforms to create a healthier rural land economy. These reforms fall into three baskets: stronger land rights for farmers, promotion of mechanized large-scale agriculture, and "townization" of rural areas.[13]

Improved Land-Use Rights. Various policies aim to strengthen farmers' right to buy, sell, and mortgage their land-use rights. To do so, all land must first be registered. Property rights cannot be effective unless the boundaries of land plots are surveyed and the boundaries and property owners are set down in a public registry. Somewhat more than half of China's rural land is registered. Completing registration for all rural land is likely to take at least another decade. Another thorny issue is ensuring that women's property rights are protected. About 90 percent of registered rural land is in the name of the male head of household, leaving most rural women at risk of destitution if they divorce.[14]

Large-Scale Agriculture. The government has long resisted large-scale, mechanized farms, primarily because the family farm was long the main rural social-safety net. If a family fell on hard times or if a migrant family member was laid off from a city job and unable to find work, one could always fall back on the family farm for shelter and sustenance. This rationale has weakened with the increase in permanent migration to the cities and the rollout of rural pension, health care, and minimum-income programs. The Ministry of Agriculture now advocates a move to larger-scale farms, and this is one factor behind the desire to make rural land more marketable.

Townization. This term refers to the practice of consolidating scattered villages into more concentrated rural towns. Villagers are moved from their original settlements into new, higher-density towns; the original village is demolished and the land returned to cultivation. This results in a net increase in cultivated land, since the new town occupies less land than the villages it replaces. Farmers retain the use rights to their agricultural land and can continue to farm it if they like; but the assumption is that a majority will prefer to transfer the use rights to their land and start working in urban jobs. This policy is an effort to continue the gradual urbanization of the rural populace but in a way that maintains or increases the supply of farmland.

Can China feed itself?

A final question about the rural economy is whether China can feed itself, or if it even needs to. This question matters for the whole world: if China were to start to import food on a large scale to feed its population of 1.4 billion people, the impact on global prices could be great. From time to time, one reads scare stories about how China's ravenous appetite for imported food will lead to ruinous worldwide food price inflation or intolerable pressure on the world's scarce supply of arable land.[15] Chinese policymakers also see the need to import food as a national security risk, and they worry about food price inflation.

These concerns over China's impending food crisis have been frequently expressed for decades and so far have always proved wrong. The pessimists have consistently underestimated China's ability to raise production of key agricultural products and livestock. Today China produces twice as much grain, four times as much oilseed, and six times as much meat as it did in 1980 (Figure 4.3). China already enjoys fairly high yields of most crops: its per-acre output of rice and wheat is among the highest in the world. But the scope for increase— through increased mechanization, improved land management techniques, and higher-yielding varieties—is in some cases still considerable. The biggest opportunity lies with corn (important mainly as feed for livestock), for which China's average yield of 6 tons per acre is well above the figures for Brazil, India, and Southeast Asia, but below the 8 to 9 tons achieved in North America.

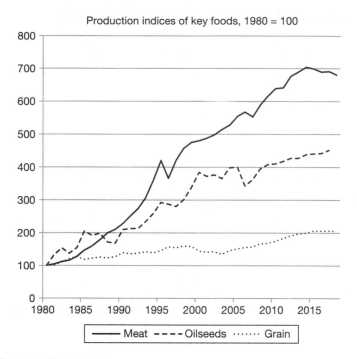

Figure 4.3. Food production.

Source: Author calculations from NBS/CEIC and US Dept of Agriculture.

On the demand side, China's total food consumption may grow but probably not by much. The average Chinese now consumes nearly 3,000 calories a day, an ample diet. South Korean consumption leveled off at about this level in the early 1990s. In Japan, average daily calorie intake has actually fallen over the past 20 years, as the population has aged. Given that China's population will replicate Japan's aging experience over the next 25 to 30 years, a large further increase in calorie consumption is unlikely.

Of course, the composition of diet matters too: as societies grow richer, they consume more meat (and dairy). This indirectly pushes up demand for grain because the creation of a pound of meat requires many pounds of feed grain. Yet China's consumption of the preferred meat, pork, is already quite high at around 80 pounds per person per year; this is about 30 percent higher than the figure for South Korea and only slightly below the 90 pounds at which Taiwanese consumption topped out in the 1990s.[16] China's government, hoping to stem the increase in chronic conditions such as obesity and diabetes that result in part from richer diets, in 2016 issued dietary guidelines aiming at a significant reduction in meat and poultry consumption.

China will not cause a worldwide food Armageddon, but it will import more food. This poses a challenge for the government, which for national security reasons has long maintained a policy of 95 percent self-sufficiency in grain. This policy has been relaxed somewhat in recent years. China still supplies more than 95 percent of its demand for cereals (principally rice, wheat, and corn). But its self-sufficiency ratio on its broader definition of grain—which includes beans and potatoes—has fallen to 83 percent, mainly because of a huge increase in imports of soybeans since the late 1990s.

It is likely that within a decade China's grain self-sufficiency will fall below 80 percent, with greater imports of both soybeans and corn thanks to higher demand for animal feed. Soybean and corn producers in the Americas and eastern Europe should be able to supply this demand. China is also actively encouraging its agricultural firms to invest in farmland in Africa, South America, Australia, and elsewhere, both to increase the total global supply of agricultural land and to ensure that China has secure sources of supply as its import needs grow.[17]

5

INDUSTRY, EXPORTS, AND TECHNOLOGY

Why did China become such a big manufacturer and exporter?

China's emergence as a great industrial, exporting, and technology power is one of the truly world-changing economic events of the last three decades. In the late 1970s, China accounted for little of the world's industrial production and less than 1 percent of its trade. By the end of 2018, it produced more than a quarter of the world's manufactured goods by value and was the world's biggest exporter, accounting for 13 percent of all global exports and 18 percent of exports of manufactures.[1]

China is now the hub for a global production network that begins with design studios in the United States and Europe; proceeds through producers of specialized components and raw materials in East and Southeast Asia; and ends up in China, where designs, materials, and components are brought together in finished products that are then sent all around the world. Increasingly, Chinese companies are producing high-technology components and finished goods on their own. A Chinese company, Huawei, is the world's biggest producer of telecommunications network equipment. Chinese firms are important producers of ships, high-speed trains, mining and construction machinery, and power generation equipment, including nuclear reactors.

How did this transformation occur? Historical advantages, lucky circumstances, and good policies all played a role.

As we pointed out in Chapter 2, China had a long history of manufacturing prowess before the Industrial Revolution. This "deep" historical advantage is real. But by itself it was not enough. Consider India. Until the eighteenth century, India's economy was almost as large as China's, and it dominated global trade in cotton textiles.[2] Like China, it has a large population and centuries of commercial and manufacturing tradition. Yet, since the 1980s its industrial and trade development has lagged; its exports are only about one-seventh China's, and it runs a persistent trade deficit of over $100 billion a year. Clearly, some other things have gone right for China in the last 40 years. This is where lucky circumstances and good policy come in.

The lucky circumstances include:

- **Good neighbors:** The successful export-driven development of Taiwan, South Korea, and especially Japan gave Chinese policymakers an easy-to-follow template for industrial development.
- **Hong Kong:** When China started its reforms, Hong Kong was already a world-class port and trading hub with modern legal and financial systems. This gave Chinese manufacturers quick access not only to global trade routes but also to much of the "soft" infrastructure needed for a modern economy.[3]
- **Timing:** China was fortunate to open up to trade just at the moment when the shipping container, invented in the 1950s, was beginning to make possible the creation of global production chains, spanning multiple countries, because of steep reductions in long-distance shipping costs.
- **A "killer app":** By the late 1980s, culturally similar Taiwan had established a sophisticated electronics industry, which moved en masse to China in the late 1990s, creating a world-class electronics manufacturing base almost overnight.

Whether consciously or not, Chinese policymakers recognized these opportunities and exploited them to the maximum extent. Two policy orientations stand out. The first is embedded in the slogan Deng Xiaoping and his colleagues invented to describe their economic program: *gaige kaifang*, or "reform and opening." Deng recognized that reforming the domestic economy would be quite difficult without an ever-greater openness to trade and investment and foreign ideas. So time and again he and his successors adopted policies that maximized opportunities for exporters, from the opening up of special economic zones (SEZs) in the early 1980s to joining the WTO in 2001.

The second was the strong emphasis on building infrastructure, especially ports, roads, power plants, and telecommunications networks, which made life easier for manufacturers up and down China's long coastline. The result was that, by the early 2000s, China had a unique and probably unrepeatable combination of low, developing-country labor costs and good, almost-rich-country infrastructure. This created an irresistible platform for export-oriented manufacturers. A further infrastructure drive in China's interior in the 2000s, focusing on expressways and high-speed rail lines, helped knit together the internal market, bringing closer to reality the old but elusive dream of "a billion Chinese customers." (Details of infrastructure development can be found in Chapter 6.)

The confluence of historical advantages, good luck, and good policy produced an unusually powerful economy. Yet the Chinese model also had some limitations. One is that the heavy reliance on direct investment by foreign multinationals meant that certain sectors, and the majority of export production, wound up captured by foreign firms. Another is that low labor costs, good infrastructure, and a large market of price-conscious domestic consumers led to a business model described below as "80 percent of the quality at 60 percent of the price." This model is viable, but it means Chinese firms face a challenge in moving up into the highest-value niches.

What was China's strategy for developing its industry?

As outlined in Chapter 3, China's industrial development since 1978 can be seen as the result of two processes: the *transition* away from a communist command economy to a more market-driven system; and the gradual adoption of an *East Asian developmental strategy*, similar to those of Japan, South Korea, and Taiwan. The first process involved a steady reallocation of resources away from the state and toward the private sector. The second involved "industrial policies" to promote particular sectors, infrastructure investments, and strong central control of the financial system. China's industrialization did not result *simply* from pro-market reform policies, or *simply* from an effective top-down developmental strategy. Both were needed.

China's industrialization was also unique in its unusually heavy reliance on foreign investment. This reliance was strong up to about 2006; since then, the government has shifted to policies that aim to reduce dependence on foreign investment and build up the capacities of domestic firms. Finally, China's industrial policy has not been static: it has evolved over time in response to new conditions and ambitions (Figure 5.1). We will now sketch out this evolution.

What was Deng Xiaoping's industrial policy?

When Deng Xiaoping took power at the end of 1978, he inherited an industrial economy that, thanks to decades of Maoist central planning, had two core problems. First, it was overly reliant on capital-intensive heavy industry, while production of consumer goods like clothing, bicycles, and electric fans was minimal. This went against China's basic factor endowments. As a poor country, it had relatively little capital but plenty of cheap labor. It was therefore more logical to structure the economy around labor-intensive light manufacturing. Second, virtually all industry was in the hands of SOEs, which had few incentives to improve their efficiency.

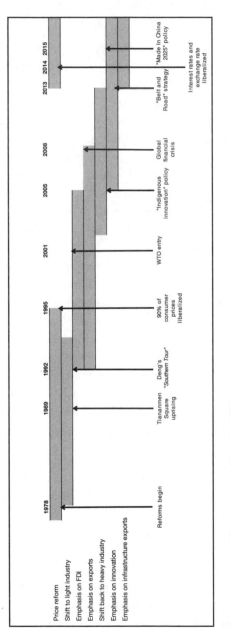

Figure 5.1. Phases of China's industrial policy since 1978.

Source: Author research.

After much trial and error, Deng's economic policymakers devised an approach with the following elements:

- A shift from capital-intensive heavy industry to labor-intensive light industry.
- A focus on light industrial exports to generate the foreign exchange needed to import capital equipment.
- The establishment of SEZs, allowing foreign companies to set up factories on preferential terms.
- Price reforms, to reduce the power of central planners and increase the role of the market.
- Increased tolerance for private enterprises.

The first two policies represented an embrace of the East Asian development model, with its emphasis on labor-intensive exports of consumer goods as the first step on the ladder to long-term economic growth. The last two (price reform and more private enterprise) were the tasks required for a successful "transition" from a communist to a more capitalist economy. The one in the middle (SEZs) was borrowed from another reformist communist country, Yugoslavia, but eventually morphed into a unique Chinese invention, the foreign direct investment–driven growth model.

Implementation of these reforms proceeded in fits and starts, thanks to constant battles between reformers led by Deng Xiaoping and conservative officials led by Chen Yun. But over a decade, the results were impressive. Between 1978 and 1990, the share of consumer goods whose prices were set by the market went from zero to 70 percent; overall industrial output rose sixfold; the SOE share of industrial production fell from 78 percent to 54 percent; and annual exports sextupled, from about $10 billion to $62 billion. In the first decade of reforms (1979–1988), the economy grew at an average annual rate of 10 percent a year, about the same as Japan's during its "miracle" industrial takeoff period in the 1950s.[4]

How did industrial policy change under Jiang Zemin and Zhu Rongji?

Impressive as the early gains were, China still faced problems as the reform era entered its second decade. Reforms unleashed a wave of pent-up consumer demand, and inflation soared above 20 percent in 1988–1989. Partial price reform meant that many products had two prices: a low plan price and a high market price. Many officials profited by buying up goods at cheap plan prices and reselling them on the free market. Popular discontent over high inflation and rampant official corruption were two important causes of the political protests that rocked Beijing and other Chinese cities in the spring of 1989, ending in the massacre of thousands of demonstrators around Tiananmen Square. And overall, China was still a poor country.

In the immediate aftermath of the Tiananmen massacre, conservative leaders brought reforms to a halt, and growth slowed. But in early 1992 Deng Xiaoping kick-started a new phase of growth with his "Southern Tour," during which he visited Shenzhen and other reform hot spots, signaling that "reform and opening" was alive and well. The next decade set China firmly on course to becoming a major industrial and trade power. Price reform accelerated: by the end of the 1990s, 95 percent of consumer goods and 90 percent of agricultural commodities and producer goods were purely market-priced (Figure 5.2). Better financial management brought inflation under control. Beginning in the mid-1990s, an SOE reform program dramatically reduced the number of state enterprises and state-sector workers, and it also greatly increased opportunities for private companies, especially in manufacturing.

The most noteworthy characteristic of this second reform phase was the strong emphasis on enticing foreign companies to invest in China and building up export industries. Foreign direct investment (FDI) had run at $2 to 3 billion a year in the 1980s and consisted mostly of small-scale Hong Kong manufacturers moving their factories across the border to the neighboring Shenzhen SEZ. After Deng's Southern Tour, FDI exploded,

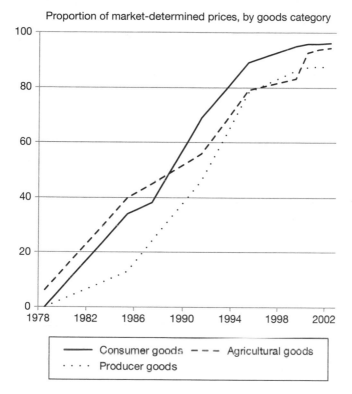

Figure 5.2. Price reform.

Source: Adapted from Lardy 2014.

peaking at $45 billion in 1997. Between 1994 and 1997, FDI accounted for nearly one-sixth of all fixed investment in China. Much of this FDI went into export manufacturing. Between 1990 and 2001, China's exports more than quadrupled, from $62 billion to $266 billion, and by the end of that period, more than half of the country's exports were produced by foreign firms.

Why did industrial policy become more statist under Hu Jintao?

During the administration of President Hu Jintao and Premier Wen Jiabao (2003–2012), industrial policy took on a more statist tinge, as the government promoted large-scale infrastructure projects, provided additional protections for SOEs, and slowed the pace of market reforms. Nonetheless, FDI and exports grew even more rapidly than in the previous decade, thanks less to government action than to a perfect storm of favorable conditions. China's entry into the WTO in late 2001 gave it more reliable access to world markets. The relocation of much of Taiwan's electronics-assembly capacity to the mainland enabled China-based exporters to benefit disproportionately from the explosion in global demand for computers and cell phones. And the world economy grew by 5 percent a year in 2003–2007, well above its long-run average. Between 2001 and 2008, China's exports grew at an astonishing rate of 27 percent a year, rising sixfold from $266 billion to $1.4 trillion (Figure 5.3).[5]

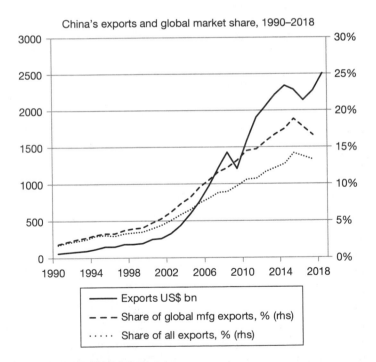

China's exports and global market share, 1990–2018

Exports US$ bn
– – – Share of global mfg exports, % (rhs)
· · · · · Share of all exports, % (rhs)

Figure 5.3. Exports and global market share.

Source: NBS, IMF, WTO.

Government industrial policy, though, did not focus on export promotion. Its main concerns were to consolidate the state sector, facilitate infrastructure, and enable Chinese firms to regain market share from the foreign companies that had poured into the country over the previous decade. The biggest SOEs were reorganized under a central government agency with a mandate to turn them into global champions. Infrastructure-intensive regional development plans such as "Develop the West" and "Revitalize the Northeast" aimed to spread the fruits of economic growth beyond the prosperous coastal provinces, which had reaped almost all the benefits from the FDI/export model.

These development efforts dovetailed with a construction surge set off by the privatization of the urban housing market under Zhu Rongji. As a result, demand for basic materials such as steel, cement, and glass soared, and China experienced perhaps the biggest heavy-industrial boom in world history. From 2000 to 2014, China's steel production rose nearly sevenfold, from 129 to 823 million tons, by which point China produced about half the world's steel and more than seven times as much as the second-biggest producer, Japan. During the same period, cement production nearly quadrupled from around 600 million to over 2.2 billion tons a year, and again China was responsible for about half of world output.[6]

When did the focus on high technology start?

Hu and Wen's industrial strategy was not just about construction and heavy industry, though. One of their most contentious initiatives was the "Indigenous Innovation" policy launched in 2006.[7] This was in some respects a continuation of technology-oriented industrial policies dating back decades. As noted in Chapter 2, Chinese leaders since the mid-nineteenth century were obsessed with closing the technological gap that had opened up between China and the industrialized West. Beginning in the mid-1980s, the reform era saw a series of

policies aimed at spurring both basic and applied scientific research and the development of industrial technology.[8]

Indigenous Innovation was more ambitious, however, in
its explicit aim to free China from its position as the last-stage
assembler of high-value components produced elsewhere; to
increase domestic companies' market share in technology-
intensive industries; and to make China a technological leader
rather than a follower. It included subsidies for research and
development (R & D) in several priority high-tech industries;
rewards for filing patents and creating technical standards;
encouragement for domestic firms and government offices
to buy Chinese-made products; and, most controversially,
stronger requirements for foreign companies to transfer key
technologies to local firms as a condition for being allowed to
invest in China.

The technology-transfer requirements and the attempts to
mandate Chinese technical standards for things such as wire-
less networks and encryption immediately sparked fierce
pushback from foreign companies, chambers of commerce,
and governments. Indigenous Innovation produced few obvious gains, other than an upsurge in the filing of mainly
worthless patents. It is true that foreign firms' share of high-
tech exports peaked at nearly 90 percent in 2005 and has since
fallen to under 70 percent. It is hard to say, though, how much
this shift owed to policy and how much simply to the maturation of China's privately owned technology companies.
Despite its questionable track record, Indigenous Innovation
set the stage for a much more aggressive technological development strategy a decade later.

How has industrial policy evolved under Xi Jinping?

By 2013, when Xi Jinping took over the government, Chinese
industry faced a number of problems. Heavy industry was
bloated by excess capacity, and too much production was still

controlled by state firms, which were much less efficient and profitable than private firms. Most economists, Chinese and foreign, agreed that the government needed to deemphasize heavy industry and do more to promote services; deregulate the prices of key inputs (notably energy, land, and capital) so that investment could become more market-driven and efficient; rationalize the sprawling SOEs; and create more space for private companies.

Over the past several years, the government has launched a variety of policy initiatives aimed at upgrading China's industrial structure. The most important are the "Third Plenum Decision" on economic reform, released in November 2013, and "Made in China 2025," an industrial plan released in May 2015.

The Third Plenum Decision was a lengthy document signaling the main directions of Xi Jinping's economic policies, without getting into much operational detail.[9] It contained two core and apparently opposed ideas. The first was that market forces would play a "decisive" role in resource allocation, an upgrade from the "important" role assigned to the market in previous party documents. The second was that the state sector would retain its "dominant" role in the economy. This seems like a contradiction. If market forces were truly decisive, the dominance of the state sector could not be guaranteed: state firms might lose out to private ones in market competition. Conversely, if state dominance were guaranteed, market forces could not be truly "decisive."

Chinese leaders see no paradox in their embrace of both a "decisive" market and a "dominant" state. State enterprises are crucial because they enable the government to pursue strategic development objectives and to intervene to stabilize the economy when times are tough. (Stimulus via state-led infrastructure spending was a big reason why China weathered the global financial crisis of 2008–2009 so successfully.) At the same time, the risk of waste and inefficiency in SOEs is high, so they must be subjected to market discipline to ensure that they remain reasonably profitable. One way to think about it is that market forces are indeed "decisive" much of the time—until they threaten the "dominance" of the state, at which point they are curbed. In practice, this means that markets generally determine the prices of *goods and services*; but they are not allowed to *transfer control of assets* from state owners to the private sector.

For a more detailed understanding of specific industrial policy goals, we must turn to Made in China 2025. This policy initiative built on the 2006 long-term technology strategy that introduced the idea of "indigenous innovation" and on the subsequent 2010 "strategic emerging industries initiative" which identified seven high-tech industries for priority support. It also drew on concepts marketed in Germany and the United States as "Industry 4.0," or "the industrial internet," relating to the improvement of industrial productivity through the collection and analysis of massive amounts of user data. Made in China 2025 has three main dimensions.

First, like Industry 4.0, it aims to accelerate the use of IT and other technologies throughout China's industrial sector in order to improve the quality and value of output. It is thus both broader and more sophisticated than earlier industrial strategies in that it sets goals for both traditional and advanced industries and addresses the whole chain of manufacturing processes and related service industries rather than narrowly focusing on handful of high-tech industries. This element of the strategy makes sense given China's development goals, and it is also innocuous from the vantage point of China's trade and investment partners.

The second and third dimensions of Made in China 2025, however, have raised hackles. The plan identifies ten high-tech priority sectors, ranging from semiconductors to robotics to new energy technologies and declares that China should assume a global leadership position in most of these industries within one or two decades. And it specifies targets for the share of domestic and global markets in these industries that should be captured by Chinese firms by 2025 or 2035—typically, in the range of 40–80 percent.[10]

These ambitions are problematic because they imply that China intends to favor domestic firms over foreign firms in its own market. If true, this would violate the spirit of Beijing's commitment under WTO to give "national treatment" to foreign companies—that is, to treat foreign companies the same way it would treat domestic ones. Many foreign companies and governments have interpreted Made in China 2025 as a statement of the Chinese government's intent to discriminate in favor of Chinese firms in order to help them gain a bigger share of the market for high-tech goods. Many fear that it will also be used to justify policies compelling foreign companies to transfer critical technologies to Chinese firms in exchange for access to the China market.

The international concern over Made in China 2025 is heightened by the amount of money China seems willing to throw at promoting its home-grown national champions. Since 2014, central, provincial, and city governments have set up around 2,000 "government guidance funds" to promote high-tech development. Ostensibly, these are venture capital funds: the government provides seed capital, but professional fund managers are supposed to decide how to invest the money and are tasked with achieving good returns on their investments. In practice, however, most of these funds seem to be thinly disguised subsidy programs, used to channel money to domestic technology companies, with little or no expectation of a commercial return.

The biggest and best-developed of these funds is the national Integrated Circuit Fund. By the end of 2018, this fund had mobilized about $20 billion, much of which supported several new memory-chip semiconductor fabs in eastern China. In addition, in late 2019, a second, $29 billion semiconductor fund was set up.[11] But the picture on the other guidance funds is far from clear. The 2,000 funds that had been set up by mid-2018 had a combined fundraising target of Rmb12.5 trillion ($1.8 trillion). Spot-checks suggest that the amount of money actually raised by these funds is a fraction of that total and that in many cases local officials use the money to subsidize real estate or infrastructure projects rather than high-tech industry. Local governments have effectively used these funds as a way to substitute for other revenue sources that had dried up.[12]

Why did investment by foreign companies play such a big role?

A feature of China's industrial development that sets it apart from its East Asian peers is the large role of FDI. ("Direct" investment refers to money that is invested directly in factories, equipment, or real estate, as opposed to "portfolio" investment, which consists mainly of the purchase of minority shareholdings in companies.) From 1985 to 2005, annual FDI inflows averaged nearly 3 percent of GDP, a very large number (Figure 5.4). For South Korea and Taiwan during their comparable high-growth eras (the early 1970s to the early 1990s), FDI inflows were only about half a percent of GDP. And in Japan

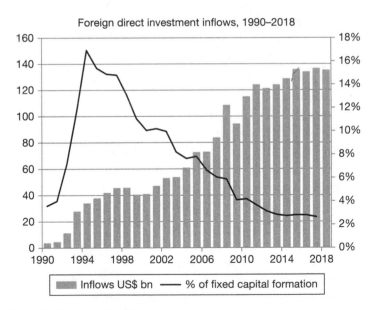

Figure 5.4. Foreign direct investment.

Source: Author calculations from NBS data.

from the mid-1950s to the mid-1970s, FDI was basically nonexistent, running at less than 0.1 percent of GDP.[13]

The role of foreign companies is particularly noticeable in China's export trade. The exports of Japan, South Korea, and Taiwan were almost exclusively booked by domestic firms. In China, this has not been true at all; since the early 1990s a third or more of exports were produced by foreign-invested firms, and the foreign share peaked at 58 percent in 2005. For exports the Chinese government classified as "high technology," the foreign role is far larger: from the early 2000s until 2012, well over 80 percent of "high-tech" exports from China were produced by foreign firms, and the foreign share is still around two-thirds (Figures 5.5 and 5.6).

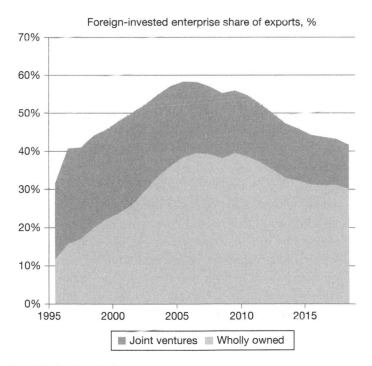

Foreign-invested enterprise share of exports, %

■ Joint ventures ■ Wholly owned

Figure 5.5. Foreign enterprise exports.
Source: NBS/CEIC.

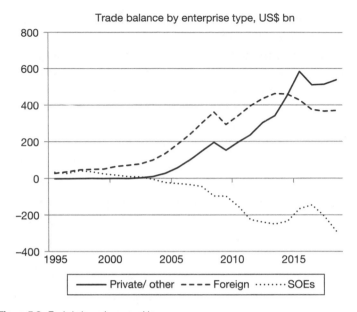

Figure 5.6. Trade balance by ownership.
Source: Author calculations from NBS/CEIC data.

As we noted in Chapter 3, this heavy reliance on FDI had at least three causes: China's desire for a speedy technological catch-up strategy; a need to offer market access for foreign companies in exchange for China's own access to international markets; and the fact that advances in shipping and logistics made it attractive for international companies to relocate much of their production in low-labor-cost countries such as China.

The opening to FDI began pragmatically. China in the late 1970s was in dire economic straits and had few ways to raise foreign exchange to buy foreign technology. A quick one was to let foreign companies set up export-oriented factories inside China—at first through a handful of SEZs in the south and later throughout the country. The policy choices that led to the later surges in FDI—in the early 1990s and again in the early 2000s after China's entry into WTO—were more strategic. Reformers knew they could accelerate reform of the domestic economy by introducing competition by big foreign firms.

Another facet of the FDI strategy was that much "foreign" investment was not really foreign. Nearly half of inbound direct investment has come from Hong Kong. In the 1980s and 1990s, most of the city-state's manufacturing firms moved their production across the border to Shenzhen and neighboring cities in Guangdong. From the late 1990s onward, Hong Kong property and infrastructure firms have poured many billions of dollars into toll roads, ports, and residential and commercial property developments. Although Hong Kong returned to rule by the mainland in 1997, Chinese statistics still count its investments as "foreign."[14]

Moreover, as much as a third of China's reported FDI may in fact be "round-tripping"—investments by Chinese individuals and companies that is routed through companies in other jurisdictions, especially Hong Kong. Until about 2005, there was a strong incentive for round-tripping in order to capture tax breaks and other benefits reserved for foreign firms.[15] Even after those benefits began to evaporate, there were still reasons for domestic companies to register themselves as "foreign"—for instance, to make it easier to take capital out of the country by disguising it as profit remittances by a foreign-invested firm.

The peak of the FDI model came in 2002–2006, when the terms of China's WTO accession agreement required it to make a series of reforms giving foreign firms more access to its market. By the end of 2006, China had met all its WTO obligations, and an increasingly prosperous domestic economy was no longer in such desperate need of foreign capital. FDI in that year accounted for 6 percent of total investment in China, down from the peak of 17 percent in 1994. By 2014, FDI accounted for less than 3 percent of investment.

Reliance on FDI has brought China substantial benefits: the technology, production techniques, and management skills brought by foreign firms have been assimilated by domestic companies and have helped them grow. Foreign firms also benefited. Despite regulations that restrict their investments, affect certain industries, or force them into joint ventures with local firms, they enjoy substantial market access and have generated large profits from their China operations.

But the relationship between the Chinese government and foreign firms is growing chillier. Since 2005, China's industrial policy has increasingly focused on building up domestic companies, most notably under Made in China 2025. Given foreign firms' large existing footprint in China, and China's commitment to equal treatment under the WTO and other international agreements, it will be a tricky task to provide support for domestic firms without sparking increased criticism from foreign companies and governments.

Does China "cheat"?

Critics often claim that China achieved its industrial and export success by "cheating" against the rules of fair trade and competition. These charges began in the early 2000s when China's exports boomed and have become much louder and more frequent since the adoption of Made in China 2025 and since the election of Donald Trump as U.S. president in November 2016. Specifically, it is alleged that China supports its industry and exports by:

- Keeping interest rates, the exchange rate, and energy prices artificially low;
- Showering its firms with subsidies;
- Imposing unreasonable restrictions on foreign companies that want to sell into the Chinese market; and
- Permitting theft of foreign firms' intellectual property rights (IPR)—or even forcing IPR transfers as a condition of market access.

Such claims always contain a mixture of economic fact and political fiction. Many trade practices that may not be "fair" are nonetheless quite common. Every country that has created a successful "catch-up" industrial economy has employed some or all of these tactics. This includes the United States, which was notorious for its disregard of other people's intellectual property for much of the nineteenth century, maintained high tariff barriers right up until World War II, and continues to subsidize politically important industries on a large scale.[16] All countries try to bend global trade and investment rules in their favor, and they succeed to the degree that their market power enables them to do so.

Broadly speaking, China's industrial success is due to skillful exploitation of its natural advantages and smart macroeconomic and industrial policies, not "cheating." Foreign companies have been important and enthusiastic contributors to this success and have willingly invested and transferred technology on a large scale in order to gain access to China's huge market and efficient production base. Although some companies have been hurt by Chinese competition, on balance foreign companies have profited handsomely from China.

However, some of China's practices clearly diverge from established global norms of fair competition, and as China has grown, these divergences have become much more problematic. Practices that richer countries could afford to ignore when China was a relatively small economy producing mainly low-technology goods seem far more threatening now that China is the world's second-biggest economy and Beijing has set ambitious targets for Chinese leadership in high-tech industries such as semiconductors, electric vehicles, and artificial intelligence.

Let us examine one by one the four main categories of unfair practices that we mentioned above.

Artificially Low Interest Rates, Exchange Rates, and Energy Prices. These were commonly cited in 2000–2010 but are less talked about today, in part because these claims were weak to begin with and have mostly been addressed by Chinese policy. Low interest rates were largely an artifact of China's very high savings rate rather than a deliberate effort to advantage industry (see Chapter 9). Since the global financial crisis of 2008, which forced the United States, Europe, and Japan to adopt ultra-low (and in some cases negative) rates for a long time, Chinese interest rates have not been especially low. The exchange rate was undervalued for a few years (roughly 2003–2007) but then, between 2007 and 2017, steadily appreciated by a total of around 40 percent and is now, roughly, both fairly valued and more market driven. China's government has long managed energy prices—but mainly to reduce volatility and not to make energy artificially cheap (see Chapter 10).

Subsidies. Subsidies are clearly an issue, especially the guidance funds being used to promote Made in China 2025, which are thinly disguised subsidy programs. Under WTO rules, subsidies are prohibited for export promotion but permitted to support production for the domestic market. Formally, guidance funds support production for the domestic market. But this seems like a fig leaf given the global market share (that is, export) targets under Made in China 2025 for many of the supported sectors.

Restrictions on Foreign Companies in China. Strangely, despite the large role foreign companies have played in China's development, it is true that China has some of the highest barriers to foreign investment of any major economy, as measured by an Organization for Economic and Cooperation and Development (OECD) index. Some of these restrictions are in the industrial sector: for instance, the requirement that foreign automobile and petrochemicals companies operate through joint ventures with Chinese firms. But the most onerous restrictions on Chinese investment are in services. These include censorship-related rules that make it virtually impossible for most international internet companies to do business in China.[17]

Intellectual Property Theft or Forced Transfer. Protection of intellectual property rights such as patents, trademarks, copyrights, and trade secrets has long been weak in China—as in virtually every other country that has ever tried to catch up with the most technologically advanced nations. For example, Europe's nascent porcelain industry in the early eighteenth century depended heavily on reports by Jesuit missionaries on Chinese ceramic techniques, which the Chinese state considered trade secrets. Theft of tea plants whose export was prohibited by China enabled the British to establish a tea industry in India. In the early nineteenth century, the first great textile complex in the United States was founded essentially on industrial espionage.[18] After World War II, Japan, South Korea, and Taiwan relied in part on reverse engineering and copying of Western technologies, in violation of Western patent rules.

The point is not that IPR violations are morally defensible, but that they are routine and typically endure until a country has enough IPR of its own to decide that it is more beneficial to protect than to steal. This shift occurred in the United States in the mid-nineteenth century and in the East Asian states in the 1980s and 1990s. It has begun in China with the establishment of specialized IPR courts and the use of criminal penalties for some violations.

All that said, China's treatment of IPR can be criticized on several grounds. First, China's development has occurred during a period when legal protections for IPR are much higher than they were in the nineteenth century or even right after World War II. China agreed to high-standard protections for IPR when it joined the WTO. So it can legitimately be held to account for its failure to meet its own commitments. Second, China's IPR violations are on an unusually large scale, and its legal system is unusually weak and subject to political control.

Finally, through both formal measures such as joint venture requirements and informal arm-twisting, the Chinese government has made technology transfer a condition for market access by foreign firms. The Chinese government argues that such transfers are voluntary and not forced, since foreign companies are free not to sign these contracts (at the price of foregoing the profits they hoped to gain by doing business in China). And foreign firms have proved crafty at signing agreements that limit the amount of really crucial technology they transfer. But there is little doubt that China's efforts to compel technology transfer lie outside acceptable practice in the developed world.[19]

Where has "industrial policy" succeeded and where has it failed?

The goals of China's industrial policy have been to create a broad set of industries, with Chinese companies progressively producing goods of greater technological sophistication and higher value, and gradually becoming more globally competitive. These aims have largely been achieved.

China has moved from being a producer of low-end textiles and cheap consumer goods in the 1980s to a country with successful and large-scale automotive, shipbuilding, machinery, electronics, chemicals, and precision instruments industries. The global competitiveness of Chinese production has steadily risen, as shown by its growing share of global manufactured exports. Studies have documented that the research-and-development intensity of Chinese exports—that is, their technological sophistication—has risen as well.[20] Moreover, growing shares of exports and the trade surplus are generated by domestic firms. For most of the 2000s, foreign enterprises accounted for more than half of exports and as much as two-thirds of the trade surplus. By 2014, the foreign share of both was under half, and by 2018, foreign companies accounted for 42 percent of exports—still a high number but the lowest since the mid-1990s.

But China has not been equally successful in all industries. In particular, it has not always done well in ensuring that the production of higher-technology goods is controlled by Chinese-owned firms. The FDI model means that certain industries have been built mainly by foreign firms, and it has sometimes proved hard for Chinese companies to break in.

Two prominent examples are automobiles and electronics. Since 2010, China has been the world's biggest passenger car market, and virtually all the vehicles sold in China are built in China. There are essentially two types of producers: (1) joint ventures between big global automakers and local firms (typically, SOEs), and (2) purely local private or SOE car firms. All the globally important American, Japanese, and European car makers have joint ventures in China, and these joint ventures dominate the industry's revenues and profits. Chinese firms produce about half the cars sold in China, but these are mainly low-end vehicles with very thin profit margins. The foreign joint ventures control around 80 percent of the industry's revenues. Chinese firms increasingly export their cars to low-income markets in the Middle East, Central Asia, and Latin America, but they have failed to make inroads in developed countries, and in general they show no signs of being able to emulate the international success of Japanese and Korean automakers.[21]

The auto industry should be borne in mind when assessing claims about China's industrial and technological prowess. As it demonstrates, Chinese companies remain far from achieving the highest global standard in products that require multiple levels of technology, intricate production processes, and high degrees of precision. Other examples include jet engines, airplanes (where China has tried for years, without much success so far, to develop homegrown commercial aircraft), semiconductors, and many consumer electronics sectors. On the other hand, Chinese firms are highly competitive in technology-intensive industries of less complexity, and in particular those in which the customers are mainly businesses rather than consumers: auto components, power generation equipment, telecom network equipment, and so on.

Electronics is another interesting case. At one level, it is a spectacular success story: China now accounts for over 40 percent of global exports of electronics goods like computers and smartphones, up from 5 percent in the year 2000. But the majority of electronics activity in China remains final-stage assembly, where profit margins are thin, and even this activity is largely controlled by foreign enterprises—especially Taiwanese firms, of which Foxconn (the main contract assembler of Apple products) is the best known. The highest-value components of the technology value chain—design and marketing of final products, design of integrated circuits, and original software development—remain in the hands of global giants such as Apple, Samsung, Intel, and Microsoft.

Persistent efforts by the Chinese government to foster local challengers to these companies have failed. Today China has no globally significant software firms, and only a small handful of important hardware companies. Two interesting examples of the latter are telecom network equipment maker Huawei and smartphone maker Xiaomi.

Huawei and Xiaomi grew using a business model that can be described as "80 percent of the quality for 60 percent of the price." Firms like this produce reliable equipment with functionality that is behind the leading edge but still good enough for most buyers—and at an unbeatable price. This makes their products very attractive to a large number of customers that want to keep up with technological trends but cannot afford the latest and greatest: poor countries that want decent cell phone networks, or lower-middle-income Chinese who want a smartphone but cannot shell out $700 for an iPhone. Many successful Chinese industrial firms employ a variant of this business model, exploiting China's low production costs and economies of scale to offer solid products at a low price. This enables them to generate large sales volumes, but their profit margins are low. They are essentially technology followers, not technology leaders.

Recently, Huawei has proved an important exception to this generalization. Since the 1990s, it has invested 10 percent of its annual revenues in R&D, and it is the largest contributor of intellectual property to the "fifth-generation" (5G) technology for mobile networks, which will start being deployed in 2020. It is a true technological leader and has surpassed its European rivals to become the world's biggest telecom network equipment maker; industry insiders consider its technology to be leading-edge.[22] Even so, it remains heavily dependent on imports of American semiconductors and has become a key target in the escalating trade and technology rivalry between the United States and China.

Can Chinese industry become more innovative?

A major preoccupation of Chinese policymakers and of outside China-watchers is whether China's economy can become more innovative. This is a tough question because experts find it hard to agree on what innovation is, how innovative China is right now, and what the ingredients are for an innovation-driven economy.[23] Without pretending to come up with a complete answer, we can make a few observations.

First, Chinese firms are generally quite good at "adaptive" innovations—taking existing products, services, or processes and modifying them, often in substantial ways, to make them more responsive to the needs of the Chinese market. This is an important type of innovation. But Chinese companies have shown little ability—so far—to develop new products, services, or processes that are adopted or emulated in other countries. This makes China different from Japan in the 1960s and 1970s. Japan pioneered some important business-process innovations—notably total quality management (TQM) in manufacturing (actually, a Japanese development of ideas conceived by the American engineer W. Edwards Deming)— that were later studied and adopted by firms in other countries. By the mid-1970s, Japan had a long roster of companies that were beginning to set global quality and technology standards for a host of industries: firms like Toyota, Sony, Panasonic, Nikon, Canon, and Seiko. Aside from Huawei, China has no such companies today. And no one is coming to China to figure out how to make factories in the United States or Europe run better.

Second, Chinese innovation policy conflates the concepts of innovation and autonomy. The Chinese term for Indigenous Innovation, *zizhu chuangxin*, could also fairly be translated as Autonomous Innovation.[24] Chinese innovation policies often seem less about creativity per se and more about reducing reliance on imported products, services, and ideas.

Autonomy and innovation are quite separate and perhaps even contradictory ideas. One can be "autonomous" or self-reliant by creating non-innovative, just-good-enough domestic substitutes for foreign goods. Made in China 2025 can be criticized not only because it discriminates against foreign firms, but also because its stress on self-reliance may lead the government to support domestic firms even when they are less innovative than international competitors.

Third, one must entertain severe doubts about the innovative potential of a society that has moved so aggressively in recent years to restrict the free exchange of ideas, which under any definition is surely an indispensable requirement for sustained innovative achievement. The Communist Party has always been relatively repressive of public information flows. But under Xi Jinping it has become much more so, by shutting down independent voices in social media, increasing censorship and blockage of both foreign and domestic websites, and harassing or closing down civil society organizations that receive foreign funding or are suspected of propagating ideas from abroad. It has also launched a campaign to cleanse university textbooks of foreign ideas and to encourage university professors to promote "Chinese" ideas in their teaching.

Finally, despite these ideological controls, the vibrant Chinese internet has proved a fertile breeding ground for genuinely innovative companies, notably Alibaba in e-commerce and mobile payments, and Tencent in social networking and gaming. The enormous amounts of data collected by these firms from their online users provide a strong basis for China to take a leadership role in the development of artificial intelligence. China's hopes for developing into a more innovation-driven economy rest heavily on the shoulders of these internet firms, which we will explore further in Chapter 14.

6

URBANIZATION
AND INFRASTRUCTURE

How fast has China urbanized?

Mass migration from country to city is a phenomenon that every country experiences as it industrializes. China is no exception to this rule but has done it faster and on a far larger scale than most other nations. On the eve of the reform era in 1978, only 18 percent of the population lived in cities, a share that had been almost static since the late 1950s. Forty years later, in 2018, the urban population had swelled to 60 percent of the total (Figure 6.1). This roughly parallels what happened in the United States in the seven decades between 1860 and 1930, when the urban share of the population rose from 20 percent to 56 percent. In other words, China urbanized about twice as fast as the United States did.

Moreover, China's urbanization has involved vastly more people than any other country's. Between 1978 and 2018, the urban population rose from 172 million to 832 million—an increase of 660 million, or about double the present U.S. population. By contrast, between 1860 and 1930, the U.S. urban population rose by just 63 million people. The only country that even comes close to China is India, which saw its urban population increase by 310 million in 1978–2018.

One way to make these large numbers easier to grasp is to imagine what China would have had to do if it decided to put each year's new urbanites in a brand-new city. To

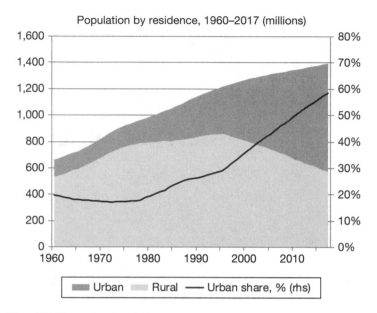

Figure 6.1 Urban and rural population.

Source: NBS/CEIC.

accommodate an urban population growing at 16 million an-
nually, China would have had to build a new city, equal in size
to greater New York City and greater Philadelphia combined,
every year for 35 years.

In absolute terms, the growth of China's cities is without
peer. In proportional terms, it is rapid but not completely unprecedented. The 42-percentage-point increase in China's
urban population share between 1978 and 2018 was about
double the average for other developing countries during the
same period. But a few other places have made the shift from
mostly rural to majority urban as fast or faster than China. In
its first three decades, the Soviet Union urbanized at about
the same rate as China since 1978. And South Korea—a much
smaller country—saw its population go from three-quarters
rural to three-quarters urban between 1955 and 1990. This involved a total increase in the urban population of about 26 million people, less than China experiences in 2 years.

Despite the enormous increase in the city population, China today remains less urbanized than virtually any other country of its income level. The rural population kept growing until it peaked at 860 million in 1995; since then it has declined to 565 million. If one assumes, as many demographers do, that the urban share of the population will level off at around three-quarters, China's high-speed urbanization process still has another 10–15 years to run.[1]

How does urbanization relate to economic growth?

Urbanization interacts with economic growth in three ways, corresponding roughly to three stages of economic development. As an economy modernizes and industrializes, factories spring up in and around cities. These factories offer wages higher than the incomes available to people working in subsistence agriculture (which, at the beginning of industrialization, is most people). These wages pull people off the farm and into the modern economy, so we can call this stage of urbanization the "magnet" phase. Because a worker's productivity is much higher in a modern factory than in traditional agriculture, this transfer of population from the traditional to the modern economy is a major contributor to faster economic growth.

After a certain point, the urbanization process itself becomes a direct contributor to economic growth, not just a side effect of industrialization; we can call this the "building-binge" phase. The workers who have been brought in to staff the factories need housing, roads, sewers, water lines, electric hookups, telephone services, and so on. Construction of all this housing and infrastructure creates new employment opportunities, and it also stokes demand for basic materials such as steel, cement, glass, aluminum, and copper. Urbanization becomes one of the processes that pushes economic growth. This second type of urbanization-associated growth is of lower quality than the first because it does not by itself create large productivity gains. For a period of time, construction of housing and infra-structure can push up the rate of investment and hence GDP growth. But once the building binge is over, the workers living in these cities are not necessarily a lot more productive than they were when living in company dormitories with minimal amenities.[2]

Once they are endowed with modern infrastructure, cities can become hubs of economic vitality. Their density of skilled workers enables the creation of knowledge networks, which generate specialization and productivity growth in particular industries. We can call this the "smart city" phase. Prominent examples of this sort of specialization include London and New York (finance), Los Angeles (entertainment), and the San Francisco–San Jose conurbation known as Silicon Valley (tech-nology). A study by the Brookings Institution found that half of economic growth in the entire world now comes from the 300 biggest metropolitan areas, largely because of specializa-tion in extremely high-value activities.[3]

China's urbanization in the first two decades of the re-form era was mainly of the first type. Workers moved from the countryside to urban factories, but for the most part they did not bring their families. Their incomes were still low, and they tended to live in factory dormitories or other company-provided housing. The rapidly rising productivity of these workers as they moved from traditional agriculture to modern industry was the single most important contributor to eco-nomic growth, accounting for as much as one-fifth of the in-crease in GDP between 1979 and 1997.[4]

After 1998, urbanization moved into its second, "building-binge" phase, for several reasons. First, economic reforms and tacit relaxations of the rules governing migrant labor accelerated the pace of rural-to-urban migration, with the result that the average annual increase in the urban popu-lation leaped from 12 million people in 1978–1998 to 21 mil-lion in 1998–2018. Second, the urban housing market was privatized in the late 1990s, leading to perhaps the biggest housing boom in world history. Finally, government policy after 1998 increasingly supported the building of infrastructure. Some of this infrastructure—such as intercity highways and railroads—made it easier for people to move to cities in search of work. And some of it—such as urban roads, subways, and water treatment plants—directly contributed to the physical growth of cities.

The challenge for China today is that the building-binge stage of urbanization is close to a plateau. Annual completion of new housing nearly quadrupled between 1998 and 2018. Housing construction is now at or near its peak and will almost certainly begin to decline in the early 2020s (Figure 6.2). Broadly the same story holds for urban infrastructure: much

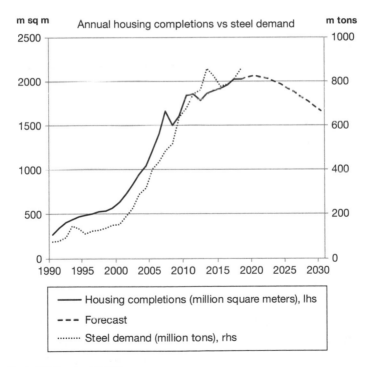

Figure 6.2 Housing and steel.

Source: Gavekal Dragonomics.

more needs to be built, but the annual amount of construction no longer needs to increase. So China is not going to get any more *growth* simply by building houses and infrastructure. Instead, it must enable its cities to move into the "smart city" phase, in which specialization and innovation become the main economic growth drivers.

What is China's "partial urbanization" problem?

China's urban population has grown rapidly. But the raw figures we quoted earlier are somewhat misleading. Just who counts as "urban" is a matter of definition, and China's urban population data are subject to various distortions. For one thing, the boundaries around Chinese cities keep expanding. As the city limits expand, large swathes of rural land are engulfed. According to the World Bank, the reclassification of previously rural land as urban accounted for 42 percent of the increase in the urban population in 2000–2010; migration contributed 43 percent and natural increase the remaining 15 percent.[5]

Because Chinese cities are officially defined by their administrative boundaries, their populations are often much larger than the number of people who actually live in recognizably urban areas. The most extreme example is the municipality of Chongqing, which is sometimes described as "the largest city in the world." In fact, it is nothing of the kind: it is a territory the size of Austria (and almost as mountainous), carved out of the larger province of Sichuan in 1997, whose population of 31 million is at least a third rural. Chongqing city itself has a population of 7–8 million, just one-quarter of the total municipality. The actual biggest city in China is Shanghai, with an urban population of 22 million. Under a broader definition, Guangdong's Pearl River Delta in 2014 overtook metropolitan Tokyo as the world's biggest urban area, with a population of 42 million.[6]

Urban geographers have carefully studied China's true urban population and have concluded that the total number is roughly the same as reported in official statistics, but the distribution is more scattered than it might appear at first. A large number of urban Chinese live in small "satellite towns" that orbit major metropolises like Beijing and Shanghai.[7]

The bigger problem—and the one that Chinese scholars mean when they refer to "partial urbanization"—is that the living conditions for Chinese urbanites are widely disparate. The lucky ones live in proper apartments and have full access to social services such as public schools for their children, medical care, and pension plans. The less lucky—who account for a third of China's urban population, or some 250 million people—live and work in the city but are not entitled to these social services, and in many cases live in substandard housing without their own kitchen or toilet (Figure 6.3).[8] Hundreds of millions of Chinese have physically moved into the cities over the past 40 years, but many of them are still waiting to be fully integrated into urban life. Put another way, China has done a good job of urbanizing *jobs* but a poor job of urbanizing *people*. Turning these "incomplete urbanites" into full urban citizens is a major challenge for the next decade.

What is the hukou system, and what impact does it have?

One of the main reasons for this "partial urbanization" is the *hukou* or residence registration system. This system has its roots in the *baojia* household registration method established by the Song Dynasty in eleventh-century China, versions of which later appeared in other Asian countries, including Vietnam, Korea, and Japan. The modern hukou, dating from 1958, is far more restrictive than the traditional *baojia*, which was used mainly for census and taxation purposes. Hukou incorporates elements of the "internal passport" system used by the Soviet Union to limit the mobility of its citizens. In addition

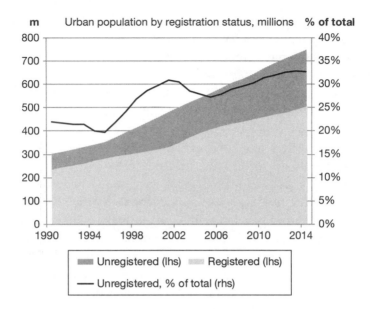

Figure 6.3 Urban population.

Note: data on unregistered population not published after 2014.

Source: NBS/CEIC.

to assigning each person a place of registration that is hard to change, the system sorts people into two categories: rural and urban. When it was strictly enforced during the Maoist era, hukou made it very difficult to obtain a job outside one's place of registration and almost impossible to migrate from the country to the city. Between 1960 and 1978, the urban share of the national population actually fell, from 20 percent to 18 percent. This repression of city growth in the 1960s and 1970s is one of the main reasons why even today China's urban population is lower than is normal for a country of its income.[9]

Enforcement broke down in the 1980s as factories sprouted in coastal cities and began to suck up labor, at first from the surrounding countryside and later from provinces hundreds of miles away. Officials eager to promote economic growth allowed a free inflow of migrant labor. But migrant workers were not permitted to bring their dependent family members because officials feared the emergence of uncontrollable slums. And if they did bring their dependents—as increasingly became the case in the 1990s and 2000s—migrant families were shut off from social services. Migrant children could not legally attend local public schools, hospitals would not accept migrants for treatment, and migrants often had difficulty renting or buying formal housing. All these services were reserved for the people who held local, urban hukou.

In a strict sense, hukou has long ceased to be a barrier to labor mobility: workers are pretty much free to go wherever there are jobs for them. But it distorts labor flows in ways that impose economic costs. The cities with the most vibrant economies and best job opportunities, like Beijing and Shanghai, also have the most restrictive immigration policies, so their populations and economies are smaller than they would be without hukou barriers. Many migrant workers are diverted from these hubs into smaller cities, where construction jobs have created a temporary demand for labor and more relaxed migration policies, but where the potential for long-term productivity growth is lower.[10]

Hukou is also a significant barrier to social mobility within cities. The average wage for migrant workers is only about 60 percent of that for urban hukou holders. Migrant families are locked into second-class status: unlike in South Korea, where migrants from the countryside quickly became indistinguishable from longer-term city dwellers, even the children of China's migrant workers face discrimination in their access to housing and other channels of upward mobility.[11]

How is the hukou system being reformed?

The national government has gingerly experimented with reforms to the hukou system. Key moves were a 2001 policy encouraging small cities and towns to grant urban hukou to migrants, a 2006 state council decision that abolished arbitrary fees on migrants, national guidelines in 2011 for relaxing hukou restrictions, and a partial step toward implementing those guidelines in 2014. On-the-ground progress has been glacial. The central conundrum is figuring out a way (1) to give migrant workers equal access to social services in the cities where they live, without (2) subjecting those cities to unbearable fiscal pressures, and (3) ensuring that migrant workers flow more or less evenly to cities of all sizes throughout the country rather than flocking to a small number of attractive cities mainly along the coast.

The third objective—ensuring migrant flow to cities of all sizes—imposes a constraint on the ability to achieve the first two, and it illustrates the tension between the policymakers' stated interest in market forces and their engrained habits of top-level planning. The most straightforward way to equalize conditions for migrant workers would be to let them go without restriction to the biggest and richest cities. These cities already have the fiscal resources to begin making social services available to all; more importantly, their sophisticated and diverse economies ensure that the productivity of migrant workers can rise quickly. This would contribute to future economic growth, which in turn would boost these cities' fiscal resources and ability to expand social services.

It is clear, however, that this solution is not on the table. The 2014 relaxation of hukou restrictions explicitly stated that migration into cities with a population above 5 million (which already accounts for 20 percent of China's urban population) would be tightly controlled, while migration into the smallest cities with less than 1 million inhabitants would be actively encouraged.[12] This decision partly reflects the political power of elites in the big cities, who want to preserve their quality of life from the degradation they fear it would suffer from an influx of low-income migrants. It also reflects a long-standing bias among policymakers against permitting the emergence of sprawling, hard-to-control megacities. This bias is not irrational. The developing world offers plenty of examples, from

Manila to Mumbai to São Paulo, of magnet cities that risk being engulfed by their own slums.

Yet, East Asia also has successful megacities such as Tokyo and Seoul (whose metropolitan area houses about half of South Korea's population), which are well-ordered hubs of creativity and innovation. Chinese authorities may be right that a Chinese megacity would probably look more like Manila than Seoul. But by deliberately restricting the growth of the country's most successful metropolises, they may slow China's progress toward becoming a more innovative society and make it harder to solve the inequities created by the hukou system.

Reform efforts now focus on creation of a "residence permit" system to operate parallel with the hukou registration system. The idea is that social services would be delinked from hukou and tied instead to a residence permit, issued by the city or town in which a person actually works and lives. Since 2010, several cities, notably Guangzhou, Shenzhen, Chongqing, Shanghai, and Tianjin, have piloted residence permit programs. Most use points systems under which migrants earn credits for years of employment, taxes paid, educational qualifications, and other criteria; they get a permit once they accumulate a certain number of points. In theory, such a system could be implemented nationwide, in which case the primary remaining function of rural hukou would be to document rural land rights. In practice, residence permit reforms have advanced slowly. They will continue to do so until the central government issues national standards for such permits and also improves the fiscal transfer system, so that cities without the resources to provide social services to migrants can receive appropriate assistance.[13]

What was the impact of urban housing privatization?

One of the great turning points in China's economic history was the decision to privatize the urban housing market. Until the late 1990s, most urban residents lived in apartments assigned to them by their work units, for which they paid a nominal rent. This legacy of the Maoist centrally planned economy meant there was little incentive for anyone to build new homes. As a result, housing was in short supply and most families lived in cramped quarters, with only about 150 square feet of living space per person.

Under Zhu Rongji's state-owned enterprise reform program, SOEs and government work units were ordered to sell off the housing they controlled to the occupants, at prices that represented a big discount on market value. How big a discount was difficult to judge, since at that time there was no real market for urban housing or land. Even at these low "insider" prices, many families had difficulty affording their apartments, so they received subsidies from the government or their employers or mortgages at concessional rates. In return for these benefits, buyers were often prevented from selling their newly acquired apartments for a period of time, typically 5 years. In general terms, the program resembled Margaret Thatcher's privatization of state-owned housing in the United Kingdom in the early 1980s—but on a larger scale.

China's housing privatization was one of the greatest wealth transfers in history, and it laid the foundations for the extraordinary housing boom of the following decade. Urban households got to buy valuable property for far less than its market value. The difference between what they paid their SOE landlords for this property and the higher price they were ultimately able to sell it for represented a transfer of wealth from the state to households. The total value of that wealth transfer was about $540 billion, or one-third of China's GDP in 2003, the year when housing privatization was largely complete.[14]

To understand its impact at an individual level, consider this simplified example. Imagine a family that buys a house in the center of a city for $100, using $50 of its own money and $50 borrowed interest-free from the family's work unit. After 5 years, when the family is finally permitted to sell, the market value of the house is $250. The family sells and has $200 left over once it has repaid the loan to the work unit. The difference between the money the family put in and what it took out—$150—can be considered a transfer of wealth from the state to the family, since the individual is allowed to collect the capital gain that the work unit would have enjoyed if it had been allowed to sell the apartment on the open market.

As its next step, the family uses this money to buy two new apartments farther from the center of town, which cost only $100 each: one to live in and the other as an investment. After another few years, the market value of each of these houses rises to $250. The family's original $50 investment has ballooned to $500, a tenfold increase. Meanwhile, it has spawned demand for two new housing units, creating business for property developers.

Of course, this example contains a number of assumptions, most importantly that house prices continue to rise at a rapid rate. House prices cannot simply rise forever—as homeowners in the United States discovered to their detriment in 2007–2008. But China has sustained fast increases in house prices for two decades, for a couple of reasons. First, the starting point for urban property prices was extraordinarily low. Because there was no active property market and most urban land before the late 1990s was controlled by state-owned work units, which in many cases had held the rights for decades, land values were far below what they would have been in a market system. The second reason was that the starting point for the housing supply was one of acute shortage. For these reasons, once market conditions took hold, there was every reason for house prices to soar until supply and demand began to balance out. Anyone able to get hold of urban property in the late 1990s or early 2000s—whether a homeowner buying at an insider price or a property company gaining redevelopment rights—was almost guaranteed to reap spectacular gains as land prices adjusted up to their true market value.

Housing privatization created an enormous benefit for tens of millions of urban Chinese households, who improved their living conditions and gained a valuable store of wealth. But these benefits came at high cost in the form of increased inequality and unfairness. Housing privatization was a great deal *if you already occupied a state-owned house.* (It was an even better deal if your family had the rights to several apartments, as sometimes occurred when both a husband and wife were assigned housing by their work units or inherited housing units from their parents.) If you did not happen to be sitting in a state-owned apartment in the late 1990s or early 2000s, or did not have the cash to get into the market in the early years, you were out of luck. Since you could no longer get a house from your work unit, you had to buy an apartment out of your own meager savings, in a market where prices (at least in some cities) were rising faster than incomes.

One consequence was that the great housing boom of 2000–2010 was driven principally by "upgrading demand" from urban hukou holders moving from an older home to a newer, better one. Relatively little demand came from new urban migrants because they simply could not afford the high prices.[15] So even though China famously was experiencing a huge migration from countryside to city, the housing market was largely an insiders' game, where the housing needs of new migrants were given short shrift, while some urban hukou holders enjoyed enormous financial gains. By 2012, a variety of studies suggested that home ownership rates among urban hukou holders were in the range of 70 to 80 percent, well above the U.S. rate that peaked at 69 percent in 2004. The rate for migrant families was 10 percent or less.[16] Instead, migrant workers lived in company dormitories, in underground apartments created in basements and air-raid shelters, or in rooms in converted farmhouses on the city outskirts.

A final point about housing privatization is that it is one of the starkest cases of urban bias in Chinese policymaking, and a major contributor to China's yawning inequality chasm. A group of urban households were given full property rights to their houses, including the rights to buy and sell and to use their house as collateral for a mortgage. Urban residents now have an absolute right to private real property if they can afford to acquire it. By contrast, the property rights of rural farmers remain far more limited. As we explained in Chapter 4, farmers mainly just have use rights, and not the right to freely buy and sell their land on the open market. (They are, however, free to have their land seized by the government for infrastructure development, at prices that are unlikely to be fair.) The quality of those use rights varies widely by region, and in many cases title is not clear. The government remains deeply reluctant to give farmers the same level of property rights as urban households. As long as this disparity continues, high levels of income and wealth inequality between cities and the countryside will persist.

Is China's housing market an unsustainable bubble?

Over the past two decades China has had one of the most extraordinary housing booms in history, with monumental increases in both the volume of housing construction and housing prices. Between 1996 and 2018, annual construction of new housing quadrupled, from 500 million 2 billion square meters. From 2003 to 2018, the average price of urban housing rose 290 percent. Average house prices in the most desirable cities, Beijing and Shanghai, rose four- or fivefold.[17]

This breakneck rise in prices, along with periodic reports of massive tracts of unsold housing in various cities, prompts recurrent fears that China's housing market is a "bubble" that is bound to burst, perhaps triggering a financial crisis. These fears have so far proven unfounded. It is worth understanding why.

In a bubble, prices of some asset (houses, shares on the stock market, tulips) rise far above their underlying value. The bubble pops when rationality returns and prices plunge to a more realistic level. This can be disastrous if people borrowed a lot of money to buy the overvalued assets because there is a lot of debt that cannot be repaid. In the Chinese housing market, prices indeed rose quite rapidly for a long time, but careful analysis suggests they did not often rise for long above realistic levels. And, relative to other markets, Chinese households have not taken on that much mortgage debt.

Three key factors lay behind the long housing boom and also made it hard to analyze. First, until the early 2000s, urban China effectively had no real estate market because most urban housing stock and land was owned by SOEs, and there had been almost no trading of these assets since the 1950s. So at the start of the housing boom urban real estate prices were far below their true market value. Second, there was a severe shortage of housing. Under these conditions, it was natural for prices to rise quite a lot before hitting their true market level. Third, as we noted above, housing privatization handed a huge capital gains windfall to many urban residents. As a result, many house purchases especially in the early years were not financed by regular income but by this windfall—which made it hard to figure out the right relationship between house prices and household income.

In fact, data show that, despite steadily rising prices, housing has become more affordable for the average urban household—especially since 2007, when the government identified high house prices as a major problem and started actively promoting affordability. Between 2007 and 2018, the price of an average urban apartment fell from nine times the average annual household income to seven times—a normal figure for densely populated Asian countries.[18] The average mortgage payment burden fell from 40 percent of monthly income to 26 percent during the same period (Figure 6.4).[19]

Looking ahead, although property markets in many individual cities may prove volatile, there is little reason to expect a national housing crisis like the one that gripped the United States in 2008. House prices are generally in line with regional norms, and central and local governments constantly adjust policies if prices rise too much. Second, buyers are not heavily indebted because minimum down payments

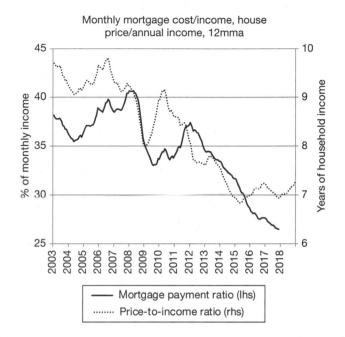

Monthly mortgage cost/income, house price/annual income, 12mma

Figure 6.4 Housing affordability.

are high—typically, 20–30 percent of the home's value and as much as 60–70 percent for investment properties.[20] Finally, the likely future increase in the urban population—around 200 million people over the next 15 to 20 years—will create a large pipeline of demand.

What problems does China's two-tier housing market create?

The real problem with China's urban housing market is not that it is a bubble, but that it is an unequal, two-tier system. This is a legacy of housing privatization, which created a lucky class of homebuyers who could afford to purchase relatively expensive housing thanks to the benefit they got from privatization, and a second unlucky class who had to buy housing purely from their own hard-earned savings. The more market-driven tier of the housing system caters to the first class: upgraders and relatively high-income families. This tier is often at risk of oversupply because too many cities became too enthusiastic about promoting high-end housing developments—since city governments, which controlled the land on which those developments were built, stood to profit handsomely. The second tier, which addresses the needs of migrants and families whose incomes are too low to enable them to buy housing on the open market, suffers from shortage.

The government began to identify this problem—too large a supply of high-end housing and an insufficient supply of affordable housing—in 2007, and by 2010 it had a full set of policies to deal with it. Sales of high-end properties were subject to severe restrictions, including higher down payment requirements, higher mortgage interest rates, and limits on how many properties a single person could buy. Meanwhile, a large-scale "social housing" program aimed to increase the supply of affordable housing for lower-income households through use of various government incentives and subsidies. The initial target was to start construction of 36 million social housing units during the twelfth Five-Year Plan period (2011–2015), or about 7 million units a year.

These policies were somewhat effective in moderating the pace of increases in house prices, as well as in creating more housing options for low-income families. But the purchase restrictions did not achieve their intended effect of reducing the excess supply of high-end housing. By early 2015, with the market segment of the housing sector under severe pressure because of the large inventories of unsold apartments, virtually all purchase restrictions were lifted.

As for the social housing program, it is best described as a mandate without a mechanism. Localities were given quotas for the number of social housing units they were supposed to build, but little advice on how it should be done and, at least at first, minimal financial support. The result, unsurprisingly, was widely divergent outcomes. Richer cities such as Shanghai developed intelligent slum-upgrading programs, which renovated dilapidated units into modern housing at reasonable cost. Third- and fourth-tier cities often responded to the mandate by hastily erecting some buildings on cheap land far away from the town center and declaring "mission accomplished," even though shoddy construction and the lack of nearby shopping and transport rendered this housing literally unlivable.

Today social housing is a patchwork of a dozen different programs, financed by a hodgepodge of local resources, bonds, and bank loans (often collateralized by land assets at unrealistically high valuations), along with transfers from the central government that are often earmarked in ways unsuitable for the local governments that receive them. The emphasis has gradually moved from construction of new units that low-income people were expected to buy to the upgrading of existing low-quality housing that can be rented out. This is welcome: earlier expectations about the amount of money low-income people could present up front to buy housing proved wildly unrealistic.[21]

Meeting urban China's housing needs will be a difficult challenge for the next couple of decades. For better or worse, the government will meet this challenge by increasing its role. Between 2000 and 2010, about two-thirds of urban housing was provided by the market; the rest was social housing or subsidized apartments built by government agencies or SOEs for their workers. Now, probably half or more of urban housing involves a direct or indirect government subsidy of some kind, and this approach is likely to continue.

Why does China build so much infrastructure?

Related to the urbanization boom has been a boom in infrastructure spending. China made significant infrastructure investments in the first two decades of the reform era, notably in roads, ports, and telecommunications networks. Investment stepped up several notches in 1998, when in response to the Asian financial crisis the government launched a fiscal stimulus program whose main component was infrastructure spending, financed by special bonds. The main item was building a national expressway network, modeled on the U.S. interstate highway system. This was achieved: the expressway system went from less than 5,000 kilometers in 1997 to 143,000 kilometers in 2014, nearly double the size of the U.S. interstate system.

Other programs followed. Ports up and down the coast were expanded to accommodate the export surge of the 2000s. At the beginning of the decade, nearly half of Chinese exports went through Hong Kong because domestic ports could not handle the load; and only one Chinese port, Shanghai, was among the world's top twenty container ports (it ranked nineteenth). By 2013, Chinese ports had expanded their volume sixfold, and they handled more container traffic than the next six countries combined. Shanghai had passed Singapore as the world's biggest container port, and five other Chinese ports ranked in the world top ten.[22]

When Guangdong province, the heart of the nation's export sector, started having occasional blackouts in 2003, investment in power plants exploded. Each year for the next decade, China installed a new power plant worth one of Great Britain's. Generation capacity quintupled from 357 gigawatts in 2002 to 1,900 gigawatts in 2018—nearly double the U.S. capacity. Large investments in telecoms and Internet network infrastructure enabled China to go from 68 million Internet users in 2003 to 800 million in 2018; the number of mobile phone users rose from 270 million to 1.3 billion during the same period. A massive program to blanket the country with high-speed passenger rail lines, modeled on Japan's bullet-train network, was launched in 2003. In 2018, China had 29,000 kilometers of high-speed rail lines and two-thirds of the global total; the network is planned to reach 38,000 kilometers by 2025. More recently, the emphasis has shifted to somewhat less sexy urban infrastructure projects such as subway networks (of which

4,000 kilometers have already been built in more than thirty cities) and sewage treatment plants.[23]

This building extravaganza had several causes. Certainly, China had legitimate infrastructure needs that economic planners strove to meet. But other factors conspired to ramp up the scale and speed of construction—and also created problems such as redundant or wasteful projects, poor construction design and quality, and inadequate coordination. Local governments competing for investment felt pressure to install as much infrastructure as possible without careful cost-benefit analysis. Low interest rates in 2003–2012 and rapidly rising revenues from land sales made it cheap for them to do so. Bureaucratic incentives also played a role: in order for a small city to rise in the nation's administrative hierarchy (meaning promotion and higher status for the city's officials), it has to meet certain infrastructure standards. Local officials faced a strong temptation to build this infrastructure to advance their own careers, regardless of whether the projects were really necessary.

How much infrastructure is useful, and how much is wasteful?

Most of the infrastructure China has installed in the past two decades is useful and productive, although there are some large exceptions. China's infrastructure mania is often criticized for wastefulness, mainly on the grounds that the volume of construction is so staggering as to beggar belief. These blanket criticisms ignore a number of factors; chief among them is China's scale. China is a continent-sized country, as big as the United States including Alaska, and with more than four times the U.S. population. On a per capita basis, there are few infrastructure indicators on which China looks overbuilt relative to the United States or other developed economies.

China's infrastructure investment decisions are also driven by a complex set of factors that are often misunderstood by people from richer countries with slower growth rates, service-driven economies, and infrastructure built so long ago that it is now taken for granted. For one thing, China's 10 percent average growth rate for most of the past three decades meant that the economy doubled in size every 7 years. All else equal, this meant that for most of the reform era, you could reasonably assume that in 7 years you would need twice as much infrastructure capacity as you had today. It often made sense to build first and ask questions later.

The complexities of investment decisions and the inappropriateness of some international comparisons are illustrated by the high-speed rail network. This project was criticized on the grounds that China had not yet reached the stage of development that justified such a fancy kit, that it was too costly, that there was no way it could pay for itself, and that it was being built too fast. The first objection is simply invalid: Japan opened the first line of its much-admired bullet-train network in 1964, when its per capita GDP was the same as China's in 2007.

The other objections, many of them raised by domestic critics, were reasonable. But there were counterarguments. High-speed rail lines are notoriously costly to build in rich countries with high labor and land costs. In China, lower costs for land, labor, and capital equipment meant per-mile construction costs were substantially less than in rich countries. Another factor was that China's existing rail network was bursting at the seams, with capacity utilization rates several times higher than those in any other major economy. In 2008, China had 6 percent of the world's railroad-track miles but carried one-quarter of the entire world's rail traffic. Building a separate dedicated passenger system would enable many passenger routes on the old network to shut down, freeing up much-needed space for freight shipments. Increased freight charges on these old lines, planners calculated, would ultimately pay for much of the capital cost of the new passenger lines.[24]

The high-speed rail network is a mixed bag, with some very profitable lines and others less so. On balance, it will prove a worthwhile addition to China's transport mix. But the way it was built also illustrates a downside to China's approach to infrastructure, namely, immense corruption. The high-speed rail project was originally designed as a 17-year program, but in the wake of the global financial crisis the powerful railways minister successfully argued for cutting back the timeline by 5 years. This provided economic stimulus but also increased the scope for graft, since oversight was naturally laxer under the accelerated timetable. The minister and several colleagues ultimately wound up in prison for siphoning off billions of dollars. This, and many other Chinese infrastructure projects, could have been completed with more efficiency and less theft if the pace had simply slowed down.[25]

Another problem is needless duplication, caused by competition between cities. The prime example of this problem is airports: dozens of cities in China have built giant vanity airports in hopes of becoming the next major hub, only to see them stagger along with a handful of flights a day. This is genuinely wasteful spending and is made possible largely by the chaotic fiscal system that makes it hard to discipline profligate local officials (see Chapter 8).

Even if we accept that most of China's infrastructure is useful, it is clear that the age of breakneck spending is drawing to a close. The return on investment in infrastructure and other capital-intensive projects has been falling since 2008, and with the economy slowing and shifting more to services, the requirement for new infrastructure will probably decline in the coming decade. Just as for housing, the "building-binge" phase of growth is almost over. This does not have to be a problem: all countries eventually reach the point where they have built most of the infrastructure they need and start focusing on using it better. But adjusting to the post-infrastructure economy will be a challenge in a system where government officials have largely been rewarded for how much visible construction they could achieve.

What is China's plan for "new-style urbanization"?

Chinese policymakers have long had conflicted views about urbanization. In the 1980s and 1990s, they tolerated the flow of migrant workers into urban factories, but they did their best to prevent families from following the workers. This retarded the growth of cities and entrenched the pernicious class division between privileged urban hukou holders and second-class migrants. In the 2000s, policymakers abandoned efforts to prevent rural families from moving en masse and embraced rapid urbanization as a driver of economic growth. But the policymakers tried to steer migrant flows away from their natural course into big, prosperous cities and encouraged the proliferation of smaller cities whose economic rationale was much less clear. Poor budget controls and local fiscal systems overly dependent on land sales created sprawling cities and towns with abundant physical infrastructure but limited prospects for productivity-driven economic growth once the building binge ended.

Scholars and central government officials recognized these problems, and under the aegis of Premier Li Keqiang the state council in 2014 released a blueprint for "new-style urbanization," meant to guide the development of China's cities over the next decade. The general idea is that future urbanization efforts will focus less on physical construction and more on developing cities' social services and human resources.

This reorientation is sensible, but it is proving hard to implement. For one thing, it depends on a revamp of local government finance that is taking much longer than originally expected. This is a particular constraint on the target of giving 100 million migrant workers—about a third of the total—full access to urban social services and housing by 2020, presumably via a residence-permit system. The goal is worthy, but no clear funding mechanism has yet been established.

7

THE ENTERPRISE SYSTEM

Which are more important: state-owned enterprises or private firms?

One of the most contentious features of China's economy is its ownership. Two narratives are common. One is that the basic story of the reform era has been the steady retreat of state-owned enterprises (SOEs) in favor of the private sector, which now accounts for the majority of economic activity. The other is that China remains an extraordinarily state-dominated economy in which SOEs command a far larger share of national assets than they do in other countries, and the vast majority of large firms in almost every economic sector are state-run.[1]

At first glance, these stories cannot both be true. Either the private sector or the state sector must be the dominant force in the economy. Yet both stories are true in some sense, and it is equally accurate to describe China as a private-led or a state-led economy. China has a large and fast-growing private sector, which in aggregate accounts for the majority of economic output and employment, and its share of many economic indicators is rising. But private firms are, on average, small. The overwhelming majority of the largest companies in China are state-owned, and state firms dominate most capital-intensive sectors. The state sector's share of national assets is far larger than in any other major economy. State enterprises command a share of resources (such as financial capital, land, and energy) much bigger than their contribution to economic output. The SOEs are also an integral part of the political power structure. They are often used as instruments of macroeconomic policy and industry regulation in place of relatively weak formal policy and regulatory instruments. So the power and importance of SOEs are much greater than implied by economic statistics alone. In addition, at least since 2013 (and arguably since 2008 or before), a goal of national economic policy has been to strengthen the role of SOEs.

A further complication is that much of China's private sector, and especially its biggest companies, is open to the charge of "crony capitalism." Many apparently private firms depend wholly or in part on investments or patronage by senior government officials. Others have large minority shareholdings by government agencies, making it questionable how independent these firms really are from state influence.

In order to understand how China arrived at this position—with a large, growing, but diffuse and perhaps cronyistic private sector, and a shrinking but concentrated and politically powerful state sector—we must first examine the historical development of what we may call the "enterprise system." This system is essentially a mechanism for organizing state ownership, but it has implications for the way in which the private sector has developed.[2]

What were the aims of SOE reform in the 1980s and 1990s?

When China began its reform process in the late 1970s, the vast majority of nonagricultural economic activity was controlled by the state, not through companies but through government ministries and bureaus at both central and local levels. The efficiency of this system was low, for several reasons.

First, the lack of market prices meant that it was impossible to know whether a "work unit" was really creating economic value. (Since there were no companies, economic activity was conducted by "work units," such as individual factories, under government agencies.) Second, this absence of knowledge about true economic value meant that work units did not face hard budget constraints, as they would have if forced to account for their profits and losses. Access to resources, such as investment budgets, thus depended more on political skill than on economic success.

Third, the production of any given product was fragmented into dozens, hundreds, or even thousands of separate work units throughout China—a legacy of the autarkic Maoist ideology that emphasized local self-sufficiency. This made it impossible to achieve economies of scale. Finally, since the government directly controlled all production, there was no separation between producers and regulators. This worked—sort of—as long as the economy was organized around a centralized plan, in which the essential regulatory function of the state was simply to ensure that inputs were distributed so that output targets could be achieved. Once the decision was taken to move in a more market-oriented direction, an obvious conflict of interest arose between the state's roles as owner of assets and as regulator of economic activity.

State-sector reform has addressed all these problems and has made some progress on each, but none has been fully solved. By the late 1990s, most prices were marketized, but a handful of important input prices—notably for land, capital, and energy—remained subject to various kinds of state control. State firms were basically made responsible for their profits and losses in the 1990s, but their continued preferential access to resources at prices not fully set by the market means that their budget constraints are still softer than those of private firms.

The other two issues—excessive fragmentation and lack of clear distinction between the government's roles as regulator and owner of assets—proved thorny and led to intricate maneuvers to create new forms of SOE organization. The desire of central officials to create larger SOEs fell afoul of local governments' determination to hang on to sources of patronage, tax revenues, and employment. Efforts to separate ownership and regulatory functions were complicated by the government's conflicting ambitions to make SOEs more efficient and profitable, and to ensure that they remained willing agents of state policy when needed.

The obvious solution to these problems would have been simply to privatize the SOEs. This has never been a serious option because even the most reform-minded officials, from Deng Xiaoping on down, were committed believers in a strong state role in economic management. They further believed that this role had to be exercised, in part, through the direct ownership of assets, rather than merely through regulatory control of the distribution of resources, as in Japan. Moreover, China's relative success in navigating the global financial crisis of 2008–2009 was viewed by many leaders as proof of the value of a large state sector. SOEs were an effective channel for the distribution of economic stimulus and hence an important stabilizer. Thus, the goal of SOE reform has always been to make the state sector a more effective instrument, not to dismantle it.

Do Chinese SOEs resemble Japan's keiretsu or Korea's chaebol?

In the 1980s, Chinese scholars and officials searching for a better form of organization for state economic activity had two nearby models to choose from: Japan's *keiretsu* and South Korea's *chaebol*. Keiretsu are networks of firms linked by cross-shareholdings, typically with a bank (called the "main bank") at the center. The main advantage of the keiretsu system is that it promotes stable and collaborative relationships between industrial firms and their financiers, and between companies and their suppliers. This system enabled big Japanese companies to engage in long-term planning and investment without having to worry about short-term fluctuations in their stock prices. Keiretsu also made Japanese firms essentially invulnerable to takeover by foreign firms, and cozy supplier relationships enabled companies to rig domestic markets so that prices and profit margins stayed relatively high. Because of their secure positions, keiretsu firms were able to offer many employees guaranteed lifetime employment.

This system worked well from the 1950s until the mid-1990s. It started to fall apart because of severe financial pressures on the main banks following the bursting of the Japanese stock-market bubble in 1990, as well as the increasing difficulty Japanese firms had in keeping up with the rapid pace of technological change in the Internet era, when commercial advantage shifted from companies good at organizing large production systems to those adept at quickly bringing new technology-based services to market.

Chaebol are diversified conglomerates, typically controlled by a founding family. Like keiretsu, they involve extensive use of cross-shareholdings among related companies. Unlike keiretsu, they are prohibited by law from owning banks. This prohibition on bank ownership was a deliberate choice made in the 1960s by the Korean government, which wanted to make the chaebol dependent on credit from state owned banks and hence responsive to the government's policy objectives.

For Chinese policymakers, the keiretsu and chaebol models were attractive because of the way in which they facilitated organization of complex economic activity at a large scale. This satisfied the demand for structures that would enable China to consolidate production in bigger units. But there was no obvious way to translate them into the Chinese context. For one thing, both keiretsu and chaebol had their origins in strong family-owned firms. China had destroyed all its large family businesses in the 1950s, so there was no obvious entrepreneurial basis for new conglomerates. In any case, China's continued commitment at least in name to a communist system dictated that the state maintain control of large-scale enterprises rather than pushing them into private hands.

Two other concerns were important. First was a reluctance to permit business groups to have their own banks.

Policymakers believed that direct government control over the banking system was crucial in order for macroeconomic policy to be effective, and they feared that too much control over their own funding would make state enterprises less responsive to government development objectives. The second was a preference for firms that focused on a single industry, which could eventually evolve into "national champions" in key sectors such as steel, petrochemicals, and autos. Both chaebol and keiretsu systems, by contrast, tended to create sprawling empires spanning many different industries.

How are SOEs organized?

After much experimentation, the system that evolved in China was that of the "business group" (*qiye jituan*).The business group was first legally defined in 1987, and over the course of the next 15 years the central government created about 200 such groups by corporatizing various ministries and production bureaus. Provincial governments replicated this procedure, initially in a haphazard and incomplete way. Two further policy moves provided the next steps in the evolution of the business group system.

The first of these was the adoption in 1995 of a comprehensive SOE reform program, under the slogan *zhuada fangxiao* ("grasp the big, release the small"). This program had two main aims. The immediate one was to clean up a morass of nonperforming loans that state enterprises had built up during the investment boom of the early 1990s, which threatened to bring down the whole economy. The strategic goal was to set state ownership on a more rational footing.

The basic idea was that there was a host of industries, such as consumer goods manufacturing and basic services such as retail shops and restaurants, where state ownership was unnecessary. Small-scale SOEs in these sectors (most of which were controlled by local governments, not the center) could be privatized or bankrupted, and these economic areas could be handed off to the private sector. But state control of what is sometimes called the "commanding heights" of the economy needed to be strengthened. These "commanding heights" included:

- Important national networks, including aviation, railways, telecoms, and power generation and distribution;
- Upstream production of oil, gas, and coal;
- Basic heavy industries such as steel, aluminum, and petrochemicals;
- Production of critical heavy machinery such as machine tools and power generation equipment;
- Infrastructure engineering for the construction of roads, dams, ports, and railways;
- "Pillar" consumer durables industries, notably automobiles; and
- Military equipment.

Under the *zhuada fangxiao* reform, state ownership of these commanding-heights sectors was organized under large-scale business groups controlled directly, in most cases, by the central government. Formal rules governing the structure of business groups were published in 1998. With a few exceptions, notably the Ministry of Railways, ministries responsible for a specific industrial sector were broken up and corporatized. By 2016, 92 percent of the state-owned companies under these centrally controlled business groups had been corporatized.[3]

A key element of this procedure was that, in most cases, the government set up not a single monopolistic state-owned corporation but several competing enterprises. The former electricity ministry was broken up into five large national power-generation companies and two regional grid companies; the telecom ministry gave way to three telecom firms; the aviation agency to three airlines, and so on. Provinces and cities were also permitted to retain control of state enterprises that they deemed strategic, but they were pressured to corporatize these firms, using the group-company structure, rather than continuing to run them simply as arms of the local government.

Another element of the reform program was the creation of subsidiaries suitable for listing on overseas stock markets. Typically, this involved the packaging of an SOE's most commercially attractive assets in the listing vehicle, while lower-return investments in infrastructure, or politically sensitive projects, were retained in the unlisted parent company. So, for example, the principal oil company, the China National Petroleum Corporation (CNPC), created a subsidiary called PetroChina that listed in Hong Kong and New York. The listed vehicle included most of CNPC's oil and gas fields and refineries, but excluded some pipeline assets and investments in politically controversial regions such as Sudan.

These SOE stock market listings were not privatizations, although stockbrokers and media reports often erroneously described them as such. In most cases, no more than 20 percent of shares were sold to the public, with the remaining 80 percent staying in the hands of the parent company—in effect, in the hands of the Chinese government. The idea behind the listings was never to privatize these firms, even gradually. Instead, the purpose was to teach big Chinese firms how to tap international capital markets to fund some of their capital expansion plans and to improve their commercial performance by exposing them to modest amounts of discipline from international shareholders.

The final move in SOE reform was the establishment of the State-Owned Assets Supervision and Administration Commission (SASAC) in 2003. The purpose of SASAC was in essence to act as the government shareholder in nearly 200 centrally controlled SOE business groups. Instead of the State Council itself trying to figure out how to exercise its ownership interests in the sprawling business empire nominally under its aegis, SASAC took on responsibility for appointing senior management and holding them accountable for meeting financial targets such as return on assets and market share, much as a controlling shareholder of a normal corporation would do. Local SASACs were also set up by provincial and city governments to oversee the smaller-scale SOEs. Financial SOEs, such as banks, are controlled not by SASAC, but by the Ministry of Finance.[4]

In addition to its job overseeing each company individually, SASAC was given two broad mandates: gradually reducing the number of centrally controlled business groups to under 100, and maximizing the aggregate value of state assets. The logic of the first target was that policymakers wanted the big SOEs to develop into globally competitive "national champion" companies and felt that this objective could only be achieved by further consolidation. At least in numeric terms, this target has been met: by 2018, SASAC had boiled down the number of SOE groups under its control to less than 100, comprising about 23,000 individual companies.[5]

The second goal has also been achieved: total SOE assets climbed to Rmb140 trillion by 2015, four times the figure a decade earlier and more than double the size of China's GDP (Figure 7.1). But size is not everything. Most indicators of SOE financial performance improved substantially up to about 2008. Since then, however, virtually all of these indicators have gone into reverse: state firms have become less profitable and more debt-ridden, as they expanded in size. In recent years, it appears that SASAC's emphasis on asset growth has led to a deterioration of the efficiency of the firms it controls.

How are SOE business groups structured?

The result of the process outlined above was the creation of a Chinese model of corporate organization as distinctive as the prior keiretsu and chaebol models in Japan and South Korea, respectively. The typical structure of a Chinese SOE business group is as follows:

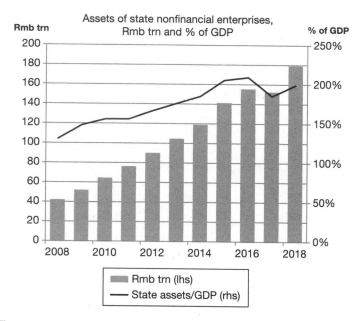

Figure 7.1 State-owned assets.
Source: NBS/CEIC.

- Top layer: unlisted parent group entity, controlled by the government via SASAC.
- Second layer: corporate subsidiaries wholly or majority-owned by the group entity. These may include subsidiaries listed on Chinese or overseas stock markets. In most cases, one of these controlled subsidiaries is a finance company.
- Third layer: minority-controlled subsidiaries and joint ventures, which usually enable the group to take an interest in peripheral activities. For instance, CNPC, one of whose core interests is the wholesale distribution of natural gas via pipelines, also has stakes in various city gas companies that deliver gas to households.
- Fourth layer: companies that have no equity relationship to the group entity or its subsidiaries but are bound by various contractual relationships.

This structure is the same for centrally controlled SOE groups owned by the central SASAC and for local SOEs owned by provincial and city SASACs.

Several features of this structure are worth noting. First, SOE business groups typically operate within a single industrial sector. This rule is somewhat elastic, and most SOE groups have a cluster of investments in sectors unrelated to their core businesses, often in property, travel services, and restaurants. But these investments are generally modest relative to the core businesses. This single-industry focus distinguishes Chinese business groups from the highly diversified Japanese and Korean conglomerates. For example, before it broke itself up in a major corporate restructuring in the late 1990s, Korea's biggest chaebol, Hyundai Group, had significant interests in automobile manufacturing, shipbuilding, chemicals, semiconductors, personal computers, property development, and department stores. No major Chinese SOE has anything approaching such a spread of businesses, although a handful of private conglomerates have emerged with chaebol-like portfolios.

Second, most SOE groups have an in-house finance company. Enterprises registered as SOE groups are entitled to a finance company; enterprises that fail to meet the requirements for group registration—as is the case for many private enterprises—may not have a finance company. In-house finance companies are a bit like the "main banks" at the heart of Japanese keiretsu, but with a couple of important differences. For one thing, they are wholly owned by the parent company, and they own no shares either in the parent or in any other group subsidiaries. For another, they are relatively small. Japanese main banks are among the biggest banks in the country; the biggest corporate finance companies in China are comparable in size to third-tier banks. The modest size and restricted role of corporate finance companies strikes a balance between objectives. On the one hand, the government wants its big SOEs to organize their finances flexibly—especially in the matter of moving money from one group company to another. But on the other hand, it does not want to lose control of the financial system by permitting the corporate finance companies to become full-fledged banks.

What impact did the SOE reform program of the 1990s have?

The *zhuada fangxiao* SOE reform program begun in 1995 achieved its two main aims. First, it cleaned up a huge bad debt problem that had grown within the SOE sector in the mid-1990s. This was often referred to as the "triangular debt" problem (companies unable to pay their suppliers, and both kinds of firms unable to pay back their bank loans). Ultimately, the debt problems were concentrated in the state-owned banks, whose nonperforming loans (NPLs) were estimated at an astonishing one-third of GDP in the late 1990s. The banks were recapitalized and relieved of their responsibility to lend to nonviable SOEs simply to maintain employment. Viable SOEs were freed to focus on improving their businesses in capital-intensive sectors. Second, *zhuada fangxiao* succeeded in getting SOES out of intrinsically competitive sectors (such as consumer goods manufacturing), while consolidating and corporatizing bigger SOEs in "commanding heights" sectors and improving their financial performance.

Over the next decade, these reforms had three major impacts. First, the number of SOEs was slashed, from 262,000 in 1997 to 110,000 in 2008, by consolidation, privatization, and bankruptcy.[6] Second, employment in the SOE sector fell from 113 million, or nearly 60 percent of total urban employment in 1995, to 64 million (20 percent of urban jobs) in 2007. And finally, the operational efficiency of SOEs improved. The average return on assets in state firms soared from 0.2 percent in 1998 to 5 percent in 2007. SOE profits rose from just 0.3 percent to 6.6 percent of GDP in the same period. This improvement resulted from a combination of reduced obligations to finance employee social welfare costs, increased competitive pressure, pressure from SASAC to hit financial targets, and subsidized access to land and capital.[7]

How has SOE reform evolved since 2008?

The pace of SOE reform slowed somewhat after the end of Zhu Rongji's premiership in 2003, and by 2008 or so it became clear that the basic orientation of SOE reform had shifted. Instead of streamlining the state sector and making it more efficient, the central government was now focused on fortifying the state sector and making SOEs larger and more effective instruments of state policy. This emphasis became especially pronounced after the 2008 global financial crisis. State firms became important channels of the massive economic stimulus launched by the government to offset the effects of the crisis. Moreover, the fact that the global crisis originated in the United States undermined the credibility of pro-market reformers in China who took the United States as their model, and strengthened the hand of conservative officials who wanted a permanent strong state role in the economy. This shift toward a more powerful state sector was summarized in a popular phrase of that time: *guo jin min tui*, or "the state advances and the private sector retreats."

After Xi Jinping came to power in 2013, there was hope that efficiency-oriented SOE reform would resume. There was much talk about subjecting SOEs to more discipline by putting them under holding companies focused on financial returns and introducing private shareholders. After much debate and bureaucratic infighting, however, Beijing adopted an SOE policy that focused almost entirely on making SOEs bigger rather than trying to improve their efficiency. This set in stone the trends already in place since 2008: SOEs are becoming bigger, less strategically focused, and far less profitable.[8]

How big is the state sector today?

Despite the pruning of SOEs over the past three decades, China today still has by far the largest state sector, relative to GDP, of any major economy. According to the Ministry of Finance, in 2015 China had about 170,000 SOEs, with combined assets of around Rmb 141 trillion, or 205 percent of GDP. The SOEs controlled by the central government account for about one-third of the total number of state firms and slightly less than half of SOE assets. The remaining two-thirds of SOEs, and a bit more than half of SOE assets, are controlled by provincial and other local governments.[9]

Cross-country comparisons are tricky because there are no consistent standards for reporting data on state firms. But it is clear that China's state sector is unusually large. In 2011, researchers at the Organization for Economic Cooperation and Development (OECD) analyzed data on all SOEs appearing in the Forbes Global 2000 list of the world's biggest companies. They found that China's major SOEs had assets equivalent to 145 percent of GDP and revenues of 26 percent of GDP (Figure 7.2). Both figures were about double the numbers for the other big emerging economies—Brazil, Russia, and India. Among developed countries, the highest levels of SOE assets relative to GDP were in South Korea (48 percent) and France (23 percent).[10]

The biggest Chinese SOEs are very big indeed, and the vast majority of really large companies in China are state-owned. In 2018, 103 mainland Chinese firms appeared in the Fortune

SOE assets and revenues, % of GDP, 2011		
Country	Assets	Revenues
China	145%	26%
India	75%	16%
Russia	64%	16%
Brazil	51%	12%
South Korea	48%	7%
France	23%	8%
Indonesia	19%	3%
Source: OECD		

Figure 7.2 The world's biggest state sector.

Global 500 list, which ranks the world's biggest firms by revenue. Of these, 67 were central SOEs and another 20 were local government SOEs. Only 16 were private firms. Of the 40 largest Chinese companies on the Fortune list, 33 were central SOEs. These included three of the four biggest companies in the entire world: Sinopec, CNPC, and State Grid.

So in terms of the assets and revenues they control, China's SOE sector is large. The picture looks different, however, when we turn to employment and contribution to GDP. Total employment by SOEs fell to 61 million people in 2017, an all-time low of 14 percent of total urban employment.

Contribution to GDP is harder to measure because Chinese data do not always distinguish precisely between state and private firms. But we can make an estimate based on information about the state role in three main production sectors: agriculture, industry, and services. In agriculture, most production is by private household farms. State firms do exist for scale production, especially in sectors like meat and dairy. A reasonable estimate of the state share of agricultural production is about 10 percent. Detailed data exists for industry, and the most careful studies show that the state share of industrial production (on a value-added basis) is about 25 percent. For services, our information is spottier. In some services, such as telecoms, state firms are clearly dominant. In many others, such as retail, restaurants, and online commerce, private firms rule. Chinese scholars estimate that output in the service sector is about evenly divided between state and nonstate companies.[11] Adding up these contributions and weighting each sector by its contribution to GDP, we conclude that SOEs account for about 35 percent of output. Roughly speaking, domestic private firms account for about 60 percent of GDP, and firms controlled by foreign investors account for the remaining 5 percent or so.

One observation that springs from these calculations is that SOEs' contribution to GDP is low relative to the vast swath of assets they control. This in turn implies that state firms extract a far lower return from their assets than do private firms. This conclusion is supported by industrial data, which show that between 2012 and 2018, industrial SOEs earned an average return on assets of just 4 percent, compared to 6.6 percent for private firms.

Are SOEs monopolies?

China's SOEs are pervasive, politically influential, and in command of resources disproportionate to their contribution to output. But with a handful of officially designated exceptions—the national railway system, the tobacco monopoly, and the salt monopoly (abolished in 2014)—SOEs do not occupy monopoly positions. A deliberate feature of the SOE reforms of the 1990s was the creation of multiple, competing state firms even in sectors marked down for central control, such aviation, telecoms, oil, and electricity generation. In less strategic industries, the degree of state-sector fragmentation is even greater: in 2011, for instance, there were 880 SOEs in coal mining, 312 in steel, and 264 in nonferrous metals processing. Detailed data on industrial enterprises fail to reveal any evidence either of an unusual concentration of industries in a small number of firms or of the excessive profits that one would expect from monopolists.[12]

The nonmonopolistic nature of the state sector helps explain why China has been able to sustain such high rates of economic growth despite its continued heavy reliance on state firms, which are clearly less efficient than private ones. One lesson from this experience is that, for countries making the transition from a socialist planned economy to a market economy, full privatization of state assets is not necessarily the critical step, as many economists believed in the 1990s. The indispensable feature of a market economy is not private property but competition. If state assets are privatized but competition mechanisms remain weak, the results will be poor: one just substitutes private monopolists or oligopolists for state-owned ones. (This was arguably Russia's experience in the 1990s.)

If, on the other hand, competition is strengthened, it is possible to leave a large share of assets in state hands and see strong economic growth. This is because more productive private firms spring up to take advantage of market opportunities that state firms miss, and even state-owned firms are forced to up their game. Even if SOEs' productivity continues to lag in the private sector, the *improvement* contributes to economic growth. The economist Barry Naughton coined the phrase "growing out of the plan" to describe China's strategy of relying on greater competition, rather than privatization, to manage its transition from plan to market.

This approach has limits, however, and China is now hitting them. Competition only works if the losing firms exit the market through bankruptcy or acquisition by stronger players. Since the conclusion of the *zhuada fangxiao* reforms in about 2005, state firms have rarely gone bankrupt or been taken over by more efficient private competitors. Since 2009, Beijing has encouraged SOEs to bulk up their assets and has allowed them to take on enormous debt to support their unprofitable investments. Finally, competition law is weak and regulatory oversight poor. An antimonopoly law was passed in 2007, but enforcement was split among three agencies, and the law has mainly been used to limit the market power of foreign firms rather than to break down anticompetitive behavior by SOEs or government agencies.[13] In short, SOEs may not be monopolies, but they are certainly insulated from competitive pressures, and their decreasing efficiency is taking a toll on economic growth.

Are China's central SOEs independent actors or agents of a government "master plan"?

This is a very thorny question. Our description of the "enterprise system" would suggest that the activities of the big SOEs are coordinated by the central government, through the share-holding agency SASAC and by the Communist Party, which directly controls appointments of top managers of about half of the most "strategic" SOEs. There is also a very active "revolving door" that shuttles both SOE bosses into important government roles and government and party officials into the leadership of key SOEs.

Yet despite the density of ties binding together SOEs, the government, and the party, SOEs do not simply follow orders from above. Like big firms in other countries, SOEs pursue their own commercial objectives, which may or may not be consistent with state aims. They lobby the government, with varying degrees of success, to change policies and regulations in their favor. Frequently, the interests of different SOEs clash, and they lobby the government in opposing directions. A common example is in trade matters, where some SOEs may seek antidumping tariffs to be imposed on foreign competitors, while other SOEs that rely on imported materials oppose the duties and may team up with foreign firms to lobby against them.[14]

In practice, SOEs operate both as fairly autonomous fiefdoms, acting in ways that they believe will increase the size and power of their businesses, and as part of an elite network of institutions that includes the party and government. Many Chinese—including some within the government—increasingly believe that power flows not from the government to the SOEs but the other way around. A popular phrase in recent years was "there are no state-owned enterprises, only an enterprise-owned state." This is an exaggeration but not a great one.[15]

How important is the private sector?

China's state sector is unusually large by international standards, and SOEs are important tools for the government in

Non-state sector share of various economic indicators, % of national total					
	Registered companies	Urban employment	Exports	Industrial output	Fixed asset investment
2000	-	55%	5%	< 30%	< 30%
2005	55%	77%	20%	-	47%
2010	74%	81%	31%	-	54%
2013	93%	83%	42%	> 60 %	60%
2018	95%	86%	48%	-	65%
Source: Author calculations from NBS/CEIC, Lardy 2014, and OECD 2007					

Figure 7.3 Private sector gains.

managing macroeconomic policy, resource flows, and infrastructure development. But the rise of the private sector has been an even bigger contributor to China's sustained high growth rates over the past three decades.

All the gains in employment since 1978, and most of the improvement in productivity, can be traced to the reallocation of resources from the state to the private sector. The private sector now accounts for about 85 percent of employment and manufacturing output, roughly two-thirds of GDP and fixed investment, half of exports and more than half of the trade surplus (Figure 7.3). Its share of most indicators has steadily increased, although the pace of private-sector gains has slowed in recent years. In 2018, China had 620 private-sector billionaires, more than any other country in the world. China's economy is largely a private-sector success story, and its ability to keep up fast growth in the future will depend mainly on private companies.[16]

How has the private sector evolved?

The rise of China's private sector since the beginning of reforms can broadly be divided into three phases. In the first period (the late 1970s until the mid-1990s), private economic activity expanded very rapidly, but its legal basis was insecure; and the dominant corporate form was the *getihu* (individual business enterprise), which by law could have no more than seven employees. Larger private firms existed, but because of the difficulty of registering a purely private company, many were often registered as "collective" enterprises, with significant shareholdings by local governments that acted as patrons and protectors—a practice known as "wearing the red hat."

The second era ran roughly from the beginning of the *zhuada fangxiao* SOE reform in 1995 until the global financial crisis year of 2008. During this phase, private property rights were strengthened, more flexible forms of corporate organization were opened up, and the state role in many sectors was radically reduced, offering private firms the chance to enter lucrative new markets and in some cases to buy up distressed SOEs or SOE assets. An important symbolic move was the decision in 2001 to permit private entrepreneurs to become Communist Party members, reversing a ban imposed following the Tiananmen demonstrations of 1989.

In this second period, the private sector boomed and rapidly increased its share of output (especially in industry) and employment. This growth is hard to measure precisely because of technical problems in Chinese company statistics, which do not distinguish clearly between private and state firms, but roughly speaking the private share of China's industrial output and fixed investment rose from less than a quarter to about two-thirds.[17] A 2007 OECD study found that the private-sector share of industrial value-added more than doubled between 1998 and 2003—from 15 percent to 33 percent.[18] Work by the economist Nicholas Lardy, which includes estimates for small-scale enterprises and nominally "foreign" firms that were really controlled by domestic private shareholders, suggests that the true private share of industrial value-added was higher: 56 percent in 2003 and 63 percent in 2007. The nonstate share of national fixed investment rose from about a quarter in the late 1990s to nearly 60 percent by the end of 2007.[19]

Is it true that "the state advances and the private sector retreats"?

The third era of private-sector evolution dates from 2008, when the expression *guojin mintui* (advance of the state, retreat of the private) became common in Chinese media. This phrase reflected a belief that the government had launched a systematic effort to roll back private-sector gains and reassert the dominant role of the state. Evidence included the proliferation of industrial policies that seemed to benefit state firms; several high-profile cases in which private firms were forced to sell out on allegedly unfavorable terms to state-owned competitors; and the consolidation of the coal industry in Shanxi Province under a group of provincial SOEs, which bought up most of the privately owned mines.

For several years, economic data did not support this story of a private-sector "retreat." Even after 2008, the private sector's shares of industrial output, exports, employment, GDP, and market shares in most economic sectors continued to rise, as did its share of bank credit. By 2011, there were only six out of forty major industrial sectors in which state firms accounted for more than 20 percent of output.[20] But the *rate* at which private firms displaced state firms slowed markedly from 2008. The number of SOEs stopped falling, stabilized, and began to rise again after 2010. Employment in SOEs stabilized. The SOE share of fixed investment began to decline much less swiftly and in some sectors began to increase.[21]

Moreover, after Xi Jinping came to power, and especially after 2015, a strong pro-SOE bias became evident in government policy, and the state share of various indicators stabilized. Beijing introduced measures to exert more influence over private firms, for instance, by more strictly enforcing the requirement that firms set up Communist Party

committees. State firms continued to command a share of resources (land, capital, and energy) far larger than their contribution to economic growth. In particular, private companies'
access to credit was restricted by a campaign to limit nonbank lending (see Chapter 9). By 2019, it was accurate to say
that in some dimensions, the state role in the economy was
increasing.

Four factors lie behind this change in trajectory. One is that
the Hu Jintao administration had in general a more statist bent
than its predecessor and was more active in using SOEs as instruments of policy. Xi Jinping evidently shares this pro-state
bias even more strongly. Second, the increase in SOE profits
in the early 2000s meant they had both the incentive and the
means to lobby more actively against reforms that would erode
their market power. Third, the government launched a massive economic stimulus program at the end of 2008 in response
to the global financial crisis. Much of the stimulus spending
went through SOEs and local governments into infrastructure
projects. As SOEs took on ever more debt to finance their supposedly essential role in preserving economic stability, the cost
of redirecting credit to more productive use rose because a reduction in SOE credit lines would force many companies into
financial hardship or bankruptcy.

Finally, the structure of the economy has shifted in a way
that favors SOEs. Between 2008 and 2018, the share of output
coming from industry and construction (where much activity
has been privatized) fell from 47 to 41 percent; the share of
services (where the state role remains much bigger) rose from
43 to 52 percent.

How will the state–private balance evolve?

To sum up, state enterprises represent a large minority
share of the economy, which is now stable after many years
of decline. Moreover, they have a claim on resources and
political influence that far exceeds their economic weight.

The private sector in aggregate accounts for the majority of economic activity but is fragmented and politically weak. The current direction of policy seems clearly to favor the state sector. How will the state–private balance of power evolve?

One crucial element of this equation is the dramatically declining efficiency of SOEs. From 1997 through 2007, the financial performance of SOEs improved, as measured by returns on assets and equity. After the global financial crisis year of 2008, however, returns on assets and equity fell by about one-half (although they picked up in 2017–2018, perhaps because of government effort to curb excess capacity and shut down zombie firms.) About 40 percent of state firms do not earn enough profit to cover their cost of capital, meaning that they must take out new loans simply to pay the interest on the old ones. Meanwhile, the performance of private firms has continued to strengthen. In 2018, private industrial companies generated a return on assets about double that of their state-owned counterparts (Figure 7.4).[22] Moreover, they achieve this result with far less debt than SOEs: in 2010–2017, the average debt-to-equity ratio was more than 30 percentage points higher for SOEs than for private firms (Figure 7.5).

The worsening performance by SOEs is both a reflection and a cause of China's recent economic slowdown. SOEs tend to be in heavy industrial sectors that have been hit hardest by the end of the "building-binge" phase of growth we described in Chapter 6. Private firms tend to be in consumer sectors that benefit from the spending power of the new middle class. So it is not surprising that, overall, SOEs have fared worse than private companies. But studies also consistently show that within a given sector, private firms outperform state firms.

To stabilize economic growth, China needs to improve its overall return on investment. As in the past, this need not mean wholesale privatization of state firms. It will, however, require opening up service industries to private-sector competition,

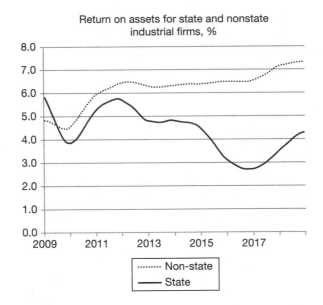

Return on assets for state and nonstate industrial firms, %

Figure 7.4 State versus private return on assets.

Source: Gavekal Dragonomics.

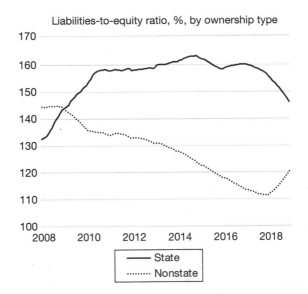

Liabilities-to-equity ratio, %, by ownership type

Figure 7.5 Corporate leverage.

Source: Gavekal Dragonomics.

just as manufacturing was opened to private firms in the 1990s; being willing to let smaller-scale SOEs—especially those controlled by local governments—go bankrupt if they cannot survive in a more competitive environment; exerting much stronger financial discipline on central SOEs; and enacting financial sector reforms to ensure that credit flows only to companies that can put the money to productive use.

As yet, there is little evidence of such reforms. SOE policy under Xi Jinping has focused mainly on making state enterprises larger and on reducing competitive pressures. The crackdown on "shadow finance" that began in late 2016 removed an important source of credit for private firms, and no replacement has yet emerged. Barriers to entry to private firms in modern service sectors such as finance, telecommunications, and health care remain very high. On the plus side, the elimination of regulatory red tape has made it much easier to start a private company, and the "supply-side structural reform" program of 2016–2018 seems to have been successful in eliminating the worst of the SOE "zombie" firms.

But on balance, not enough is being done to ensure that China's corporate sector remains profitable and productive. For China's economy to keep growing at a rapid pace (say 5 percent or more during the 2020s), enterprise efficiency must be improved. These efficiency gains must come from both an expansion of the space in which private firms are allowed to operate and a rationalization of the state sector.

8

THE GOVERNMENT
FINANCE SYSTEM

Why does the fiscal system matter?

There are two reasons for understanding China's fiscal system. The first is about power relations. In a country as large and diverse as China, relations between the central and local governments are tricky to manage. The fiscal system explains how power is divided among the different levels of government. The second reason is macroeconomic: knowing how China's government raises and spends its money, and how much it needs to borrow to achieve its goals, are essential to judging the nature and sustainability of China's growth.

How powerful are local governments compared to the central government?

As we observed in Chapter 1, China is formally centralized but in practice highly decentralized. A recurrent theme throughout its history has been the struggle between central and local governments, a struggle summed up in the Chinese expression *shang you zhengce, xia you duice*—which, loosely translated, means "the leaders make policies and people below find ways around them."

Decentralization can be described either quantitatively or qualitatively. By the simplest quantitative measure—the proportion of fiscal revenue and expenditure handled by local governments—China is by a wide margin the most decentralized country on earth: local governments command over 50 percent of government revenues and are responsible for 85 percent of expenditure. In OECD countries, the averages are about 20 percent and one-third, respectively. Most developing countries tend to be even more centralized.[1]

This extreme decentralization is worth bearing in mind when one hears people talking about China as an authoritarian country where the central government can just snap its fingers and make anything happen. One can also go too far in the direction of claiming that China is a fragmented country where local actors do whatever they want, regardless of what Beijing might say. Remember that "local governments" in the Chinese context includes the provinces, which have a median population of 46 million and are therefore essentially nation-sized units. If we consider provinces as part of the central government, then the "local" fiscal shares of revenues fall to about one-third for revenues and half for expenditures—still high figures but less extreme than the headline numbers.[2]

Two other considerations mitigate the picture of a decentralized China. While it is true that local governments command a large share of revenue collections, they have little or no formal ability to set their own tax policies or tax rates. In the United States, every state and local government sets its own mix of taxes and tax rates based on local conditions. Some state governments (such as California) rely heavily on personal income taxes, while others (such as New Hampshire) have no income tax at all but depend mainly on sales taxes. In China, Beijing determines what kinds of taxes are allowed, sets their rates, and dictates how the revenues will be shared; localities have little leeway to adjust these parameters.

Furthermore, on a qualitative basis, the central government's hold over localities is substantial. This is visible in the personnel system, substantially controlled by the party's Central Organization Department in Beijing, which systematically rotates senior officials between provinces in order to limit the authority of local networks. The party's Central Commission for Discipline Inspection, the anticorruption watchdog, is also frequently used to break up local power constellations.[3]

Still, for every mechanism the central authorities build to limit the autonomy of local officials, local officials are quick to build a workaround. A persistent issue in the fiscal system has been the rampant local practice of using extrabudgetary revenue sources (ranging from miscellaneous fees to land sales and leases) to finance extrabudgetary expenditures. Despite a formal ban on local government borrowing, China's local governments now have a large debt burden.

A final point is that we should not uncritically accept stories about who the good guys and bad guys are in the central–local power struggle. Central officials moan that their wise policies are thwarted by short-sighted, greedy, and corrupt local functionaries. Local officials complain that their efforts to deal with pressing problems are undermined by senseless or contradictory edicts from arrogant, out-of-touch, and corrupt bureaucrats in Beijing. Both claims are often justified. Rather than assigning black hats and white hats, we should do our best to understand the forces that drive the power struggle: the conflicting demands for central control and local autonomy in a large country, and the incentives that drive officials at all levels to pursue ends that are sometimes in the public interest and sometimes not.

What impact does decentralized government have on economic development?

From an economic standpoint, the high degree of effective decentralization brings both advantages and drawbacks. The main advantage is that decentralized authority permits policy experiments on a large scale. Sometimes the central government conducts these experiments deliberately by designating certain cities or regions as "pilot areas" for specific policies. The largest experiments were of course the special economic zones set up in the early 1980s, which had entirely different tax and business policies from the rest of the country. But sometimes Beijing's approach is more passive: it knows that practices in a certain locality diverge from national norms but tolerates them either in recognition of inevitable local variation or in the hope that some interesting innovation will arise that can then be applied more broadly. This ability to experiment has been an important ingredient in China's success and differentiates it from another large developing country, India, which can be considered China's inverse in that it is formally decentralized but in practice highly centralized in many ways.[4]

The drawbacks are that economic activity winds up being very fragmented, and local governments often lack accountability for their actions. When we further consider the major incentive structures imposed on localities by the center since the early 1980s— rewarding officials for their ability to maximize GDP growth and maintain social stability—and the general tendency to focus more on capital accumulation than on economic efficiency, it is easy to see how undesirable consequences might arise.[5]

These factors combine to produce the characteristic pathologies of Chinese local government: an obsession with large-scale, capital-intensive industrial and infrastructure projects, and a reluctance to permit loss-making enterprises to simply go bankrupt and exit the market. Capital-intensive projects are favored because they are highly visible; thus, they are a good way to impress visiting officials from higher up in the bureaucracy, who can influence one's prospects for promotion. They also contribute immediately to reported GDP while they are being built because of all the investment dollars required during their construction.

If a factory runs into trouble, local officials have both the incentives and the means to keep it in business, even if doing so makes no economic sense. Reported GDP will suffer if the plant stops producing, and the laid-off workers could present a threat to social stability. Local governments control supplies of land and electric power and other utilities; have influence over the credit policies of local bank branches; are able to strong-arm local companies and government units to purchase goods from preferred local suppliers; and can set up trade barriers that make it hard for companies from other jurisdictions either to compete or to acquire local champions.

The power of localities to prevent the entry of new market players has substantially eroded, but their ability to keep terminally ill businesses on life support is as strong as ever. This helps explain the endurance of excess capacity and the proliferation of small players in many industries—why, for example, there are still at least 120 automobile manufacturers in China, sponsored mostly by local governments, even though central policy for more than two decades has pushed hard for industry consolidation. When the economy's main job is to accumulate as much capital as possible—as it was in China until a few years ago—this sort of waste is manageable. But now that the economy's main job is to squeeze the highest possible return out of all its assets, the incentives of local governments need to be changed.[6]

What was the significance of the 1994 tax reform?

The central–local struggle is illustrated by reform-era fiscal history system, which divides neatly into two phases, separated by a major tax reform in 1994.

Before 1994, the theme was decentralization. During the planned-economy era, most revenue consisted of operating surpluses from state-owned enterprises (SOEs) rather than taxes, which were virtually nonexistent. This revenue was collected, mostly at the local level, and remitted to the central government. The center then sent money back down to the provinces each year to fund the next year's investment quota and to cover the administrative expenses of the local governments.[7]

Early in the reform era, policymakers made two major changes. First, they began to devolve the responsibility for investment decisions down to the enterprises. Second, to encourage local officials to promote market-driven economic activity, they allowed localities to retain any tax revenues they collected above a fixed annual quota that had to be sent to Beijing. These shifts were in keeping with the general move to reduce the roles of state planning and central control as well as to permit market forces greater play.

The effect on government budgets was dramatic. Total government revenues fell from over 30 percent of GDP in 1978 to less than 11 percent in 1994, as SOEs no longer sent their profits to the treasury. As the free market began to take root in the late 1980s, the proportion of revenue controlled by the central government fell from a peak of 41 percent in 1984 to just 22 percent in 1993. By the early 1990s, policymakers in Beijing began to worry that the central government did not have enough revenue to finance its activities. Developing countries normally collect at least 20 percent of GDP in total government revenue, and for rich countries the figure usually exceeds 30 percent. They also worried that with such a huge share of revenue controlled by local governments, Beijing did not have enough leverage to keep localities in line and enforce national policies.

The tax reform of 1994 aimed to solve these two problems by creating a system that would (1) increase total government revenues and (2) ensure that the central government directly controlled at least half of those revenues. Under the new arrangement, central and local governments were each given a fixed share of each tax in a way that guaranteed the central government would get the majority of revenue. Stronger central oversight, and improved mechanisms for collecting the most important tax, value-added tax (VAT), aimed to increase the overall revenue pie.

The 1994 reform had an immediate and permanent impact on the central–local revenue split. The central share of revenues leapt from 22 percent in 1993 to 56 percent in 1994 and stayed above 50 percent through 2010. The impact on total revenue collection was slower to emerge but impressive. After bottoming out at just over 10 percent of GDP in 1996, total government revenue inexorably rose to 22 percent of GDP in 2015 (Figure 8.1).[8]

The 1994 reform had two other lasting impacts. First, it enhanced Beijing's power by giving the central government greater control over the national budget and much greater visibility on the true extent of the state's fiscal resources. Second, it imposed a structural operating deficit on local governments, since localities were assigned a minority of revenues but a majority of expenditures— initially, about 70 percent. Technically, localities ran balanced budgets, because transfers from the central government covered their shortfalls. Only the central government was permitted to run a formal deficit and to issue bonds to finance that deficit. But in practice, the transfer

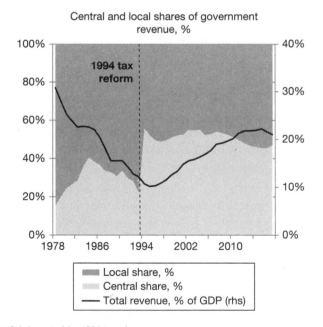

Figure 8.1 Impact of the 1994 tax reform.

Source: Ministry of Finance.

system worked poorly, and localities felt immense pressure to raise extra revenues to cover their expenses. This pressure only mounted as their pretransfer shortfalls rose from about 3 percent of GDP in the mid-1990s to 8 percent by 2009 and 10 percent by 2016 (Figure 8.2).

In the 1990s, the favored tactic for raising extra funds was to impose ad hoc fees on whatever might occur to the imagination of the local bureaucrat. This produced a chaos of off-the-books tax collection (or extortion), and the burden fell heaviest on those who had the least ability to fight back—generally speaking, farmers. The central government responded with the "tax-for-fee" reform, which restored order by converting most of these fees to taxes, with published rates and assigned recipients. The tax-for-fee reform was largely completed by 2003.

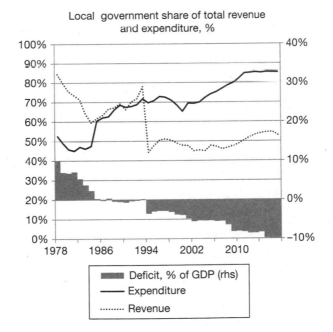

Figure 8.2 Local funding gap.

Source: Ministry of Finance.

But at the same time, Beijing was forcing local governments to take on an ever-wider array of responsibilities. The central government did little to ensure that they had the tax base to fulfill these duties—a practice criticized in the United States in the 1980s with the phrase "unfunded mandates." The SOE reform in the late 1990s reduced or eliminated enterprises' requirement to cover education, health care, and pension benefits. Responsibility for funding these social services—and for providing welfare payments and retraining services for tens of millions of laid-off SOE workers—increasingly fell on local governments.

Moreover, as the pace of urbanization increased, localities faced mounting pressure to build housing and urban infrastructure such as roads, power and water lines, and sewage systems. Between 2000 and 2011, local governments' share of total government expenditures rose from 69 percent to a staggering 85 percent. In absolute terms, it rose more than ninefold, from Rmb 1 trillion to Rmb 9.3 trillion. (During the same period, central government expenditures only tripled.) To fund these ballooning programs, localities turned to the biggest asset on their books: land.

How does the land-based local financing system work?

Starting in the early 2000s, city governments started to experiment with raising finance from the urban land they controlled. This was now possible because the housing privatization of 1998–2003 created a large-scale market for urban land in which private developers were eager to get hold of city–center plots for redevelopment into modern housing, offices, and retail space. Because the price of urban land had been artificially suppressed, the difference between the current land price and its expected value after redevelopment was enormous. Recognizing this state of affairs, local governments began to borrow against the expected increase in land values.

The scale of the opportunity is illustrated by one of the first major deals, arranged by the China Development Bank (CDB) in Tianjin in 2003. In that year Tianjin's mayor announced a 5-year infrastructure development project with a price tag of Rmb 170 billion ($21 billion)—six times the city's combined infrastructure spending in the previous 14 years and more than five times the city's annual revenue. This seemingly outlandish plan was largely financed by a line of credit from the CDB, which reckoned that, while the infrastructure projects themselves (roads, subways, parks, and so on) would produce little revenue, Tianjin could raise enough money from land sales to cover the Rmb 72 billion in principal and interest payments over the 15-year life of its loan. That forecast proved far too conservative. In the first 6 years of the project, Tianjin raised Rmb 95 billion from land sales, and in year 7 it raised Rmb 73 billion—enough in a single year to pay off its loan.[9]

This experience, more or less, was replicated in hundreds of cities around China. To get around the formal prohibition on local government borrowing, cities usually transferred land assets into a special-purpose company; such companies are called "local government financing vehicles." This company would then use the land as collateral for a bank loan. Repayment of the loan was financed by sales or leases of the land. Since land values skyrocketed during the early 2000s, the collateral often wound up worth far more than was necessary to repay the loans, so at the end of the project whatever was left over could be used as collateral for a new loan. Between 2008 and 2018, the gross value of these off-budget land sales was on average equal to about half of local governments' budgetary revenues. After accounting for the cost of clearing the land and installing infrastructure, the net value of land sales made up about 20 percent of localities' total revenues.

In its early years, this model proved an effective way to finance rapid, large-scale urban improvements; it is one reason why most Chinese cities have better infrastructure than is usual in countries of similar income. The central government was fully aware of the technique, and most of the finance was supplied by the CDB, a centrally controlled policy bank.

But after 2008, the land-based finance model spiraled out of control. In response to the global financial crisis, Beijing approved a Rmb 4 trillion ($590 billion) economic stimulus program, most of which went into infrastructure projects. To fund this activity, local governments borrowed heavily from commercial banks. These banks were less adept than the CDB and lent against land values that were unrealistically high, or sometimes did not ask for any collateral at all. The result was a tsunami of debt, much of which local governments had no hope of repaying. By the middle of 2013, the National Audit Office estimated that local governments had liabilities of almost Rmb 18 trillion, nearly double the figure for 2010. Local liabilities equated to one-third of GDP and were half again as much as the liabilities of the central government.[10]

How big is the government debt problem?

This explosion of local government debt attracted a lot of attention and rightly so. Unregulated borrowing by localities was at the heart of many previous emerging-market financial crises, notably the Brazilian debt crisis of the 1980s. It was reasonable to worry that China might face a comparable problem. This was especially true since the central government statistics on local debt were opaque and sometimes contradictory, suggesting either that the central authorities were deliberately trying to obscure the magnitude of the problem or (perhaps worse) that they themselves did not really know how much debt was out there.

Amplifying concerns over the debt problem is the extreme opacity of China's fiscal statistics, resulting mainly from the hodge-podge of off-budget mechanisms used by local governments to raise and spend money. China's official budget data report that the combined deficit of central and local governments averaged 1.5 percent of GDP in 2000–2014, and 3.8 percent in 2015–2018, when local government spending was more accurately recorded. It also claims that government debt was about 38 percent of GDP in 2018—but this only counts bond issuance by central and local governments. The IMF, however, estimates that the true budget deficit rose from 5 percent of GDP in 2010 to over 11 percent in 2018, once all local government spending is counted. Moreover, it reckons that true government debt was around 73 percent of GDP in 2018 (including all off-balance sheet borrowing by local governments as well as nonbudgetary debt by agencies such as the Ministry of Railways).[11]

The government debt problem is large but probably still manageable. Gross government debt in excess of 70 percent is common among OECD countries; the United States, the United Kingdom, Canada, and France have public debt loads above 90 percent of GDP. Moreover, much of China's public debt finances infrastructure that is likely to have a positive impact on economic growth eventually, whereas much rich-country government debt finances redistributive welfare spending. If it can be restructured to reduce the excessive reliance on rising land values, local government debt need not prompt a fiscal crisis. China's more serious debt problem stems from ineffi- cient SOEs that borrow ever more money to finance ever less- profitable investments. (See Chapters 7 and 9 for details.)

The issue with local government debt is not that it risks sparking a financial crisis but that it reflects a deeply flawed and unsustainable fiscal system that in turn springs from the tricky political relationship between central and local governments.

How is the government trying to fix China's fiscal problems?

As our discussion so far has shown, the fiscal system in place since 1994 created a number of problems:

- Local governments had expenditure responsibilities far in excess of their direct revenue resources, which encour- aged them to seek ad hoc and unsustainable additional sources of revenue, such as land sales.
- Despite the formal prohibition on borrowing, localities incurred huge debts, which were often structured in an inappropriate way.

- Local governments resorted to ad hoc financing and borrowing because the central–local transfer system, which was supposed to balance their budgets, worked poorly.
- The structure of local government revenues encouraged excessive investment in capital-intensive industry and infrastructure.

Solving these problems is the target of a series of fiscal reform efforts that began in 2014. A revised Budget Law, passed in September 2014, restricted the ability of officials to rely on off-budget funds and imposed stronger reporting requirements.[12] In 2015, local governments were required to start converting their off-balance sheet borrowings via "local government financing vehicles" into bonds. The result was a torrent: in 2015–2018, localities accounted for three-quarters of all government bond issuance, and by the end of 2018 they had Rmb 18 trillion ($2.6 trillion) of bonds outstanding, more than the central government (Figure 8.3). This frenzy of bond issuance caused China's official government debt burden to double to 37 percent of GDP. Remember, however, that for the most part this was not new debt, but simply the conversion of previously hidden off-balance sheet liabilities into visible, public liabilities.

Finally, in August 2016, the State Council announced a 4-year fiscal reform program. The three main aims of the program are to reassign some local expenditure responsibilities to the central government; bring order to the chaotic system of transfers from the central to local governments; and increase the transparency and accountability of government spending at all levels. These changes are expected to be codified in a new fiscal law in 2020.

Under the plan, the central government would increase its share of spending on environmental protection, resource management, and social services. This reallocation is likely to push its share of total government spending up from the present 15 percent to at least 25 percent and probably quite a bit higher, although details are still scarce.

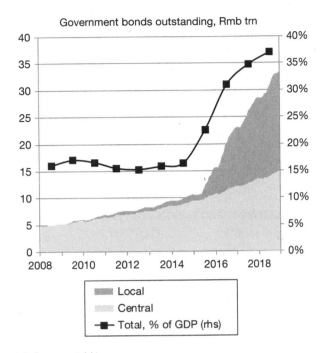

Figure 8.3 Government debt.
Source: Ministry of Finance.

Increasing the center's spending responsibilities will reduce the need for transfers from Beijing to local governments, which in some jurisdictions account for more than half of local revenues. Even so, the transfer system desperately needs to be fixed. There are over 200 separate transfer programs with different rules, schedules, and formulas. Transfers go first from Beijing to provincial governments, which then distribute them on uncertain schedules and in highly variable ways to lower levels of government. Transfers to the provinces are overseen by just a handful of officials in the Ministry of Finance, so it is difficult for Beijing to track the distribution of transfers after the money goes to provincial capitals.

Many of the transfers are earmarked for specific purposes that may not suit the actual needs of the recipient agency.

Some of the general-purpose transfer programs are based on formulas that deliver the most money to the richest localities, and the least to the poorest—exactly the opposite of what is needed to reduce China's stark regional income inequalities. The overall result is that local governments often do not know how much transfer money they will receive, when they will get it, and what they can use it for. This naturally gives them an incentive to hunt for other sources of revenue that they control and that are more predictable.[13]

How will fiscal reform affect central–local relations and economic development?

The political aims of the current fiscal reform are clear. Like the 1994 reform, it is a centralizing program whose intention is to strengthen the power of the central government and to subject the localities to greater discipline in various ways. Forcing localities to rely on bond issues for their borrowing needs, rather than on loans from compliant local bank branches, will impose market discipline. Localities that can build a good credit record will be able to go to the capital markets; more profligate governments may not be able to borrow at all.

The new Budget Law strengthens discipline at higher levels of government by imposing tighter accounting standards and reducing the scope for raising and spending extrabudgetary revenue. In exchange for accepting this greater oversight, local governments will gain relief from unfunded mandates and will have greater flexibility in using transfer funds from the central government.

The economic aims are also clear. The intention is to change the incentives of local officials so that they are less inclined to promote infrastructure, capital-intensive industry, and land speculation. Instead, the hope is that they will shift their economic-development priorities to consumer-oriented service sectors.[14] Perhaps more important, the idea is for local officials gradually to stop thinking of government as a glorified chamber of commerce whose main aim is to make life easy for business and to start focusing on the delivery of public goods and services—health care, welfare, education, a clean environment—as their main job.

What kind of taxes does the government impose?

An important characteristic of the Chinese tax system is that it relies very little on taxes on personal income or property, which are crucial parts of the tax systems of advanced countries. More than half of government revenues come from VAT (which is mainly paid by companies) and the corporate income tax (Figure 8.4). The personal income tax accounts for just 8 percent of revenues, and while this share has been creeping up in recent years, it is still far below international norms. In the United States, for instance, 86 percent of federal revenues come from personal income taxes and payroll taxes. A relatively small share of Chinese workers pay any income tax at all.[15] Capital gains taxes are routinely avoided, and except for a few small pilots, there is no tax on the value of real property, which as we have seen is a major store of wealth for urban households (see Chapter 6).

The main reason for China's enterprise-focused tax structure is that it is a lot easier to collect taxes from a relatively small number of companies than from hundreds of millions of wage earners. This is especially true for VAT, which has built-in incentives for compliance. When a company pays its VAT, it can deduct the VAT it paid when buying goods and materials from its suppliers. It is relatively easy for tax officials to force the biggest enterprises to pay their full tax bill because there are so few of them. These enterprises thus have a strong incentive to force their suppliers to charge VAT and provide them with proper tax receipts. Those suppliers in turn have the same incentive for their suppliers and so on down the chain. Taxes on corporate revenues and profits are easier to evade through accounting tricks that enable firms to understate their sales and earnings.

Sources of government budgetary revenue, 2018			
Revenue item	Rmb bn	% of tax	% of total
Value added taxes	6,250	40%	34%
Corporate income tax	3,532	23%	19%
Urban land, housing and construction taxes	1,576	10%	9%
Individual income tax	1,387	9%	8%
Consumption taxes	1,063	7%	6%
Other taxes	1,832	12%	10%
TOTAL TAX REVENUE	15,640		85%
Non-tax revenue	2,695		15%
TOTAL REVENUE	18,335		
Source: Ministry of Finance			

Figure 8.4 Structure of government revenue.

It is interesting to speculate whether a subconscious political motive is also at play. Tom Paine's famous slogan, "no taxation without representation" has enduring relevance: a government that directly taxes its citizens gives those citizens a strong incentive to demand greater accountability for how their money is spent. It is a short step from that demand to the desire for more representative government. By essentially exempting the majority of wage earners from the income tax and by not taxing the vast earnings on the capital invested in the nation's booming property and stock markets, the government (intentionally or not) defuses a potential source of political activism.

Despite these incentives, the government is now moving to ramp up collection of personal income tax. A new individual income tax law that went into effect in early 2019 cut tax rates for most households but eliminated tax breaks for certain types of income such as bonuses, and promised tougher efforts to collect taxes on nonwage income, such as gains from selling or renting property, royalties, and profit-sharing. To drive home the point, several high-profile people, including China's most popular actress, Fan Bingbing, were detained in 2018 and compelled to pay millions of dollars in back taxes.

Another tax advocated by the Ministry of Finance, but politically difficult to implement, is a tax on property values, such as most American localities use to fund their school systems. The lack of property tax encourages investors to buy as many properties as possible and hold them (vacant, if need be) for as long as possible until they can reap a capital gain. Imposing a property tax would make a lot of economic sense and would probably lead to a more sensible pattern of development in China's cities. But it has been vigorously opposed by property owners and by local governments, who would see a net revenue loss when they switch to a property tax from the current system of simply selling land outright.[16]

How does the government spend its money?

The structure of its spending offers a handy snapshot of a government's priorities and theory of governance. We can divide China's budget into four main categories. The first, which we may term *social management*, accounts for about a third of spending and includes not only spending on social welfare programs, pensions, and the health care system, but various local development projects. The second category, *education and science and technology*, consumes about 20 percent of the budget. *Resource management*, which mainly relates to agricultural support but also includes environmental protection and resource extraction, accounts for another 17 percent. Finally, *security*—comprising both national defense and internal policing—accounts for 11 percent of spending (Figure 8.5).[17]

This breakdown prompts a few observations. First, spending on social welfare programs is a far smaller share of China's budget than is typical in advanced countries. One challenge for China's leaders in the coming decades will be to build the more generous social safety net required by an older population,

Budgetary expenditure by category, 2018		
	Rmb bn	% of total
Social management	**7,156**	**32%**
Social security and employment	*2,701*	*12%*
Urban/rural community affairs	*2,212*	*10%*
Health and family planning	*1,562*	*7%*
Education, culture, science and technology	**4,404**	**20%**
Education	*3,217*	*15%*
Science and technology	*833*	*4%*
Resource management	**3,680**	**17%**
Agriculture, forestry, and water conservation	*2,109*	*10%*
Environmental protection	*630*	*3%*
Resource exploration	*508*	*2%*
Security	**2,565**	**12%**
Domestic security	*1,378*	*6%*
National defense and diplomacy	*1,128*	*5%*
Interest on government debt	**740**	**3%**
General administration	**1,837**	**8%**
Other	**1,709**	**8%**
Total expenditure	**22,091**	
Source: Ministry of Finance		

Figure 8.5 Structure of Government expenditure.

without falling into the trap of excessive entitlement spending that bedevils so many developed-economy governments. Second, spending on education and science and technology is relatively high, reflecting the government's desire to build the "human capital" needed to power a high-technology economy. Finally, spending on national defense as a share of the budget (5.4 percent) or of GDP (1.3 percent) is in line with its level of development.[18] Indeed, China spends more on internal security than on defense, although the internal security budget is a small fraction of the broader social welfare budget.

More broadly, these spending priorities illustrate that the CCP has a complex strategy for governance and legitimacy: it is not just a police state but a police state that also devotes enormous energy and funds to improve the material conditions, opportunities, and living environment of its citizens. It is important to keep this observation in mind in Chapter 15 where we consider China's future growth prospects and its place on the international stage.

9

THE FINANCIAL SYSTEM

What role do China's banks play in financing growth?

China has a bank-dominated financial system. About 70 percent of corporate finance is provided either by banks or by other lenders that act like banks. Only about 30 percent comes from the capital markets—issuance of stocks and bonds (Figure 9.1). In this respect, China lies squarely in the tradition of East Asian developmental states, all of which mainly used banks to finance their growth. This pattern is also found in many continental European economies, such as Germany and France, although those countries also have better-developed corporate bond and stock markets than Asian countries. China's system differs most sharply from those of the United States and the United Kingdom, both of which have unusually large capital markets and banking systems with an unusually low share of total financial assets. That said, the nature of both banks and the financial system has changed enormously in the past four decades, and the role of the capital markets has increased substantially.[1]

At the beginning of reforms, banks were simply the distribution agents for investment funds that came out of the state budget. In the 1980s and 1990s, more banks were established. They began to issue real loans, but these loans were driven more by central and local policy directives than by commercial

	Rmb bn	% of total
Enterprise loans	7,639	70%
Corporate bonds	2,049	19%
Equity finance	1,211	11%
Source: PBOC, author calculations		

Figure 9.1 Corporate financing flows, 2018.
Source: PBOC, author calculations.

considerations. In the late 1990s banks were restructured along more commercial lines, and they began to diversify into household mortgages, credit cards, and other forms of consumer lending.

Starting in 2010, the bank share of financial activity began to decline as nonbank lending companies (the so-called shadow banks), and the bond and stock markets, began to play a larger role in a more diverse financial ecosystem. Beginning in late 2016, the government launched a fierce campaign to rein in nonbank lenders, which by 2019 greatly reduced their importance. At the same time, the bond market grew rapidly, as Beijing pushed local governments to restructure their vast bank debts into revenue bonds. Yet banks remain the core of the financial system, and their lending remains subject to much political influence from central and local governments.

During the planned economy period, China effectively had one bank, the People's Bank of China (PBOC), which was both the central bank and the sole commercial bank. The Bank of China was in essence the unit of the PBOC that handled foreign exchange transactions, and the China Construction Bank was a unit of the Ministry of Finance (MOF) that distributed funds for investment projects. A network of rural credit cooperatives enabled collection of deposits from farm families and the distribution of credit to small-scale rural enterprises. Under the communist system, the PBOC "monobank" was simply the fiscal agent of the state, moving funds into state enterprises to enable them to buy their supplies and pay their workers, and transmitting enterprise surpluses back to the central treasury.

In the early 1980s, the PBOC was gradually turned into a regular central bank, and commercial lending functions were separated out into the "Big Four" commercial banks directly controlled by the MOF—the Bank of China, the China Construction Bank, the Industrial and Commercial Bank of China, and the Agricultural Bank of China. The Big Four dominated China's financial system from the mid-1980s until the early 2000s, for most of that period accounting for two-thirds or more of total bank credit. Until the late 1990s, the Big Four continued to act more as state fiscal agents than as proper banks. Their main job was to collect deposits from individuals and companies and to extend working-capital loans to state-owned enterprises (SOEs). They made virtually no loans to private firms or households. Basic elements of consumer finance that we take for granted, such as personal checking accounts and credit cards, did not exist.

This model hit a crisis in the late 1990s. Following Deng Xiaoping's southern tour of 1992 (see Chapter 1), the nation went on an investment spree, and SOEs—especially those controlled by local governments—invested heavily in new capacity to produce goods for which there were often no markets. Inventories piled up in warehouses, and companies could not repay their loans. Bad loans in the Big Four reached a staggering one-third of GDP in 1998.[2] A leading international analyst concluded that "China's four major banks as a group have a negative net worth and are thus insolvent."[3] The economy risked suffocating under the weight of dead capital.

Premier Zhu Rongji organized a restructuring plan that solved the problem. First, most bad loans were extracted from the banks and placed in specialized asset management companies. The banks got fresh capital from the MOF and were told they no longer had to lend to zombie SOEs; instead, their job was to finance viable businesses and give mortgages to families buying homes in the freshly privatized housing market. Next, in 2001–2006, the Big Four were reorganized as shareholding companies, found "strategic shareholders" (mainly foreign commercial and investment banks) that gave them infusions of capital and bolstered their international credibility, and were listed on international stock markets.[4]

While it restructured the banks, the government made other moves to create a better financial system. In 1994, it set up three "policy" banks to finance government-directed projects that would likely not generate a commercial rate of return.[5] In the late 1990s, a dozen or so smaller "second-tier" or "shareholding" banks were encouraged to expand their operations. These banks were also state-owned, but their shareholders were a congeries of local governments and other SOEs, rather than the MOF. At least in theory, they were nimbler than the Big Four because they were not subservient to the central government and operated only in the most vibrant regions. Urban credit cooperatives were organized into what are now about 170 city-level banks, and rural credit cooperatives were restructured into several thousand rural banks. Thanks to this proliferation of new lenders, by 2018 the Big Four's share of total bank loans shrank to about a third.[6] Finally, regulation was made more professional by the creation of the China Banking Regulatory Commission (CBRC). Led for its first decade by an experienced reform-oriented banker, Liu Mingkang, the CBRC did a good job of ensuring that banks adopted modern risk-management practices and stayed well capitalized.

As a result of all these factors—a stronger capital structure, increased competition, a healthier universe of borrowers, discipline from domestic and international stockholders, and a vigilant regulator—the quality of China's banks has improved, and they finance a much wider array of activities at present than in the 1990s. For instance, consumer lending, virtually nonexistent in 2000, in 2018 accounted for 28 percent of outstanding bank loans and consists mainly of home mortgages.[7]

What was the role of "financial repression" in China's growth?

Aside from the predominance of banks, the other key feature of China's financial system is "financial repression"—policies designed to channel funds away from household and corporate savers and toward the government. As we discussed in Chapter 3, East Asian developmental states used a broad set of financial repression tools to maximize the government's control over money flows, and China followed suit. These include:

- Tightly regulated interest rates, which effectively taxed savers to keep borrowing costs low for companies and the government;
- Rules to prevent banks or nonbank financial institutions from skirting the deposit-rate caps by offering other, higher-yielding financial products;
- An undervalued exchange rate (encouraging investment in export industries and discouraging purchases of imported consumer goods or borrowing in foreign currencies);
- Capital controls (to prevent savers from escaping the low yields at home by investing their money abroad).

The main aim of such policies is to increase the availability of funds for investment in infrastructure, basic industries such as steel and petrochemicals, and export manufacturing. Every country uses a different mix of tools. China only slowly groped its way to a financial repression package in the 1980s and 1990s, and since 2010 has reduced its reliance on most of them, with the notable exception of capital controls.

Between 1980 and 1995, the exchange rate was gradually depreciated in order to promote exports, and capital movements were strictly controlled. But domestic interest rates were not held especially low: Zhu Rongji hiked them sharply in 1994 to tame double-digit inflation, and he kept deposit rates well above the rate of inflation through the end of his premiership in 2003. In 2004, however, the new government of Hu Jintao and Wen Jiabao adopted a classic financial repression strategy. In 2004–2013, the average real deposit rate was negative 0.3 percent.[8] The main reason was probably the bank bailout of the late 1990s. This bailout was in essence a series of accounting tricks, and to rebuild their true capital base, the banks needed to have abnormally high profits for a long time. One way to guarantee such profits was to hold banks' funding cost (deposit rates) at very low levels, while letting them lend out funds at much higher rates.[9] Another reason to keep interest rates low was to ensure cheap funding for ambitious infrastructure programs.

Full-scale financial repression is hard to sustain for a very long time: eventually, savers will look for ways to earn a higher return, and whether legally or not will start to move their money out of the regulated banks. In China, this pressure helped fuel the rise of "shadow banking" from about 2010 onward.

What was behind the rise of "shadow banking"?

After the 2008 global financial crisis, regulators and financial sector analysts started to pay attention to so-called shadow banking, which the IMF defines as "financial intermediaries or activities involved in credit intermediation outside the regular banking system, and therefore lacking a formal safety net"— or in simpler language, banking done off the balance sheets of regular banks. In some countries with highly developed financial systems, notably the United States and the United Kingdom, these "shadow banking" activities were bigger than the formal banking systems, and many believed that they contributed to the financial crisis.[10]

By 2010, shadow banking began to emerge in China through two channels. Banks and trust companies started offering "wealth management products," which gave investors higher rates of interest than bank deposits; and more loans began to be made outside the traditional banks. At first, most of these nonbanks were trust companies, lightly regulated institutions that collect funds from wealthy individuals and companies and invest in a range of credit instruments. But then a host of others joined in: brokerages, securities companies, asset managers, and insurers all set up lending arms.

The expansion of nonbank loan activity was dramatic: from 2010 through 2013, annual growth in bank lending stayed fairly stable at around 14 percent, but a massive increase in shadow lending drove total credit growth to a peak of 23 percent in early 2013. Even after the government started curbing overall credit growth, shadow finance kept expanding rapidly until the end of 2016, when it peaked at Rmb 11.5 trillion, nearly half of all new loans (Figures 9.2 and 9.3).

This explosion of nonbank finance responded to various needs of households, borrowers, and lenders. For years, households had been stuck with few ways to earn a decent return

% of total financial system assets, 2007 and 2018			
Institution type	2007	2018	Change 2018/2007, pp
Banks	**86.2%**	**74.1%**	**-12.1**
Policy banks	7.1%	7.5%	0.4
State-owned commercial*	46.7%	27.5%	-19.2
Other (shareholding, city, rural)	32.4%	39.1%	6.7
Non-banks	**13.8%**	**25.9%**	**13.1**
Trusts	1.5%	5.2%	3.7
Insurance companies	4.7%	5.1%	0.4
Other**	7.6%	15.6%	8.0
Total system assets, Rmb trillion	**62**	**362**	
% of GDP	224%	402%	

* Big 4, Bank of Communications, Postal Savings Bank

** Asset managers, mutual and hedge funds, securities firms

Source: PBOC, CEIC, Wind, Ministry of Finance

Figure 9.2 Financial assets by institution.

% of total credit assets, 2007 and 2018			
Asset type	2007	2018	Change 2018/2007, pp
Bank loans	62.9%	57.0%	-5.5
Shadow loans	0.0%	8.2%	8.8
Bonds	28.8%	33.8%	5.0
Central govt and policy bank	*17.7%*	*11.8%*	*-5.9*
Local government	*0.0%*	*7.3%*	*7.3*
Financial institutions	*0.8%*	*2.4%*	*1.6*
Corporate/other	*10.3%*	*13.2%*	*1.9*
Central bank bills	8.3%	0.0%	-8.3
Total credit assets, Rmb trillion	**44**	**247**	
% of GDP	163%	274%	
Source: PBOC, CEIC, Wind, Ministry of Finance			

Figure 9.3 Credit assets by type.

on their savings, since their main option was to put money in a bank account that paid a rate of interest lower than inflation. The panoply of higher-yielding products available in rich countries—money market funds, mutual funds, real estate investment trusts, and so on—was simply not available. By 2010, many Chinese households had enough savings to make it worthwhile to chase higher returns, and inflation was creeping higher. They flocked to higher-yielding wealth management products. The rise of these products parallels the rise of money market funds in the United States in the 1970s, which was also a response to growing consumer wealth and regulated deposit rates falling behind inflation.[11]

Plenty of borrowers were eager to gain access to financing that banks were unable to extend. Many of these were private companies, which had good businesses but had trouble getting bank loans. This was partly because of structural biases favoring state firms. An SOE typically had a lot of fixed assets, such as land or equipment, to use as collateral. If it experienced trouble repaying a loan, its supervising government agency (its "mother-in-law") could help broker a deal with their lenders. And it often carried an implicit guarantee—a tacit promise by the government that the company would not be allowed to go bankrupt, leaving its lenders in the lurch.

With less fixed assets, no government "mother-in-law," and no implicit guarantee, private firms often looked too risky to banks. Another set of eager borrowers was local governments, which were required by the central government to make expensive investments in infrastructure and social welfare programs, but often lacked the revenues to do so. Technically, until 2015 local governments had almost no borrowing authority, but for years they had gotten around this restriction by setting up shell companies into which they injected government-held land assets that served as collateral (see Chapter 8).

Finally, both shadow lenders and some banks had huge incentives to ramp up shadow lending. For several years after 2010, China's economy boomed, with annual growth rates of 7–10 percent. Many private companies were willing to pay high interest rates to finance their fast-growing businesses, so lending to them, while somewhat risky, could also be very profitable. Moreover, banks had good reasons to facilitate this lending by running funds through shadow lenders, rather than making loans directly. The central one was that China's bank regulators, following international standards, required banks to hold at least $8 of capital for every $100 of loans they issued; but anything classified as an "investment" required only $2–3 of capital.[12]

This meant that banks that wanted to rapidly expand their lending (and profits) had a strong incentive to pretend that their loans were actually "investments." So instead of issuing a loan directly to a company or local government, they would buy an "investment product" from a trust company or other shadow lender, which would then make the loan. Sometimes two or three different nonbank institutions were involved in moving money from the banks to the ultimate borrowers.

For several years, regulators tolerated this explosion of credit because it served their purpose of deregulating the financial system, providing higher returns to savers and making credit available to a wider range of borrowers. But by the end of 2016 they began to be concerned that the risks of shadow banking outweighed its benefits.[13]

Why did the government crack down on shadow banking?

Shadow banking created three major risks in China. First, it contributed to a rapid rise in national leverage, or the amount of debt in the economy relative to output. China's debt-to-GDP ratio was relatively stable at around 140 percent until the 2008 global recession; in the ensuing decade, it soared to about 260 percent by 2017. While neither the level nor the increase of debt reliably presages a big financial crisis, both factors substantially raised the risk of such a crisis. Second, the relations between all the different institutions involved in shadow banking became ever more complex, so it became hard for regulators to know how much debt there really was and how risky the loans were. Finally, the shadow system created a class of undercapitalized banks. The country's 170 or so city-level commercial banks were among the most enthusiastic funders of shadow activity, and loaded up their balance sheets with "investments" in shadow banking products that were really disguised loans. Because of the low capital requirements for these "investments," many of these banks had far less capital than they really needed.

In response to these risks, regulators led by the People's Bank of China launched a comprehensive financial de-risking campaign in late 2016. The aims were to reduce the overall rate of credit growth and severely restrict all shadow banking activities, and to restore the banks as the main sources for credit.

The groundwork for this campaign had been laid over the prior 2 years with several regulatory changes, notably the passage of a new banking law in 2015 and the authorization for local governments to issue both general revenue bonds and special infrastructure project bonds, which aimed to free them from their reliance on shadow lenders. Additional measures followed, notably the establishment of the Financial Development and Stability Committee (FDSC) under the State Council in 2017 and the merging of the bank and insurance regulators into a single body, the China Bank and Insurance Regulatory Commission (CBIRC) in 2018. These moves brought some order to a chaotic regulatory system and made clear that the State Council, not any individual financial regulator, had ultimate responsibility for ensuring financial stability.

The de-risking campaign was well managed and achieved most of its basic goals. Between late 2016 and late 2019, annual credit growth slowed from over 16 percent to 10 percent, and the national debt-to-GDP ratio stabilized. Banks effectively stopped their "investments" in shadow lenders, and the volume of shadow lending contracted sharply (Figure 9.4).

What is the future of financial regulation?

Though successful, the de-risking campaign left several problems in its wake. The main difficulty was that, by shutting down the shadow lenders, the government made it much harder for private firms to obtain credit. Banks still had all the old reasons to be cautious about lending to private firms, and in fact as the shadow sector grew, they actually cut back on the provision of credit to provide companies. According to one estimate, the private-sector share of new corporate bank lending fell from over 50 percent in 2010–2013 to 11 percent in 2016.[14]

The challenge in the coming years therefore will be to resume in a more formal way the deregulation of the financial sector that the shadow banking boom achieved informally. One key step is the full liberalization of interest rates, which remain subject to various controls by regulators. In principle, caps on bank lending rates were abolished in 2004, and banks

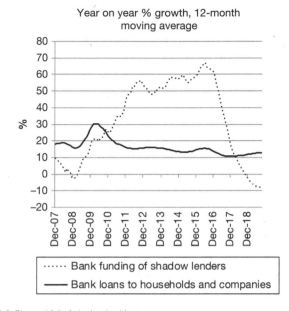

Figure 9.4 Rise and fall of shadow banking.
Source: PBOC, Gavekal Dragonomics.

theoretically became free to set their own deposit rates about a decade later. In practice, however, banks tend to set their loan and deposit rates very close to benchmarks set by the PBOC, and they receive extensive guidance from the PBOC and the bank regulator on where they should direct their lending and what interest rates they should charge.

If interest rates are fully deregulated and political influence on bank-lending decisions is lessened, it may be possible to increase the share of credit going to private companies and thereby improve economic efficiency. But this financial deregulation directly conflicts with other government goals: maintaining active support for state enterprises and using directed bank credit as a way of achieving economic targets. It is not clear how this tension between efficiency-oriented deregulation and the continued desire for top-down control will be resolved.

What is the role of the bond market?

Although China remains a bank-dominated financial system, the role of capital markets has increased substantially in recent years. Of particular importance is the bond market, whose development has been the focus of intense efforts by the PBOC since 2002. Until then, China's bond market was small and stagnant, consisting mainly of government bonds issued by the Ministry of Finance, quasi-government bonds issued by the policy banks, and bonds issued by the largest SOEs under a strict quota system ("enterprise bonds"). These bonds were bought by banks and insurance companies which mainly held them to maturity; trading was thin.

There were two problems. First, the ability to access credit was limited to those companies (mainly, SOEs) that could get bank loans. As long as this was the case, the distribution of credit would be subject to political constraints; to achieve a more economical distribution of credit, additional channels of credit creation were required. Second, the lack of actively traded money markets meant it was impossible for PBOC to run a conventional monetary policy in which the central bank controls a short-term interest rate and subsequent market trading causes other interest rates to move in response. Instead of this "price-based" monetary policy, which is generally considered to be more economically efficient, PBOC had to conduct a "quantity-based" monetary policy, under which it controlled the volume of loans issued by banks under a quota system.

In the decade 2002–2012, under PBOC's leadership, a host of new fixed-income instruments were created, starting with short-term bills issued by the central bank in 2002 and continuing with asset-backed securities, medium- and long-term bonds for nonstate companies, and local government bonds. The latter were first introduced in 2009, but their volume was tightly limited; in 2015, localities received authority to issue bonds much more freely in order to replace the huge land-backed loans they had taken from banks over the previous decade. By 2019, China's bond market was one of the largest

in the world, with Rmb94 trillion ($13.5 trillion) of total issu-
ance. A little less than two-thirds of this amount was still by
public sector entities (governments and policy banks), and
most of the rest was by SOEs and local government financing
vehicles. But larger private firms have also become active
issuers.

The next step was to open the market to foreign investors.
Although foreign institutions were allowed to invest in some
bonds under a quota system as early as 2002, and central banks
and sovereign wealth funds got unlimited access to the main
bond markets in 2010, most were reluctant because of concerns
about the market's liquidity and the potential impact of capital
controls on their ability to take money out of the market when
they needed to. Many of these concerns were allayed by the
launch of the "Bond Connect" scheme in 2017, under which
foreign institutions could buy and sell Chinese bonds using
accounts in Hong Kong. By late 2019, foreign investors held
about Rmb 2 trillion of Chinese bonds, more than double the
figure in 2016 and about 2 percent of the total market. Foreign
participation is likely to increase as China's market is included
in the global bond indices that dictate the weights of different
bond markets in major institutional bond portfolios.[15]

How did the stock market develop?

China's stock market is a large, complicated beast. The first
stock market launched in Shenzhen in 1991 and grew rapidly. But for two decades that market and the much larger one
that soon followed in Shanghai were a colorful sideshow to
the financial system, subject to swings between speculative
bubbles and regulatory freezes, with little relationship to the
real economy. For years, most large Chinese firms sought listings on international stock markets in Hong Kong, Singapore,
New York, and London. This included famous private Internet
companies such as Alibaba and Tencent, whose original shareholders included foreign venture capital funds.

But starting in about 2008, private firms started listing en masse in the domestic market, in part because the two main markets set up various submarkets with less stringent listing requirements. Over the next decade, the number of domestically listed firms swelled, and a variety of regulatory problems that slowed the market's development were gradually solved. By the end of 2019, China's domestic stock market boasted nearly 5,000 firms (more than any other country except India); another 1,000 or so Chinese companies are listed in Hong Kong and about 350 in other countries. The capitalization of domestically listed stocks was about $7 trillion, putting China second, albeit a distant one, behind the $30 trillion U.S. stock market. Including all the offshore listed firms pushes China's total up to $11 trillion. About 60 percent of these firms (both by number and by market capitalization) are private-sector companies.[16]

As with the bond market, large-scale international interest in China's domestic stock market is a relatively recent phenomenon and only really took off with a Hong Kong-based investment channel and the market's long-delayed inclusion in key global indices. In 2015, the Stock Connect scheme was launched, allowing international investors to buy Shanghai-listed stocks using a Hong Kong brokerage account. A Connect scheme to the more tech-oriented Shenzhen market followed in 2016. As with bonds, the Connect schemes allayed investor concerns that capital controls would prevent them from freely pulling money out of the market. In large part because of the Connect schemes, MSCI (the leading provider of global stock market indices) began including domestic Chinese stocks in 2018 and is slowly increasing their weights.

What is the risk that China will hit a financial crisis?

One of the most common worries about China is that it will encounter a severe financial crisis. This worry arises partly from the track record of emerging markets in general and partly from problems specific to China's financial sector.

Fast-growth emerging economies are prone to financial crisis. The litany of the last three decades includes Brazil and other Latin American countries (1982–1984), Mexico (1994), South Korea and several Southeast Asian countries (1997), Russia (1998), and Argentina (1998–2002). Why should China prove immune to the financial shocks that beset other big emerging economies? Of particular concern is the fast rise in the national debt-to-GDP ratio from 140 percent in 2008 to around 260 percent in 2016. This leverage ratio subsequently stabilized as a result of the financial de-risking campaign, but it is still very high by the standards of other developing economies, and a rapid *increase* in debt such as China experienced in 2008–2016 is often associated with crisis, regardless of the level of debt.[17]

Yet several factors suggest that China is unlikely to experience a dramatic financial crisis like the ones that engulfed the United States in 2008 or many Asian countries a decade earlier. More realistic worries are that China's high level of debt limits the government's ability to respond to economic downturns, and in the long run could lead to a substantial slowdown in the country's economic growth rate.

A debt-to-GDP ratio of 260 percent may sound scary, but many advanced economies, including the United States and Japan, have similar or higher ratios. With its faster-trending economic growth rate, China will have more income to service its debts than slow-growth countries with higher debt levels. It also has plenty of assets that could be sold to pay down debts, such as land controlled by local governments or plant and equipment owned by SOEs.

Equally, the rapid rise in debt after 2008 is often cited as a sure-fire signal for crisis, but it is not necessarily so. Most developed countries have seen substantial and in some cases very rapid increases in debt-to-GDP ratios since the 1960s, and there is no particular pattern of association between these increases and financial crisis. A notable example is Australia, which since 1993 has seen its private-sector debt (i.e., borrowing by companies and households, but not the government), nearly double, during which time it has never experienced a recession, let alone a financial crisis. In the United States, private-sector debt rose from 50 percent of GDP in the early 1950s to 150 percent in the early 2000s, without triggering a crisis. A financial meltdown occurred only after a later surge in debt during the 2003–2007 housing bubble.

Debt can rise for many reasons, not just profligacy and inefficiency. The steady rise in debt in most rich countries since the 1950s is largely attributable to innovations in corporate finance (bonds and commercial paper) and consumer credit (flexible mortgages, home equity lines, credit cards) that enabled both companies and households to sustainably finance more of their assets with debt rather than with equity. (This process is called "financial deepening.") In China after 2008, rising debt was partly attributable to financial deepening, as more and more households took on mortgages to buy apartments, and as private companies previously shut out from the financial system found ways to take on debt to finance their growth. It is also true that much debt financed infrastructure projects by local governments, some of which will never deliver a financial return.

Moreover, a full-blown financial crisis requires not just a high level of debt, but also a trigger. The classic trigger for emerging-market debt crisis is an inability to pay back foreign lenders, which can spark capital outflows, a collapse in the currency, and decimation of the domestic financial system. This is essentially what occurred in the Asian financial crisis of 1997–1998. Another classic trigger is a shortage of "liquidity"—easily available funds. This shortage leads to rapid sales of assets at low prices, damaging the banks that accepted those assets as collateral for loans. This is basically what occurred in the United States after Lehman Brothers went into bankruptcy in 2008.

No such trigger is likely to be pulled in China—in part because the government is aware of the risk and has tried to immunize the financial sector against it. Inability to pay foreign debt is not a problem because foreign debts are small—about 10 percent of GDP—and foreign reserves of about $3 trillion give the central bank plenty of ammunition to ward off a speculative attack on the currency. A domestic liquidity squeeze is also unlikely because the domestic savings rate is very high (about 40 percent of GDP) and much of that saving is still funneled into bank deposits, the safest form of funding for a financial system.[18] Moreover, the government owns virtually all of the main financial institutions, as well as most of the most problematic borrowers (local governments and SOEs). It can therefore control the pace at which bad debts are recognized and prevent panic sales of assets.

The real challenges posed by China's heavy reliance on debt-fueled growth after 2008 lie elsewhere. First, the government's very understandable desire not to let debt rise further means that it has fewer tools to combat an economic downturn. This became evident in 2018–2019, when China's economy slowed sharply as a result of the domestic financial de-risking campaign, a drop in exports as a result of the trade war with the United States, and a broader deceleration in global trade. Because of its determination to continue de-risking the financial sector and prevent leverage from rising, the authorities did not permit an acceleration of credit growth until early 2019, and even then the credit expansion was very small. Given that China's debt-to-GDP ratio is relatively normal for a developed country but quite high for a developing country, it is likely that for some years to come policymakers will try to prevent debt from growing much faster than GDP; this will limit its ability to stimulate the economy during slowdowns.

Given this constraint, it is crucial that each dollar of credit generate as much economic benefit as possible. So a goal of financial policy in the coming years should be to increase the amount of credit that goes to high-return projects and decrease the amount flowing to low-return projects. In essence, this means increasing credit to private companies, which generate a high return on investment, and reducing credit flows to SOEs (which consistently underperform their private peers) and to local governments, whose infrastructure investments are delivering ever-lower returns. As we noted earlier, this need to redirect resources from the relatively low-productivity state sector to a high-productivity private sector makes economic sense but collides with the Xi Jinping government's desire to maintain a large state sector.

This conflict raises the second risk from China's debt pile. If the government continues to insist on organizing the financial system so that a disproportionate share of credit flows to low-return state sector projects, the sustainable growth rate of the economy is likely to decline over time. As we will argue in Chapter 14, given good policies, it should be possible for China's economy to keep growing at a rate of 5 percent or more a year at least through 2025, and perhaps longer. But it will be hard to maintain this growth rate if the financial system continues to pour money into relatively low-yielding investments. In the absence of more aggressive market-oriented reform to the financial system, there is some risk that China's economy in the 2020s could "Japanify": that is, fall into a low-growth, high-debt pattern similar to the one that engulfed Japan in the 1990s.[19]

Why has China controlled its exchange rate so tightly?

Aside from the domestic banking system and interest rates, the other key component of any financial system is the currency's exchange rate. China has a managed exchange rate, not a free-floating one. Contrary to a widespread view in the financial media and U.S. Congress, China has never really had a policy of deliberate undervaluation to ramp up its exports. Since 1979, the main aims of exchange-rate policy have been to ensure that (1) prices in China were reasonably comparable to those in the rest of the world; (2) China's exports stayed competitive (but exporters also faced pressure to keep moving up the value chain); and (3) businesses had a stable and predictable investment environment.

In general, the last goal—stability for investors—has been the most important, but the balance of objectives has shifted over time, along with changes in China's economy. We can define four major periods of exchange-rate management: managed depreciation (1979–1995); a fixed exchange rate against the U.S. dollar (1995–2005); managed appreciation (2005–2015); and a managed float since late 2015 (Figure 9.5).

From 1979 to 1994, the renminbi was steadily devalued, from 1.5 to 8.7 against the dollar. This was because, during the 1980s, the main task of the exchange rate was to enable a move from a communist-style import-substitution economy to an East Asian export-oriented one. In the planned economy period, China—like virtually every other communist country—had a severely overvalued exchange rate, reflecting the communist economic principle that domestic investment in

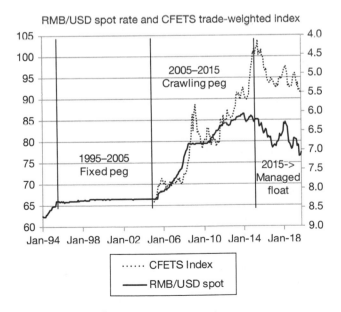

Figure 9.5 The renminbi exchange rate.

heavy industry, rather than international trade, was the route to wealth. A high exchange rate was useful because it made imports of capital goods and raw materials cheap.

The new export-driven growth model required an exchange rate that was, if anything, a little undervalued, so that China's exports would be competitive on the global markets. Over the first 15 years of reform, China let its exchange rate gradually fall to a more realistic level. It also maintained two exchange rates: a high official rate, used, for example, when foreign tourists converted their money into renminbi; and a second, market-oriented rate that was available only to licensed foreign trade organizations.

In 1994, the two exchange rates were combined (at the lower market rate), and over the next couple of years the authorities let the exchange rate float fairly freely in an effort to figure out the renminbi's true international market value.[20] By the end of 1995, the rate had settled at 8.3 to the dollar, and this was adopted as the fixed rate for the next decade, with only a small daily trading range permitted.

Why did China shift from steady devaluation to a fixed rate against the dollar? The reason is that the main job had changed: from making the renminbi safe for Chinese exporters to making the renminbi safe for foreign investors. Foreign companies were pouring into China in the 1990s and building huge numbers of export-oriented factories. Such investors wanted reassurance that their big investments would not be rendered worthless by dramatic swings in the exchange rate. China's exchange rate thus needed to meet two conditions: it had to be low enough to ensure that China's exports would remain competitive, but it also had to be close enough to the true market level that it could be maintained for a long time with little variation.

Almost immediately after its adoption, the fixed exchange rate faced a challenge. During the Asian financial crisis of 1997–1998, several neighboring Asian countries, many of which had export baskets that competed directly with China's, were forced to devalue their currencies massively. Most observers assumed that China would devalue the renminbi as well in order to keep its exporters in business.

They were wrong. China did not devalue: in fact, it tightened the peg to the U.S. dollar by reducing the permitted daily trading band to a minuscule 0.1 percent. Instead of succumbing to the temptation to devalue, it doubled down on its fixed currency bet. Why? Basically, because the principle of long-run stability for investors trumped the expedient of short-term support for exporters. For a couple of years, the costs were high: export growth ground nearly to a halt, and the trade surplus shrank. But foreign investors were heartened by Beijing's commitment to a stable exchange rate, and foreign direct investment (FDI) continued to pour into the country. By 2001, China had established a clear reputation as one of the best places in Asia to do business, and exports were growing again at double-digit rates.

By 2004, China's trade surplus was exploding, and critics in the United States began to argue that an undervalued currency was helping Chinese factories steal market share from American firms. Note that China's currency in 2004 had exactly the same value against the U.S. dollar as in 1998. China had not devalued its currency to gain exports. But two things had happened. First, Chinese workers had become far more productive because industrial reforms made them move from inefficient SOEs to better-managed private and foreign firms. And second, the U.S. dollar weakened sharply after 2000. The renminbi, pegged to the dollar, got cheaper against many other currencies, and this helped Chinese exporters.

In 2005, China abandoned the fixed-dollar peg and let the renminbi "crawl up" against the dollar. The initial pace of appreciation was slow, but after China's current account surplus hit $400 billion, or 10 percent of GDP, in 2007, the renminbi's rise accelerated. By the end of 2013, after 8 years of gradual appreciation, the renminbi touched a rate of 6 to the dollar, making it nearly 40 percent more valuable than in 2005. Thanks in large part to this shift, the current account had shrunk to a much less scary 2 percent of GDP.

The fourth stage of Beijing's currency management began in late 2015, when the PBOC abandoned its targeting of the U.S. dollar in favor of a basket of the currencies of China's major trade partners, and also allowed the market to play a bigger role in determining daily movements. Since this new system took effect, the renminbi's value has bounced up and down against the dollar, as most currencies do, although the pace of these movements has clearly been moderated by PBOC efforts to reduce exchange-rate volatility.

The introduction of this "managed float" occurred against the backdrop of a mini balance-of-payments crisis. During the previous "managed appreciation" era, the renminbi could only do two things against the US dollar: rise or remain stable. It could not go down. This posed no problems until late 2014, when the real or trade-weighted value of the dollar surged.[21] This forced the real, trade-weighted value of the renminbi to strengthen as well, until the currency was seriously over-valued. Once Chinese companies realized that the renminbi was overvalued, they knew that sooner or later its value would fall. So they began selling renminbi and renminbi assets, and buying dollars and dollar assets. In other words, China began to see large-scale capital flight. With private capital flowing out, the only way the PBOC could maintain a constant renminbi exchange rate against the dollar was to spend its foreign exchange reserves to buy up the renminbi that other people were selling. Between June 2014 and December 2016, China's foreign reserves fell from $4 trillion to $3 trillion—a loss of a trillion dollars—largely because of this effort to prop up the currency.

By switching to a managed float against a trade-weighted basket, PBOC no longer had to care about defending a par-ticular rate against the dollar, so it could stop spending its reserves. Over 2016, the renminbi gradually depreciated and capital flight ended (in part because of the imposition of stricter capital controls making it harder to move money out of the country); when confidence was restored, the renminbi once more rose in value in 2017. Foreign exchange reserves have remained stable at around $3 trillion.

The managed-float regime showed its worth again in 2018–2019 after the United States launched a trade war, eventually imposing tariffs of up to 25 percent on half of China's exports to the United States. The renminbi depreciated by 10 percent against the dollar (because of market action, not intervention by the PBOC) and by a slightly smaller amount against the trade-weighted basket. This offset some of the rise in China's export prices caused by the tariffs and the effort to keep China's exporters competitive.

Again, however, the new managed float currency mechanism is not mainly designed to make life easy for Chinese exporters. The main aims are to make the exchange rate more flexible so that it can more easily be used to offset external shocks (such as the trade war) and to give international investors more confidence that the value of the renminbi is driven more by the market than by the whims of Beijing bureaucrats. This latter goal is important given the long, slow effort to make the renminbi an important international currency.

Why is China trying to make the renminbi an international currency?

Beginning in 2009, China began a push to increase the international use of the renminbi, which until then had been minimal. Key features of the program were increasing the ability of Hong Kong residents to open renminbi bank accounts, boosting the use of renminbi in the invoicing of China's trade flows, and opening a renminbi bond market in Hong Kong. (Renminbi bonds issued outside of the Chinese mainland are colloquially known as "dim sum" bonds.)

The initial results of this program were impressive. By the end of 2014, outstanding dim sum bonds totaled Rmb 400 billion ($65 billion); renminbi deposits in Hong Kong totaled Rmb 1 trillion, or 12 percent of total deposits in the territory; and 22 percent of China's trade was settled in renminbi. Issuance of renminbi bonds expanded beyond Hong Kong to other financial centers, notably Singapore and London. From a standing start only 5 years earlier, this was a large increase in the renminbi's international presence, comparable in many ways to the internationalization of the Japanese yen in the 1980s.[22]

But after this fast start, international use of the renminbi stalled. In 2019, the renminbi still ranked just eighth on the list of the most frequently traded currencies on foreign exchange markets and was involved in 4 percent of global currency trades by value. The shares of the three main global currencies—the U.S. dollar, the euro, and the yen—were, respectively, 88 percent, 32 percent, and 17 percent. (Because every trade involves two currencies, the total for all currencies is 200 percent.) Renminbi deposits in Hong Kong were just Rmb 707 billion, down nearly a third from 5 years earlier and only 5 percent of deposits in the territory. The dim sum bond market was down to Rmb 200 billion, half its size, in 2014. The share of China's international trade invoiced in renminbi had fallen to under 20 percent. China's share of the international reserve holdings of central banks hovered around 2 percent, compared to 62 percent for the U.S. dollar and 20 percent for the euro.[23]

This pattern raises two questions: why did the renminbi internationalize so rapidly in 2009–2015, and why did the momentum stall afterward? The reasons for the initial internationalization are straightforward. First, by 2009, it was quite odd for the currency of a trading nation of China's size not to be internationally traded. China became the world's biggest exporter in 2009 and overtook the United States as the world's biggest trading nation (imports plus exports) in 2013. With so many countries and companies shipping goods to and from China, it is natural that more of them would want to conduct that trade in China's currency—just as international use of the deutschemark and yen soared in the 1970s, when West Germany and Japan became major trading powers.

There were also policy reasons behind the renminbi's abrupt takeoff. Following the 2008 global financial crisis, China's closed financial system was not damaged, but its trade flows were: exports fell by nearly 20 percent in the following year, in part because global trade depends heavily on letters of credit issued in U.S. dollars. Chinese officials concluded that to insure against a future crisis, it should reduce its reliance on the U.S. dollar funding system.

Another factor was the PBOC's desire to force the pace of China's domestic financial liberalization. Financial reformers at the central bank realized that future economic growth depended in improving the efficiency of capital allocation. But many financial institutions and the SOEs that benefited from cheap capital and a closed system opposed financial liberalization. To get around this resistance, the PBOC started building up the renminbi market in Hong Kong. The idea was to create a place outside of mainland China where renminbi interest rates could be set by the market. Once that small-scale, controlled experiment succeeded, it would be easier to make the case for liberalizing interest rates on the mainland.[24]

The rapid early progress of renminbi internationalization led to predictions that it was only a matter of time before the renminbi became a major international currency and perhaps supplanted the U.S. dollar as the world's central currency.[25] These predictions seemed to be validated in November 2015, when the IMF announced that the renminbi would be the fifth currency included in its special drawing rights (SDR), an artificial reserve currency.[26] But SDR inclusion turned out to be a highwater mark of the renminbi's ascent, rather than the beginning of an era of dominance.

Why have efforts to internationalize the renminbi stalled?

The basic constraint on the renminbi becoming an important international or reserve currency is the Chinese government's desire to control its financial system, capital flows in and out of the country, and the exchange rate. The dollar consolidated its position as the indispensable currency in the decades following World War II in part because the United States was willing to tolerate a buildup of dollars outside the country (mainly in Europe) to finance a wide range of trade and investment, even though this technically violated the capital controls then in place. After the breakdown of the Bretton Woods system of fixed exchange rates in 1971, which also led to the elimination of capital controls, the United States was willing to run perpetual trade deficits in order to ensure that the rest of the world had an ample supply of dollars; it opened its Treasury bond market so that non-U.S. institutions had a safe place to park their dollar balances; and it allowed the value of the dollar to fluctuate widely in response to economic conditions.[27]

The Chinese government is unwilling to do any of these things, at least not quickly. Its commitment to running trade surpluses makes it hard to create a channel that will reliably funnel renminbi to the rest of the world. Although the exchange rate has been liberalized, Beijing still wants to confine its movements to a narrow range in the name of economic stability. This means it must maintain capital controls to prevent capital flows from pushing the renminbi's value rapidly up or down. These capital controls make it hard for China to fully open its domestic bond market to international investors, since international investors will be reluctant to put large sums of money in a market without assurance that they can freely take their money out whenever they want.

The conflict between the renminbi internationalization program and the government's desire for tight financial controls was dramatically illustrated in January 2016, just 2 months after the announcement of SDR inclusion. As noted above, China was facing large scale capital outflows, and speculators were driving down the value of renminbi traded offshore in Hong Kong well below the currency's rate in the closed domestic market in Shanghai. After spending hundreds of billions of dollars of its reserves defending the value of the renminbi, the PBOC finally resorted to sterner measures: it cut off renminbi liquidity to the Hong Kong money markets, making it prohibitively costly for traders to place bets against the currency. It also instituted strict capital controls to curb capital flight. These measures stabilized the exchange rate. But they also destroyed the credibility of the offshore renminbi market and created a lasting suspicion that international investors who put their money in the onshore bond market in Shanghai would not be able to get it out when they needed to.[28]

In short, Beijing's desire to tightly control its exchange rate and financial system means that individuals and companies outside of China find it hard to obtain renminbi; cannot use renminbi for many transactions outside of China; and have no convenient place (equivalent to the U.S. Treasury market) to invest their renminbi holdings. It is perfectly possible, given the gradual opening of China's financial markets, that the renminbi could become a secondary reserve currency, like the yen or the Swiss franc, within the next decade. Its chances of replacing the U.S. dollar, however, are close to zero.

10

ENERGY AND
THE ENVIRONMENT

In the preceding chapters, we have examined three of the systems that support China's economic structure: the financial, fiscal, and enterprise systems. In this chapter, we will look at the fourth major system, energy. This is in some ways the most complex system because China's energy use is tied up in two other major issues: the nation's air pollution problem and global climate change. Securing diverse, stable supplies of energy to fuel its future growth is also a big factor in China's emerging geopolitical strategy.

How much energy does China use?

China is the world's biggest user of energy, accounting for a quarter of global consumption. China burns 40 percent more energy than the United States and nearly twice as much as the European Union. It is by far the world's biggest user of coal, accounting for about half of global consumption. Consequently, China is also the world's biggest contributor to carbon dioxide (CO_2) emissions that are the main driver of global warming.

Of course, China has a lot of people and a very large industrial economy, so it is not surprising that it would use a lot of energy. The more important question is: Does China use a lot or a little energy relative to its population and economic weight? To answer this question, we have to convert all of China's energy consumption—whether from oil, coal, gas, nuclear, or renewables—into standard units and then divide by its population and GDP. The results, which convert all energy use into their equivalents in barrels of oil, are shown in Figure 10.1.

On a per capita basis, China does not look so bad. It consumed the equivalent of seventeen barrels of oil per person in 2018, slightly above the world average, and less than a third of the fifty-two barrels consumed by the average American. But when we turn to the economic comparison, China's numbers are dismal. It needs to burn the equivalent of 1,763 barrels of oil to generate a million dollars' worth of economic output, more than twice the figure of the United States and three times that of the European Union. China is by a sizable margin the world's most energy-intensive major economy.[1]

Total primary energy consumption				
Billion barrels of oil equivalent (boe)				
	World	China	United States	European Union
Oil	34	5	7	5
Natural gas	24	2	5	3
Coal	28	14	2	2
Nuclear/hydro/renewables	16	4	3	3
Total	102	24	17	12
Energy per capita and per unit GDP				
	World	China	United States	European Union
Energy use per capita, boe	13	17	52	24
Energy use per US$m of GDP	1,184	1,763	823	660
Source: BP Statistical Review of World Energy 2019, World Bank, author calculations				

Figure 10.1 China's energy use in global context.

Why is China's energy intensity so high?

There are three reasons for China's high energy intensity: its economic structure, the structure of its energy demand and inefficiencies. China's economy relies far more on manufacturing, and industry generally than that of any other major country. The industrial sector uses a lot more energy for each dollar of output than the service or agriculture sectors, so an economy that relies mainly on industry will consume more energy than an economy of equal size that is based mainly on services.

Until very recently, nearly half of China's economic output came from industry, compared to less than a quarter for the United States. That figure fell to about 40 percent by 2019, but it is still quite high by international standards. Moreover, an unusually high proportion of China's industry is heavy industry: manufacturing steel; smelting aluminum and other metals; refining petrochemicals; and making cement, glass, and so on. These industries are especially energy-intensive. Given a structure of production so reliant on energy-hogging industries, rather than the energy-light services that dominate advanced economies, it is no surprise that China's energy intensity is very elevated.

The second factor is the structure of China's energy supply, specifically its reliance on coal, which accounts for nearly two-thirds of its electric power generation. (By contrast, coal fuels less than a quarter of power production in Europe and 30 percent in the United States.) This leads to relatively high energy intensity because coal is a less efficient fuel for power production than the main alternative, natural gas: it takes about 25 percent more coal than gas to produce a unit of electricity.[2] Economically, China's heavy reliance on coal makes sense because it has abundant domestic supplies, whereas natural gas must largely be imported at a high cost (China has 13 percent of global coal reserves, but 3 percent of gas reserves and less than 2 percent of oil reserves).[3] Unfortunately, the heavy use of coal imposes great environmental costs, as we shall see later in this chapter.

The third factor, efficiency, is less straightforward because China's use of energy is not inefficient across the board. Its coal-fired power plants, for instance, are on average about 25 percent more efficient in their conversion of coal into electricity than are U.S. coal power plants. This is because the average American plant is 40 years old, and many even date back to the 1950s and 1960s, whereas most Chinese plants (and all of the 100 largest) were installed after 2005, thus taking advantage of newer and more effective technology. Similarly, China's fuel efficiency standards for vehicles, first adopted in 2004 and then progressively strengthened in 2008, are stricter than those in the United States and most developing countries, though still behind those in Europe, Japan, and South Korea.[4]

There are, however, numerous ways in which China's use of energy—and natural resources more generally—is quite inefficient. One of the most significant of these inefficiencies is in buildings. During the construction boom of the past 20 years, Chinese houses and office buildings went up at a frantic pace, and little attention was paid to sealing or insulation to minimize heating and air conditioning costs.

Another major source of inefficiency is in industry, which accounts for about two-thirds of the nation's electricity consumption and is also a major user of other types of energy (for example, burning coal to heat industrial boilers). In some cases, these inefficiencies arise because firms use outdated equipment. But this is less and less the case due to government campaigns to shut down obsolete production lines. The bigger issue is the way in which local governments support unprofitable local industries. Local governments will sometimes set artificially low prices for inputs like coal and electricity to keep plants humming, thereby maintaining employment and tax revenues. As a result, a lot of energy is used for relatively little contribution to economic value added. From an energy efficiency perspective, it would be better to shut down these plants and, if need be, import the products they used to make from locations that can produce them more efficiently.[5]

What kinds of energy does China use, and how is the mix changing?

The first word that comes to mind when examining China's energy system is "coal," a resource that China relies on far more heavily than any other major country does. Coal accounts for 58 percent of total primary energy demand, more than double the world average of 27 percent (Figure 10.2). Half of all coal consumed in China goes into power plants. Most of the rest is used in industry for purposes such as cement production and heating boilers.

Coal is abundant in China and relatively cheap, but it is also a major source of air pollution and climate-warming emissions of CO_2. Consequently, the government has spent most of the last decade trying to diversify its sources of energy by ramping up the use of natural gas, nuclear power, and renewables. These efforts have had some success: in the past decade, for example, annual output of both nuclear power and hydropower has more than doubled, and electricity from renewable sources has risen almost twentyfold. This has dented coal's dominance: its shares of primary energy consumption and electricity output has fallen by 12 and 15 percentage points, respectively, since 2005. But given the huge installed base of

Fuel shares of total national primary energy consumption, %				
	China	**United States**	**European Union**	**World**
Coal	58%	14%	13%	27%
Oil	20%	40%	38%	34%
Natural gas	7%	31%	23%	24%
Nuclear	2%	8%	11%	4%
Hydropower	8%	3%	5%	7%
Renewables	4%	5%	9%	4%
Source: BP Statistical Review of World Energy 2019, World Bank, author calculations				

Figure 10.2 China's energy mix in global context.

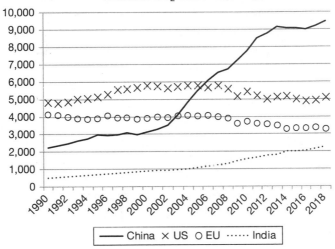

Figure 10.3 CO_2 emissions.
Source: Enerdata Yearbook 2019.

coal power plants, some projections suggest that coal may still account for around half of China's energy mix as late as 2050.[6]

The most recent data show that coal use peaked in 2013 and that its share of China's energy consumption could decline more rapidly than previously expected. Unfortunately, this data is subject to frequent revision; the latest update, while confirming the 2013 peak, revised upward total consumption in that year to 4.2 billion tons. Consumption in 2018 (3.8 billion tons) was double what it was as recently as 2003. Moreover, estimates of CO_2 emissions show a plateau in 2013–2017 and then a slight uptick in 2018 as the government relaxed environmental and emissions controls in an effort to revive flagging economic growth (Figure 10.3).[7]

How much does China rely on imported energy?

Despite its enormous energy use, China has traditionally satisfied most of its demand from domestic sources. This is

gradually changing, however, as China's energy mix diversi-
fies. It still sources more than 90 percent of its principal fuel,
coal, at home, and its gigantic reserves mean that imports
of coal will always be relatively modest compared to total
demand.

The story for oil is different. China was self-sufficient in oil
until 1993, when it became a net importer. Since then, import
reliance has steadily increased, and in 2013 China surpassed
the United States as the world's biggest oil importer. In 2018,
it imported 9 million barrels a day, representing 70 percent of
its needs. A similar story is being told in natural gas, where
imports rose from almost nothing in 2005 to over 40 percent of
demand in 2018.[8] In theory, China could greatly increase its gas
production, as the United States has, by unlocking its reserves
of shale gas, which by some estimates are bigger than those of
the United States. But doing so will be very difficult because
the geology of China's shale formations is markedly different
from that of the United States, and new and expensive extraction technologies may be required. It is likely that China will
continue to be a big purchaser of liquefied natural gas from
Australia and Indonesia and also of gas brought in by pipeline
from Central and Southeast Asia.

China's increasing reliance on imported oil and gas has strategic consequences. Despite efforts to diversify its sources of
supply, China continues to rely on the Middle East for more
than half of its oil imports. This situation creates two risks.
First, oil supplies from this politically volatile region could
be disrupted by war or social unrest. Second, most of this oil
reaches China by tankers that must travel through the narrow
Strait of Malacca between Malaysia and Sumatra. In the event
of conflict with the United States, it would be easy for the U.S.
Navy to severely crimp China's oil supply by blockading this
passage.

Because of these risks, the Chinese government has a strong
interest in continuing to develop new and less vulnerable
sources of oil supply and transport. This interest means that

China will probably continue to be an active investor in new oil and gas fields and pipelines in Central and Southeast Asia.[9]

What impact does China's energy use have on climate change?

In 2005, China became the world's biggest emitter of the greenhouse gases that cause climate change. By 2014, the last year for which fully comparable international data are available, China accounted for 30 percent of global greenhouse gas emissions, more than the United States and European Union combined. About 85 percent of China's total emissions are CO_2. And again, the main culprit is extreme reliance on coal, which releases far more CO_2 when it is burned than other fossil fuels: twice as much as natural gas and about 40 percent more than oil. So the single most important variable determining China's future impact on global warming is its rate of coal consumption.[10]

China's leaders have been concerned about the nation's impact on global warming since 2005. But initially their stance on international climate negotiations was defensive. They argued, first, that China's per capita emissions were much lower than those in most rich countries; and second, that early industrializers such as the United Kingdom and the United States should shoulder a much larger share of the burden of reducing carbon emissions because of their long history of pumping CO_2 into the atmosphere. Countries like China that came late to the development game should have a chance to get rich first before working hard to reduce their emissions. Finally, they claimed that part of China's emissions are in effect really the responsibility of wealthy countries, insofar as multinational companies moved much of their production to China and hence also "exported" their pollution.

By 2015, when it reached a symbolically important agreement with the United States and other nations in international climate talks in Paris, China had quietly retreated from these positions. The first argument is untenable because China's greenhouse gas emissions blew past the global per capita average by 2010 and kept rising fast at least until 2014. The second may have some moral justice to it, but it is essentially irrelevant because the emissions reductions required to stabilize the global temperature are so large that they cannot possibly be achieved if the world's single biggest emitter opts out. The third made little sense to begin with, since most of China's CO_2 emissions came from heavy industries like steel and cement that cater to domestic construction demand, not from export-oriented consumer goods factories that foreign companies established.

China has now committed to a target of capping its CO_2 emissions by 2030, through a combination of (1) shifts in the structure of the economy to make it less energy-intensive; (2) changes in the energy mix to rely less on coal and more on cleaner fossil fuels (such as natural gas) and renewables; and (3) promotion of energy efficiency. Progress is occurring on all these fronts, but most climate analysts agree that this progress needs to be accelerated if the target of limiting global temperature rise to 2 degrees Celsius over preindustrial levels is to be met.[11]

The government has strong incentives to make these reforms. For one thing, it is clear that sustained and balanced long-run economic growth depends on reducing the country's energy intensity. For another, the policies needed to reduce China's contribution to climate change are the same policies required to bring under control the country's terrible air pollution problem, which is a matter of increasing social concern.

How bad are China's environmental problems?

China's environmental damage has attracted worldwide notice and with good reason. Rapid industrialization has exacted a toll in extreme degradation of the country's air, water, and soil. In January 2013, Chinese and global news media focused the world's attention on an especially terrible smog episode in Beijing—the so-called Airpocalypse—when the skies darkened under a load of particulates measured at nearly 800 micrograms per cubic meter, more than thirty times the maximum level considered safe by the World Health Organization. This dreadful event became a catalyst for more serious governmental action to combat pollution.[12]

China's environmental challenges need to be put in international and historical perspective. Every country that has grown rich has gotten quite dirty along the way. Today the headlines are filled with stories about toxic smog in Chinese cities and chemical spills in Chinese rivers. It is easy to forget that in the 1970s, almost identical headlines were being written about Japan and that in the 1960s, the United States faced severe air pollution problems in big cities like Pittsburgh and Los Angeles, rivers in industrial regions caught on fire, and localities were rendered unfit to inhabit because of chemical pollution. It took decades to clean up these environmental disasters, and much work still needs to be done. Even "Airpocalypse" was, unfortunately, far from unprecedented. Estimates suggest that particulate concentrations during London's deadly Great Smog of December 1952, which resulted in over 4,000 identifiable deaths in five days and as many as 8,000 more in subsequent months, may have been as much as five times higher than those registered in Beijing in January 2013.[13]

The point is not to gloss over China's environmental problems, which are extraordinarily bad. Rather, it is to resist the tempting assumption that these problems are uniquely attributable to shortcomings in China's economic growth model or political system. It is more accurate to see them as severe variants of a syndrome that has afflicted every industrializing country.

How severe? Figure 10.4 tries to answer that question. It compares the score on Yale University's comprehensive Environmental Performance Index (EPI) with per capita income (adjusted for purchasing power) for thirty of the world's most important economies. The list includes all the major developed

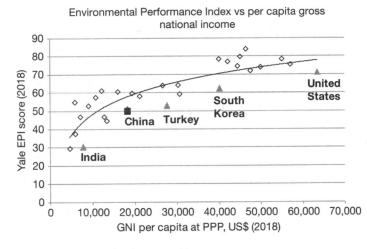

Figure 10.4 Environmental performance and income.
Source: Yale Environmental Performance Index, World Bank.

economies; all of the industrializing nations of Asia (including aspirants such as Vietnam and Bangladesh); and most other large emerging economies (e.g., Russia, Brazil, South Africa, Mexico, and Turkey). It excludes city-states and countries with small or sparse populations or no significant industry, for instance, Singapore, Saudi Arabia, and New Zealand.

Two facts jump out. First, there is a strong correlation between a country's income level and its environmental performance. This supports the common intuition that nations care little about pollution when they are poor and then grow markedly cleaner as they get richer. The improvement in environmental performance seems to be especially sharp for countries entering middle-income territory (roughly $10,000 to $20,000 according to this measure)—again, supporting the idea that environmental protection rises higher on the national agenda when an enlarged middle class starts demanding safer air and water.[14]

Second, China's performance, while not a huge outlier, is on the poor side: its EPI score is about 12 percent lower than predicted by its income level. Four other countries have EPI scores at least 10 percent lower than suggested by income levels: India, Turkey, South Korea, and the United States.

These observations suggest a framework for thinking about China's environmental issues. Some of its pollution problems can be considered "normal" attributes of its recent rapid industrialization and relatively low income, but not all. As a relative "environmental underperformer," it shares important characteristics with other members of that club. Like South Korea, it is an "East Asian developmental state" that places an unusually high premium on maximizing economic growth through forced-march industrialization. Like India and the United States, it is a very large country: it makes sense that it will be harder to coordinate environmental protection over a large land area and population than in the compact western European countries that dominate the top of the rankings. And like the United States, China aspires to be a superpower and so has a natural tendency to subordinate "soft" concerns, such as the environment, to ambitions for industrial and technological development that lay the foundations for global power. It is also likely that China's weak legal institutions and feeble civil society make it harder to mobilize environmental protection efforts.

How likely is China to address its environmental and climate problems?

All these considerations suggest that China is likely to remain an environmental underperformer for many years to come. A review of the mechanisms by which other countries have addressed their environmental problems leads to a similar conclusion. Successful environmental improvement programs in the rich countries of Europe, North America, and Japan have typically included some combination of the following elements:

- Strong environmental laws, strictly enforced;
- Market mechanisms such as pollution permit trading schemes;

- Legal redress via class-action lawsuits against major polluting companies;
- Activism by environmental nongovernmental organizations (NGOs); and
- Media exposés.

The nature of China's political system means that it will rely almost exclusively on the first instrument, with modest support at best from the other four. Media exposure of pollution problems is to some extent tolerated: in this area as in others, the central government is happy for the press to unearth problems that local officials would rather keep buried. But once the authorities in Beijing think they know enough, they tend to clamp down on reporting. A classic example of this pattern came in March 2015, when veteran CCTV investigative reporter Chai Jing distributed a scathing documentary about air pollution, *Under the Dome*, over the Internet. Within days, the video was watched by over a hundred million people. Then the censors stepped in, forced the video to be removed from all websites, and closed off social media discussions. In a freer country, this documentary could have prompted a large-scale, long-running national debate on how to balance the imperatives of environmental protection and economic growth. In China, this conversation was strangled in the cradle.

Similarly, the central authorities keep environmental NGOs and legal activism on a tight leash. A significant reform announced in late 2014 was a set of guidelines under which approved environmental NGOs would be permitted to file lawsuits against polluting companies in specialized environmental courts. This was a step forward, but the impact has been limited, since the central government vets in advance the organizations that are allowed to bring suit.

The authorities have shown enthusiasm for emissions trading schemes, especially for CO_2 emissions. In principle, this is a good thing: a permit trading system was a key component of the United States' successful drive to reduce emissions of sulfur dioxide (the main cause of acid rain) following passage of the Clean Air Act of 1990. In practice, however, these systems are difficult to implement and require both robust market infrastructure and a vigilant and powerful regulator. It is not obvious that China is close to satisfying the basic conditions needed for a successful emissions-trading system.

Can top-down pollution control work?

China's environmental protection drive will depend largely on top-down administrative action. The effectiveness of these administrative measures in turn depends on the quality of their design and—perhaps more importantly—on the political will of the central government to address the problems.

Because of the depth of the problems and the government's demonstrated obsession with economic growth (not to mention scary events like "Airpocalypse"), it is easy to be cynical about Beijing's commitment to an environmental agenda. But the truth is that the fight against air pollution has made progress in recent years, is now a declared priority of the national government, and is likely to see an acceleration of gains in the near future. Progress on water and soil pollution, however, has been much slower.

China's air pollution derives overwhelmingly from the burning of coal. Estimates vary but typically find that coal combustion accounts for at least 50 percent of air-polluting emissions, mainly thanks to the electric power, cement, glass, and metals-smelting industries. The contribution from automobile emissions is lower, probably 15 to 20 percent. This distribution of pollution culprits has several implications. On the downside, the heavily polluting industries are politically powerful and resist efforts to clean them up. On the other hand, the relatively concentrated nature of the problem makes it simpler to attack. Moreover, reduced reliance on coal is an aim not just of environmentalists but also of the bureaucrats managing China's energy strategy and industrial policy. This convergence of interests makes it more likely that coal use will be reined in and made cleaner.[15]

Energy efficiency and reduced reliance on coal became important policy objectives in 2005, when the government began to be concerned that China's highly energy-intensive growth model was unsustainable. An important but clearly secondary worry was that excessive reliance on coal (which then accounted for over 70 percent of primary energy use and over 80 percent of power generation) would worsen local air pollution and increase China's already enormous contribution to the emissions of greenhouse gases that cause climate change. Beijing therefore set a target of reducing energy intensity—the amount of energy needed to generate one yuan of GDP—by 20 percent by 2010. It also began to focus on reducing the nation's reliance on coal by pushing large investments in cleaner-burning natural gas, hydropower, nuclear power, and renewable sources such as wind and solar power.

These efforts had a measurable impact. The centerpiece of the energy efficiency drive was the "1,000 Enterprises Program," which set individual efficiency targets for the country's biggest firms in heavy industry. After a few years, this system was adopted by most provinces as well. Energy intensity fell by 19 percent in 2005–2010, just shy of the target. By 2018, energy intensity had fallen by 42 percent since the 2005 peak, an average gain of 4.2 percent a year. Coal's share of primary energy, which peaked at around 73 percent in 2005, dropped to 58 percent in 2018. It is likely that China's coal demand has peaked and will decline further from here.[16]

In addition to policy, structural economic changes played a large role in these gains. Most energy is used by industry; services require far less energy to generate a unit of GDP. Until 2013, industry was a larger part of the economy in services, but services are now a larger sector and are growing faster. Construction of housing—which as we saw in Chapter 6 tripled between 1996 and 2010—was the biggest single source of demand for the materials whose production drives energy use and air pollution: steel, cement, and glass. But growth in housing construction has slowed sharply and is probably past its peak.

A final component in reducing energy intensity is gradual reform of prices. For the most part, China's energy prices are not especially low: electricity prices for industrial users are slightly higher than the global average; pump prices for gasoline and diesel fuel since 2008 have ranged from 20 to 40 percent above U.S. levels and are about the same as those in Canada and Australia; and the contract price for coal used by power plants, which began to be deregulated in the early 2000s, tripled between 2005 and 2014 and is now basically the same as the global spot price.[17]

But it is also true that China's energy prices remain subject to various controls by the government and do not respond fully to changes in supply and demand. Electricity prices, for instance, remain tightly regulated and have not risen nearly as much as the price of the main power-plant fuel, coal. Under price reforms that began in 2009, gasoline and diesel prices fluctuate with crude oil prices, with a short lag, but the government's pricing formula prevents a full pass-through to consumers of very high crude oil prices. This means that when crude oil prices are high (as they were from 2010 to 2014), there is less incentive than in a full market system for users to make energy-saving investments in more fuel-efficient cars or industrial equipment. For controlling air pollution, the electricity price is most important, since electricity demand largely determines the demand for coal. Steps toward making electricity pricing more market based began in 2014 but are still far from complete.

All in all, progress in reducing air pollution has been significant. In September 2013, in response to Airpocalypse the government rolled out a national air pollution action plan that imposed targets on provinces to reduce the small PM2.5 particulates that are the major source of smog in northern China, as well as larger PM10 particles. Over the next 4 years, the national average PM2.5 level fell by over 25 percent, from over 70 to 52 micrograms per cubic meter ((μ/m3). Further campaigns to cut back on construction and heavy industry in north China during the winters of 2017–2019 seem to have produced further reductions. The gains in Beijing were particularly striking: PM2.5 concentrations fell from 89 μ/m3 in 2014 to 51 in 2018. Emissions of sulfur dioxide (which creates acid rain) have fallen significantly, thanks to cleaner and more efficient coal-fired power plants. Harvard researchers found that China's 4-year reduction in particulate pollution was comparable to the decline in the United States over a 30-year period after the first Clean Air Act of 1970.[18]

The relative success of the air pollution effort shows both the power and the limits of top-down action. The reductions in targeted pollutants have been impressive, swift, and noticeable. But they came with unintended side-effects: due to complex atmospheric chemistry, the fall in PM2.5 levels caused a big rise in ozone, a key component of urban smog.[19] Moreover, as an economic slowdown hit the country in 2018–2019, environmental curbs were relaxed and pollution levels rose again. Progress on air pollution is likely to continue both because it has become a political priority and because of the natural restructuring of the economy to a less polluting path. But gains will be uneven, and even optimistic officials believe it will be another 15 years before the air in most Chinese cities approaches levels that would be considered acceptable in the developed world. Work on other critical environmental issues, such as cleaning up contaminated rivers, lakes, and soil, has barely begun. Environmental damage will continue to be a huge problem for years to come.

11

DEMOGRAPHICS AND THE LABOR MARKET

What is the "demographic dividend"?

The "demographic dividend" refers to a period during which the proportion of nonworking, dependent people in a population falls substantially. This usually occurs in a traditional agricultural society in which birth rates start out very high because many children die in infancy: for a family to be sure it will have several surviving children, it needs to have a lot of births. Then, as better sanitation and health care become available, child and infant mortality drops. Eventually, families respond to this increased survival rate by having fewer children. In many cases, this tendency is encouraged by the government's birth control policies.

The result of these shifts is a two-stage evolution of the population age structure. In the first stage, the number of people of working age rises rapidly, due to the population boom that occurred while child mortality rates were falling but fertility rates were still high. Meanwhile, the rate at which people have babies slows. In consequence, the country winds up having a relatively large number of productive, working-age people and a shrinking proportion of dependent children. Put another way, the "dependency ratio"—the ratio between the number of young and old people on the one hand, and the number of working-age people on the other—falls.

This age-structure shift does not guarantee faster economic growth, but it can help. With more productive workers and relatively few dependent mouths to feed, families can save more of their income. If the country has an effective mechanism for capturing those savings and recycling them into investments in infrastructure and manufacturing, a virtuous cycle can be created in which higher saving leads to greater opportunities for income growth. Faster income growth in turn encourages people to put off having children while they pursue economic opportunities. This in turn leads to further declines in the fertility rate, higher savings, and so on.

Unfortunately, after a few decades, this process starts to go into reverse. The "bulge" of productive workers turns into a bulge of retirees, who make increasing demands on the nation's health care and pension systems. Meanwhile, the next generation of workers is much smaller. So instead of having a large number of workers supporting a small number of (mainly young) dependents, the country now has a small number of workers supporting a large number of (mainly old) dependents. This stage, when the population ages rapidly, is called the demographic transition and tends to be associated with slower economic growth rates.

How has the demographic dividend worked in China?

Most of China's East Asian peers (Japan, South Korea, and Taiwan) enjoyed a solid demographic dividend, and this was a contributing factor in their high-growth eras. China's demographic dividend was unusually large and long-lasting.

To understand why, we need to go back to the late 1950s and early 1960s. For around 3 years, from 1959 through 1962, large parts of China suffered near-famine conditions, thanks to disastrous economic policies during the 1958–1959 "Great Leap Forward," when millions of farmers were pulled off the land to engage in ill-advised rural industries such as small-scale steel plants. Although the Chinese government has never officially acknowledged the great famine, demographers have shown that it probably caused 30 to 40 million deaths.[1]

After this catastrophe, fertility soared, and in the decade 1963–1973 China had a tremendous baby boom during which the population rose from 680 million to 880 million. Contributing factors included the natural tendency toward rapid population growth after wars or natural disasters, government policies that encouraged large families (largely based on Mao Zedong's belief that a more populous country was a more powerful one), and improvements in sanitation and health care that dramatically decreased infant, childhood, and maternal mortality.

By the early 1970s, government officials became worried that the population was expanding too rapidly and that it would become difficult for the nation to feed itself or provide enough jobs. In 1973, it introduced the "later, longer, fewer" campaign, which encouraged couples to marry later, space children more widely, and limit their offspring to two in cities and three in the countryside.[2] In the 1970s, the fertility rate plunged from 5.8 to 2.4, partly due to these policies and partly thanks to the normal impact of lower childhood mortality. Despite this impressive drop, which brought China's fertility close to the "replacement rate" of 2.1, which enables a stable population size, the government in 1980 introduced the draconian "one-child" policy, which contributed to a further fall in the birth rate in the 1980s and 1990s.

The combination of excessive deaths during the famine years (which reduced the number of people entering retirement in the 1980s), the big baby boom of the 1960s, and the large fertility drop that began in the 1970s produced a deep, long-lasting demographic dividend (Figure 11.1). Between 1975 and 2010, the dependency ratio—the number of young (under 15) and old (over 65) people for every 100 working-age people—fell from 80 to 36. During the same period, the

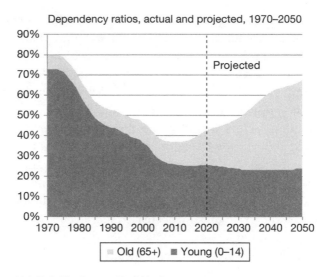

Dependency ratios, actual and projected, 1970–2050

Figure 11.1 End of the demographic dividend.
Source: United Nations World Population Prospects.

national savings rate rose from 33 percent of GDP to over 50 percent, real annual growth in investment spending averaged 12 percent, and the economy grew at an average rate of about 10 percent a year. The relationship between demographics and economic growth is far from straightforward, and it would be wrong to say that this big demographic dividend caused China's fast economic growth. But it was clearly an important favorable condition. The demographic dividend helped create the opportunity for fast economic growth, and the reforms that began in 1978 enabled that opportunity to be realized.

What about China's "demographic transition" to an older population?

Unfortunately, China is now coming out on the other side of the demographic dividend, and in the coming years the dependency ratio will rise. The fall in dependency occurred entirely because the young people of the 1960s–1970s baby boom became workers. The rise in dependency over the next few decades will occur entirely because those baby-boom workers are turning into retirees. In 2020, a bit less than one in five Chinese is over the age of 60; that figure will rise to one in four by 2030, and one in three by 2050. The burden on the pension, health care, and social services systems will grow enormously. In 2020, there are about five people of working age (20–64) for every person of retirement age (65 or older). By 2035, there will be just over three workers per retiree, about the same as in the United States today. And by 2050 there will be only two—about the same figure as in present-day Japan, a famously "old" society. In the space of less than three decades China will move from being a relatively young society to a very old one (Figure 11.2).

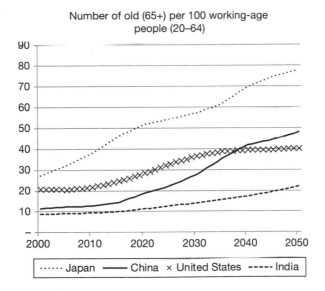

Figure 11.2 The aging population.

Source: United Nations World Population Prospects.

What does the aging population mean for the labor force and economic growth?

China's future demographic trajectory is certainly one of rapid aging, and this will put downward pressure on economic growth and push up the fiscal burden of the social security system. A common phrase describing this situation is that China risks "getting old before it gets rich." But contrary to the common saying, demography is not destiny when it comes to economic growth. Demographic trends are an important constraint, in part because once established they can take decades to reverse. But economies have a lot of room to maneuver within the limits set by demography.

For China, the immediate problem for the next decade or so is that the working-age population, which grew rapidly for many years, is starting to shrink. But the working-age population is not necessarily the same as the labor force. The labor force consists only of people who are either working or actively seeking work. The share of people in any age cohort who are working or actively seeking work is called the labor force participation rate. A striking fact in China is that the labor force participation rate is very high until people hit their late 40s, and then it declines precipitously (Figure 11.3). At age 48, 80 percent of urban residents are active in the workforce. By age 50, that share drops to 70 percent; and by age 60, only 29 percent. The decline in participation is particularly acute among women in their 40s and 50s.

The conclusion is that China still has the ability to increase its labor force, even though the working-age population has started to decline. To do this, it must increase the participation rate, especially among older workers in the 45–65 age range, who will constitute nearly half of the working-age population by 2030. There are many ways to achieve this goal. One is to increase statutory retirement ages, which are quite low in many government agencies and SOEs (60 for men and 55 for women). Another way is to improve access to education— not

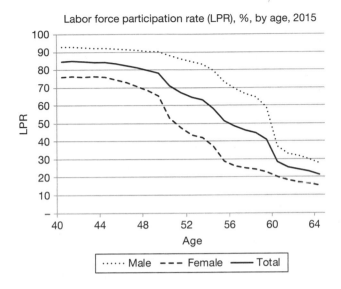

Figure 11.3 Labor participation.

Source: CEIC, Gavekal Dragonomics.

only traditional schooling but also adult education and on-the-job training. Increasing workers' ability to get training at different stages of their careers will improve their chances of adapting to changes in the economy and staying employed for longer. Finally, shifting the emphasis of the economy away from industry and toward services will help because services are more labor-intensive than industry, and it will create a larger number of physically undemanding jobs that people can keep doing through their 60s.

A final consideration is that the economic impact of labor is partly a function of the number of workers, but more importantly of the productivity of those workers. The importance of labor productivity is illustrated by the fact that China's economy is still only about three-quarters the size of the U.S. economy, even though China's labor force is nearly five times bigger. This implies that, on average, a Chinese worker produces only about one-sixth of what her U.S. counterpart does. So to offset the economic impact of a shrinking working-age population, the government should focus not just on increasing participation but also on boosting productivity. Improved efficiency and productivity are indeed goals in the government's economic reform agenda, which we will consider in more detail in Chapter 14.[3]

There is, unfortunately, a bit of a problem here. As we have seen, one of the most effective ways to increase the participation rate is to shift the economy to a focus on services, which is more labor-intensive than industry. But labor productivity in services tends to be lower and to enjoy lower growth rates than labor productivity in industry. (This is because it is harder to boost a service worker's output by simply linking her up with a machine.) So, as the economy inexorably shifts toward services, productivity growth will trend lower. The good news is that there is almost certainly a lot of "low-hanging fruit" in the form of service industries—including logistics, finance, manufacturing-related services, and health care—that are heavily dominated by inefficient SOEs. Simply by opening up these sectors to increased competition from the private sector, there is potential to unlock productivity gains that are more rapid than one would normally expect in services.[4]

What is the importance of the one-child policy?

As a population-control measure, the significance of the one-child policy is far less than is generally believed. The major decline in China's fertility rate occurred in the 1970s—before the one-child policy was adopted in 1980. During the 1980s, enforcement of the new policy was chaotic and fluctuating: sometimes savage, with widespread reports of forced abortions and forced sterilizations; and sometimes relaxed, leading to surges of births in the countryside. By the late 1980s, the policy was codified in a more pragmatic way, with a blanket exception for rural families (who were permitted to have a second child if their first was a girl) and more relaxed quotas for ethnic minorities. It might more accurately be called the "one-and-a-half-child policy," since under perfect enforcement, only 60 percent of families would be limited to one child, and the fertility rate would be about 1.5.[5] This policy remained in full effect for a quarter-century, until a slight easing in late 2013. In late 2015, policy was changed to allow all couples to have two children.

The impact of the policy is far from clear. In 1980 the fertility rate was 2.4; by 1990 it was around 2.1, which is the replacement level. By 2000 it was down to 1.4, and since then it has fluctuated between 1.4 and 1.5. It is impossible to know how much of this reduction came from the policy and how much resulted from factors such as the migration of vast numbers of country dwellers to the city (migrant worker families have fewer children than families that stay on the farm). In recent decades, other East Asian countries without similarly restrictive birth control policies have seen even more rapid reductions in their fertility rates, to about China's level. In South Korea, fertility fell from 2.8 in 1980 to 1.6 in 1990 and reached 1.2 in 2010; in Thailand during the same 1980–2010 period, the rate fell from 3.4 to 1.4.[6]

It is hard to avoid the conclusion that the one-child policy was one of the worst major policies of the reform era. It was unnecessary when it was introduced; savage at times, and consistently intrusive and demeaning to the women who had to endure annual birth-control examinations even if they were not forced into abortions or sterilization; and far more long-lasting than it should have been. The main reason it endured is bureaucratic inertia: the State Family Planning Commission (SFPC) that enforced it had 500,000 employees and six million part-time workers, and it collected millions of dollars in fines every year. It had every incentive to keep the policy in place simply to protect all these jobs and revenues, and it did so by constantly overstating the fertility rate and claiming that its services were still urgently needed.[7] Only after the 2010 census conclusively proved that the fertility rate was far lower than the SFPC had claimed, and after the SFPC was deprived of its separate status and put under the Ministry of Health, could the policy finally start relaxing.

In November 2013, the government announced that urban couples in which either the husband or the wife was an only child could have a second child. (Previously, only couples where both people were only children could have a second child.) This was a timid reform, but even on its own limited terms, it had far less impact than the government hoped. In the first year, only 1.1 million couples applied for permission to have a second child, far below the 12 million eligible, and below the 2 million officials had hoped for. The policy was further relaxed in November 2015 to permit all couples to have two children. Births briefly surged in 2016 but fell back again in 2017.

The evidence so far is that urban China is not immune to the low-birthrate dynamics now common in most other East Asian countries, which are driven by the high cost of raising children, cramped living spaces, and limited availability of affordable childcare. Just as the one-child policy probably contributed little to China's falling birthrate, ending the policy will do little to encourage Chinese to start having more babies. Removing the hand of the state from family childbearing decisions will be a great improvement in personal liberty. But the direct economic benefit of eliminating the one-child policy will be negligible.

Why did Chinese workers start moving from the countryside to the city?

The story of China's labor market in the reform era has been one of steady movement of workers out of agriculture and into urban employment in industry and services, and out of the state sector into the private sector. At the outset of the reform era in 1978, 70 percent of workers were engaged in agriculture in the countryside, and nearly all city workers worked either for state-owned or "collective" enterprises. By 2018, only 26 percent of workers were in agriculture, and only 14 percent of urban workers were employed by SOEs and collectives. A careful study of China's messy and incomplete employment data by the scholar Nicholas Lardy concluded that two-thirds of China's urban labor force in 2011 worked in privately controlled companies—and more impressively, that 95 percent of net urban job creation since 1978 has been generated by private firms.[8]

The first wave of off-farm employment growth came in the 1980s, with the creation of township and village enterprises (TVEs), or small-scale rural industrial firms, which we discussed in Chapter 4. Employment by TVEs grew rapidly after agriculture was liberalized in the late 1980s; it exploded in the aftermath of reforms in 1983–1984 letting farmers engage in marketing their own produce and freely seek work off the farm. From 28 million in 1978, TVE employment rose to 70 million in 1985 and surged to an astonishing 123 million in 1993—nearly 20 percent of the entire nation's active workforce.[9]

At first, the great majority of TVE employment was in "collective" enterprises controlled by local governments.[10] In some cases, these firms were actually run by private entrepreneurs, who thought it wise, given the ambiguous status of private business in those days, to seek political cover by enlisting government shareholders. (These companies were often described as "wearing a red hat.") In other cases, TVEs were sponsored by local governments eager to generate sources of economic growth and fiscal revenue, and whose officials were also interested in getting some off-the-books income for themselves. Whether these hybrid companies were "really" private or "really" state-owned is a moot point. In order for startup companies to succeed in the political environment of the time, a combination of entrepreneurial energy and political patronage was required, and TVEs provided the necessary structure. Today, however, the vast majority of TVE employment is clearly in private firms. This is because privately owned TVEs grew much faster than collectively owned ones, and many ostensibly "collective" or state-owned TVEs threw off their "red hats."

What was the impact of SOE reform on the labor market?

After the employment boom of the late 1980s and early 1990s, the next major turning point came in the late 1990s, when the government embarked on a massive reorganization of SOEs, which in 1995 still employed about 60 percent of urban workers but were increasingly plagued by inefficiency and financial losses (see Chapter 5). Between 1995 and 2005, employment in urban SOEs fell by nearly 50 million people, from 113 million to 64 million, and around 30 million people were officially laid off. Most of the job losses occurred in industrial firms. Other SOE workforce reductions were achieved by early retirement plans or privatization of the companies. The SOE share of urban employment plummeted to 23 percent in 2005. Over the decade, total job losses in the state sector equated to 20 percent of the average urban workforce during that period.[11]

To put these statistics in perspective, in its decade of retrenchment China's total state-sector job losses were more than five times the number of jobs the U.S. economy shed between 2008 and 2010 in the Great Recession (9 million). The 30 million industrial layoffs were more than four times the total number of jobs lost in the U.S. manufacturing sector from 1979 to 2009 (8 million).[12] In some ways, the slashing of China's state sector was comparable to the Great Depression, when the U.S. unemployment rate soared to 25 percent.

But in fact China did not go through a great depression. During the decade of these massive layoffs, total urban employment actually increased by 90 million people, a gain of nearly 50 percent. There were four reasons for this extraordinary result. First, the government effectively deregulated manufacturing, allowing a surge of more efficient private companies to take over the production gaps left by the shrinking state sector. Second, trade liberalization, culminating in China's entry into the WTO in 2001, enabled many of these new manufacturing companies to tap into booming global demand. Third, a host of new service businesses (such as transport firms and restaurants) launched to cater to the needs of the manufacturing firms and their employees. Finally, increased government spending on infrastructure and the real estate boom unleashed by the housing privatization, boosted the demand for construction workers.

How big an unemployment problem does China have, and are wages rising?

This generally positive picture glosses over some problems. First, plenty of people got left out of the party. China does not publish reliable unemployment statistics, but estimates by labor scholars suggest that the urban unemployment rate rose from under 7 percent in 1996 to over 11 percent by 2002. In the subsequent economic boom, the unemployment rate fell, and it remained at a relatively low level even after the 2008 global financial crisis. Government surveys of a selection of economic sectors show an urban unemployment rate of around 5 percent since 2015; various scholarly estimates are somewhat higher. The general conclusion is that, while China has created lots of jobs, maintaining full employment for its huge working-age population remains a challenge.[13]

A second problem was that because of the enormous labor glut—caused not only by the state-sector layoffs but by a swelling in the working-age population of nearly 200 million between 1995 and 2005—wages for ordinary workers did not rise fast enough to prevent the emergence of serious income and wealth inequality. As with so much else in China, the story is complicated. Manufacturing wages rose far more rapidly in China than in other low-income countries in the 1990s and 2000s. In 1994, for instance, a Chinese factory worker made $500 a year, only a quarter of the wage of his counterpart in

Thailand. By 2008, the Chinese worker was earning $3,500 a year, nearly 25 percent more than the Thai worker. This is an impressive gain.

But manufacturing accounts for only one-quarter to one-third of urban employment. Most of the rest consists of relatively low-wage jobs in construction and services. Wages in these sectors also rose but not as fast as in manufacturing. And in general, wages did not rise nearly as fast as the income of the owners of capital. (As we discuss later in this chapter, these trends appear to have changed since 2010, in labor's favor). So, in aggregate, labor's share of national income fell from 54 percent in 1995 to 47 percent by 2008, while the corporate profit share rose. The Gini coefficient, a standard measure of income inequality, rose from a fairly unexceptional level of around 0.32 in the early 1990s to an uncomfortably high 0.43 by 2010. (We will explore the dimensions of inequality in detail in Chapter 13.)[14]

What is the Lewis Turning Point, and what does it mean for China?

The term *Lewis Turning Point* derives from the work of Sir W. Arthur Lewis, a West Indian economist who won the Nobel Prize in Economic Sciences in 1979. In the 1950s, Lewis developed a simple model for a developing economy, which, though subject to criticism on various grounds, is useful for a stylistic understanding of the stages that a country like China goes through on its route to industrialization.[15]

Lewis imagined an economy with two sectors: a subsistence agricultural sector and a modern industrial sector. Higher wages in modern industry draw labor out of the countryside, but because the supply of surplus agricultural labor is so large, companies can get away with raising wages at a slower pace than the rate of productivity growth. In this first stage, the economy sees rapid accumulation of capital, a rise in the corporate profit share of national income, and a fall in the labor share.

At a certain point, however, the supply of surplus rural labor begins to dry up, and then companies have to start raising wages much more aggressively. In this second stage, a reallocation of national income away from the capitalists and toward the workers can occur, as long as the capitalists do not keep wages low by importing workers from abroad or by moving their investments to low-wage countries. The transition from the first to the second stage is called the Lewis turning point.[16]

The Lewis model is helpful in understanding developments in China's economy and labor market over the last quarter-century. In the 1990s and early 2000s, China had a virtually unlimited supply of labor, thanks to the demographic dividend and mass layoffs in the SOE sector. This enabled a large expansion of industry and the building of huge amounts of infrastructure. A greater share of the financial gain from this economic activity flowed to the capitalists through rising profits than to workers through rising wages—although, as we noted above, wages also increased quite rapidly. Consequently, the investment share of GDP (financed by corporate profits) rose, and the consumption share of GDP (funded by worker wages) fell.

Beginning in about 2005, however, the labor supply began to top out. This was first visible in the supply of young workers (ages 15–24), which peaked in 2005 and began to fall in 2010. By 2023, the supply of these young workers will have fallen by one-third from its peak level.[17] The overall working-age population (ages 15–64) peaked at a little over one billion in 2015 and is now declining, though slowly: by 2040, this cohort will be just under 900 million, down 12 percent from its peak.

The impact of a gradually more restricted labor supply has been evident both in wages and in migration patterns. Soon after the supply of young workers stopped growing in 2005, export-oriented factories in Guangdong that depended heavily on migrant labor started reporting labor shortages. Since the young worker population started to decline in 2010, wage growth for migrant workers and for relatively low-skilled jobs in general has accelerated; these wages are now growing faster than those for white-collar jobs.[18] This trend was exacerbated by the central government's decision in the late 1990s to dramatically increase university enrollments. That decision was taken in part because of a desire to upgrade the quality of the workforce but, more importantly to keep young people out of a labor force that the government believed was already glutted. Between 2000 and 2011, annual graduations from tertiary institutions rose from less than one million to more than six million. These graduates were not interested in factory work, but a paucity of white-collar jobs awaited them. By 2018, the pool of new graduates was 7.5 million, but employment prospects were better because of a big increase in the number of jobs in finance, law, education, and other modern services.

Generally speaking, wage growth in China has been very rapid. As Figure 11.4 shows, between 2008 and 2017, the average real wage in China doubled, far exceeding the gains in most other countries. Despite numerous forecasts that higher labor costs would cut the competitiveness of Chinese exports and cause the country to lose good manufacturing jobs to cheaper competitors elsewhere in Asia, companies have successfully adapted to higher labor costs by improving production efficiency and moving up the value chain. Rising wages in China are an unalloyed good: they improve the standard of living, but they do not undermine the economy's ability to keep growing.[19]

There is thus little doubt that China has begun to enter its Lewis turning point—although it will be a rather extended "point," lasting a decade or more. One consequence—faster growth in wages relative to corporate profits—is already evident both in the wage data just cited and in the fact that the investment/GDP ratio has leveled off and the consumption/GDP ratio is starting to climb. Another subtler consequence is

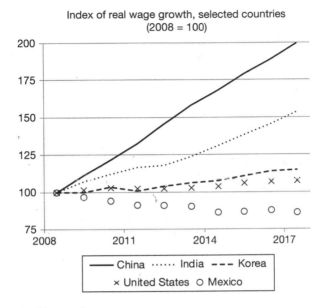

Figure 11.4 Wage growth.

Source: ILO Global Wage Database.

a likely change in migration patterns. Young workers are quite happy to move to wherever the jobs are, but after the age of 30, their willingness to move decreases because they have stronger family ties that hold them in place. By 2017, the average age of migrant workers was nearly 40, about 5 years older than a decade earlier; and by 2015 the growth in the nation's migrant labor workforce had slowed to a crawl.

How many more workers can move from the countryside to the cities?

Migration from countryside to city has been one of the great facts of China over the past three decades. In 1982, only 7 million people in all of China worked outside their native county. By 2012, that figure was 163 million. Another 99 million migrated within their own county to find work (usually moving from the country to the main county town), bringing the total number of migrants to 262 million, or a bit more than a quarter of the working-age population. Eighty-five percent of these migrant workers started out in rural areas.

There is a common perception that China's great migration consists mainly of workers moving from the poor interior of the country to the rich coast. This is only partly true. About 40 percent of migrants work in the central and western provinces, and 43 percent originate in the coastal provinces. Only about one-third of migrants work outside their home province. The main story of China's great labor migration is not movement from hinterland to coast. Rather, it is one of people moving from rural areas to urban areas—mostly nearby towns, but sometimes distant cities—to pursue higher wages.[20]

How much longer will this migratory pattern endure, and how many more people will make the move? It is hard to be precise, but it is clear that here we enter the realm of educated guesswork. Broadly speaking it appears that China's rural to-urban migration is about three-quarters complete. In 2014, the World Bank estimated that the excess rural labor supply (i.e., workers not needed to maintain the present level of agricultural production) was somewhere around 100 million people. Accounting for future increases in agricultural productivity, the Bank expected that somewhere around 120 to 135 million workers were likely to move from country to city between 2012 and 2030—that is, about half as many as made the move before 2012.

Recent data roughly confirm this estimate. In 2010, out of a total increase in the urban population of 24 million, migrants from rural areas accounted for 13.4 million, or about 60 percent. By 2017, rural migrants added just 4.9 million to the urban population, just a quarter of the total increase in city populations. Rural-to urban migration will continue on a large scale, but the wave is well past its peak. Despite this slowdown, China's total urban population is on track to grow to about 1 billion (70 percent of the national population) by 2030.[21]

How bad are conditions for Chinese workers, and is there hope that they will get better?

The answer to this question depends entirely on the point of comparison. Conditions for Chinese workers are worse than for those in rich countries today, but arguably better than those in many other developing countries and definitely better than conditions in China two or three decades ago.

Working conditions for many Chinese are undeniably harsh. Long hours and compulsory overtime are routine in many factories; safety conditions in factories, mines, and other hazardous workplaces fall well short of Western standards; and employers have wide latitude to fire workers, dock their pay, or impose other arbitrary punishments. Workers have little recourse and no ability to organize independent labor unions. (There is a single nationwide union organized by the Communist Party, but it does little to advance worker rights and it often acts as an agent for management.)

It is also true that certain types of labor abuse common in other developing countries are much less common in China and that the government has made efforts to strengthen worker protections in some areas. Child labor, for instance, remains common in India and other South Asian nations but is a minor issue in China, where the government has successfully imposed near-universal education through age 15.[22] A major campaign on mine safety beginning in the late 1990s brought the number of coal-mine deaths down from a horrific 7,000 in 1997 to 1,000 in 2013. A labor contract law effective in 2008 makes it far more difficult for employers in the formal sector to fire employees without cause, and it sets generous standards for maternity leave, sick leave, and compensation for the early abrogation of a contract.

Market forces are also strengthening labor's hand. When labor was superabundant, as it was until 2005 or so, employers could get away with a lot. But under the increasingly constrained labor market conditions that have taken hold in the past decade, workers' bargaining power has increased substantially. This is visible first and foremost in rising wages. Workers have taken advantage of their stronger position to agitate not just for higher wages but also for better conditions and fairer treatment.

In short, the picture of Chinese workers as virtual slaves toiling in concentration-camp conditions is a caricature—and a patronizing one at that, since it implicitly denies any agency to the workers, who constantly make active decisions not only to leave the torpor of subsistence agriculture for a more materially rewarding life but also to move from bad employers to better ones.[23] Both the current state of Chinese working conditions and their upward trajectory echo the earlier experience of Japan, South Korea, and Taiwan. Establishing a consistently humane working environment will take longer in China because of the vast numbers of people involved. But progress is being made in that direction.

12

THE EMERGING CONSUMER ECONOMY

Is China's growth "unbalanced"? How much does it matter?

China from 1980 until a few years ago has been mainly an investment-driven economy. Growth has been powered by capital spending on basic industries, export-oriented factories, infrastructure, and housing. In the "expenditure" accounting that economists use to break down GDP, the share of investment (technically, "gross fixed capital formation") steadily rose, while consumption's share steadily fell.[1] In 1981, capital formation accounted for 28 percent of the economy and spending by households for 53 percent. Three decades later, the investment share had soared to 45 percent—the highest figure ever recorded for a major economy—while consumer spending had fallen to just 36 percent.[2]

Most of the increase in investment and the decline in consumption occurred between 2000 and 2010. Since 2010, due to a combination of structural changes in the economy and government policy, investment's share in the economy has fallen somewhat and consumption's share has gradually risen. But overall, China's consumer spending is unusually low relative to the size of the economy (Figure 12.1).

These data have caused much confusion. Some commentary suggests that there is something wrong with China's economic model because growth has been "unbalanced," with

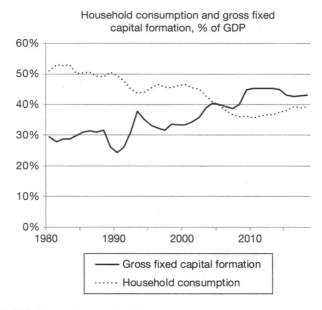

Figure 12.1 Investment/consumption balance.
Source: NBS.

investment growing much faster than consumption. A corollary is that Chinese consumer spending is unusually weak and that therefore government policy should seek to boost it.

There is some truth in both propositions, but neither should be accepted uncritically. The first one, that unbalanced growth is intrinsically undesirable, goes against the experience of post–World War II East Asia, whose growth model China has largely copied. All the countries in this region that grew wealthy—Japan, South Korea, and Taiwan—went through a period of "unbalanced" growth during which investment grew much faster than consumption. Because of these different growth rates, the investment share of GDP grows substantially in such periods, and the consumption share naturally falls.[3]

The reason is simple. To make the transition from a mainly agricultural to a mainly industrial economy, countries must install a huge amount of fixed capital: factories, infrastructure, and modern housing. During this installation process, invest-ment spending grows very rapidly. Household incomes and spending also enjoy strong gains, as workers move from low-wage agricultural jobs to higher-paying industrial ones. But for a while, these gains do not keep up with the breakneck pace of investment. Once the "installation" phase is over, in-vestment spending slows down, household spending becomes the main engine of the economy, and the consumption share of GDP begins to rise again. In other words, a period of "un-balanced" growth can be a natural stage for a country moving from low-income to high-income status.

Was China's "unbalanced" growth bad for consumers?

A stylized example can clarify why a period of "unbalanced" capital-intensive growth is not necessarily bad for household welfare. Imagine a poor country with a per capita GDP of $1,000, in which 80 percent of national income ($800 on average) comes from farmers selling their crops. The farmers, who constitute almost the entire population, spend seven dollars out of every eight they earn buying clothing and other necessities they cannot make for themselves. Thus, in this economy, each person spends about $700 a year, and consumption's share of GDP is 70 percent.

Then suppose this country undergoes a successful industri-alization drive. During this period, capitalists build factories and infrastructure, and farmers start to move to higher-wage jobs in the cities. By the end of this period, about half of na-tional income goes to the capitalists, who mostly reinvest these profits in new factories. So the household income share of the economy falls from 80 percent to 50 percent. Moreover, fam-ilies now have to save one dollar out of every three they earn, because they must buy expensive urban housing, provide against medical emergencies, and have a nest egg for their old age. This means the household consumption share of GDP has fallen in half, from 70 percent to 33 percent. Per capita GDP, though, has risen to $10,000.

Is the average household better or worse off as a result of this process? If you look at the aggregate ratios, they seem to be worse off. The household share of national income has fallen by 30 percentage points; the average consumer only feels safe spending two of every three dollars she earns, instead of seven out of eight; and consumption's share of GDP has fallen by half.

Yet if you look instead at how much money the average consumer has to spend, it is clear that her life has improved a great deal. In the old agricultural economy, each consumer spent $700 a year. In the new industrial economy, average spending is $3,350 a year—a nearly fivefold increase.[4] The fact that the household consumption share of GDP has fallen by half is dwarfed by the fact that GDP has grown by a factor of 10. In other words, average household has a smaller (proportionate) slice of a much bigger pie. The reason the income pie grew so much was that intensive investment—"unbalanced growth"—created large numbers of new jobs in high-wage manufacturing sectors.

This imaginary example actually describes pretty well what has happened in China. Between 1995 and 2017, average per capita consumer spending rose sixfold in terms of real, inflation-adjusted U.S. dollars—an average annual growth rate of nearly 9 percent. This was more than double the rate of increase in the next fastest-growing big economies (India and Indonesia) and far above the rates experienced by the rich economies and by middle-income countries in Latin America. This explosive growth in consumer spending occurred even as the consumption share of the economy fell by about 15 percentage points and as the household saving rate rose from about 25 cents of every dollar of income to 39 cents. The spending power of consumers in China's "unbalanced" economy grew much faster than that of consumers living in more "balanced" economies (Figure 12.2).

The new spending power of Chinese consumers is visible in a wealth of particular examples. Here are two. First, China

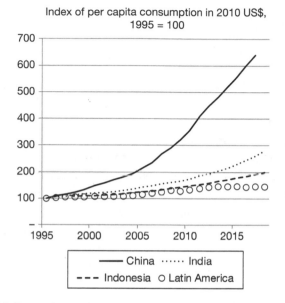

Index of per capita consumption in 2010 US$,
1995 = 100

Figure 12.2 Consumption growth.

became the world's biggest passenger car market in 2010, and by 2017 annual sales of around 25 million units were now about 60 percent higher than in the United States. Second, Chinese consumers are increasingly taking their money abroad. China surpassed Germany as the world's leading source of international tourist trips in 2012, and by 2018 it recorded 155 million such trips, nearly four times the number a decade earlier. Spending by Chinese international tourists was about $277 billion, roughly five times the decade-earlier number.[5]

Of course, this does not mean that intensive investment is the only way for a country to grow rich or that all investment is a good thing. China's pre-1980 period, together with the history of the Soviet Union, provide examples of investment-intensive economies that did not lead to vibrant consumer spending. This was because those economies invested mainly in heavy industries like steel and petrochemicals, deliberately suppressed production of consumer goods, and failed to achieve the productivity gains needed for sustained wage growth.

Nor does it mean that China's situation today is without flaws. Far from it. The capital spending share of GDP is extraordinarily high, even for an East Asian economy; returns on investment have been falling since 2008; and evidence of wasted investment is everywhere in "ghost cities," empty shopping malls, and factories churning out more steel, cement, and glass than the nation can absorb. Perhaps more important, China's capital-intensive stage of growth created far more income inequality than was the case in Japan, South Korea, and Taiwan. The society China has created is much less economically efficient and socially fair than its East Asian models.

Clearly, the investment-heavy phase of growth is nearing its end, and in the future the economy will have to be driven by consumer spending and by more selective, high-return investments. We will explore this "rebalancing" of the growth model in Chapter 14. For the moment, it is enough to observe that China's consumer spending has in fact grown very rapidly for many years. From a policy perspective, the task of "rebalancing" has less to do with boosting consumer spending—which is already doing fine on its own—than with increasing the efficiency and productivity of investment and ensuring that the profits from capital are properly taxed and redistributed into appropriate social goods.

Why is the consumption share of China's economy so low?

Unfortunately, this is a technical question that has no definitive answer. According to official data, household spending in 2013 was just 36 percent of GDP. Virtually every other major economy in the world has a household consumption rate of 50 to 65 percent of GDP.[6] As we have just argued, China's low figure does not indicate that consumption is weak; in fact it is quite strong. What it mainly shows is that China's investment boom was unusually large: consumer spending grew very fast over the last quarter-century, but investment spending grew even faster.

A couple of other factors are at work. One is that consumer spending is almost certainly undercounted. This reflects the bias of the Chinese statistical system. Because economic policymakers are mainly concerned with promoting investment and industry, the data on investment and industry are detailed and accurate. The data on consumer spending, wages, and services are of much lower quality and almost certainly miss a lot of activity. It is increasingly accepted that Chinese consumption data understate the true value of housing services and probably miss much spending on transport and leisure as well.[7] Plausible upward revisions of these sectors produce a consumption ratio somewhere between 40 and 45 percent— still low but not as dire as the official figure. Some Chinese economists have argued, with weaker evidence, that the true consumption ratio may be as high as 45 to 50 percent, or at the low end of the normal range for a country at China's stage of development.[8]

Another point is that China's present low consumption rate is in part an artifact of its unusually low consumption rate at the beginning of economic reforms. When Japan started its most investment-intensive stage of growth, in 1955, household spending was 66 percent of GDP; the comparable figures for Taiwan and South Korea were 62 percent and 71 percent. After a decade or more of heavy investment, these ratios all fell into the low 50s before gradually recovering. But at the beginning of China's reform process in 1980, the consumption ratio was already barely above 50 percent. Most likely this figure reflects the structure of the planned-economy period, when consumption was deliberately suppressed in favor of large-scale state investments in heavy industry. Although that economic structure gradually disappeared, influential vestiges remain, such as the tendency of some urban consumer spending to come in the form of in-kind benefits from work units (gifts of food at the Lunar New Year, all-expenses-paid company outings, etc.).

This again supports the notion that true consumer spending may be higher than is shown in official statistics.

What is China's "middle class"?

So far we have talked about consumption in the abstract language of macroeconomics, as a component of GDP. Yet, when businesses or ordinary people talk about consumption in China, they mainly refer to the spending of the urban middle class. About half of the Chinese population still lives in the countryside, working mainly in farm-related activities, and of course they account for a large share of purchases of basic necessities. But their incomes are low: the average rural household has the same income as one in the poorest 10 percent of urban households. So the bulk of consumer spending in the "modern economy"—purchases of branded consumer goods and of transport, leisure, finance, education, and health care services—is done by urban households.

Before trying to pin down how many people are in this urban consuming class and how much money they have to spend, it is worth clarifying the term *middle class*. Although the words imply a group of people in the middle of a country's income distribution, the term is generally used in a much fuzzier way. It refers to the group that shares certain characteristics broadly considered typical of the mainstream of people in a modern urbanized economy. They work for a living, in jobs that pay them enough so that they can buy their own house, a car, and other consumer durables such as televisions, computers, and air conditioners. They invest significantly in education, and they usually hope their children will work at white-collar jobs rather than on a factory floor. And because they typically own property, they pay a lot of attention to ensuring that their property rights are secure.

China has many such people, but we should bear in mind two characteristics that distinguish the Chinese "middle class" from the "middle class" in developed countries. First, the

Chinese middle class is neither the middle nor the majority of society. In this chapter, we will offer a generous estimate that the middle class comprises a bit less than 40 percent of the national population, enjoying incomes in the upper third of China's income distribution. In other words, the people with a middle-class lifestyle in China constitute an elite, rather than a majority "middle class" in the American or European sense. This has an important political implication: the Chinese middle class is unlikely to become an advocate for political change anytime soon, since it is a privileged minority that benefits disproportionately from the present system.

The second characteristic is that one can qualify as a member of the Chinese middle class with an income far lower than that required for middle-class status in the United States, western Europe, or Japan. So when we start looking at the size of China's middle class, it is important to remember that, on average, Chinese middle-class people have less spending power than middle-class people in developed countries.

How big is the "middle class"?

There are as many estimates of the size of China's middle class as there are of consulting firms with clients selling consumer goods.[9] As we have just shown, "middle class" is an amorphous concept, so it can be plausibly defined in many ways, producing estimates of widely differing size. Bearing this caution in mind, we offer an approach to estimating the population of what might better be termed China's "modern consuming class."

The World Bank defines the middle class in all countries as the people who spend $10 to $100 each day on consumer goods and services. Using this definition, the World Bank calculated that China had 157 million middle-class consumers in 2010, or about 11 percent of the population. This was a large increase from just 2 percent in 2000 but considerably lower than the middle-class share of the populations in Brazil and South

Korea when those countries were at China's present level of development.[10] Extrapolating from that figure based on economic growth rates since then, we find it plausible that by 2020 this group roughly doubled to 300–320 million, or somewhat less than a quarter of China's population.

A broader calculation relies on well-established income thresholds at which people in most countries start to buy important categories of goods and services. Households with incomes of at least $8,000 a year start to buy brand-name goods rather than cheap knockoffs. At $13,000 a year, they start to buy automobiles—and since purchases of cars and houses are tightly correlated, this is also roughly the threshold level for widespread home ownership. At $20,000, they become significant purchasers of modern services: health care, education, tourism and leisure, and financial services. At somewhere above $30,000, they tend to upgrade to higher-cost, premium versions of the goods and services they are already used to buying.[11]

We can thus define several different tiers of active consumers (Figure 12.3). At the top are the affluent consumers (minimum household income $20,000) who can reasonably be considered part of the "global middle class." There are about 320 million people in this group—which of course also includes a significant number of people who are not "middle class" but rich by any standard. Broadening out, the group of people who probably own their home and can at least contemplate an automobile purchase (minimum household income $13,000) is another 200 million, so the total of people who could be considered middle class or above in a purely Chinese context is about 520 million, or 37 percent of the total population. Finally, another 250 million or so people have enough income (at least $8,000 a year) to be active purchasers of some consumer goods beyond the necessities. In all, we can say that about 775 million Chinese, or 56 percent of the population, belong to the "modern consuming classes."

Estimate for 2018		
Income bracket	**Million people**	**% of national population**
Upper affluent	126	9%
Affluent	196	14%
Global middle class	**322**	**23%**
Established consumers	197	14%
Domestic middle class	**519**	**37%**
Emerging consumers	255	18%
Total consumer class	**774**	**56%**
Lower incomes	**613**	**44%**

Definitions:

Upper affluent: Household income above $33,000
Affluent: Household income between $20,000 and $32,000
Established: Household income between $13,000 and $20,000
Emerging: Household income between $8,000 and $13,000
Lower incomes: Household income below $8,000

Source: Adapted from Cui, Gatley and Batson 2016

Figure 12.3 Measuring the middle class.

These are indeed large numbers, and they help explain why the China market has become a cynosure for global consumer brands, as well as producing its own giant consumer-oriented firms, such as Alibaba and Tencent. But the average purchasing power even of China's "global middle class" remains far lower than the average in the United States and other developed countries. Based on official data, total household consumption in China in 2018 was about $5.5 trillion. In the United States, the equivalent "personal consumption expenditure" was $14 trillion. Even if we assume that 80 percent of total household consumption in China is done by the 320 million people we have defined as "global middle class" or above, average annual per capita consumption in that group is only about one-third the average for the entire U.S. population.

What do China's consumers buy?

Over the past few decades, China's urban consumers have gone through successive waves of buying trends. In the 1980s, when incomes were very low, people focused on goods such as bicycles, electric fans, and basic furniture sets. In the 1990s, they started to buy pricier household goods, such as washing machines and air conditioners, and by the end of the decade, China became the world's fastest-growing cell phone market.

The early 2000s brought a huge upsurge in purchases of automobiles, and the private housing boom created large new markets for home furnishings and appliances. Then after 2010 there was a wave of increased demand for services and experiences—financial services, international tourism, the movie box office—as well as steady upgrading to higher-priced segments. For instance, sales of higher-priced SUV cars began to grow much faster than those of cheaper sedans. The average shopping basket for "affluent" Chinese consumers (the 23 percent or so of the population whose household income is above $20,000) is now fairly similar to that of ordinary households in South Korea and Taiwan.

These shifting consumption booms were driven by the household income dynamics shown in Figure 12.4. This shows the number of new households each year crossing each of the four income thresholds we defined in Figure 12.3. Why is this important? Because it turns out that patterns of consumer adoption of new products and services are discontinuous. Below a certain income threshold, no one buys Product X. But once that threshold is crossed, everyone rushes to buy product X. This tendency leads to the familiar S-curve patterns that many consumer products and services experience: a period of modest sales, followed by a period of explosive growth, followed in turn by a plateau at a stable, higher level of demand.

So, concretely, the boom in household appliances and cell phones was driven by the rapid increase in the "emerging" consumer bracket. In 2000–2002, an average of 5 million such

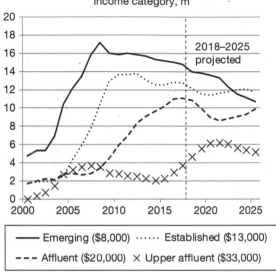

Number of new households entering each
income category, m

2018–2025
projected

— Emerging ($8,000)   ⋯⋯ Established ($13,000)
--- Affluent ($20,000) × Upper affluent ($33,000)

Figure 12.4 Waves of consumption growth.

households were created each year, and by 2008, China had
17 million more newly emerging households. The subsequent
waves of demand for cars, financial services, and so on were
driven by the rapid increase in higher-income households,
which dramatically increased the addressable market for these
products and services.

The thing that is immediately noticeable is that most of these
big waves are now in the past. The projections, which assume
the gradual slowdown in GDP growth that is already in evidence, suggest that the annual increase in households at each
income bracket has already stabilized or will do so in the early
2020s. This means that the days of turbo-charged, double-digit
growth rates for most broad categories are over. This pattern
is already starkly evident in the automobile market. From
2005 to 2016, China's passenger car market was the wonder
of the world, growing at an average rate of 18 percent a year,

from 4 million vehicles to over 24 million. But in 2017 growth slowed, and in 2018 car sales registered their first-ever decline (4 percent), a fall that continued in 2019. Changes in automobile taxes, stiffer emission standards, and other policies played a role, and it is likely that car sales will resume their upward path. But if they do, the annual growth rates are likely to be on the order of just 2–3 percent a year.[12]

The news is not all bad. As Figure 12.5 shows, the total number of middle-class households will continue to grow for some years, and most of that growth will be concentrated in the "affluent" $20,000-and-up segment. So demand for a wide range of consumer products and services will continue to grow, and growth for higher-priced premium brands may

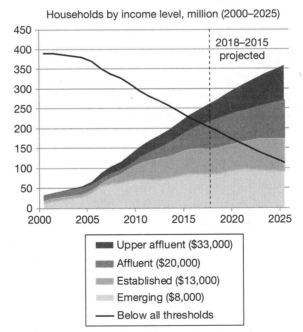

Figure 12.5 China's consumption tiers.

Note: $ figures refer to minimum income for each bracket.

Source: Gavekal Dragonomics research.

tend to be a bit stronger. But, as with cars, growth in demand in most categories will be far lower than in the past. For companies, this means that their focus will shift from increasing the volume of what they sell to extracting higher prices and profits from each customer.

This pattern is visible even in e-commerce, one of the biggest growth stories of the last decade. Online shopping has taken over a much larger share of the retail pie in China than in more developed countries: 20 percent in 2019 compared to 11 percent in the United States. This is partly because China never had time to develop the system of efficient big-box stores and modern retail chains that emerged in the developed world over several decades and partly because the rapid adoption of smartphones meant that it was easy for online retailers to reach a vast population of customers.

Another factor is that an abundance of low-cost labor made it possible for e-commerce companies to hire armies of delivery people, who roam the cities on electric bicycles and motorcycles, delivering most goods within one or two days after an online order is placed. The potential growth of the market was reflected in the 2014 initial public offering of China's biggest ecommerce firm, Alibaba, which valued the company at over $230 billion—significantly more than Amazon, even though Amazon's annual sales were about ten times Alibaba's.

Alibaba and its competitors are still seeing annual sales growth of 20–30 percent a year—but this is down from earlier growth rates of 50 percent or more and will probably slow even more in the future. So Chinese e-commerce firms are now spending more time figuring out how to increase average revenue per customers (since the number of customers will eventually stop growing) and linking their online portals to bricks-and-mortar retail outlets.

Aside from the rise of e-commerce, the biggest trend in Chinese consumer behavior—and one with greater macroeconomic significance than online shopping—is a sharp rise in consumption of services. As we have noted, service consumption begins to pick up sharply among households making more than $20,000 a year. Such households, having already satisfied their main material needs, devote an increasing share of their income to extras like leisure and tourism; additional spending on education for their children (or perhaps even for themselves); more expensive health care; health and retirement services for their parents; and financial services to generate a higher return on their savings than that afforded by bank deposits. Overall, the service share of GDP rose from 43 percent in 2018 to 52 percent in 2018. The service sector is now growing faster than the traditional growth engines of industry and construction.

How good is China's "social safety net"?

Much discussion of consumption in China has focused on the relative lack of a social "safety net": public programs for health insurance, unemployment insurance, pensions, and so on. A common story is that consumer spending in China is relatively weak because families feel compelled to engage in "precautionary saving," devoting an ever-larger share of their income to finance expected future health care, education, and retirement costs. The evidence for this story is that the household savings rate rose from less than 20 cents for every dollar of disposable income in the late 1990s to around 30 cents by 2012 (since then, it has declined only slightly).[13] An improved social insurance system is therefore an important precondition for a more robust consumer economy.

This story sounds plausible. The traditional social safety net for urban workers until the late 1990s came through state-owned enterprises, which provided guaranteed employment, housing, medical care, pensions, and schooling for employees and their children. This welfare system was dismantled by the SOE reforms of 1995–2005, and at first there was no replacement for it. Urban families had to buy their own housing, and they increasingly paid medical expenses and school fees out-of-pocket. Rural families suffered in different ways. Their main traditional safety net was simply the family farm, which could provide a subsistence living if all else failed; and this was unaffected. But the availability of state-provided medical care in rural areas deteriorated sharply in the 1990s.

These failures of government social welfare spending coincided with a rise in the household savings rate and a decline in the consumption share of GDP. So it was natural to conclude that lower welfare spending contributed to weaker consumption and that strengthening the social safety net would boost consumer spending. On closer inspection, the argument has numerous problems.

For one thing, growth in household consumption began to accelerate just as the old social safety net fell apart. In 2001, the trend growth rate in per capita consumer spending was 7.3 percent a year; by 2008, when new social programs had been launched but not yet fully funded, this figure had risen to 10 percent. By 2013, trend consumption growth had climbed to 10.6 percent, even though the household savings rate continued to rise. By 2017, when a significant social net was in place and household saving rates declined, trend consumer spending growth was down to 7.4 percent.[14] The acceleration from the late 1990s until the early 2010s does not quite fit with the "precautionary savings" story. But it does square well with the story we told earlier in the chapter, about how rapid industrialization can create large income gains that enable the average consumer to spend a lot more dollars each year, even as she saves a higher percentage of each dollar she earns.

Another interesting point is that, at least in their early stages, expensive social welfare programs are more likely to be negative than positive for household incomes. This is because they have to be funded, and the main source of funding is levies on employers and employees that fall disproportionately on workers. Once a welfare system is up and running, present workers can benefit from the contributions that earlier workers made into social security funds. But the first generation of workers enjoys no such benefit. Moreover, the largest share of health care and pension benefits goes to older retirees. Today China has about five people of working age for every one of retirement age, meaning that more people are paying into social welfare funds than are extracting benefits. This is obviously good in the long run, but it is hard to see how it could be beneficial for total consumer spending in the short run.[15]

It can be concluded then that creating a social safety net is likely to have a modest impact at best on consumer behavior, especially during the period when households are putting more into the welfare system through tax payments than they are receiving in benefits. Much more important is the rate of income growth. If household income grows fast, so will consumer spending, even if the safety net is riddled with holes. The deceleration in household spending growth from 2012 to 2017, despite the increase in social spending, can be almost entirely explained by the overall slowdown in GDP growth during that period, which dragged household income growth down with it. A social safety net is an important component of a just and equitable society, but it is not a consumption policy.

What sort of safety net is the government weaving?

One of the significant achievements of the Hu Jintao administration was the establishment of a comprehensive set of nationwide social programs, replacing the old SOE-based welfare system. In addition to expanding the minimum-income program that ensures a basic livelihood for the poor who are unable to find work, Hu's government established separate nationwide health insurance programs for urban and rural residents; abolished tuition and other fees for the 9 years of education that are compulsory under Chinese law; greatly expanded coverage of basic pension schemes; and began a large-scale program to subsidize housing for low-income urban residents.

The minimum income program began in 1997 as a measure to prevent laid-off SOE workers from falling into destitution. In 2007, it was extended to include poor rural families, and about 3 percent of the urban population and 8 percent of the rural population are beneficiaries. Comprehensive national health insurance began to be rolled out in 2009 and consists of two urban insurance plans (a mandatory one for formal-sector workers, funded mainly by employer and employee contributions, and a voluntary one for informal-sector workers, which relies more on government subsidies) and a plan for rural residents. In 2018, 96 percent of households, both urban and rural, are now covered by government health insurance. However, benefit levels, though rising, remain very meager. In that year, 68 percent of urban and rural people were covered by government pensions, four times the figure in 2003, although again the benefit levels in most cases are very basic.

Another important initiative was the establishment of "social housing" programs in 2010 in order to increase the availability of affordable housing for low-income urban households. Between 2005 and 2018, total government spending on health, education, and social security rose from 5 percent to 8.5 percent of GDP and from 28 percent to 34 percent of the government budget. These figures would be even higher if subsidies for social housing were included.[16]

These achievements are substantial, but it is obvious that much more needs to be done. Benefit levels for both pensions and health insurance must be raised significantly. More important, most social programs do a poor job of covering the migrant workers who constitute as much as a third of the urban population. Extending coverage to these disadvantaged workers and financing increased benefits will be very difficult to achieve. A particular difficulty is that benefit levels must be raised to make them meaningful—but not raised so much that they impose an unbearable fiscal burden in 30 to 40 years when China becomes a much older society, with far fewer workers supporting far more retirees. Yet, solving the social welfare puzzle is essential if China is to bridge the vast gulf of income and social inequality that has arisen as a result of the rapid economic growth of the past three decades.

What policies should the government take to promote consumption?

Earlier we observed that the government need not bend over backward to boost consumer spending, which has been growing quite robustly for many years. We also argued that expansion of the social safety net, while important for other reasons, is unlikely to have much impact on consumer spending, at least in the short run. Does this mean the government should do nothing to make the economy more consumer-friendly? Not at all. There are two broad policy areas where the government can reasonably act to increase the scope for a vibrant consumer economy to emerge.

The first relates to income distribution. The main reason that household consumption has such a small share of the economy is not because consumers are reluctant to spend, but because the household share of national income is relatively small. The best way to get households to spend more is to increase their incomes.

As one would expect during an era of capital-intensive industrialization, an increasing share of national income since the early 2000s has gone to companies that have reaped large profits from their investments and have mostly reinvested those profits in more industrial capacity. A goal of economic policy should now be to ensure that this trend is reversed and that the household share of national income starts to rise. This can be done in several ways. Increased environmental and resource taxes can reduce corporate profits that arise simply from ignoring the true costs of "externalities," such as environmental damage or resource depletion. Allowing the cost of capital to be determined by the market rather than by government policy will effectively raise costs for heavy industrial firms (especially SOEs).

This means that firms will have to make their investments more efficient; it will also encourage them to simply forgo new investments when the prospective returns are not high enough. Then, instead of constantly recycling profits into new investment, they may choose to return some of their profits to shareholders through higher dividends; that money then becomes available for consumption spending. Ensuring stronger competition will also tend to reduce corporate profits. Consumers benefit through lower prices and will have more money left over to spend elsewhere.

The second major area where government policy can be useful is in promoting the development of services and deemphasizing industry. A shift from industry to services tends to redirect income away from the corporate sector and into households because services generally use much more labor and much less capital than does industry. So a higher share of a service company's revenue goes into workers' pockets in the form of wages.

Most of these initiatives have been built into government policy, at least in theory. The twelfth Five-Year Plan (2011–2015) explicitly targeted raising the household share of national income and embraced the aim of making services replace industry as the main driver of economic production. These goals were repeated in the thirteenth plan (2016–2020). Another bit of good news comes from demographics. As we documented in Chapter 9, the supply of young workers is shrinking rapidly, forcing employers to raise wages more sharply than in the past. A number of market and policy factors are thus conspiring to give households a bigger share of national income. This should be beneficial for consumer markets in the future.

Unfortunately, many obstacles remain. Much of the bias toward industry and investment arises from incentives built into the fiscal system, so much depends on the central government's ability to push through its complex fiscal reform plan. Corporations (both state-owned and private) and officials at all levels of government profit handsomely from the present system and so will fiercely resist the necessary reforms. The next two chapters will examine in more detail the costs of the present growth model and what the government needs to do to change it.

13

THE SOCIAL COMPACT

So far we have painted a relatively positive picture: China's growth has been sustained at a high rate for four decades, most of the population has benefited, and its political and economic systems have adapted fairly well to constantly changing conditions. But any process of rapid change such as China has experienced inevitably creates huge social stresses. In this chapter, we will focus on two interlinked problems that, if left unaddressed, could undermine the political and economic order: inequality and corruption.

How bad is income inequality in China?

As both Chinese officials and international agencies such as the World Bank often point out, China's economic growth since the 1980s has literally lifted hundreds of millions of people out of poverty. This is a great achievement. But the fruits of growth have been distributed very unevenly. By virtually any measure of income or wealth, China is now one of the more unequal societies on earth. Perhaps more important, it is the country where inequality has grown most rapidly in the past few decades.

One standard measure of income inequality is the Gini coefficient (or index), developed by the Italian economist Corrado Gini in 1912 in which 0 represents perfect equality and 1 the state where all income is controlled by a single person. In practice, most countries have a Gini index of somewhere between 0.2 and 0.6. Rich countries with well-developed social welfare systems (e.g., in Scandinavia) fall at the bottom of the range; commodity-based economies where wealth is very concentrated (e.g., in Africa and Latin America) tend to be near the top. The median Gini for the Organization for Economic Cooperation and Development (OECD), a club of middle- and high-income democracies, is 0.31.[1]

Estimates of China's Gini vary, but virtually all agree on two basic conclusions: China's income inequality is very high, and it rose substantially at least until 2008. China's income inequality is substantially greater than that of all developed countries, though lower than that of some large developing countries. More important, it is much greater than in the successful East Asian economies it emulates: Japan, South Korea, and Taiwan. In addition, China's income inequality, starting from a low base in 1980, rose rapidly for at least the first 30 years of the reform era.[2]

That said, it is worth exploring the nuances through Figures 13.1 and 13.2, based on the most comprehensive database on global income inequality. The first figure shows the Gini coefficients for several countries, based on disposable income—that is, after all taxes have been paid and social welfare transfers have been received. (This is the standard way to report Gini numbers). It shows that China's inequality rose sharply from 1990 to 2010, arriving at a high peak level of over 0.43. Income inequality is clearly much higher in China than in developed countries such as the United States, Germany, and South Korea.

But it also shows a few other things. One is that rising income inequality was a global trend over that period (except in Brazil, where stratospheric inequality was made slightly less so under the populist president Lula da Silva in the early 2000s). It also shows that, though high, China is still less unequal than the other two biggest developing countries, Brazil

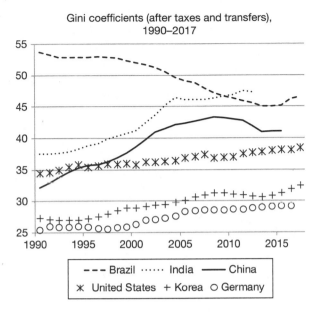

Figure 13.1 Income inequality.

Source: Standardized World Income Inequality Database, version 8.1.

and India. Finally, it shows that inequality began to decline somewhat after 2010, a finding corroborated by other research.

Figure 13.2 is even more interesting. Here we look at inequality in just two countries, the United States and China, both before and after the impact of taxes and transfers. We can see that based on the primary distribution of income—that is, before taxes and transfers—the United States is substantially more unequal than China, with a Gini coefficient of over 50. Yet after taking account of taxes and transfers, the United States is much less unequal than China. Most American politicians scurry away from the label "socialist," but in fact the United States has a very progressive tax system and a wide range of social welfare programs that take the sting out of its very unequal income distribution. Conversely, China—despite being run by an ostensibly "communist" party—has a very

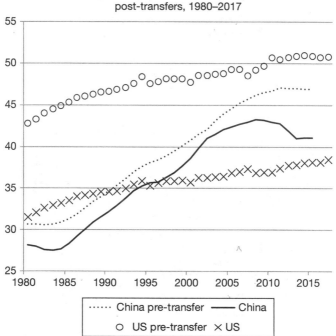

Figure 13.2 Impact of social transfers.

Source: Standardized World Income Inequality Database, version 8.1.

weak social safety net and a tax system that does little to shift income from rich to poor.

The other point clearly visible in this chart is that all of the reduction in China's inequality since 2010 has come through increased social transfers, not through a reduction in the inequality of primary income distribution. This finding is not surprising: reducing income inequality and improving the quality of social programs such as unemployment insurance, minimum basic income, pensions, and health insurance became a national policy theme starting in 2005. The results of those efforts were slow in coming but are now noticeable. By contrast, exhortations in successive 5-year plans beginning in

2010 to reduce the disparities in primary income distribution appear to have had limited effect.[3]

What are the sources of income inequality?

To understand where inequality comes from, we must first understand its full dimensions. The Gini coefficient is commonly cited because it is comparatively easy to calculate, but it only measures inequality among the incomes of all individuals. It does not capture inequality in wealth, which is probably more extreme in China than income inequality. One credible estimate suggests that the top 10 percent of Chinese households own about 85 percent of assets in the country, much higher than their 57 percent share of total income.[4] Moreover, some dimensions of inequality relate to groups, not individuals: the gap between urban and rural incomes; and the disparity between the rich coastal provinces, which benefited from foreign direct investment and exports, and the hinterland provinces that were left behind.

However one defines inequality, its sources can be divided into two broad categories. First, increased inequality is to some degree the natural outcome of a period of rapid economic development, when a country shifts from agriculture to industry; this is true for any country, not just China. The reason, as outlined by the economist Simon Kuznets in 1955 and elaborated by later development economists, is that in the early stages of economic development, the relatively few people lucky enough to have access to the modern economy—either through owing capital or through having the skills to get a job in the modern sector—see their incomes rise very quickly, while those left behind in traditional agriculture face relatively stagnant incomes. As development continues, a greater proportion of the population gets drawn into the modern economy, and inequality tends to moderate.[5] This process is most likely part of what lies behind China's high inequality. In particular, it helps explain the rising gap between urban and rural incomes before

2010 and the big wealth gap between coastal and hinterland provinces.

Second are factors specific to China that have made its inequality problem far worse than those experienced by other fast-growing East Asian countries—especially Japan, South Korea, and Taiwan, which managed the industrial transition without big rises in inequality. Chief among these factors is the differing property rights regimes for rural and urban households, which led to unequal access to capital. Urban households enjoyed a gigantic wealth transfer in the 1998–2003 housing privatization (see Chapter 6). By contrast, farmers often had their land confiscated at below-market rates by local governments. In addition, China's taxes on capital gains are modest and inconsistently enforced.

What are the prospects for a decline in inequality?

As noted above, inequality as measured by the Gini coefficient seems to have peaked in 2010 and has declined somewhat since then. This is also visible in group income data. In the early 2000s, incomes for the lowest 40 percent of the population grew much more slowly than those for the top 40 percent. By 2007, the two groups had converged, and beginning in 2010 incomes were growing faster for lower-income people than for high-income people.

This shift owes something to organic changes in the economy. Chief among these is demographics: as the supply of young migrant workers has begun to shrink, firms must bid their wages higher. Meanwhile, the supply of young people competing for high-end jobs in management, finance, and technology has grown rapidly, thanks to a huge increase in the number of college graduates, from one million a year in 2000 to over seven million a year today. As a result, since 2009 wages in predominantly blue-collar sectors (construction, manufacturing, retail, and agriculture) have grown much faster than wages in white-collar sectors. This trend was reinforced by the government's massive infrastructure stimulus program in 2009–2010, which created millions of new construction jobs.[6] This progress is heartening but modest. A tightening labor market ameliorates inequity in wage income; it will do nothing to improve the distribution of assets and reduce inequality arising from ownership of capital.

Government policies have also played a role. The twelfth Five-Year Plan (2011–2015) was the first to highlight the need to make income distribution less unequal. The plan's approach was a set of policies designed to reduce incentives for capital-intensive investments and to encourage the growth of service sectors that are much more labor-intensive. All else being equal, this will tend to reduce the growth of income from capital and to accelerate wage growth for ordinary Chinese. But as Figure 13.2 showed, most of the decline in the Gini coefficient since 2010 has not come from an improvement in primary income distribution. Instead, it resulted from an increase in social transfers and efforts to make the tax system more progressive.

Since 2005, Beijing has slowly but steadily worked to build a comprehensive social safety net including unemployment protection, minimum income schemes, universal health insurance, and urban and rural pension plans. By 2020, most of these programs covered virtually the entire population, although benefit levels for public health insurance and pensions remain relatively low because the government is concerned about how much these systems will cost in a few decades' time when the population is much older. Tax policy may also have played a small role: a major cut in personal income taxes in January 2019 was designed to deliver much bigger cuts to low- and middle-income households than to rich ones. About three-quarters of Chinese households are effectively exempt from personal income tax, having incomes below the minimum liability threshold.

On balance, though, the government has devoted less energy to reducing individual income inequality than to initiating policies intended to narrow regional and urban/rural income gaps. Programs to boost rural incomes have included: a relaxation of rules requiring farmers to grow grain, enabling them to increase production of more profitable cash crops; the easing and finally abolition of taxes and fees on agricultural production; a major push to build farm-to-market roads, helping farmers gain access to richer urban consumers; and stepped-up investments in food-processing industries. To address the coast/hinterland divide, Beijing has unleashed a series of infrastructure development programs targeting first the far west, then the rustbelt northeast, and finally the central provinces.

All these programs are subject to criticism on grounds of efficiency, but they contributed to arresting or reversing the two types of inequality they intended to address. By 2004, growth in rural consumption began to catch up to urban levels, and the urban-rural income gap began to shrink in 2009.[7] In 2005, only a half-dozen provinces had urban wages within 10 percent of the national average. The rest of the country was divided between a handful of provinces, mainly on the coast, with much higher than average wages, and a vast mass of interior provinces with much lower incomes.

By 2011, this provincial wage gap had closed: half of the provinces had urban wages within 10 percent of the national average, and only the coastal megacities of Beijing, Tianjin, and Shanghai had wages more than 10 percent above the national norm.[8] Most measures of provincial inequality continued to narrow through 2016, but there is some evidence that progress began to slow thereafter. This is not surprising given that the coastal provinces have benefited disproportionately from the new technology-related economy, while inland provinces remain heavily dependent on old smokestack industries like coal and steel that are headed for permanent decline.[9]

The progress is real. Yet to bring China's inequality in line with the much lower levels seen in the advanced East Asian economies, much more aggressive policies will be required. In particular, the government must increase and enforce capital income as well as roll back the vast accumulations of assets in the hands of a small number of officials and tycoons. In other words, it must tackle the problem of corruption.

How bad is China's corruption problem?

Corruption has clearly been endemic throughout the reform era, although its shape has shifted with time. In the 1980s, one of the biggest sources of corruption was the two-track price system, under which factories committed to sell a certain amount of their output at relatively low planned prices, but they could sell any excess production on the free market at higher prices. This system created an incentive for officials to use their influence to purchase goods at low plan prices and then resell them at higher market prices. As suggested earlier, outrage at this kind of corruption was an important contributor to the Tiananmen Square protests of 1989.

The subsequent price reforms, which eliminated the two-track system and led to the acceptance of market pricing for almost all goods except a handful of strategic commodities, eliminated this channel of corruption. In the booming 1990s, an important source of corruption was smuggling. This was profitable because high tariffs and nontariff barriers made many goods far more expensive in China than on the global market. In 1992, China's weighted average tariff was 32 percent, and duties on some popular goods (such as automobiles) were 100 percent or more. In addition, more than half of all imports were subject to various kinds of nontariff restrictions that impeded their import.[10]

By the mid-1990s, smuggling was a gigantic business turning over billions of dollars a year. The effect was visible in macroeconomic statistics. In 1998, foreign exchange reserves grew by only $5 billion, even though the official trade surplus and foreign direct investment inflows were each around $45 billion. The difference of more than $80 billion—nearly 8 percent of GDP—mostly represented money that flew out of China in payment for smuggled goods and other forms of capital flight. Smuggling disappeared as a major form of corruption thanks to draconian crackdowns on big smuggling rings in south China; but more importantly because tariffs and nontariff barriers were sharply reduced in the late 1990s and early 2000s, making the game not worth the candle.

In the first decade of the 2000s, the construction boom in urban China offered rich opportunities for rake-offs from land deals and infrastructure projects. Because local governments controlled the land supply, officials could extract bribes for directing prime plots to particular developers. And, as in any construction boom, officials routinely received kickbacks on infrastructure contracts. Since China was undergoing the biggest construction boom in history, the scale of corruption was similarly unprecedented, with top officials frequently squirreling away hundreds of millions of dollars in black income. Construction-related corruption almost certainly surged in 2009–2010, when the government launched its economic stimulus program, most of which went into infrastructure spending.[11]

There have of course been numerous other channels for corruption. Officials could get payoffs for delivering any of the many licenses and approvals required for setting up a new business or for executing any major investment project. In many jurisdictions, official appointments and promotions were for sale. For the elite sitting at the top of the system, the initial public offerings (IPOs) of major companies offered a comparatively clean way to get rich quick. Either to speed up the tortuous IPO approval process or, more likely, to buy influence for other purposes, company officials often gave officials or their family members cheap or free shares ahead of the listing, enabling them to pocket huge profits when the shares started trading.[12]

Profiteering from corruption ran right to the top of the political system. The biggest case that the government has acknowledged was that of Zhou Yongkang, who served on the Politburo standing committee in 2007–2012 and ran the nation's security services. In 2014, Zhou was formally investigated for corruption and expelled from the party; police claimed to have confiscated assets of $14.5 billion from Zhou, his family members, and his business associates. That amount would rank Zhou as seventh in the list of China's richest people compiled annually by the Shanghai-based Hurun Report. Foreign media have also documented extensive wealth in the immediate family of former prime minister Wen Jiabao ($3 billion, according to the *New York Times*) and current president Xi Jinping ($55 million in Hong Kong property and investments in companies worth $2 billion, according to Bloomberg News). The widespread perception that, in the party and government, no one's hands are clean of corruption is probably accurate.[13]

Why didn't corruption stop economic growth?

Given the magnitude and ubiquity of corruption—and its apparently rising scale at least until 2013, when the new president, Xi Jinping, launched a massive anticorruption campaign—it is worth asking why the wheels haven't come off the Chinese system by now. A solid body of research finds a robust inverse correlation between corruption and economic growth: the more corrupt a country is, the lower its long-run growth rate. Of course, recent history is filled with examples of dictators who accumulated vast wealth by looting their countries but eventually saw their regimes crumble: the Duvaliers in Haiti, Mobutu Sese Seko in Zaire, Marcos in the Philippines and Suharto in Indonesia immediately come to mind. China managed to be incredibly corrupt while at the same time sustaining an economic growth rate of around 10 percent for more than three decades and creating a political system that does not look in the least fragile. How could this be?

One answer, offered periodically by pessimistic analysts, is that it is just a matter of time: uncontrollable corruption will eventually force the system into either political collapse or economic sclerosis.[14] But despite the passage of time, such predictions have failed to pan out. Clearly, something else is going on, and three factors seem to be at play.

First, for much of the reform era, corruption was in essence a side effect of reforms that also brought powerful economic benefits. As long as the benefits from restructuring outweighed the stealing by corruption, the system as a whole was sustainable. Moreover, especially in the 1980s and 1990s, certain types of corruption (not all) could be seen as rational economic behavior rather than just looting. The most obvious examples are the arbitrage of plans and market prices in the 1980s, as well as some of the smuggling activity in the 1990s. Under the dual-track price system, the authorities tried to maintain in-plan price controls for many goods, not because those prices were appropriate or economically efficient, but simply because it was politically inconvenient to dismantle the old planned-economy price system all at once. The result was artificial shortages of some goods and chronically high inflation. Officials who diverted goods from the plan to the market were, among other things, responding to the market signal that those goods were in high demand and short supply. Once prices were marketized, this type of graft disappeared.

The case of smuggling is similar. Some smuggling was just crime, as when Fujian entrepreneur Lai Changxing bribed dozens of officials to enable him to bring in billions of dollars' worth of crude oil and luxury cars without paying duties.[15] But much of it could be seen as a private-sector effort to reduce import tariffs. In Guangdong in the late 1990s, businesses routinely imported some of their materials and components, or finished goods they wanted to sell on the mainland, indirectly via Hong Kong. First, the goods would be sold to an agent, or "converter," in Hong Kong. A week or two later those same goods would be purchased by the business in Guangdong from another agent, at a markup of 15 to 20 percent over what the converter paid. Everyone knew that customs officials had been paid off in between, but no one asked questions, and the practice was considered virtually legitimate. In these sorts of transactions, businesspeople were in effect reducing the import tariff from a noneconomic rate (typically 40–70 percent) to one that made commerce profitable. As with dual-track-price-related corruption, this practice vanished once tariffs were lowered to more reasonable levels.

Second, tolerance for some corruption was the deal that the leadership offered to officials in order to marshal their support for reforms. At the start of the reform era and for years after, many officials had reached their positions by toeing the line of communist ideology, and they did not necessarily know how to conduct their new job of promoting business activity. Letting them keep part of the proceeds from the new market economy—giving them some "skin in the game"—provided a material incentive for officials to go along with market reforms.

Finally, this tacit license to steal was not unlimited. Beginning in the early 1980s, the Communist Party waged a continuous and occasionally intense fight against corruption. "Economic crime" cases recorded by the central prosecution agency surged from less than 10,000 in 1980 to nearly 80,000 in 1989 in the aftermath of the Tiananmen protests. Prosecutions continued at a rate of more than 50,000 a year until the late 1990s, when they dropped—most likely because opportunities for large-scale corruption abated with the elimination of controlled prices and high tariffs, and the legitimation of private-sector economic activity reduced officials' incentive to extract bribes simply to let private companies stay in business. Prosecutions averaged 30,000 a year in the decade leading up to the 2008 global financial crisis. At the same time, though, the number of higher-level officials prosecuted continued to rise, as did the severity of penalties.

Researchers have found that, at most, one in ten corrupt officials are ever charged with corruption; but those that are charged are almost invariably convicted, and they face harsh sanctions, including prison terms of 10 years or more or even death sentences, of which 700 were passed down in corruption cases in the decade to 2008. The point about this activity is not that it was comprehensive, but that it established some constraints, so that corruption was confined to the role of successful parasite: it lived off its host (a rapidly growing economy) without killing it.[16]

This description of why corruption and robust economic growth could coexist is plausible for the first quarter-century or so of the reform period, but becomes less convincing after about 2005, when the construction-led corruption boom was in full swing. This is because, first of all, the more recent corruption seems less a side effect of a generally beneficial economic reform process and more purely predatory. The two single biggest sources of corrupt wealth in recent years were skim-offs from infrastructure projects (which may have been economically useful but could not be seen as part of an "economic reform" program) and profits from land extracted from farmers at far below its true market value (which was simply exploitation of farmers' inadequate legal property rights). Moreover, the scale of the thieving—routinely running into the hundreds of millions, if not billions, of dollars—was extraordinary. By the end of the Hu Jintao era, many in the Chinese elite began to fear that economic reform had run aground, corruption had run out of control, andthe country was at serious risk of running off the rails.

Is Xi Jinping's anticorruption campaign a real solution to the problem?

After Xi Jinping took over from Hu Jintao as secretary-general of the Communist Party (in November 2012) and as state president and head of the military (in March 2013), he immediately launched a massive anticorruption campaign, pledging that he would spare no efforts to snare "both tigers and flies"— both high- and low-level offenders. This campaign, led by Wang Qishan, a member of the politburo standing committee and head of the Central Commission on Discipline Inspection (CCDI), the party's disciplinary agency, continued at full force for Xi's entire first term, through 2017. After Wang's elevation to vice-president in 2018, the campaign continued, and by 2020 an estimated 1.5 million government officials had been disciplined in some way, including at least 120 at the vice-ministerial level or above.[17] Virtually every province and every agency of the party–state was affected. It is by a wide margin the longest-lasting and most intense antigraft drive in the party's history.

The central question is whether this campaign is really a serious effort to root out corruption, or if it is—like many previous anticorruption surges—simply a witch hunt to crush the current leader's political enemies. Since we cannot read Xi's mind, we cannot know for sure, but most likely the campaign has at least three dimensions. There is little doubt that it was, in part, designed to destroy rival political networks, especially at the beginning. Key "tiger" targets have been Zhou Yongkang, the former security boss, who had turned the intelligence services into an almost autonomous power base; two senior generals closely linked to former president Jiang Zemin; and Ling Jihua, the powerful former private secretary for Hu Jintao.

But the extraordinary breadth and duration of the campaign, along with other parallel initiatives such as an intraparty ideological campaign, and crackdowns on the media and academia, show that the antigraft drive is part of a bigger governance strategy. The 2013 party document outlining the goals of the anticorruption campaign presented it as exactly that: an element of a broad-based effort to improve the party's governance capacity.[18]

This aim was formalized in March 2018, when the National People's Congress adopted constitutional and legal changes that established a new branch of government devoted to discipline and anticorruption under a National Supervision Commission in Beijing. This new bureaucracy will be responsible not just for rooting out corruption, but also for ensuring that officials at all levels of government comply with centrally mandated policies.[19] This makes clear that the anticorruption drive is not simply a war against Xi's enemies, or a short-term "strike hard" campaign to weed out a few evildoers, but an effort to end the implicit political-economy bargain in place since the early 1980s: a relatively high tolerance of corruption as part of the price to be paid for giving officials incentives to prioritize economic growth. While that bargain produced impressive economic returns, the resulting corruption eventually threatened the CCP's legitimacy. Xi's solution to that crisis of legitimacy is to impose much tighter top-down centralized political control. It remains to be seen whether this solution is sustainable in a country as large and diverse as China.

Why haven't inequality and corruption caused more social unrest?

On the face of it, one might expect that rapidly widening income inequality and rampant official corruption would lead to widespread social unrest, as the people with lower incomes grow angry at the rich people and officials skimming off most of the benefits of the growing economy. This should be especially true in China, where a communist ideology of equality was strictly enforced for over three decades before the reform era.

Yet the available evidence does not indicate China is a simmering cauldron of discontent, at least not more than any other large and complex society. No doubt, there are many protests. In 2006, the Ministry of Public Security published data reporting 87,000 "mass incidents" the prior year, and while no systematic data has been published since, occasional reports in official media suggest that the number of such incidents or of "public order disturbances" has grown substantially. But these terms are hazy. Most incidents that find their way into these statistics are likely small-scale events arising from local grievances.[20]

Survey work suggests that Chinese citizens are not unusually unhappy with their lot and have a generally positive outlook for their personal economic prospects. A careful set of surveys by Harvard sociologist Martin Whyte in 2004 and 2009 concluded that, despite increasing concerns over unfairness, "China's social volcano of potential anger at distributive injustice was clearly still dormant in 2009." The annual Global Attitudes and Trends survey by the Pew Research Center shows that, at least until 2016 (the last survey date), well over 80 percent of Chinese respondents reported being satisfied with the state of the economy and were confident their children would have a better financial future.[21]

One answer to the question of why rising inequality has not spawned greater obvious discontent is that inequality is a by-product of even faster gains in average incomes. For most of the past four decades, all boats have been rising, and most people pay more attention to their own boat than to the boats that have risen higher. For instance, during the period 1998–2008, when income inequality was rising the fastest, average per capita income in China grew by an astonishing 229 percent, ten times the global average of 24 percent and far ahead of the rates for India (34 percent) and other developing Asian economies (68 percent).[22] Moreover, it is likely that the gradually improving provision of social services means that people see their quality of life improving across a broad range of social goods, not just income.[23]

It may be that for many Chinese the huge improvement in their own opportunities is a more important fact than the general rise in inequality. In short, they may have bought into Deng Xiaoping's motto early in the reform era that "some people and some regions should be allowed to prosper before others." This psychology may seem alien to people from highly egalitarian societies, such as Scandinavia or Japan. But it is not that different from the prevailing ethos in the less egalitarian United States, where most people apparently believe that unequal economic outcomes are an acceptable counterpart of wide-open opportunity for bettering one's own lot.

It is possible, of course, that people would like to protest much more, but China's authoritarian political system simply crushes all demonstrations before they have time to spread. There is definitely truth to this: the Communist Party maintains an elaborate internal security apparatus, whose budget exceeds that of the military, and is quite vigilant about cracking down on all forms of social disturbance.[24] But by itself, this answer is incomplete. Regimes that rely purely on repression and fail to deal with underlying causes do not last long, and China's record of sustained economic success, relative political stability over three generations of leaders since 1989, and the broadly positive attitudes revealed by surveys are not consistent with a simplistic picture of a cowed populace suppressing its anger from fear.

Detailed research indicates that the Communist Party's legitimacy derives from far more varied sources than just economic growth and political repression. In a set of detailed surveys conducted in 2010 and 2014 with a respected social science team at Peking University, the American scholar Bruce Dickson found that large majorities of urban Chinese gave the party high marks for providing social stability and public goods. While there was a widespread perception that government officials were corrupt from top to bottom, corruption did not in itself seem to be a strong reason for dissatisfaction with the regime as a whole.

Surprisingly, 70 percent of those who agreed with the statement "almost all central officials are corrupt" also expressed support for the party's rule. Several explanations could account for this finding. Historically, widespread corruption has always been a feature of Chinese governance, so people may simply accept it as a fact of life, especially if they are confident that they can make the system work in their favor. There is also a pronounced tendency for Chinese to be more critical of local than central officials. So in many cases complaints about corruption relate to specific local grievances rather than to the system as a whole. Whatever the reasons, there is little indication that the Communist Party faces an imminent crisis of legitimacy.[25]

14

CHANGING
THE GROWTH MODEL

Why does China need to change its growth model?

Since reforms began in 1979, China has become one of the world's greatest economic success stories. At no point during those decades did success come easily: the economic miracle required persistent hard work and creativity by millions of Chinese workers and entrepreneurs, as well as skillful management by policymakers, under conditions that never seemed to stabilize for more than 3 or 4 years at a time. But today, China faces a challenge that is arguably greater than any it has had to overcome in the past. This challenge is to shift away from a growth model based mainly on the mobilization of resources to one based primarily on the efficiency of resource use. Another way of putting it is that China has spent the last three decades installing the assets needed for a modern economy. Now its job is to maximize the return on those assets.

The stakes are high. By the end of 2019, China's GDP growth had fallen to 6 percent—far below the 10 percent average rate it sustained from 1980 to 2012—and a further decline in the coming years is all but certain. This decline is partly a natural maturation process: no economy can keep growing at 10 percent a year forever. The precedents of Japan, South Korea, and Taiwan all suggest that, with the right policy mix, China could keep growing at around 5 percent a year well into the

2020s—an impressive achievement for what is now a $14 trillion economy. Without the right policies though, there is real risk that China's growth miracle could come to an end and the country could stagnate in a mire of unproductive capital, crushing debt, and inexorable demographic decline.

How does China's growth model need to change?

As we have seen in the preceding chapters, since 1979, China has moved away from a state-dominated, planned economy to a dynamic mixed economy in which market forces and the private sector have played more important roles. From one perspective, this task was complex, requiring an intricate series of reforms in financial, fiscal, enterprise, governance, and legal systems and an ability to respond flexibly to the often-unintended consequences of these changes. But from another point of view, the underlying task was straightforward: to put more resources to use.

This mandate mainly meant putting more capital into the system. China has always had an abundant labor supply, and even at the beginning of the reform era its workers were relatively healthy and well educated by the standards of low-income countries, so they had plenty of productive potential. But for that productive potential to be unleashed, these workers needed to be brought out of their low-productivity agricultural occupations and paired with capital in all its forms. This capital included industrial technology and modern management techniques, and plenty of infrastructure: the networks needed to run these modern businesses (electricity and telecoms), the links to global markets (ports and airports), and the tools enabling workers to move to where the jobs were, and to knit together the domestic market (housing, roads and railways).

In short, the biggest single task for China in the decades after 1980 was to increase its capital stock: the total value of equipment, buildings, and other forms of physical capital. An advanced industrialized economy typically has a capital stock worth around three times its annual GDP (although as these economies shift to high technology and investment-light services, this capital-to-output ratio tends to fall; Germany saw its ratio fall from three to two between 1980 and 2015). A poor country, such as China was in the early 1980s, might have a capital stock that is one-and-a-half times its annual GDP or even less. The first job for any country that wants to move from poor to rich is therefore to increase its capital stock.

Three conclusions follow from this observation. First, by simple arithmetic, in order for the capital stock to rise relative to GDP, investment in capital must obviously grow much faster than GDP for a long time. Here's a simple example. Let's say a country starts out with a capital stock that is one-and-a-half times its GDP and aims to reach an industrial country's capital/GDP ratio of three-to-one over 30 years, with the economy growing at an average rate of 6 percent a year. For this country to achieve its aim, the capital stock must grow each year by 8.5 percent—more than a third faster than GDP. If we further assume that capital in this country depreciates at a rate of 5 percent a year, then the country's investment rate—that is, the share of annual GDP that is devoted to new capital investments—will nearly double over the three-decade period, from 19 percent to 37 percent.

This simplified example captures fairly well the experience of the successful post–World War II East Asian economies. All of them invested intensively in industry, infrastructure, and housing over several decades, building up their capital stock; all of them saw their investment rates rise from somewhere in the twenties to somewhere in the high thirties; and at the end of the process Japan, South Korea, and Taiwan all achieved at least upper-middle-income status, with household living standards half or more of the U.S. average. In China's case, between 1980 and 2012 the investment rate rose from 28 percent to an unusually high 45 percent, and the capital stock rose from about 1.6 to 2.5 times GDP (see Figure 14.1 and also Figure 12.1 for the investment rate). Conversely, the crucial

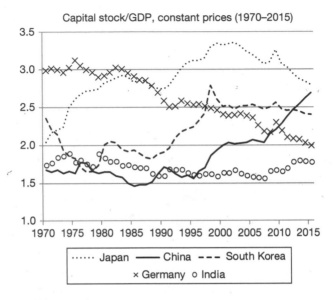

Figure 14.1 Capital stock.

Source: IMF Investment and Capital Stock Dataset.

characteristic of countries that have failed to sustain a drive into the club of upper-income nations (for instance, Brazil, India, and Thailand) is that they have been unable to keep capital investment growing at a sufficiently high rate.[1]

The second point is that, at least during the early stages of this capital accumulation phase, the marginal efficiency with which capital is used, while not irrelevant, is of secondary importance. Obviously, new capital projects must meet some basic productivity standard: building a bridge that is not connected to a road on either end is a pure waste of money, as is building an export-oriented sneaker factory 1,000 miles from the nearest port. Capital investments must be broadly appropriate to the country's level of economic development and linked to well-functioning markets, so that industries do not keep producing goods for which there is no demand and infrastructure helps enable the creation of new productive businesses. These conditions differentiate an effective period of capital accumulation, such as China has enjoyed over the past three decades, from misguided capital accumulation—which is what China endured in the preceding Maoist era, when it built too many steel plants and not enough farm-to-market roads or consumer goods factories.

On the whole, though, it is more vital for poor countries to focus on putting in as much appropriate capital as possible than to try to maximize the marginal productivity of each individual project—as long as they have functioning market institutions, a decent labor force, a reasonable standard of governance, and economic policies that create a predictable investment environment for businesses. Under these conditions, most new capital investments are likely to generate large returns quite quickly, thanks to the ability of infrastructure and new technology to dramatically boost productivity from its very low starting point. This is the "advantage of backwardness" that we talked about in Chapter 1. The aggregate benefit of adding lots of new capital to the system far outweighs the marginal loss incurred by some projects failing along the way.

The third point, though, is that even if this capital-intensive stage of growth is perfectly executed, it has an expiration date. At some stage, a country's capital stock approaches the rich-country level. There is then little benefit to be achieved by simply throwing more capital into the system. Businesses already have the equipment they need to compete effectively. Workers are already so productive that their output cannot be increased by a factor of 2 or 3 simply by pairing them up with a new machine. Most of the roads, railways, ports, and power plants that the country needs have been built. When this happens, robust economic growth can no longer be achieved simply by adding capital. Instead, growth must come from increasing the amount of output that a given unit of capital can produce—that is, by increasing the efficiency of resource use. One consequence of this shift is that the economy will grow much more slowly than in the past because instead of two major sources of growth (the addition of new capital and improved productivity), there is really only one (productivity).

Returning to Figure 14.1, we can see the relevance of this discussion to China. By 2015 (the last year of firm data) China's capital output ratio was 2.7, fairly high by any standard, and the continued investment-intensive growth of 2015–2020 means that by now it is higher still. It is hard to believe that this massive investment spree is delivering good returns. Indeed, most measures show that the productivity of capital is declining sharply.

The high economic growth rates of China's reform era can be boiled down to two factors: (1) the mobilization of resources that greatly increased the country's capital stock; and (2) the gradual shift of control of those resources from the state sector to the private sector, which ensured that over time and, on average, the efficiency of resource use gradually improved, even if some investment got wasted along the way. Now, however, China has installed so much capital that the era of resource mobilization is drawing to an end. In the future, growth must rely less on additions of capital and more on efficiency gains.

What does it mean to say that China's growth is "imbalanced"?

Many analysts describe China's economic problems today in terms of "imbalances." In the past, the story goes, China relied far too much on investment, industry, and exports to power its growth and too little on household consumption. Household spending typically represents 60 to 70 percent of final demand in rich countries but in recent years has accounted for less than 40 percent of Chinese demand. China's main task, therefore, is to achieve a better "balance" among the different sources of growth: investment, consumption, and exports. In practice, the prescription is usually to cut back the investment rate and increase consumer spending.

The concept of "imbalances" is in some respects a useful way to describe China's position, but it needs refining. First, as we saw in Chapter 12, a period of "unbalanced," investment-heavy growth is a perfectly normal stage of development for a country moving rapidly from agrarian poverty to industrial wealth, and up to a point some "imbalance" is actually a sign of success, not failure. Our discussion of the capital stock, however, makes it evident that by now China's heavy reliance on capital spending is a problem in urgent need of correction. Second, "imbalances" exist in several dimensions, and sometimes the correction of one imbalance leads to an increase in another. So rather than getting hung up on the idea that an imbalance is intrinsically bad, we should consider imbalances as signposts that may point to economic problems such as inefficiency, misallocation of resources, or unsustainable patterns of production.

China's economy has been described as "imbalanced" in various ways: too much investment, not enough consumption; too much industrial production and not enough services; too much reliance on exports and not enough on domestic demand; too much reliance on debt rather than equity to finance growth; and too much reliance on state enterprises and not enough on the private sector. Policymakers have been addressing these issues since about 2006, with widely varying degrees of enthusiasm and success.

A combination of policy moves and organic economic changes has led to a sharply reduced reliance on exports, a significant increase in the service share of economic output, and a very modest rise in the contribution of consumption to economic growth. The reliance on capital spending and debt financing have (with great difficulty) been curbed somewhat, but the level of debt remains high, and the productivity of capital is in sharp decline. Finally, under Xi Jinping's leadership, the trend of the preceding 35 years of a shrinking state role in the economy has been arrested, and the SOE share of some economic indicators has risen. Since SOEs use much more debt than private firms, tend to invest in relatively low-return projects, and contribute little to stimulating consumer demand, limiting the role of state firms must play a key role in correcting the deficiencies of the present growth model and setting China on a sustainable growth path in the 2020s.

How did China's economic imbalances evolve in the early 2000s?

The idea that China's growth was dangerously "imbalanced" began to take hold in the early 2000s, when both the trade surplus and the investment share of GDP began to expand rapidly. From 1990 to 2004, China consistently ran a positive balance of trade, with annual surpluses of around 2 percent of GDP. Exports grew fast, but so did imports—both of raw materials and capital goods—so the trade balance stayed fairly stable relative to the whole economy.

Starting in 2005, the surplus began to balloon, reaching a peak of nearly 9 percent of GDP in 2007. In the same year, the broader current account balance (which includes trade in services and income on international investments in addition to goods trade) hit 10 percent of GDP. These are extremely high numbers for a large economy. The United States, whose trade deficits are legendary, usually runs a current account deficit of 1 to 2 percent of GDP, which rose to a peak of just under 6 percent on the eve of the financial crisis.

Similarly, the investment share of GDP, which fluctuated at 32 to 36 percent in the decade up to 2002, began to surge as China poured billions of dollars into manufacturing, housing, and infrastructure. By 2008, investment was about 40 percent of GDP, exceeding the top levels reached by Japan, South Korea, and Taiwan during their most capital-intensive phases of growth.

These trends partly reflected the natural peak of the capital-intensive growth phase but were exacerbated by peculiarities of the Chinese economic situation and policy environment. Investment surged to an unusual degree in the early 2000s because of housing privatization, which suddenly unleashed a wave of pent-up demand for urban housing. Manufacturing and exports boomed because investments by foreign companies in outsourced production facilities in the late 1990s and early 2000s began to pay off, especially after China joined the WTO in late 2001 and became a full participant in the global trading system. For much of the period 2002–2007, policymakers kept interest rates and energy prices lower than they would have been in a market economy (making it cheaper to invest), and tolerated an exchange rate that was increasingly undervalued in real terms (boosting exports).

Chinese leaders had begun to recognize these problems and to take limited action: the renminbi was allowed to appreciate beginning in 2005, and energy efficiency targets adopted in 2006 had in part the goal of raising the cost of investment. These steps were very cautious and did little to rein in the growth of exports and investment—a fact acknowledged by Premier Wen Jiabao, who in his annual work report in 2007 described China's economy as "unbalanced, unstable, uncoordinated and unsustainable." But whatever plans the government may have had to address these problems were thrown off course by the events of 2008.

What was the impact of the 2008 global financial crisis?

The global financial crisis that began in September 2008 had a profound impact on China, despite the fact that its own, closed financial system was not directly affected. The main effect came through exports. As trade finance dried up and the global economy weakened, demand for Chinese exports plummeted by 20 percent over the next year—by far the biggest annual fall in export value in Chinese history. The impact on employment was swift: an estimated 23 million workers in export-oriented factories were laid off by the Lunar New Year holiday in February 2009 and were told not to come back to work after the vacation. In response, China unleashed an infrastructure-focused economic stimulus program with a headline value of

Rmb 4 trillion (about $590 billion at the then-current exchange rate), or 12 percent of GDP. Over the next 2 years, the actual stimulus was probably closer to Rmb 11 trillion.[2] At a time when every government in the world was launching stimulus programs, China's was the biggest both relative to the size of its economy and in absolute terms.

The announced, immediate objective of the stimulus program was to maintain an economic growth rate of at least 8 percent—the rate Chinese leaders believed was necessary to ensure satisfactory employment growth. In this they were successful: GDP growth averaged over 9.5 percent a year in 2009–2011.

At a deeper level, the stimulus program and a variety of subsequent policy measures reflected a shift of course in economic strategy. The leadership realized that China's unusually large export sector—with peak exports equal to 35 percent of GDP (triple the figure for Japan) and a current account surplus of 10 percent of GDP (by far the largest of any major economy)—was more of a vulnerability than a strength. The problem with relying so much on exports is that if your trading partners run into trouble, so do you. Chinese policymakers decided that future economic growth would have to come mainly from domestic demand, not exports. In this they were also successful: the current account surplus fell from 10 percent in 2007 to under 2 percent by 2013. By 2018, the trend level of the current account surplus was about 1 percent—although China continued to run a substantial merchandise trade surplus of about 3 percent of GDP (Figure 14.2).

Domestic demand, of course, has two main components: investment spending and household consumption. In the short run, it was unrealistic to expect Chinese consumers to suddenly start spending a lot more money—especially since many of them had lost their jobs in the export slowdown. In general, changes in consumption patterns tend to occur very slowly. So to stimulate domestic demand, the leaders did the only thing they could: push up investment through government spending

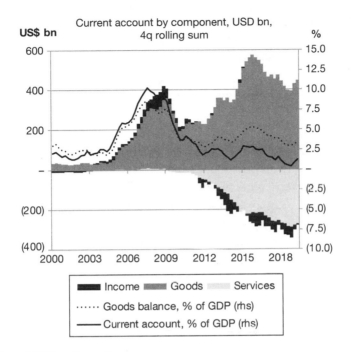

Figure 14.2 Current account.

Source: State Administration of Foreign Exchange.

on infrastructure and private spending on housing. As a result, investment surged from 40 percent of GDP in 2008 to an astonishing 45 percent in 2010, a level it roughly maintained for the next 4 years (see Figure 12.1 in the chapter on consumption). In other words, China reduced its external "imbalance" (the trade surplus) by increasing its domestic "imbalance" (the high investment rate). By 2019, after several years of determined efforts to curb wasteful investment, the investment ratio was still a stratospheric 43 percent of GDP.

Another consequence of the global crisis was that it prompted a decision to make the renminbi an international currency rather than a purely domestic one. The basic reasons that policymakers decided to push on this front were (1) they believed the global crisis was caused in part by the

U.S. government's abuse of the dollar's position as the main global currency; and (2) they worried that overreliance on the dollar for trade invoicing made China vulnerable at times—as in late 2008—when dollar-denominated trade finance dried up (see Chapter 9 for details).

Why is productivity growth slowing?

The stimulus program got China past the global crisis in better shape than any other major economy. But the artificial boost it gave to the economy papered over the fundamental structural challenge: the "mobilization" phase of growth was at the end of its natural lifespan, and important reforms were needed to ensure that the "efficiency" phase of growth could begin.

The last 3 years of the Hu Jintao administration (2010–2012) saw very few concrete structural reform achievements. This was less because of a failure of diagnosis than because of a lack of political will to enforce solutions. The twelfth Five-Year Plan, for 2011–2015, contains a number of targets showing an understanding that many of the traditional growth sources were exhausted and that new ones needed to be cultivated. In particular, the plan expressed the intent to increase consumption's share in the economy and to promote that aim by ensuring that a higher proportion of national income flowed to households (who are likely to spend their income) rather than corporations or the government (which mainly invest).

But the authorities did not come up with specific policies to realize these goals. Unable to attack the economy's structural problems, but fearful of letting GDP growth slip, the government instead tolerated a huge buildup of debt by local governments and corporations, mainly to fund investment projects that propped up reported growth while the money was being spent, but whose returns—and hence contribution to future growth—were quite low. Virtually every indicator of investment efficiency shows a severe deterioration in the 5 years after the global financial crisis. According to a 2015 report by the OECD, the average return on capital, which rose from 10 percent to a spectacular

17 percent between 2000 and 2006, had fallen to 9 percent by 2014. The "incremental capital output ratio," which measures how many dollars of new investment are required to create a dollar of GDP growth, was fairly steady at between 3 and 4 for virtually all of the reform period up through 2007. It began to climb after the global crisis and by 2017 was nearly 6.[3]

Perhaps most tellingly, the contribution to growth from productivity began to shrivel. The OECD found that, between 2000 and 2007, economic growth came about equally from capital accumulation and productivity. This accords with the story we just told that China's growth in the first three decades of the reform era came in roughly equal parts from the state's ability to marshal capital resources and from productivity gains achieved by gradually moving more and more of the economy into private hands.

But in the years 2008–2012, the OECD found that about three-quarters of growth on average came from capital accumulation, and a quarter or less from productivity growth. By 2012, productivity contributed only about one-sixth of GDP growth.[4] This deterioration can be explained in part by the corporate-sector dynamics we described in Chapter 5. Returns in state-owned companies fell sharply after 2008, but despite their poor performance, SOEs retained a large share of the economy, thanks to their political connections. Another factor, especially since 2012, has been the increased share in the economy of services, which have structurally lower productivity growth than industry (Figure 14.3).

Measures of the productivity of capital are necessarily rather technical. A clearer picture of China's productivity problem emerges from a single indicator: debt, or more precisely the level of debt compared to the size of the economy. This debt-to-GDP ratio is commonly termed "leverage." As Figure 14.4 shows, the total borrowings of households, nonfinancial companies, and the government stayed roughly stable at around 140–150 percent of GDP for several years, until the financial crisis. After the crisis, the debt ratio surged by about 40 percentage points in 2 years. After a short plateau, it began

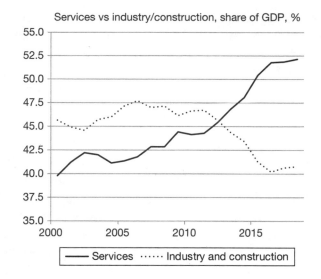

Figure 14.3 Structure of production.

Source: NBS/CEIC.

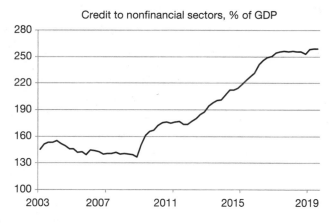

Figure 14.4 Rising leverage.

Note: Estimate of shadow credit included only from 2006 onward.

Source: NBS/CEIC, MOF, Wind.

climbing again in 2012, reaching 255 percent of GDP by early 2017. After that, a determined effort to rein in the fast-growing shadow banking sector succeeded in stabilizing this ratio (see Chapter 9).

What this means is quite straightforward. Most debt is taken on to finance productive investments. As long as the return on those investments is reasonably high, debt and GDP grow at about the same rate, and the ratio between the two remains stable. As we saw in Chapter 9, a rising debt-to-GDP ratio can mean one of two things. It could be that the financial system is becoming more sophisticated, enabling households and companies sustainably to take on more debt. This is what happened in the United States between 1960 and 2000 with the rise of credit cards, home equity loans, and other forms of consumer finance. Or it could be that people are taking on more and more debt to finance projects with a lower and lower return. While it is true that China's financial system has become more sophisticated in recent years, the evidence is strong that much of the extra debt incurred since 2008 was taken on by local governments and SOEs to finance low-productivity projects.

Obviously, this process cannot continue forever: at some point, the return on investment becomes so low that the debts cannot be repaid. At that point, one of two things can happen: there can be a financial crisis (because many loans go into default, hurting the banks); or the economy can go into recession (because even if special arrangements enable borrowers to avoid default, too much capital is tied up in projects delivering no economic benefit).

Whatever indicator you choose, the conclusion is clear: China's economy has become less productive, and much more reliant on debt, since 2008. This state of affairs derives in part from ineffective macroeconomic policy during the latter years of the Hu Jintao administration. But more importantly, it reflects the central fact we stressed at the beginning of this chapter. Those days are over when China could grow at a fast pace in large part by accumulating capital, secure in the knowledge that this capital would almost automatically deliver high returns. Policymakers must focus on fostering an economy where efficient use of resources, rather than addition of new resources, becomes the main source of growth.

How has Xi Jinping managed the economy?

Xi Jinping took power between November 2012 and March 2013, and almost immediately set about revamping the governance not just of the economy but of all of Chinese society. We will assess the impact of his broader governance strategy in detail in Chapter 15. In contrast to the somewhat scattershot style of the Hu–Wen era, Xi quickly moved to establish a tightly disciplined, top-down approach to economic management. This approach also appeared to be motivated by a different set of aims than those that had driven economic policy in the preceding three decades—or if the aims were not different, the points of emphasis were.

As we noted in Chapter 3, the Communist Party has long had two objectives. The first (and always the primary one) is to maintain its monopoly on political power. The second is to maximize economic growth. In holding to these two aims, in that order, Xi is no different than Hu, Jiang, and Deng were before him. What is different is that under the three previous leaders, the need to sustain economic growth tended to frame and constrain other decisions. This is implicit in Deng's axiom *fazhan cai shi ying daoli*, "development is the only hard truth," or "development is the iron law." Under that axiom, the underlying policy question was: "what adaptations do we need to make to the governance system—consistent with keeping the CCP's monopoly position—in order to achieve the desired level of economic growth?" For Xi, however, governance is always central. His overriding aim since taking power has been to create a more cohesive governance structure, with the party directing the activities of both government and civil society.

So the question is now, "given a fixed and increasingly top-down governance structure, how must economic policy adapt to achieve the desired level of economic growth?"[5]

Four key elements of economic management under Xi stand out. First was the "Third Plenum" decision of 2013, which outlined a host of economic reform priorities. Next was the Made in China 2025 industrial policy, released in 2015, an ambitious blueprint for industrial upgrading. Third was "supply-side structural reform," an effort that began in late 2015 to rein in excess capacity industrial sectors such as steel and coal. Finally, there was the financial de-risking campaign, beginning in late 2016, which aimed to bring rising leverage under control and eliminate the excesses of shadow banking.

What was the "third plenum" decision?

Xi's first indications of his economic priorities came with the "Decision" released in November 2013 by the Third Plenum of the Eighteenth Party Congress.[6] This decision, which contained sixty distinct economic reform objectives, was considered by many at the time of its release as an ambitious and basically market-oriented program, much in the tradition of the reforms of the Deng and Jiang eras.

Actually, it contained two broad directives. The first was that market forces should play a "decisive" role in resource allocation. Prior party documents had assigned market forces a merely "important" role. Specific agenda items included the removal of remaining price controls, a bigger role for private investment, and deregulation of protected markets. Second, however, it clearly reaffirmed a long-standing principle that the state sector should have a "dominant role" in the economy. At first, many analysts both inside and outside China focused on the first statement and assumed that the Decision was in essence a call for more market-oriented reform, with the invocations of the state role a political sop to conservative forces.

In reality, the two statements are of equal weight, and it is important to understand their combined meaning. At first, they seem directly contradictory. If market forces are really decisive, then the dominant role of the state cannot be guaranteed: state firms might lose out to private ones in the market. Conversely, if the dominant role of the state is guaranteed, then market outcomes must sometimes be suppressed and therefore cannot be "decisive." The easy explanation is that the Decision was essentially a political document, with various things thrown in to satisfy different constituencies, with little regard for consistency.

But the pattern of economic management that has emerged in the years since suggests that it is indeed the government's intent to combine state and market forces. The vision is that of an economy where the state remains firmly in command, not least through its control of "commanding heights" state enterprises, but where market tools are used to improve efficiency. In practice, this means the government will pursue reforms that increase the role of the market in setting prices but will avoid reforms that permit the market to transfer control of assets from the state to the private sector. Given that one of the biggest problems in the Chinese economy is the very low productivity of state-owned assets, it is questionable whether this reform program will deliver the boost needed to sustain high-speed growth in the long run.

What is Made in China 2025?

In June 2015, the government published an industrial policy strategy, Made in China 2025, which outlined plans to upgrade China's manufacturing capacities and its technology-intensive industries. As we noted in our detailed discussion of initiative in Chapter 5, this was by no means a wholly new program, but built on decades of efforts to promote technology-intensive industries.

At one level, Made in China 2025 seems a clear response to the challenge we identified earlier: to move China away from its traditional reliance on mobilization of capital resources to fuel growth toward a growth model dependent more on technological upgrading to drive productivity gains. But two aspects turned the program into a point of contention with China's trading partners. The first was explicit market-share targets for Chinese-owned firms (for both the China and global markets) which made it seem that a basic purpose of the plan was to favor Chinese companies over their foreign companies. The second was the establishment of apparently well-funded "government guidance funds" to channel massive subsidies to these favored local firms. Criticism of the program became so intense—especially by Trump Administration officials in the United States during the escalating trade tensions of 2017–2019—that the government retired the term "Made in China 2025" and ordered government agencies and media not to use it. The underlying policy framework, however, stayed in place.

Two general observations about Made in China 2015 are germane. First, it provides more evidence that the basic orientation of economic policy under Xi is "state capitalist." That is, economic assets are controlled mainly by profit-seeking companies, but the state intervenes heavily in various ways to direct investment flows to priority industries. While the conceptual boundary between China-style "state capitalism" and Western-style "market capitalism" are quite fuzzy (governments everywhere intervene in a variety of ways to promote or protect favored sectors), it is fair to say that Chinese government interventions in the economy are substantially larger in scale, different in quality, and less constrained than interventions in the advanced industrial nations.

Second, as China tries to upgrade its technological capacities, it will increasingly be seen as a competitive threat by rich countries that previously saw it mainly as an attractive market or a convenient source of low-cost manufacturing production. Even if it pursued technological upgrading in ways that were identical to those employed in Western countries, to the degree these efforts were successful, the rise of technologically proficient firms would be perceived as a threat to established industry leaders. So there will always be strong political incentives for companies in the advanced countries, and the governments that represent them, to complain that China is advancing by unfair means.

These two factors—the substantial gulf between China's political-economy arrangements and those of the advanced industrial nations, and the fact that China is increasingly competitive (rather than just complementary to) those nations— lie behind the trade tensions with the United States that arose beginning in 2017 and that we will discuss in more detail in Chapter 15. Moreover, they raise the question of whether and how the global trade and investment system can adapt to incorporate an actor of China's size whose economic system differs so much from those for whom the system was originally built.

What is supply-side structural reform?

By 2015, policymakers became concerned that the huge buildup of heavy industry over the previous decade or more had led to substantial excess capacity, especially in steel and coal, where China's annual production was, respectively. 800 million and 3.8 billion tons—in both cases, roughly half of the global total. This excess capacity had several adverse impacts. Overproduction led to a collapse in prices not only for coal and steel themselves, but also for the suppliers of equipment to those industries, who had expanded their own capacity to keep up with their customers. The producer price index, which measures the prices businesses pay for their inputs and equipment, fell into negative (deflationary) territory in early 2012. As a result, much of China's heavy industrial base risked being engulfed in a deflationary quagmire, with falling profits and high debts that they were unable to repay.

Excessive heavy industrial production also was bad for the environment, since these industries contributed a disproportionate share of emissions of PM2.5 and CO_2, both directly from their own operations and indirectly via their voracious demand for electricity, most of which was generated by coal-fired power plants. As pressure to clean up the dense smog in north China mounted following the "Airpocalypse" event of January 2013, restraining heavy industrial production became a key tool. Finally, producers of steel and other metal products in other countries were increasingly incensed by China's excess production, which depressed global prices and made it hard for them to compete.

The solution to these problems was a program of "supply-side structural reform," whose main aim was to constrain the capacity and supply of heavy industrial goods, thereby lifting the pricing power and profitability of the remaining companies, and stopping the vicious deflationary spiral.[7] Starting in late 2015, it had immediate positive impact. Steel production barely rose in 2016 and gained only slightly in 2017, despite a huge boom in the urban housing sector, its main customer. Coal production (which had actually peaked in 2013) fell by 9 percent in 2016, thanks to the closing of many small mines. The producer price index moved into positive territory in late 2016, and by early 2017 producer price inflation was running at 7 percent; industrial profits recovered as well.[8]

By 2018, however, supply-side structural reform had begun to collide with other economic objectives, notably the political need to keep GDP growth above 6 percent despite a significant slowdown driven by long-term forces, financial tightening, and trade tensions with the United States. The main mechanism for sustaining growth was housing and infrastructure construction, which increased demand for heavy industrial products. In 2018, crude steel production rose 12 percent over the previous year, and in the first 9 months of 2019 it rose another 8 percent. The initial success of supply-side structural reform and its ultimate shelving in favor of other priorities show both the benefits and limitations of the top-down, state-managed economic policymaking of the Xi era. It can produce impressive results in the short term. But it is much less clear whether it can deliver a long-run structural shift to an economy driven more by efficiency and productivity gains.

What was the impact of the financial de-risking campaign?

Managing financial risk has been a constant challenge throughout Xi's term in office. As we saw in Chapter 9, China's response to the global financial crisis was to launch a massive debt-financed stimulus package that was successful but that also set China on a course toward ever-rising "leverage"—the amount of debt relative to GDP. At the same time, the emergence of an affluent middle class spurred the demand for new financial products, many of which financed a buildup of debt among companies and local governments via the "shadow finance" sector. While it is clear that the proliferation of debt increased the risk of financial-sector stress or crisis, it is equally the case that cracking down on this debt could be extremely damaging to economic growth. So the government must always balance the objectives of reducing financial risk and supporting economic growth.

When Xi and his colleagues took over the government in March 2013, they inherited an out-of-control financial sector in which credit was growing by 23 percent a year, up from 16 percent a year earlier.[9] For the next 2 years, the authorities tightened monetary policy and got the credit growth rate down to 13 percent. Initially, there was little impact on economic growth, but by 2015 industry was slowing sharply and deflation was taking hold. Policymakers complemented the supply-side structural reforms, which constrained supply of industrial products, with easier monetary policy which, among other things, made it easier for people to get mortgages, thereby boosting demand for housing. By early 2016, credit was growing by 18 percent again, most of the acceleration coming from shadow banking.

By the end of 2016, officials were confident that the economy was on stable footing, but they were alarmed by the risks of the explosion in shadow finance (described in detail in Chapter 9). So they launched a comprehensive crackdown on nonbank lending, which was still ongoing as of late 2019. This gradually eliminated much shadow lending, restored the banks to their central position as the issuers of credit, and got credit growth back down below 10 percent by late 2018. Notably, even as officials responded to slowing economic growth with easier credit policy in 2019, they continued their crackdown on shadow finance.

Associated with this management of financial risk from 2013 onward was a broad set of fiscal reforms, including a new budget law imposing greater transparency on local government spending; a phaseout of the old land-based financing system in favor of letting local governments issue revenue bonds; and changes in revenue and expenditure assignments designed to make local government finance more sustainable and to incentivize localities to promote services, consumer spending, and productivity-enhancing technology investments instead of physical infrastructure. These reforms helped slow the growth of local governments' debt and made their activities more open to scrutiny, although it is debatable how much progress has been made on the wider aims.

Is China's growth model changing?

The general picture of economic policy under Xi Jinping is a determined effort to corral the nation's disparate and unruly energies and direct them toward creating an economy that is technologically more advanced, more self-reliant, highly competitive in international markets but more dependent on domestic demand, and with many of its wasteful financial excesses wrung out. The administration's aim is also to create a state capitalist system under which markets are generally allowed to govern resource allocation. However, the government reserves the right to intervene to prevent volatility or to suppress market outcomes that do not align with its long-run vision of the economic structure.

Moreover, the state retains outsized influence in the economy through direct ownership of state-owned enterprises that account for around a third of output (a far greater share than that in any other major economy) and of virtually every important entity in the financial system. Notable by its absence from our earlier list of key economic initiatives of the Xi era was SOE reform. In some ways this is unfair, since a lot of bureaucratic energy has been devoted to SOE issues. But it would be more accurate to describe these efforts as "reorganization" rather than "reform."

Not only has there been no significant privatization or closure of SOEs, as in the great state-sector reforms of 1995–2005, but other plans to turn the SOEs into more purely commercial entities—for example, by putting them under one or more financial management agencies, modeled on Singapore's Temasek, to reduce political influence and make them focus more on purely financial returns—have quietly been shelved. A much touted "mixed-ownership" plan, which had promised to introduce private shareholders into SOEs, fizzled. Instead it became a way to recapitalize poor-performing SOEs by bringing in a greater diversity of state-owned shareholders.

Is this policy mix sufficient to put China's economy on a sustainable growth path in the 2020s? GDP growth has steadily slowed during Xi's tenure, from nearly 8 percent in 2013 to barely 6 percent in 2019, and growth rates in the early 2020s are likely to be lower still. This is mainly due to long-term forces pushing China to a lower equilibrium growth rate. But the question is whether China settles into a stable-trend growth rate of somewhere around 5 percent for most of the 2020s, or whether the current deceleration keeps going until growth falls to 2–3 percent or even lower, which for a country at China's level of income is not much better than stagnation. As we have argued, achieving the former outcome requires a significant shift in favor of growth driven mainly by efficiency and productivity gains rather than capital accumulation.

On the positive side, as we saw at the beginning of this chapter, the economy is slowly moving away from its traditional industry/investment focus and toward a new services/consumption focus, and reliance on exports has declined somewhat. Consumer incomes and spending have continued to grow at slightly faster rates than the economy as a whole. A notable feature of the last decade was the emergence of a dynamic Internet-based consumer economy, led by private firms such as Alibaba and Tencent. Moreover, at some cost, the financial de-risking campaign seems to have brought the growth of leverage under control. In addition, unwillingness to let leverage rise much more now seems a permanent constraint on macroeconomic policy. All these trends, if continued, increase the odds that China will make a "soft landing" at a growth rate of around 5 percent in the early 2020s.

Other signs, however, are not so positive. Chief among these is the Xi government's insistence on maintaining the outsized state share of the economy. Since state firms persistently deliver a much lower return on capital than private firms, the resources devoted to SOEs are a clear-cut misallocation of capital and will reduce economywide efficiency and productivity. Until we see clear signs that SOEs are being restructured and privatized, and that the sectors they dominate are being opened up to much more vigorous competition from private firms, capital productivity will likely continue to languish, growth will continue to slow, leverage will continue to rise, and questions will persist about whether China can make a smooth transition to its new growth model.

Can economic reforms succeed without political reforms?

For as long as China has tried to combine a dynamic and ever more market-driven economy with an authoritarian political system, observers from the West and numerous domestic critics have argued that this combination was unsustainable. Eventually, the argument goes, China would have to change its political system to become more open and representative, or the economy would stop growing.[10]

This prediction is based on plausible precedents. In nineteenth-century Europe, industrialization and the rise of an urban middle class led to the destruction of old aristocratic orders and the gradual emergence of representative government. In Asia after World War II, both South Korea and Taiwan experienced rapid growth under authoritarian regimes, and then they made the transition to democracy in the late 1980s and early 1990s as their growing middle classes demanded more voice in government. The most successful postcommunist countries in eastern Europe, such as Poland, Hungary, and the Czech Republic, embraced capitalism and liberal democracy together.

Of the fifty-eight economies whose per capita gross national income (GNI) exceeded the global average in 2018, all but seven are at least nominally democracies, in the sense that they hold regular contested elections for the country's top leader in which all adult citizens can vote. The exceptions (including Brunei, Saudi Arabia, and several other Middle East emirates) are all countries with small populations whose economies depend mainly on exports of oil and gas, a natural formula for authoritarian oligarchy. Among the major economies, the only one other than China that is not really democratic in any meaningful sense is Russia. It seems likely that the Communist Party's twin desires to turn China into a great economic power and to retain its own political monopoly are incompatible, and sooner or later one of those goals must give way.[11]

So far, though, this prediction has proved wrong. Xi Jinping's top-down reform program aims at a sort of "Leninist capitalism" in which the economy will be driven more by market efficiency, while the party's power will be strengthened, not weakened. There are several reasons to think this strategy could be effective, at least for the next few years.

First, the acquiescence of the governed appears to remain relatively high. China is a large country and many people have many grievances—about inequality, corruption, pollution, expropriation of land, and so on. But such discontent is natural in any fast-changing society. As we saw in Chapter 13, surveys suggest that the large majority of Chinese remain satisfied with the country's direction and that their discontent is largely directed at the abuses of local officials, not at the system as a whole.

Second, the party does not simply crush dissent; it also makes a real effort to address the underlying material causes of discontent. Many elements of Xi's governance program, if successfully implemented, may address some of the most serious causes of social unrest. The anticorruption campaign could constrain the rapacity of local officials. The drive for industrial efficiency, together with changes in the tax system, may drive many polluting factories out of business and make it more cost-effective for the remaining plants to install pollution-abatement equipment. If Xi succeeds, his program will enhance the party's legitimacy by showing that it is capable of delivering difficult changes that are beneficial not just to a narrow elite but to a broad majority of people. (Admittedly, there are a lot of "ifs" in this prognosis.)

Third, the natural class advocate of a more open political system is not obviously interested in change. The urban middle class is generally seen as the group that pushes hardest for political openness. This group has been growing fast in China, but it is still a minority: it may comprise 300–350 million people, or less than a quarter of the population. On the whole, members of this group benefit disproportionately from the current system—notably through the privatization of state-owned housing, which gave them a valuable tax-free asset; and through the quotas for university admission, which are heavily skewed in favor of urbanites.

In a more representative system, the interests of this group would almost certainly lose out to the interests of poor rural people, who are twice as numerous as the urban middle class. As long as the Communist Party continues to deliver the goods, in the form of a rising standard of living (not just financial but environmental), expanding opportunities, and reasonably secure property rights, the urban middle class is unlikely to agitate for political change.

Finally, we ought to question the premise of this whole discussion, namely, that China's economy has changed dramatically while its political system has been static. This is not really true. The governance system of 2020 bears little resemblance to that of 1979. Back then, China was literally a land without laws—Mao had dispensed with laws and courts, preferring to rule by decree—and the majority of officials had no qualifications other than obedience to the ruler. The only reliable means by which a new ruler could come to power was for the old one to die.

In the intervening 35 years, China has established a comprehensive body of law and regulation that enables the country to be governed, for the most part, in a rational and predictable way (though not always fairly). Officials must demonstrate some kind of competence to be promoted, and the technocratic skills of the upper echelons of the bureaucracy are formidable. Starting in 1993, the party has pulled off three successive peaceful transfers of power from one living leader to another. These achievements represent a significant improvement in the systems of governance, even if they fall well short of both the Western ideal of representative democracy and the Chinese ideal of benevolent government.

So there is a fair chance that Xi's "Leninist capitalism" strategy will succeed in sustaining China's unique combination of market economy and authoritarian political system well into the 2020s. But this strategy is far from cost-free. The obvious victims of this approach are innovation and creativity. Although its leaders often mouth the idea that China must become a more innovative society, it is impossible to imagine creativity blossoming as long as the state places draconian restrictions on the right of people to express their views, share information, organize independently to solve social problems, challenge authority, and freely collaborate with like-minded people from other countries. In the short run, this lack of innovation need not stifle the economy, since there is plenty of growth yet to be squeezed out from industrial efficiency, service-sector deregulation, and the like. Ultimately, though, a more open and less paranoid political system will be required for Chinese society to remain vibrant as it grows older and richer.

15

CHINA AND THE WORLD: IS CONFLICT INEVITABLE?

For most of this book, we have considered China mainly on its own terms—as a large and interesting story of national development. But China's rise also has important international dimensions, which became more acute following Xi Jinping's adoption of an assertive foreign policy stance beginning in 2013 and the United States' adoption of a confrontational stance toward China after the election of Donald Trump as president in 2016. China's increasing efforts to flex its muscles internationally, and the intensifying geopolitical rivalry between the world's two largest economies, raise two broad questions. First, is the global system able to absorb a rising China whose political system and values differ so radically from those of the industrialized democracies that built that system? And second, what will be the consequences of the U.S.–China rivalry? This concluding chapter will provide a framework for addressing these questions.

What is the nature of the present global political-economic order?

Before we consider China's position in the world, it is useful to define what we mean by "the world," namely, its overall political and economic arrangements. Since 1945, these arrangements have been built around the position of the United

States as the dominant military power, the global technological leader, and the biggest national economy. The unique status of the United States at the end of World War II—when, by some estimates, it accounted for about half of the entire world economy—enabled it to take the leading role in establishing a set of global institutions, including the United Nations, the World Bank, the International Monetary Fund, the Organization for Economic Cooperation and Development (OECD), and the General Agreement on Tariffs and Trade (GATT, later the World Trade Organization or WTO), which defined the "rules of the game" for international politics, trade, and investment. In addition, less formal institutions such as the G-7 group of large economies enable U.S. leaders to share ideas and coordinate actions with the leaders of other important, friendly countries.

The United States undergirds this multilateral civil architecture with a military alliance structure that encompasses Canada; most western European nations; key Asian nations, including Japan, South Korea, and Australia; a global naval presence that polices the seas, much as the British Navy did in the two centuries before World War II; and a network of over 500 military installations in forty-five countries.[1]

The final component of this system is financial: the international economic and trade system is built around the U.S. dollar. The dollar was the anchor of the so-called Bretton Woods system of fixed exchange rates that lasted from the end of World War II until 1971, when President Richard Nixon took the dollar off the gold standard and the present system of freely floating exchange rates came into existence. Since then, the dollar has continued as the main global currency. On average, around 60 percent of central bank currency reserves are held in dollars, around two-thirds of global trade is conducted in dollars, and the prices of virtually all globally traded commodities (such as oil, iron ore, copper, wheat, and soybeans) are quoted in dollars.

The benefit to the United States is that, as the issuer of the global currency, it uniquely has an unconstrained ability to use its own money to buy all its imports and borrow from foreigners. (Other countries must at least occasionally use a foreign currency—usually dollars—to settle their import bills or borrow.) Therefore, the United States never has to worry, as other nations do, that its debts will suddenly become unmanageable due to a currency depreciation. Because it can safely borrow more than other countries, the United States can finance expensive luxuries—such as a large military—to a degree that other large countries are hard-pressed to match.[2]

This system—sometimes described as the "rules-based international order" by its supporters and as "US hegemony" by its critics—has proved to be powerful and resilient. It outlasted its only significant rival so far, the international communist bloc led by the Soviet Union, which collapsed in 1991. It also survived the breakup of the postwar fixed exchange rate system and efforts by the major oil-producing nations via the Organization of Petroleum Exporting Countries (OPEC) to push up the price of oil in the 1970s. This system has endured despite a steady diminution in the relative economic position of the United States, as the rise of powerful economies, including Japan and Germany in the 1970s, and China and India more recently, reduced U.S. share of global economic output to 24 percent.

What will happen when (and if) China becomes the world's biggest economy?

One challenge that the present global system has not yet had to face is the United States' loss of its position as the world's biggest single economy, a status it has held since the 1870s, when it surpassed the United Kingdom. At some point in the next two decades, it is likely—though by no means certain—that China will overtake the United States and become the world's biggest economy.[3] It is not easy to say when this will occur, and the shifts of the past few years counsel caution in making forecasts of this kind. In the aftermath of the 2008 global crisis, when China was still growing at double-digit rates and the United States was mired in low growth and pessimism, straight-line extrapolations suggested China could become number one by 2020.

In fact, China is still nowhere close to number one. In 2019, the U.S. economy was 50 percent larger than China's, producing about $21 trillion of goods and services to China's $14 trillion.[4] If both countries maintain their present trend of nominal GDP growth rates (4 percent for the United States and 7 percent for China), China will finally become the world's biggest economy in 2033. If, as is possible, China's growth rate slows markedly in the late 2020s, due to unfavorable demographics or other factors, that catch-up date could come later, or never. Even if it does catch up, it is by no means certain that it could sustain the rapid growth needed to stay ahead. As we showed in Chapter 11, China's population will start shrinking in the late 2020s, and by 2050 its society will be as old as Japan's today. The United States is projected to have a younger population that is still growing.[5]

But let us suppose that a decade from now China overtakes the United States to become the world's biggest economy. What will that mean?

The short answer is: not necessarily much. China's population is more than four times that of the United States, so it is hardly odd that China should eventually have larger output. When China surpasses the United States as the world's biggest economy, it will by definition have a per capita income only one-fourth as high (because its population is four times greater). So it will be a larger economy than that of the United States but also a poorer one. How this economic bulk translates into global influence will depend on technological capacity and political positioning.

History shows that the biggest economy is not always the most important one. In 1800, China was still the world's biggest economy. But its global influence was far less than that of the European nations led by Great Britain because it had fallen far behind Europe in the pace of technological change. It was the superiority of European technology, rather than the size of European economies in GDP terms, that proved the decisive factor in the nineteenth century.

Conversely, the United States became the world's biggest economy in the mid-1870s and was already a leader in the invention of new technologies. But it was not until seven decades later, after World War II, that it emerged decisively as the most important power. In the interim, Britain's vast colonial empire and control of trade networks, the dominant status of the pound sterling, London's position as the hub of global finance, and a strongly isolationist tilt to American policy meant that the United Kingdom still exerted greater influence.

So to address the question of China's future global impact, we need to think less about the size of its economy and more about its demonstrated impact so far, the intentions of China's leaders to modify or even supplant the present geopolitical order, and the country's technological capacities.

How does China's economic strength translate into international influence?

China is clearly using its burgeoning economic muscle to achieve greater political influence abroad. This development is causing concern in the United States and Europe because, unlike the two previous economic powers to arise since World War II (Germany and Japan), China is not part of the U.S. alliance structure and is an independent geopolitical actor with its own military capability. China's gain in political influence has been substantial but somewhat less than one might reasonably expect given its economic record. China's economy is now about two-thirds as big as the that of the United States, but on most dimensions the U.S lead in global power and influence is much greater.

One reason for this is that, until recently, China pursued a deliberately restrained foreign policy, guided by Deng Xiaoping's cautious slogan in the early 1990s: *taoguang yanghui*, a traditional expression meaning roughly "lie low and bide your time."[6] In practice, this policy meant focusing diplomatic efforts on fostering stable and reasonably cordial ties with as many countries as possible and avoiding both provocations and leadership roles in the international arena. A key objective in the early days of the reform era was to ensure that most countries broke diplomatic relations with Taiwan and recognized the People's Republic. This strategy was successful. From a position of almost complete diplomatic isolation in the late 1970s, China succeeded in establishing productive relations with virtually every country in the world by 2000, as well as in reducing the number of nations recognizing Taiwan to an insignificant handful.

In the early 2000s, China's foreign policy became more proactive. The government started encouraging its companies to "go out" (*zou chuqu*) and invest globally, in part to secure access to natural resources such as oil, iron ore, and copper that it needed for its capital-intensive growth at home. After a slow start, Chinese outward direct investment started to pick up sharply from 2007, and since 2015 it has averaged about $150 billion a year. China now ranks second behind the United States (roughly $300 billion a year) in annual flows of outward investment (Figure 15.1).

These numbers are impressive but must be put in perspective. First, China's investment outflows are less as a share of GDP (11 percent) than those of the United States (15 percent). So, relative to the size of its economy, China is a less active international direct investor than the United States. Second, after several years of explosive growth, China's outward direct investment flows have leveled off and show no signs of overtaking those of the United States. Third, because the United States has been investing abroad for much longer, its total stock of outward investments is much larger: about

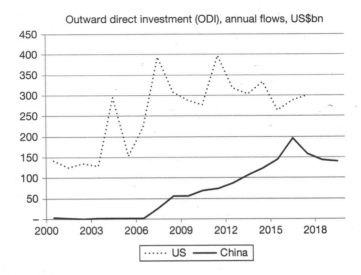

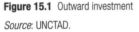

Figure 15.1 Outward investment

Source: UNCTAD.

$6 trillion compared to China's approximately $1.9 trillion. Finally, China's outflows of portfolio capital (holdings of foreign stocks and bonds) are trivial: $500 billion or 4 percent of GDP in 2018, compared to $20 trillion or 100 percent of GDP for the United States. If we use the volume of international investment as a simple index of a country's capacity to exert influence abroad, China clearly lags behind the United States, both in absolute terms and relative to the size of its economy.[7]

Aside from investment, there are at least two other channels by which a country can exert international economic influence: trade and loans. One noteworthy development is the increased number of countries reporting China as their top trade partner. Between 2010 and 2015, this figure rose from twenty-six to forty-one; in the same period, the number of countries reporting the United States as their top trade partner fell from thirty-five to twenty-nine (Figure 15.2). For rich countries, China is an important supplier of low-cost consumer goods, especially electronics. It is also a big buyer of capital goods

Number of countries counting China/US as top trade partner				
	China		United States	
	2010	2015	2010	2015
Top import source	26	46	33	23
Top export destination	18	19	37	38
Top total trade partner	26	41	35	29
Source: WTO				

Figure 15.2 China's trade leverage grows.

such as industrial equipment, airplanes, and components such as semiconductors. For commodity-producing countries, China has become the most important customer for products like crude oil, iron ore, copper, other metals, soybeans, palm oil, and sugar.

Broadly speaking, China's rising participation in global trade is beneficial, but it also creates serious challenges. For rich countries, China's rise as a low-cost manufacturing power has made it hard to sustain traditional high-wage manufacturing sectors. Commodity producers in the developing world have profited handsomely from China's increased demand for their products, but they need to prepare themselves for the day when China's "building binge" phase of growth ends. For smaller countries, exposure to China's market also means exposure to Chinese pressure. On several occasions, China has blocked access to its market for companies from countries with whom it has political disputes, and it has used this leverage to extract concessions.[8]

Two qualifications are in order. First, a closer look at Figure 15.2 shows that virtually all of China's gains in trade relationships are the result of its importance as a supplier, not as a market. Between 2010 and 2015 the number of countries reporting China as their top import source nearly doubled, from twenty-six to forty-five. But the number reporting China as their top export destination barely budged. The United States is the top export market for twice as many countries as China, and China does not appear to be gaining ground on this indicator. This reflects the fact that China's imports are highly concentrated in a few categories—commodities and some capital goods—and the economy is relatively closed to imports of a broader range of consumer goods.

Moreover, as China deepens its domestic supply chains for many finished goods, its demand for imported components and capital goods could fall. So, relative to the United States, China does not have as much leverage from being a major market for other people's exports.[9] We should not overstate this case: China is indeed a major and fast-growing market for the goods of foreign companies—as long as those goods are produced by factories inside China rather than imported. For instance, in 2017 U.S. companies and their affiliates registered sales of $544 billion in China, nearly triple the $187 billion in exports by U.S. companies to China in the same year.

The second caveat is that, to the degree that countries are reliant on imports from China, in many cases what they really rely on is goods produced by multinational companies in China. As we showed in Chapter 5, foreign firms still account for over 40 percent of China's exports. The overall conclusion is that China's growing trade relations with and importance as a market for many countries are major facts and potential sources of political leverage; but these trade relations also reflect complex webs of interdependence rather than a simple dynamic in which China can exercise unfettered power because of its market size.

A final vector of influence is China's increasing importance as a lender, especially to developing countries. Assessing the scale of China's international lending activities is hard because China participates only to a limited degree in international debt databases and because much of Chinese lending to developing countries involves Chinese policy or commercial banks extending project loans to Chinese engineering or construction companies rather than to host country governments or companies. In some cases, these loans are ultimately guaranteed by host country governments, or (in the case of resource-extraction projects) secured by shipments of oil, minerals, or other commodities. Thus, they may in fact represent actual or contingent liabilities of the host government. As loans from Chinese banks to Chinese companies, however, they do not show up in cross-border debt data.

China's role as a creditor to the rest of the world has risen dramatically since the early 2000s. Much less clear is exactly how big this role is and to what degree it is problematic. An IMF study found that in 2016, China on average accounted for a bit over 11 percent of the external debt of fifty-nine low-income developing countries. This was a large increase from essentially zero a decade before but still well below the shares of multilateral institutions such as the IMF and World Bank (42 percent) or other individual country lenders (43 percent).[10]

China is the most important contributor of flows of new credit to these countries, but in terms of the total stock of debt it is just one of several important lenders. A more alarming 2019 assessment by a group of Western economists, which tried to identify hidden Chinese lending not reported in official statistics, estimated that for the top fifty recipients of Chinese loans, China accounted for about 40 percent of total external debt.[11] While this estimate is subject to challenge on the ground that loans by Chinese policy banks to Chinese companies operating in another country perhaps should not count as a debt of that country, many developing countries are now heavily dependent in various ways on flows of credit from China.

The question is: is this a problem, and if so. how big a one? China's rise as a global creditor has prompted several types of criticism. In the early days of its lending to developing countries, a common fear was that it would spawn corruption and waste by offering huge loans at very low rates and without the conditions for good governance and environmental sustainability often imposed by lenders such as the World Bank. Subsequent research has shown that much of China's lending is done at or close to commercial terms, and in many cases (as noted above) project loans are not issued to host governments or companies but to Chinese engineering firms, in part to minimize the risk of misappropriation.

The criticisms accordingly changed: Chinese loans risked engulfing poor countries in "debt traps." Also, the practice of keeping loan funds out of the hands of local companies or governments meant that Chinese lending was less beneficial to host countries' economies or balance of payments than lending from other sources. Some critics also alleged, with scant evidence, that China had a deliberate policy of lending countries more than they could repay, so that China could then seize the assets used as collateral.[12]

The rapid rise in China's international lending does raise real issues, but some of these critiques seem driven less by evidence than by a prior assumption that China's activity is intrinsically harmful and should be treated with suspicion. China's greater role as a global creditor is a natural consequence of its economic rise. Moreover, many of the problems associated with its loans can be attributed to the relative inexperience of Chinese lending institutions outside their own borders and to failures of governance in borrower countries. These faults were exacerbated by excessively grandiose ambitions for the Belt and Road infrastructure initiative (discussed below), which is now being scaled back.

In some cases, Chinese loan issuance did involve corrupt deals with local governments.[13] There are serious concerns about the environmental impact of China's enthusiastic financing of dams and coal-fired power plants and about the general rise in indebtedness in developing countries that is driven largely but not entirely by China. Perhaps the most important problem with China's international lending activity is its lack of transparency: China does not participate fully in international debt databases, making it harder to figure out how much of a debt-sustainability problem poor countries really have.

How has Xi Jinping changed China's international profile?

China's foreign policy took a stronger activist turn in 2013 after Xi Jinping took power. Xi has decisively broken with the old "lie-low" approach in at least three dimensions. First, he has more aggressively asserted China's territorial claims in the South China Sea, which are disputed by Vietnam, the Philippines, and other neighbors. This position has involved building artificial islands around various reefs and shoals, and using these as military installations. A related maritime development was the establishment of an air defense identification zone in the East China Sea, overlapping with a similar zone claimed by Japan.

Second, Xi promoted a policy of "military-civil fusion"—essentially a vision for emulating the military-industrial complex of the United States—which suggests a desire to increase the ability of China's military to project force outside its borders.[14] Third, Xi launched the Belt and Road Initiative, which formalized China's rising international investments in engineering projects into a program of what one might call "infrastructure diplomacy."

This shift has occasioned much anxiety and criticism. In particular, the smaller countries in China's periphery have good reason to worry about the long-run impact of a more assertive stance by a large authoritarian and illiberal state with considerable economic leverage. But these developments should also be kept in perspective.

It is a natural consequence of China's economic rise that Beijing should seek to increase its regional and global influence. While this bid for greater influence is discomfiting, it is also constrained by China's need to maintain its participation in the open global trade and investment system from which it benefits enormously. China's bid for influence today is a far cry from its disruptive foreign policy of the 1960s and 1970s, when it actively supported insurrections and revolutions around the world.

China's efforts to expand its influence have focused mainly on its immediate neighborhood in Asia and have met with some success and considerable resistance. Japan and South Korea are firm members of the U.S. military alliance system, as is Taiwan *de facto*, if not *de jure*. China's influence in the weakest countries of Southeast Asia (Cambodia and Laos) is growing, but its sway elsewhere is contested. Vietnam harbors centuries-old resentment against its large northern neighbor and has actively courted closer ties with and greater investment flows from Japan. Myanmar had tight relations with Beijing under its former military regime, but fear of becoming a Chinese vassal state was one factor contributing to a dramatic political and economic liberalization. This stance led to dissolution of the military junta in 2011 and strengthened ties with the West.

Central Asian nations such as Kazakhstan and Turkmenistan welcome Chinese investment to unlock their mineral wealth and improve transport infrastructure, but they also strive to maintain their independence by playing off China against their traditional patron, Russia. In recent years, there has been rising alarm in Australia about Chinese efforts to buy influence among politicians, but this threat has been countered by a long-overdue tightening of the country's campaign finance and espionage laws.[15]

Since 1980, China has been no more inclined to use force outside its own borders than has India and significantly less so than China itself during the Maoist era.[16] Its record of intervention—which almost exclusively takes the form of influence-buying, rather than military action or efforts to overthrow governments—pales in comparison to that of the United States over the past 125 years. American military interventions have long been a routine feature of global affairs. Countries affected include the Philippines, Cuba, Panama, and Nicaragua before World War II, and Afghanistan, Iraq, the former Yugoslavia, and Libya since the end of the Cold War. By one estimate, during the Cold War, the United States tried to change the government of another country seventy-two times.[17]

Finally, U.S. and European officials have been asking for years that China take a more active role in global affairs.[18] Some of Xi's initiatives are clearly efforts to assert political dominance; others can be interpreted as a response to this call to become a better global citizen. At a meeting in Beijing with President Obama in November 2014, Xi pledged to work together with the United States to achieve a global accord to combat climate change. This was a significant shift from 5 years earlier, when a crucial climate policy meeting in Copenhagen failed to reach agreement, largely because of antagonism between the United States and China. China's bid to spearhead infrastructure investment in neighboring countries of Asia, while incorporating a great deal of self-interest, is also in part a legitimate effort to finance international "public goods" that will provide widespread material benefit.

China's leaders are apparently now seeking to translate their country's economic strength into greater influence in Asia and the world. This effort is natural and has created a combination of political challenges and potential economic benefits. China will certainly gain influence relative to established regional powers: Russia in Central Asia, Japan in Southeast Asia. China may also succeed in eroding, to some degree, U.S. influence in Asia. Its success in that regard will probably depend less on its own actions and more on whether the United States seeks to strengthen its robust alliance structure in Asia or—as has sometimes seemed the case during the Trump Administration—let it atrophy.

What is the Belt and Road Initiative?

Starting in the early 2000s, Chinese construction and engineering firms steadily increased their international activities, taking the expertise they gained in China's domestic infrastructure build-out to bid on road, rail, dam, power and telecommunications projects around the world, especially in developing countries. Annual revenues from overseas construction projects rose from almost nothing in 2000 to $120 billion in 2012. In September 2013, Xi Jinping formally launched the One Belt, One Road Program—later relabeled the Belt and Road Initiative, which set a formal government objective of building a network of infrastructure links connecting China with the rest of the world.

The "Belt" refers to a New Silk Road set of transport projects linking western China with Central Asia and, ultimately, Europe. The "Road" refers to a Maritime Silk Road program consisting of rail, road, and port projects connecting southwest China with the Indian Ocean, the Middle East, and Africa. To help finance these projects, Xi authorized the creation of a Silk Road Fund from China's own budget and, more ambitiously, a multilateral Asian Infrastructure Investment Bank (AIIB). In reality, most funding for China's international engineering projects is provided by the state policy banks (China Development Bank and the Export-Import Bank of China) and state-controlled commercial banks.

Several motivations lay behind this "infrastructure diplomacy." Many projects could help China secure supplies of energy and other natural resources through routes that cannot easily be interdicted by the U.S. military. Another aim is to create new corridors of economic activity and linkages to the rich markets of Europe that could enhance economic development in China's landlocked central and western regions. The construction projects themselves will provide much-needed business for Chinese engineering firms and materials suppliers, which now face a stagnant market at home. Underwriting much-needed infrastructure in developing countries is one way for China to expand its political influence.[19]

The Belt and Road Initiative is a good example of how China is growing both as a global economic and political power and as a provider of international "public goods." China's official position is that the Belt and Road is a benign effort to plug infrastructure gaps, enhance global trade and investment flows, and spur development in poor countries. There is some truth in this portrayal. Critics allege that it is largely a scheme to increase China's political influence around the world, and there is much truth in that too. Just as the United States sought to cement its global position after World War II by creating a community of economic interests through mechanisms such as the Marshall Plan, the World Bank, the IMF, and the trading arrangements that grew into the World Trade Organization, Beijing wants to create a community of economic interests through improved physical connectivity and it hopes that China's political influence will correspondingly rise.

In this case as in so many others, straight-line extrapolations of the growth of China's power have proved misleading. After Xi's speech launching the Belt and Road, China's overseas construction revenues grew rapidly for several more years, peaking at $170 billion in 2017. As a result, the country's external lending (much of it tied to infrastructure projects) more than doubled, to $710 billion at the end of 2018. But revenues from construction projects flatlined in 2018 and fell in 2019; external lending also stopped growing in 2019. Causes for this reversal included political backlash, the financial failure of some projects, and difficulty in identifying attractive new projects. China will continue to play an important role in financing and building infrastructure around the world, but the growth of this role will be constrained by the need to make projects more sustainable (financially, environmentally and politically), and by the reluctance of many countries to become overly reliant on Chinese assistance.[20]

How close is China to becoming a global technological leader?

China has undeniably made rapid technological progress over the last three decades. Through industrial upgrading plans such as Made in China 2025, it is investing tens of billions of dollars in accelerating this technological progress. But "progress" is not the same as "leadership," and analyzing "China's" position in global technological value chains is tricky because an unusually large proportion of the technology-intensive production that occurs within China is done by foreign-owned companies, and in many sectors Chinese end-producers are substantially reliant on high-value imported components. Chinese technology companies increasingly dominate their domestic market, but they have had less success in international markets.

One simple index of China's technological capacities is the smartphone. A majority of the world's smartphones are produced in China. By 2018, about 85 percent of the domestic market (by unit sales) was controlled by domestic firms. Low-cost Chinese cell phones are common in developing countries, although they do not have a major share of developed-country markets. China's top producer, Huawei, now ranks as one of the world's three most important smartphone makers, along with Apple and Samsung, and is competitive in rich-country markets. But its ability to maintain its market share was thrown into serious question after the firm was placed on a U.S. export-control blacklist in May 2019, restricting the ability of U.S. technology companies to supply Huawei with key components.

At first, Huawei located alternative suppliers for most of its hardware needs. But even these suppliers rely on manufacturing supply chains that depend on American equipment. If Washington bans the use of U.S.-designed machinery to make components for Huawei, the company may not be able to survive in its present form.

Moreover, the acknowledged global leader in smartphone technology remains Apple, leadership that is reflected in its disproportionate share of global profits from smartphone sales: 62 percent in 2018 compared to 17 percent for Samsung and 8 percent for Huawei.[21] Apple produces most of its phones in China, but assembly is controlled by a Taiwanese manufacturing firm, Foxconn. The share of an iPhone's wholesale value attributable to Chinese components is relatively low but has risen rapidly: from 4 percent for the first iPhone in 2009 to 25 percent for the iPhone X in 2018.[22]

The signal sent by smartphones is thus decidedly mixed. In this sector at least, Chinese companies have made rapid progress and occupy important positions as producers of both finished phones and components. But they remain much more successful in their protected domestic market than internationally (especially in rich-country markets), continue to be significantly reliant on imported components and software, and cannot as yet be fairly described as "leaders."

Widening the lens beyond smartphones, a McKinsey Global Institute study of eighty-one technology-intensive value chains found a wide range of capacities for Chinese firms. In some sectors, such as solar panels and high-speed trains, Chinese producers accounted for most or all of the value chain. In others, such as wind turbines, electric vehicles, and agricultural machinery, Chinese assemblers dominated the domestic market but depended substantially on foreign-made components and inputs. In many of the most complex sectors, such as semiconductors and commercial aircraft, Chinese companies are laggards and do not occupy important positions in the global value chain.[23] Another report, by the Center for Strategic and International Studies, also found that the results of China's intensive investments in innovation were quite mixed and that the country's overall level of technological innovation was well ahead of most developing countries and well behind the most advanced economies.[24]

Of course, these assessments are only snapshots, and China's position will improve in the coming years. So we need to understand the factors that will enable and constrain China's technological development. The most basic observation is that what matters at the end of the day is not inputs but outputs. Much media coverage and many policy studies latch on to readily available data on inputs—such as total spending on research and development, or the amount of money raised by government industrial policy funds—and assume that all this money will yield commensurate results. Yet, China's track record suggests otherwise: heavy spending on industrial policy has sometimes fostered local champions, as in solar panels and wind turbines; sometimes produced very meager results, as in semiconductors or aircraft; and sometimes contributed to the growth of a vibrant industry in which much of the financial return has gone to foreign companies, as in automobiles.

Another pitfall is to assume that all technological progress in China results from heavy-handed state intervention. In fact the opposite is often the case. One of the most vibrant and innovative sectors of China's economy is the internet, where the state played a key role in building the basic infrastructure. The successful companies, however—e-commerce giant Alibaba and messaging and gaming company Tencent, among many others—were all entrepreneurial private firms that benefited somewhat from protectionism that kept the big American Internet companies at bay, but for the most part honed their innovation skills in an arena of cutthroat free-market competition.[25]

A better way of thinking about China's technological prospects is suggested in the McKinsey Global Institute study, which notes that for a country to move up the technology value chain, four things are needed: large-scale investments, access to large markets, mechanisms for acquiring technology and know-how, and an effective system for encouraging competition and innovation.[26] China clearly has the capacity to make large-scale investments, using both government and private-sector funds. It has a large market of increasingly wealthy and sophisticated consumers.

Because of the foreign companies' extensive participation in manufacturing, China does have good capacity for gaining access to technology and know-how developed elsewhere. Its competition and innovation ecosystem is improving but flawed. While some markets—notably the Internet and electronics manufacturing—are highly competitive, others are distorted by government subsidies, intervention, or policies that limit competition by international companies. Basic research is well funded, but the distribution of research funds is much more corrupt and politicized than is the case in North America, Europe, or Japan. In some fields, the pace of innovation is retarded by the state's authoritarian controls on information flows.

In sum, China has made impressive technological progress in the past two decades, and its technology firms increasingly occupy leadership positions in their domestic market. Chinese companies produce a substantial and rising share of the value of globalized production chains located in China. The most successful Chinese technology firms are no longer just copycats but are innovators in their own right. A handful of Chinese companies have moved outside their home market and established genuine global leadership positions—most notably Huawei, which is the recognized world pacesetter in 5G mobile technology. But the number of world-leading technology companies from China is far fewer than the number from the United States today, or Japan in the 1970s and 1980s. Few Chinese innovations are being widely adopted or emulated in other countries.

In order to keep up its fast pace of technological progress, China needs to maintain a high level of integration with global markets and production chains and improve its innovation ecosystem. As we argued at the end of Chapter 5, China's ability to do these things is compromised by the state's obsession with technological autonomy and information control. The quest for autonomy means that the state will often support a second-best solution, as long as it is homegrown, over a superior foreign one. This creates an environment in which firms find it more profitable to be just good enough for the domestic market than to make the extra effort to reach the global leading edge. Information control stifles the knowledge sharing and collaboration across disciplinary and national boundaries that is essential for large-scale innovation. Continued technological progress is perfectly possible under such conditions; technological leadership may not be.

Does China want to remake the global system with its own rules and institutions?

China is a large, committed stakeholder in the global governance system. It has opened up its domestic market to foreign investment and international competition far more than any of its East Asian models (Japan, South Korea, and Taiwan) or any of its large developing-country peers (Brazil, India, and Russia). It has joined virtually every major international economic agreement or convention, and it plays by the rules of those agreements about as consistently as do other major economic powers, including the United States. It has, in fact, joined some agreements that the United States has refused to, notably the United Nations Convention on the Law of the Sea (UNCLOS). The reason for this pattern is simple: China has reaped enormous economic advantages by integrating itself into the international order. Since, as we have shown above, its continued technological advance depends critically on further integration with the global economy, it has a strong self-interest in preserving the main features of that system.

At the same time, China also wants a greater say in how the rules of the international system are set and is setting up alternative arrangements in cases where the international system does not meet its needs. This desire is understandable but deeply problematic. The postwar international order was established and run by industrialized democracies with broadly liberal political systems, capitalist market economies, and a relatively low level of state ownership of assets. It is not easy for such a club to accommodate a large new member that has an illiberal, authoritarian political system (which under Xi Jinping is becoming more authoritarian rather than less) and a state-capitalist economy in which a large share of economic activity, both at home and abroad, is subject to direct state ownership and control. The established powers have thus resisted, to some degree, China's efforts to gain more influence in global rules-setting and have raised the alarm when China has set up alternative institutions.

Alternative institutions sponsored by China include the Shanghai Cooperation Organization (SCO), a political and security grouping founded in 2001 comprising China, Russia, and several Central Asian republics; a free-trade agreement with the Association of Southeast Asian Nations (ASEAN) that spawned a broader free-trade agreement, the Regional Comprehensive Economic Partnership (RCEP); and two multilateral lending institutions: the New Development Bank (originally called the BRICS Bank, with Brazil, Russia, India, and South Africa as the other founding members) and the Asian Infrastructure Investment Bank (AIIB).

The impact of these initiatives has been marginal. China launched AIIB in late 2015 as a complement to the Belt and Road Initiative to increase funding sources for international infrastructure projects. It invited dozens of nations, including the most significant economies in Asia and Europe, to join the AIIB as founding members. The U.S. government urged many of its allies, notably Australia and South Korea, not to participate, but in the end around sixty countries, including many U.S. allies in Europe and Asia, joined. AIIB has turned out to be a rather conventional multilateral lender, with governance and lending standards closely modeled on those of the World Bank and the Asian Development Bank. With total disbursements of $5 billion in its first two years in operation (2017–2018), it is well behind not only the World Bank (which disburses over $30 billion a year), but the ADB and other multilateral banks in Africa and Latin America as well.

RCEP emerged from a more limited free-trade agreement between China and the ASEAN countries. Countries negotiating for entry also included Japan, India, South Korea, Australia and New Zealand. Although China has actively participated in negotiations, the original impetus for the deal came from ASEAN, not Beijing. Moreover, while the proposed deal would include many countries, the agreement's scope is far more narrow than the ambitious Trans-Pacific Partnership (TPP) which the United States negotiated with eleven other

Asia-Pacific economies, before withdrawing in early 2017. RCEP would mainly liberalize trade in goods, with many exceptions, whereas TPP also included high-standard rules on investment, subsidies, state-owned enterprises, and intellectual property. As of late 2019, RCEP negotiations were stalled, with India reluctant to sign on and Japan unwilling to join the pact without India, for fear that without India, China's influence would be too strong. Even if RCEP is ratified, it is unlikely to make a major change in regional or global trading patterns.

Why has U.S. policy toward China shifted?

As our discussion shows, China's economic rise has enabled the country to exert much more political influence around the world than in the past, and under Xi Jinping's leadership it has become far more assertive in promoting its interests and values. But China's ability to alter the global "rules of the game" is constrained by its economy's dependence on international trade and investment flows to support its technological development. Another deterrent is that many other countries in Asia maintain formal alliances or less formal security arrangements with the United States, which they are reluctant to abandon. China's attempt to remake global infrastructure via the Belt and Road Initiative has hit capacity constraints and political resistance. So, while China's political clout is clearly growing, it is still rather less than might be implied by its status as the world's second biggest economy and biggest trading nation, with a 15 percent share of global GDP.

Even so, China's rising economic and political status has set off alarm bells in Washington and has led to a dramatic change in the United States' stance toward China. In order to assess China's future role in the global order, we need first to understand why the United States has decided to change its China policy, and what impact this shift is likely to have.

In 1979, the United States normalized diplomatic relations with the People's Republic of China, ending a period of nearly three decades during which Washington did not recognize the CCP regime. The initial rationale for the rapprochement, from the U.S. side, was the desire to enlist China as a counterweight to the Soviet Union during the Cold War. China, which had effectively broken with its fellow communist regime by 1960, was also looking for a counterweight to Soviet power. After Deng Xiaoping assumed control of China in 1978, it was also looking for a partner to aid its economic development.

The generally constructive relationship between the two countries was tested first by the Tiananmen Square demonstrations and subsequent crackdown of 1989, which led to the imposition of economic sanctions by the United States, and then by the collapse of the Soviet Union in 1991, which eliminated the original basis of this unlikely partnership between two large powers with sharply opposed political and ideological systems. Through the 1990s, frictions were persistent, especially given that under U.S. law, Chinese eligibility for "most favored nation" trading status depended on an annual certification by the White House that China's human rights conditions were within acceptable bounds.[27]

Yet, during this period, a consensus crystallized in Washington around a policy stance usually referred to as "constructive engagement." This policy held that it was in the United States' national interest not to treat China as an adversary, but instead to foster its economic rise and encourage its integration with global economic institutions and with the U.S. economy.

The economic rationale for this policy was straightforward: China represented a huge potential market for U.S. firms. The central security rationale was not, as it is sometimes now portrayed, that economic growth and integration would inexorably cause China to evolve into a liberal democracy. Rather, it was the calculation that, given that China's political system was likely to remain divergent from the norms of the industrialized democracies, greater economic integration would (1) constrain China to play by the rules of the "global economic game," thereby becoming a broadly constructive force rather than a disruptive one as the Soviet Union had been; and (2) reduce the risk of U.S.–China frictions escalating into armed conflict, by raising the costs of such a conflict. A major achievement of this policy was China's accession to the WTO in December 2001, after fifteen years of intensive negotiations. Up until the election of Donald Trump in 2016, the idea of "constructive engagement" was the basic framework for U.S. relations with China.[28]

The Trump Administration adopted a more adversarial stance in which China was formally identified as a "strategic competitor."[29] In addition, in early 2018, it launched a trade war which by late 2019 had resulted in special tariffs of 10–25 percent being imposed on some $375 billion in Chinese imports to the United States. In August 2018, Congress also passed legislation tightening controls on the export of critical technologies, a law whose main target was China. In retaliation, China imposed tariffs on over $100 billion in imports from the United States and also restricted imports of many agricultural products, notably soybeans.

The trade war and the labeling of China as a strategic competitor are related but distinct policies. The trade war was driven personally by Trump, who has a long history as an economic nationalist and advocate of managed trade. Although China was the biggest target, it was by no means the only one: massive tariffs on imported steel and aluminum mainly targeted countries allied or aligned with the United States, including Canada, Brazil, Japan, and Germany. Trump also used tariff threats to renegotiate a long-standing free-trade agreement with Canada and Mexico. The "strategic competitor" narrative was driven mainly by bureaucrats in the National Security Council and the Defense Department. While Trump went along with it, he has shown little interest in actively promoting this approach. Across the political spectrum in Washington, the strategic-competitor idea commands broad, if often qualified, support, whereas support for the trade war is narrower.

Several reasons account for the shift from "constructive engagement" to a more adversarial stance. One is simply that China has become a lot bigger and more powerful and seems on its way not only to surpassing the United States as the world's biggest economy but also acting as a peer competitor in the economic, technological, and military spheres.

Another reason was the changes in Chinese policy under Xi Jinping after 2013. The Made in China 2025 industrial policy was seen as an effort to subsidize Chinese firms so that they could displace American competitors in a host of high-value, technology-intensive fields; the military-civil fusion program was seen as an effort to ensure that any technological gains in the commercial sector would translate into a strengthening of China's military capabilities; the buildup of artificial island bases in the South China Sea was viewed as a signal of China's intent to displace the United States as the main power in maritime Asia; and the Belt and Road Initiative was regarded as an effort to build up China's geopolitical influence throughout the world. Moreover, Xi's centralization of power, increasingly authoritarian tactics, and expansion of the CCP's role in all aspects of society reduced the hope that China's political system might converge with the democratic norms of the United States and its allies.

These security-related concerns dovetailed with economic discontents, which played a role in Trump's election. Although China's rise as a manufacturing power was probably on net beneficial for the U.S. economy, since it enabled U.S. companies to increase efficiency by lowering production costs and reduced the prices of a wide range of consumer and industrial goods, these benefits came at the cost of an accelerated decline in U.S. manufacturing employment, with job losses concentrated in the traditional Midwest industrial heartland. The U.S. political system did a poor job of protecting workers hurt by competition from low-labor-cost countries (notably but not exclusively China) and from automation. One important macroeconomic consequence was that the benefit of China's rise flowed disproportionately to owners of capital, whose share of national income rose at the expense of workers.

The rising sense that many communities were being left behind—and that China's growth came not through fair competition but by "cheating" on the rules of the WTO—boosted support for the protectionist and economic nationalist policies that Trump championed. At the elite level, there was rising concern that the transfer of manufacturing capacity from the United States to China would not only slow down the United States' economic growth, but also harm its national security by reducing the country's ability to produce the industrial goods needed for national defense.[30]

An active debate has arisen among the U.S. policy elite about what the appropriate posture toward China should be in the coming decades. Most likely, this debate will take several years to resolve because of the complexity of the U.S.–China relationship and the nature of the interests at stake. Simplifying greatly, we may conceptualize this debate as pitting three broad perspectives against one another. One is the national-security-oriented view that China's rise is, at the very least, a serious challenge to U.S. global leadership and to specific U.S. security interests in Asia, and perhaps even an existential threat to the U.S.-led international order. Allied to this view is the economic nationalist perspective that American prosperity is threatened by a predatory China and that the interdependence of the two economies should be reduced.

The second view, grounded in economics and business, sees U.S.–China economic interdependence as beneficial for both commercial and security reasons. From this vantage point, China's enormous and fast-growing market is an important source of future growth for American firms. The ability of U.S. firms to remain at the global technological leading edge will depend on their ability to participate in this market, taking advantage of the profits, human resources, and production efficiencies that it offers. The scope of U.S. business engagement with China is already so huge that it cannot be unwound or scaled back without inflicting great damage on the U.S. economy. Since 2015, China has accounted for around 16 percent of total U.S. trade, comparable to Japan in the 1980s and far greater than the trading relationship with the Soviet Union and its successor states. And, U.S. companies have a large presence in China's domestic market: in 2017, about 70,000 U.S. companies had some kind of operation in China and generated $544 billion in sales there, more than triple the value of U.S. exports to China (Figures 15.3 and 15.4).[31]

The third perspective focuses on the increasingly illiberal drift of China's political system. In this values-based view, China's increasingly authoritarian and repressive policies at home and mounting efforts to influence public opinion and silence criticism of the CCP regime abroad represent serious threats to the core values not just of the United States but of the liberal world order more generally.

A new American strategy toward China will have to accommodate, at least to some degree, the nation's national security, commercial, and values interests. Crafting such a policy will be no easy task. U.S. policy toward China in the coming years will focus more on competition and conflict, and less on cooperation and collaboration, than was the case before 2016. But efforts to launch a full-on strategy of containment, similar to the U.S. strategy against the Soviet Union during the Cold War, will be blunted by economic interests, which can mount a credible argument that continued economic interdependence is not only beneficial for the United States commercially, but also serves long-run security interests by constraining China's ability to fundamentally change the global economic order and by raising the cost of armed conflict.[32]

What is the future of China's role in the global order?

We are now in a position to assess the scale and nature of the challenge that China's rise poses to the global order and to its central power, the United States. "Realist" diplomatic

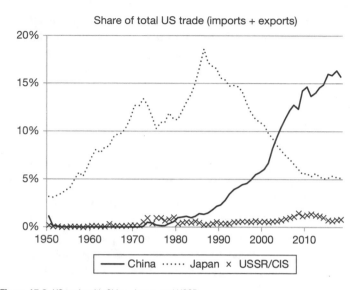

Figure 15.3 US trade with China, Japan, and USSR.

Note: Data for USSR through 1991 and for the Commonwealth of Independent States (CIS) after 1991.

Source: US Census Bureau.

historians argue that the transition from one great power to another has never gone smoothly and that the United States and China are doomed to face off in a great political or military confrontation sooner or later. Media pundits trumpet every new action by China as yet another sign of the "inexorable march of power from West to East."[33] Advocates for the American military-industrial complex are quick to claim that every quiver of the Chinese state betrays an existential threat justifying a large increase in their budgets. According to global public opinion surveys, show that majorities in many countries believe that China will replace or has already replaced the United States as the world's leading power; and that hostility towards China is rising rapidly in the United States.[34]

China's rise is a large and difficult fact, and raises a host of serious strategic questions. There is significant and rising risk

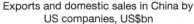

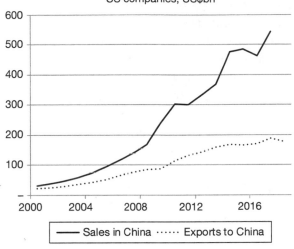

Figure 15.4 The China market for US firms.

Source: Bureau of Economic Analysis.

that the U.S.–China rivalry will spawn severe conflicts in the coming years. Yet there are also reasons to think that the global system may be able to manage China's rise peacefully.

Remember the description we gave of the global system at the beginning of this chapter. This system is complex, multilayered, and robust, and has already survived severe tests. It depends not just on the economic size and technological capacities of the United States, but on a sophisticated array of multilateral institutions, knowledge and financial networks, and military alliances. It has been built up over seven decades since the end of World War II upon deep foundations laid over the previous century through the emergence of modern industrial capitalism in Europe and the United States; the creation of flexible and responsive liberal political systems; and the statecraft of running a global commercial empire, which Great Britain pioneered and the United States has inherited and improved.

The breadth, depth, and strength of this global system weakens the relevance of one-on-one comparisons between China and the United States. China's economy may or may not overtake the United States as the world's biggest economy. But its future economic growth will still depend to a substantial degree on its ability to integrate with the global system. As its weight grows, China will gain a greater voice in how that system is run, as it should. But its ability to transform the deeply rooted principles on which that system rests can be constrained, if the incumbents in the system—not just the United States but also Europe, Japan, and other industrial democracies—adhere to a common vision.

It is reasonable to wonder whether that common vision will endure. Under the leadership of President Trump, the U.S. commitment to this order has come into question. One of Trump's first acts as president was to withdraw from the TPP, an economic pact encompassing most of the major Asia-Pacific economies except China and one supported by both Republican and Democratic administrations in the past. The strategic purpose of TPP was to create a powerful economic zone with rules on trade, investment, and intellectual property, and limits on subsidies and state-owned enterprises, written according to American standards. China would then face the choice of applying for membership—thereby gaining economic benefits but at the cost of making its system conform more to Western norms—or staying out, thereby preserving its own system but at substantial economic cost. The almost universal appraisal of both economic and defense experts was that the TPP would have been an important bulwark of the American-led order against a challenge from China. Famously, Ashton Carter, Secretary of Defense under President Obama, said that "passing TPP is as important to me as another aircraft carrier."[35]

Trump followed up this move with a wide-ranging trade war in which he imposed high tariffs, often on specious national security grounds, not just on Chinese goods, but also on imports from allies and friendly countries such as Japan, the European Union, Mexico, and Brazil. He also cast doubt on U.S. support for the NATO alliance and generally promoted a unilateralist "America first" agenda that downplayed the importance of U.S. alliances and multilateral institutions. If Trump or a successor really does tear down the postwar global system and returns the world to an era of individual competing nation-states, this would greatly strengthen China's position and greatly weaken that of the United States. At present, however, the global system faces severe pressure but has not yet cracked.

By the same token, China's capacity to conjure up some alternative, competing system should not be overrated. What would be the basis for such a system? It cannot be technological leadership, since China, though making rapid technological progress, is not yet the world leader. It cannot be a military alliance structure, since China has no alliances and no credible prospects of creating any. It cannot be a regional power bloc, since all of its neighbors view China with a degree of mistrust and are busy with hedging and balancing strategies to constrain China's influence. It could perhaps be a claim that China has discovered more effective methods of governance and economic management, and hence a stronger claim to global legitimacy and moral leadership.

One deep anxiety caused by China's rise stems from the supposed paradox of its dynamic economy and its authoritarian political system. For years, critics have claimed that this combination was unsustainable and that eventually China would be forced to accept the true faith of liberal democracy. For years this critique has proved wrong. The worry—especially in the United States, whose elites subscribe to a monotheistic view of the unique rightness of the American system and the essential imperfection of all other systems—is that China has shown how to combine economic growth with repressive politics. The perceived risk is that more countries will be seduced into this path and away from the combination of free-market capitalism and electoral democracy favored by the United States and its allies.

China's governance system is founded on principles very different from those of Western democracies: the CCP rejects elections as the criterion of political legitimacy, in favor of effective governance combined with tight repression. This stance achieves broad acquiescence in Chinese society because it essentially restates the principle of *tian ming*, or the Mandate of Heaven, which was the basis of legitimacy in China's imperial system. For 1,500 years, China's bureaucracy and ruling house justified their rule by claiming to run a well-ordered land where roads, canals, irrigation systems, and dikes were maintained; commercial activities were vibrant and well regulated; and social stability was maintained. Breakdowns in this order signaled the loss of the right to rule. The Communist Party makes essentially the same claim.

This social contract applies within the predominantly ethnic Chinese areas of mainland China, but does not exist in ethnic minority regions. This became painfully evident in 2018, when the world became aware of an extraordinary campaign of repression in Xinjiang, a vast western region whose main indigenous population is the Uighurs, an Islamic people who speak a Turkic language. Ostensibly in response to terrorist violence, Beijing rounded up as many as a million Uighurs and placed them in "reeducation camps," blanketing the region with surveillance cameras and police checkpoints. This repression campaign, which sparked broad international outrage, was implemented by a senior official who had employed similar techniques of repression in Tibet.[36]

Equally, the CCP social contract does not hold in Hong Kong, which remains a crucial link between China's economy and the rest of the world. In June 2019, more than a million Hong Kongers took to the streets to protest a bill that would have enabled people to be extradited from Hong Kong, which has a highly regarded independent legal system built on British foundations, to mainland China. Over the next several months the territory was wracked by demonstrations of increasing violence, which exposed deep dissatisfactions among the majority of people in Hong Kong, both with their material living conditions and with the prospect that their civil liberties are likely to be eroded by increasing interference by Beijing.[37]

These events underscored both the gulf in values between China and the West and the increased willingness of the Xi Jinping government to use harshly repressive tactics. This heightens legitimate anxieties about China's ability to function peaceably within the global system. There is also rising concern about China acting outside its borders in ways that directly conflict with Western liberal values: abductions in other countries of Chinese nationals for trials at home on criminal or political charges; efforts to influence the United Nations human rights commission to minimize criticism of human rights abuses in China and other authoritarian regimes; and efforts to covertly influence political and academic discourse.[38]

Responding to the challenge of a much larger and more powerful China whose values differ so substantially from those underpinning the U.S,-led international order is a hard task. It involves, first, recognizing that China is not going away and that the challenge is a permanent one. Despite the problems of debt, structural economic transition, an aging population, and so on, China will almost certainly remain a large and relatively fast-growing economy for some years to come, and neither domestic issues nor a campaign of economic pressure by the United States is likely to alter that trajectory.

Similarly, China's system of values, different as it is from that of the West, is not some fragile recent invention but is deeply rooted in Chinese traditions of governance. It is validated for most Chinese people by the nation's developmental successes since 1980. China's governance system has many flaws but has generally proved effective. And it has adapted substantially in response to shifting conditions, even if the Communist Party's monopoly remains intact. Most importantly, outsiders can do little to change it—just as outsiders can do little to change the aspects of the American system they might deplore, such as the capture of the political system by big campaign donors, institutionalized racism, excessive consumption of energy and other resources, and capital punishment.

The stubbornly illiberal nature of China's political system and its lack of convergence with the liberal norms and values of the global system make China's further integration into that system tricky, but not impossible. The global system has accommodated many different kinds of regimes in the past, not just liberal democracies. Moreover, there is no reason why all of the participation of China's government and companies in world affairs must occur within the preexisting frameworks of the U.S.-led system. The world is a large place, with diverse needs; different sources of funding and ideas should therefore be encouraged. Only after much more testing will it become clear which elements of the Chinese model are exportable. (There are good grounds for believing that these will be few.) Moreover, the more Chinese companies and agencies work abroad, the more they will be forced to come to terms with international norms and practices. Chinese-led organizations may compete with or complement existing global institutions, but they cannot yet replace them.

China will never be content to be a U.S. vassal. But in the long run, it may lack the capacity to dislodge the United States from its dominance. The deep uncertainty over China's long-run demographic and economic outlook, and the untapped expansive potential of the U.S. economy, not to mention the richness and robustness of the U.S.-led world order, reduce the odds that China will unseat the United States as the world's technological, cultural, and political leader—assuming that the U.S. acts wisely to shore up its own strengths, a proposition that is now open to much doubt. China demonstrated pragmatism and caution under successive leaders after 1980, and the more assertive policies of Xi Jinping have already begun to run into serious political, economic, and financial constraints only 5 years after being launched. We cannot rule out the possibility that either I or a future Chinese leader will steer the country back in a more pragmatic direction.

It is not impossible to engineer an accommodation under which China enjoys increased prestige and influence—to the extent it can earn it—but the U.S.-led system remains the core of the world's political and economic arrangements. "Containment"—the strategy that ultimately proved successful against the brittle and stagnant Soviet system—is unlikely to work against China, which has proved itself dynamic and adaptable. There is room in the world for both the U.S. and the Chinese systems, as long as people on both sides can agree that this peaceful coexistence is a goal worth striving for.

Appendix

WHAT WILL BE THE IMPACT OF THE COVID-19 EPIDEMIC?

As this book was being readied for publication in early 2020, China grappled with an epidemic of a severe respiratory disease, Covid-19, caused by a new coronavirus related to the virus behind the 2003 SARS (severe acute respiratory syndrome) epidemic. At first it seemed that the epidemic might be limited to China and a few neighboring Asian countries, as SARS was, and that the economic and social impacts, while severe, would be short-lived and limited in scope. This assumption proved too optimistic. While Covid-19 was less lethal than SARS, it was far more contagious, and caused enough severe cases to overwhelm local health-care systems—as in the Chinese city of Wuhan in January 2020 and in northern Italy the next month.

To contain the disease's spread, China essentially shut down its economy for two months beginning in late January. Most other major economies, including the United States, followed suit in mid-to-late March. In China, the immediate impact was a collapse in GDP growth to approximately minus 7 percent year on year in the first quarter of 2020, easily the biggest downturn since the beginning of economic reforms in 1979. Early estimates suggested that the impact on the US and European economies could be at least as large, and the US faced the possibility of an unemployment rate not seen since the Great Depression. Massive monetary and fiscal support programs were launched to offset this damage. These were clearly necessary—but also raised the question of how governments would manage their wider budget deficits and higher debt levels after the epidemic was controlled.

At the time of writing it is far too early to analyze the impact of Covid-19 on China's economic trajectory or China's place in the world with high confidence. But we can make two preliminary observations.

First, the initial response of Chinese policymakers to the economic stress of the epidemic was notable for its conservatism. The People's Bank of China made small cuts to interest rates, and the government raised the ability of local authorities to issue bonds to finance infrastructure projects. But there was nothing like the explosion of debt-fueled infrastructure spending following the 2008 global financial crises, or the credit and investment boosts used to cushion downturns in 2012 and 2015.

China's decision not to fire its fiscal and monetary shotguns also differed sharply from the epidemic response of US and European governments. Within days of realizing the need for long economic lockdowns, both the European Central Bank and the Federal Reserve revived programs of "quantitative easing"—essentially large-scale money printing. The Fed slashed its policy interest rate effectively to zero. And many governments launched huge fiscal support programs to support businesses and workers. The first US fiscal package of March 27 totaled $2 trillion, or nearly 10 percent of GDP— double the size, both in dollars and relative to GDP, of the $787 billion stimulus package passed in 2009 after the global financial crisis.

This is not to imply that Beijing stood idly by while its economy cratered. It launched a plethora of targeted measures, including: tax holidays, suspension of mandatory social security contributions, special loans for small and medium enterprises, vouchers to spur household consumption, and policies to unclog logistics bottlenecks. And as the economic picture in the rest of the world worsens, China will inevitably need to roll out more fiscal support to offset the damage to its export sector. Yet its approach has been cautious and piece-meal, in striking contrast to its past pattern and to the US and European responses. Why?

There seem to be two basic reasons. First, Chinese policy-makers probably underestimated the economic toll of the epidemic. Their economic shutdown coincided with the annual Lunar New Year holiday, when the economy slows to a crawl for two weeks anyway. They probably reckoned that the fallout from deepening and lengthening a normal seasonal lull would not be that great. They also may have failed to predict that the rest of the world economy was going to be devastated too.

The deeper reason, though, is that policymakers were deeply scarred by the long-run consequences of the 2009 stim-ulus, and the lesser but still very large credit expansion of 2012–2013 at the end of the Hu Jintao era. Those sprees did support economic growth, but at the cost of a much higher national debt burden, fiscal irresponsibility by local govern-ments, and a big increase in systemic financial risk. Since late 2016 the central government has been struggling to stabilize debt, more tightly regulate local-government budgets, and reduce systemic risk by curbing shadow finance. Even as the economy slowed in 2018–2019, Beijing stuck to this agenda, on the belief that fiscal and financial discipline was the foun-dation for sustained rapid economic growth in the 2020s. The restrained Covid-19 response indicates that this resolve has not cracked. So it appears that while the epidemic will give China (and the rest of the world) a very bad economic year, it probably will not materially alter the broad direction of gov-ernment economic policy.

Moving past Covid-19's impact on individual economies, the epidemic could also have a noteworthy impact on global governance and China's role in it. But at this early date it is hard to tell whether China's international stature will be raised or reduced.

On the positive side, China handled Covid-19 far better than it did SARS, when the central government covered up the outbreak for months and was reluctant to share information with international health authorities. This time round, China alerted the World Health Organization (WHO) and other nation's health ministries to the existence of the coronavirus in late December 2019, less than three weeks after the first reported case. Several days later, Chinese researchers sequenced the virus's genome and released their findings to the world, speeding up the search for treatments and a vaccine.

After some initial delays, Beijing's January 23 decision to shut the country down dramatically slowed the spread of the virus, and bought the rest of the world valuable time to prepare for their own outbreaks. (Unfortunately, many countries—in particular the United States—squandered this time and suffered worse epidemics as a result.) As it began to emerge from its own lockdown in late March, China began sending supplies and expertise around the world to help other countries manage the disease. The Communist Party lost no time in organizing a huge domestic and international propaganda campaign to tout its success in managing the epidemic and the contributions it was making to global public health.

Yet there are also some serious negatives. Local health officials in Wuhan, where the outbreak originated, kept the public in the dark about the outbreak for weeks after it became clear how serious the disease was. The central government was complicit in this cover-up, continuing to downplay the epidemic in domestic media even as it was sharing information with international health authorities. A group of doctors in Wuhan who defied the local government and sought to spread the word about the disease through social media were detained by local police, silenced, and forced to write self-criticisms. One of them, ophthalmologist Li Wenliang, subsequently died of Covid-19.

And even after the central government acknowledged the extent of the problem, doubts lingered about the reliability of the statistics it published. Eventually—and only after independent media reports and international pressure—the government admitted that, unlike other countries and against the practice recommended by the WHO, it did not include asymptomatic cases in its tally of confirmed cases. This kept its own reported case load down and enabled the government to claim an early and complete victory, but it could have led other countries to underestimate the speed of the virus's spread.

These positives and negatives underscore several patterns that we have observed repeatedly throughout this book. On the one hand, China has a system of governance which is sometimes slow to react and often operates in ways that are not maximally efficient from an economic point of view. Yet when it does react, it is generally effective at achieving its central aims. And over time, its cooperation with other governments and with international institutions has broadly, though unevenly, increased. Its high level of state capacity, technological sophistication (as evidenced by the speed with which its researchers sequenced the coronavirus genome), and rising interest in international engagement suggest that China is well placed to increase its global influence.

Against this, however, we must set China's endemic lack of transparency, the ruling party's paranoid unwillingness to permit any information to be disseminated except through official, controlled government channels, and the brutal suppression of any individual who tries to present an alternative point of view. These harsh restrictions on information and civil liberties are not just out of step with the norms prevailing among the vast majority of advanced societies whose ranks China aspires to join. They also make it hard for other governments to accept that China can ever be a trustworthy partner in international institutions, which are increasingly information-driven and require high standards of data transparency and a willingness of countries not only to take credit for their strengths but to account openly for their weaknesses. Will the Covid-19 epidemic advance or retard China's progress toward becoming a genuine world leader in something other than economic growth? The jury is still out.

—April 5, 2020

FOR FURTHER READING

These suggestions, presenting the most important, easily accessible sources for each chapter in the book, seek to guide readers who wish to delve further into particular topics. Additional sources are in the detailed endnotes for each chapter. As this book is aimed at a nonspecialist readership in English, the sources cited in this bibliographic note and in the endnotes are largely in English. Readers with Chinese-language reading ability will find abundant references to Chinese academic work and primary sources in the books and articles listed here. All cited articles from the *China Economic Quarterly* or the Gavekal Dragonomics research service are available to the public at the website: http://www.china-economy-book.com.

General Overviews

Those who want a more detailed understanding of China' economic development during the reform era, and the challenges it now faces, are referred to four weighty tomes. The authoritative textbook treatment is Barry Naughton, *The Chinese Economy: Adaptation and Growth* (Cambridge, MA: MIT Press, 2018), which updates a first edition published in 2007. Loren Brandt and Thomas G. Rawski (eds.), *China's Great Economic Transformation* (Cambridge: Cambridge University Press, 2008) is an excellent, though often dense, collection of essays by the world's top China scholars.

Also essential are two big reports prepared jointly by the World Bank and the Development Research Center of the State Council, China's leading think-tank. These are *China 2030: Building a Modern, Harmonious and Creative Society* (2013, http://documents.worldbank.org/curated/en/2013/03/17494829/); and *Urban China: Toward*

Efficient, Inclusive and Sustainable Urbanization (2014, http://www.
worldbank.org/en/country/china/publication/urban-china-
toward-efficient-inclusive-sustainable-urbanization). Both reports,
invaluable compendia of the best economic research on China, are
cited extensively throughout this book. In the rest of this section and
in the notes, *China 2030* is cited as World Bank/DRC 2013, and *Urban
China* as World Bank/DRC 2014. Some updates on the issues covered
in those reports are in the World Bank's *China: Systematic Country
Diagnostic* (2018, http://documents.worldbank.org/curated/en/
147231519162198351/China-Systematic-Country-Diagnostic-towards-a-
more-inclusive-and-sustainable-development).

Chapter 1: Why China Matters
See the suggestions for Chapter 15.

Chapter 2: Population, Geography, and History
The standard text on modern Chinese history is Jonathan Spence, *The
Search for Modern China*, 3rd ed. (New York: W. W. Norton, 2012). For
China's imperial history up to 1800, there is an equally large tome, F. W.
Mote, *Imperial China 900–1800* (Cambridge, MA: Harvard University
Press, 1999). Shorter and more accessible is Valerie Hansen, *The Open
Empire: A History of China to 1800*, 2nd ed. (New York: W. W. Norton,
2015). An authoritative economic history of premodern China is
Richard von Glahn, *The Economic History of China: From Antiquity to the
Nineteenth Century* (Cambridge: Cambridge University Press, 2016).
Angus Maddison in *The World Economy* (Paris: OECD, 2007) presents
the standard estimates of China's GDP over the past 2,000 years.
A still-controversial view of China's economic position around 1800 is
Kenneth Pomeranz, *The Great Divergence: China, Europe and the Making
of the Modern World* (Princeton, NJ: Princeton University Press, 2001).
The best history of the pivotal events of the Opium War which opened
the "century of humiliation" is Stephen R. Platt, *Imperial Twilight: The
Opium War and the End of China's Last Golden Age* (New York: Alfred
A. Knopf, 2018). Platt covers the subsequent trauma of the Taiping
Rebellion in *Autumn in the Heavenly Kingdom: China, The West and the
Epic Story of the Taiping Civil War* (New York: Vintage, 2012). A vivid
fictional, but deeply researched, description of the opium trade that
also contains interesting insights into the foundations of China's
manufacturing process is Amitav Ghosh, *River of Smoke* (Farrar, Straus,
& Giroux, 2011).

Chapter 3: China's Political Economy
For an accessible and up-to-date introduction to China's governance
system, see Sebastian Heilmann (ed.), *China's Political System*
(Lanham, MD: Rowman and Littlefield, 2017). An older but still
useful discussion is Kenneth Lieberthal, *Governing China: From
Revolution to Reform*, 2nd ed. (New York: W. W. Norton, 2003). The
indispensable introduction to China's Communist Party is Richard
McGregor, *The Party: The Secret World of China's Communist Rulers*
(New York: Penguin Books, 2011), by a former *Financial Times*
bureau chief in Beijing. David Shambaugh, *China's Communist
Party: Atrophy and Adaptation* (Berkeley: University of California
Press, 2009) is more academic but quite readable; it is especially
good on the lessons learned from the fall of the Soviet Union. An
indispensable study of the party personnel system is Frank N. Pieke,
The Good Communist: Elite Training and State Building in Today's China
(Cambridge: Cambridge University Press, 2009). Ezra Vogel, *Deng
Xiaoping and the Transformation of China* (Cambridge, MA: Belknap
Press, 2013), offers a wealth of valuable party's-eye detail of the
critical 1980s, when the parameters of China's reform era were laid
down. Finally, a dense but provocative analysis of the tensions
between central and local governments is Pierre Landry, *Decentralized
Authoritarianism in China: The Communist Party's Control of Local Elites
in the Post-Mao Era* (Cambridge: Cambridge University Press, 2008).

A readable distillation of the literature on East Asian developmental
states and how China's development strategy compares to that of its
neighbors is Joe Studwell, *How Asia Works: Success and Failure in the
World's Most Dynamic Region* (New York: Grove Press, 2013). The classic
academic accounts include Robert Wade, *Governing the Market: Economic
Theory and the Role of Government in East Asian Industrialization*
(Princeton, NJ: Princeton University Press, 2003); Alice Amsden, *Asia's
Next Giant: South Korea and Late Industrialization* (New York: Oxford
University Press, 1992); and Chalmers Johnston, *MITI and the Japanese
Miracle: The Growth of Industrial Policy, 1925–75* (Cambridge, MA: MIT
Press, 1982).

For a capsule summary of all the major themes of the reform era,
see Ross Garnaut, Ligang Song, and Fang Cai (eds.), *China's 40 Years
of Reform and Development, 1978–2018* (Canberra: Australian National
University Press, 2018). A vivid and fascinating account of the reform
discussions in the 1980s and 1990s, and the influence of foreign

ideas, is Julian Gewirtz, *Unlikely Partners: Chinese Reformers, Western Economists, and the Making of Global China* (Cambridge, MA: Harvard University Press, 2017). Finally, an academic exposition of a basic thesis very similar to my own—that China must be considered a unique combination of East Asian developmental state and postcommunist transitional economy—is Barry Naughton and Kellee S. Tsai (eds.), *State Capitalism, Institutional Adaptation, and the Chinese Miracle* (Cambridge: Cambridge University Press, 2015), especially the introductory chapter by Tsai and Naughton, "State Capitalism and the Chinese Economic Miracle" (1–24).

Chapter 4: Agriculture, Land, and the Rural Economy
A good summary of China's agricultural development is Jikun Huang, Keijiro Otsuka, and Scott Rozelle, "Agriculture in China's Development: Past Disappointments, Recent Successes, and Future Challenges," in Brandt and Rawski (eds.), *China's Great Economic Transformation,* 467–505. A standard description of the rise of rural industry under the aegis of local governments is Jean C. Oi, *Rural China Takes Off: Institutional Foundations of Economic Reform* (Stanford, CA: Stanford University Press, 1999). Land issues are comprehensively covered in World Bank/DRC 2014.

Chapter 5: Industry, Exports, and Technology
The classic account of China's industrial reforms in the early reform era is Barry Naughton, *Growing Out of the Plan: Chinese Economic Reform, 1978–1993* (Cambridge: Cambridge University Press, 1996). More detail, for a longer period of time, is available in Naughton 2018 (*The Chinese Economy: Adaptation and Growth*). A concise summary of the reforms that led to the shift from the import-substitution model to the export-led model is Nicholas Lardy, *Foreign Trade and Economic Reform in China, 1978–1991* (Cambridge: Cambridge University Press, 1993). A later treatment of China's foreign trade on the eve of WTO accession is Nicholas Lardy, *Integrating China into the Global Economy* (Washington, DC: Brookings Institution, 2001). The best treatment of the Made in China 2025 industrial plan is Jost Wuebbeke et al, "Made in China 2025: The Making of a High-Tech Superpower and Consequences for Industrial Companies," Mercator Institute for China Studies, December 2016. https://www.merics.org/en/papers-on-china/made-china-2025.

Chapter 6: Urbanization and Infrastructure
World Bank/DRC 2014 is an exhaustive treatment of urbanization issues, with extensive references to scholarly literature in English

and Chinese. Another detailed overview is *OECD Urban Policy Reviews: China 2015* (Paris: OECD Publishing, 2015). A lively popular treatment of China's urbanization push is by my colleague Tom Miller, *China's Urban Billion: The Story behind the Biggest Migration in Human History* (London: Asian Arguments, 2012).

Chapter 7: The Enterprise System
Nicholas Lardy, *Markets over Mao: The Rise of Private Business in China* (Washington, DC: Peterson Institute of International Economics, 2014), forcefully advances the thesis that the private sector has steadily progressed throughout the reform era and that China's impressive economic growth has depended heavily on this advance. Note, however, that in a subsequent book, *The State Strikes Back: The End of Economic Reform in China?* (Washington, DC: Peterson Institute of International Economics, 2019), Lardy concedes that in recent years the advance of the private sector has slowed and in some cases has reversed itself. Yasheng Huang, *Capitalism with Chinese Characteristics: Entrepreneurship and the State* (Cambridge: Cambridge University Press, 2008) argues, in contrast, that a brief experiment with a relatively free private sector in the 1980s gave way to a state-driven economic model in the 1990s and 2000s. Tsai and Naughton (2014; cited above for Chapter 3) also make a compelling case against underestimating the state role. My account of the structure of state-owned enterprise groups is drawn mainly from Li-Wen Lin and Curtis J. Milhaupt, "We Are the (National) Champions: Understanding the Mechanisms of State Capitalism in China," *Stanford Law Review* 65 (April 2013): 697–759. See also Curtis J. Milhaupt and Wentong Zheng, "Beyond Ownership: State Capitalism and the Chinese Firm," *Georgetown Law Journal*, 103, 665–722).

Chapter 8: The Government Finance System
The most recent good survey of fiscal issues is Philippe Wingender, *Intergovernmental Fiscal Reform in China*, IMF Working Paper WP/18/88, April 2018. An accessible, though slightly dated, overview is Lou Jiwei (ed.), *Public Finance in China: Reform and Growth for a Harmonious Society* (Washington, DC: World Bank, 2008). (Lou Jiwei was one of the architects of the 1994 tax reform and was minister of finance in 2013–2016.) World Bank/DRC 2014 contains a good discussion of fiscal issues (54–62 and 371–446). *OECD Urban Policy Reviews: China 2015* presents a comprehensive treatment of the fiscal system and related governance issues (159–228). A technical discussion of the central-local transfer

system is Xiao Wang and Richard Herd, "The System of Revenue Sharing and Fiscal Transfers in China," OECD Economics Department Working Papers, No. 1030 (Paris: OECD Publishing, 2013). An easy-to-read comparison of central–local governance problems in both China and India—which reminds us that the problems of effectively managing a huge country are not unique to China—is William Antholis, *Inside Out India and China: Local Politics Go Global* (Washington, DC: Brookings Institution, 2013). This work reminds us that the problems of effectively managing a huge country are not unique to China.

Chapter 9: The Financial System
The dean of China financial experts is Nicholas Lardy, who has devoted much of his time since the late 1990s to untangling the mysteries of this opaque system. Those interested in a deeper understanding of Chinese finance should consult three of his books. (1) *China's Unfinished Economic Revolution* (Washington, DC: Brookings Institution, 1998) describes the evolution of the banking system in the first two decades of reform and how it led to the effective bankruptcy of Chinese banks in the late 1990s. (2) *Sustaining China's Economic Growth after the Global Financial Crisis* (Washington, DC: Peterson Institute of International Economics, 2012) analyzes the mechanisms of financial repression and makes the case for interest rate liberalization as the key to unlocking future growth. (3) *Markets over Mao* (cited above in Chapter 5) provocatively argues that a majority of bank credit now goes to the private sector. A curmudgeonly but intensely well-informed look at China's capital markets by two former bankers is Carl Walter and Fraser Howie, *Red Capitalism: The Fragile Financial Foundation of China's Extraordinary Rise* (Hoboken, NJ: John Wiley, 2012).

Chapter 10: Energy and the Environment
The foundation for understanding China's energy system is the work done by the China Energy Group (CEG) at the Lawrence Berkeley Laboratory, under Mark Levine. CEG has done excellent work monitoring the structure of China's energy use and modeling the future trajectory of energy consumption and greenhouse gas emissions. Its most important publication is the China Energy Databook, now in its ninth edition (free download from https://china.lbl.gov/china-energy-databook), which contains a wealth of time series data on energy production, consumption, and prices. A distilled version is *Key Energy Statistics 2016* (https://china.lbl.gov/publications/key-china-energy-statistics-2016). CEG also offers hundreds of shorter papers on

virtually every aspect of China's energy system on its publications page
(https://china.lbl.gov/publications).

A good introduction to the structure of China's energy production
and use and possible future trends is *Reinventing Fire: China: A
Roadmap for China's Revolution in Energy Consumption and Production
to 2050* (National Development and Reform Commission, Lawrence
Berkeley National Laboratory, Rocky Mountain Institute and Energy
Foundation China, 2016). An academic overview is Philip Andrews-
Speed, *The Governance of Energy in China: Transition to a Low-Carbon
Economy* (London: Palgrave Macmillan, 2012). Two useful compendia
of international energy data are the *BP Statistical Review of World Energy*
and the Enerdata Global Energy Statistical Yearbook 2019 (https://
yearbook.enerdata.net/).

For a general summary of China's environmental problems, see
Elizabeth Economy, *The River Runs Black: The Environmental Challenge
to China's Future*, 2nd ed. (Ithaca, NY: Cornell University Press, 2010);
Ma Jun, *China's Water Crisis* (Hong Kong: Pacific Century Press,
2004); and Jonathan Watts, *When a Billion Chinese Jump: How China
Will Save Mankind—Or Destroy It* (New York: Scribner, 2010). The Yale
Environmental Performance Index (http://epi.yale.edu/epi) provides
excellent internationally comparable data on all types of environmental
degradation. Comprehensive data on greenhouse gas emissions is in
the ClimateWatch database managed by the World Resources Institute
(https://www.climatewatchdata.org).

Chapter 11: Demographics and the Labor Market
The standard work on China's demography is Judith Banister, *China's
Changing Population* (Stanford, CA: Stanford University Press, 1987).
Although it obviously does not cover recent developments, it is the
authoritative account of deaths from China's great famine of 1958–1961,
the subsequent population boom, and the efforts to control population
growth in the 1970s and 1980s that culminated in the one-child policy.
For a detailed account of the great famine by a dogged and heroic
Chinese journalist, see Yang Jisheng, *Tombstone: The Untold Story of
Mao's Great Famine* (New York: Farrar, Straus & Giroux, 2012).

An excellent forward-looking overview of labor market,
demographic, and educational issues and their impact on economic
growth is Hongbin Li, Prashant Loyalka, Scott Rozelle, and Binzhen
Wu, "Human Capital and China's Future Growth," *Journal of Economic
Perspectives* (Winter 2017): 1–26. An earlier good treatment of the labor
market is Fang Cai, Albert Park, and Yaohui Zhao, "The Chinese

Labor Market in the Reform Era," in Brandt and Rawski, *China's Great Economic Transformation*, 167–214. The idea of the "Lewis turning point" derives from W. Arthur Lewis, "Economic Development with Unlimited Supplies of Labour," *Manchester School of Economic and Social Studies* 22 (1954): 139–191, (http://www.globelicsacademy.net/2008/2008_lectures/lewis%20unlimited%20labor%20supply%201954.pdf). A brief summary and explanation of its relevance to China are in World Bank/DRC 2014, 89. This essay is essential reading for anyone who wants to understand the dynamics of growth in a developing economy and how they differ from those of rich countries.

Chapter 12: The Emerging Consumer Economy
Detailed scholarly study of the Chinese consumer economy remains a thing of the future. I have instead relied heavily on commercial research, including work done by my colleagues at Gavekal Dragonomics, which is available at the firm's public website, http://www.china-economy-book.com. The best discussions of the size of China's middle class, the "middle-income trap," and the construction of the social safety net are in World Bank/DRC 2014, 104–105 and 198–214.

Chapter 13: The Social Compact
The classic statement of the view that inequality arises naturally during a period of rapid industrialization and then declines as an economy matures is Simon Kuznets, "Economic Growth and Income Inequality," *American Economic Review* 45, no. 1 (1955): 1–28; available at https://28.pdf. World Bank/DRC 2014 contains much good discussion of China's inequality problems. For internationally comparable inequality data, see the Standardized World Income Inequality Database (SWIID), version 8.1, https://dataverse.harvard.edu/dataset.xhtml?persistentId=doi:10.7910/DVN/LM4OWF.

For the discussion of corruption, I have relied extensively on Andrew Wedeman's excellent *Double Paradox: Rapid Growth and Rising Corruption in China* (Ithaca, NY: Cornell University Press, 2012). The best statement of the view that rampant corruption risks stifling economic growth and undermining the political system is Minxin Pei, *China's Crony Capitalism: The Dynamics of Regime Decay* (Cambridge, MA: Harvard University Press, 2016), which updates his earlier *China's Trapped Transition: The Limits of Developmental Autocracy* (Cambridge, MA: Harvard University Press, 2006).

Chapter 14: Changing the Growth Model
Amid the flood of discussions since the 2008 global financial crisis about China's need to "rebalance" or "change its growth model," two works stand out. One is World Bank/DRC 2013, which was consciously designed as a comprehensive reform agenda for the next two decades. The other is the *Economic Survey of China 2015* by the OECD, available at http://www.oecd.org/eco/surveys/economic-survey-china.htm), a detailed and rigorous assessment of China's current challenges and the reforms needed to address them.

Chapter 15: China and the World: Is Conflict Inevitable?
An enormous literature on China's role in the world and the appropriate responses to it has emerged in the past decade, catalyzed by two shifts: Xi Jinping's adoption of a more assertive international policy, and especially the launch of the Belt and Road Initiative in 2013; and the Trump Administration's adoption of a more adversarial stance toward China beginning in 2017. This list is a starter's guide to the main thematic areas.

First, since the vast majority of the following citations are in English, presenting a Western point of view, it is worth noting two volumes that present Chinese perspectives. China's most prominent international relations scholar is Yan Xuetong, whose *Ancient Chinese Thought: Modern Chinese Power* (Princeton, NJ: Princeton University Press, 2011) offers a good summary of how the Chinese elite see their nation's place in the world. Nina Hachigian (ed.), *Debating China: The US-China Relationship in Ten Conversations* (New York: Oxford University Press, 2014) usefully pairs American and Chinese views.

A good overview of assessment of China's economic engagements with the rest of the world is Jonathan Woetzel et al., *China and the World: Inside the Dynamics of a Changing Relationship*, McKinsey Global Institute (July 2019). For China's technological capacities, a balanced assessment is Scott Kennedy, *The Fat Tech Dragon: Benchmarking China's Innovation Drive* (Washington, DC: Center for Strategic and International Studies, 2017). A less balanced but provocative view, which contains an excellent summary of the development of China's internet, is by Kai-fu Lee, who headed Google's China office in 2006–2010: *AI Superpowers: China, Silicon Valley and the New World Order* (Boston: Houghton Mifflin, 2018). The U.S. Defense Department paper that led to the adoption of stricter controls on exports and investments is Michael Brown and Pavneet Singh, *China's Technology Transfer Strategy: How Chinese Investments in Emerging Technology Enable a*

Strategic Competitor to Access the Crown Jewels of U.S. Innovation (Defense Innovation Unit Experimental, 2018).

On trade, the key work on the impact of Chinese imports on the U.S. labor market is a series of articles principally authored by MIT Economist David H. Autor: David H. Autor, David Dorn, and Gordon H. Hanson, "The China Syndrome: Local Labor Market Effects of Import Competition in the United States," National Bureau of Economic Research (NBER) Working Paper 18054 (May 2012); Autor, Dorn, and Hanson, "The China Shock: Learning from Labor Market Adjustment to Large Changes in Trade," NBER Working Paper 21906 (January 2016); David H. Autor, "Trade and Labor Markets: Lessons from China's Rise," IZA World of Labor (February 2018). A careful treatment of the problems China poses for the WTO is Mark Wu, "The 'China Inc.' Challenge to Global Trade Governance," *Harvard International Law Journal* (Spring 2016), 57: 261–324. A comprehensive analysis of China's role in global governance more generally is Scott Kennedy (ed.), *Global Governance and China* (New York: Routledge, 2017).

On the Belt and Road Initiative, a good starting point is the work of David Dollar, scholar at the Brookings Institution who previously served in Beijing as head of the World Bank office and as US Treasury attaché. See inter alia Amar Bhattacharya, David Dollar et al., "China's Belt and Road: The Geopolitics of Global Infrastructure Development," Brookings Institution (April 2019) and "China's Engagement with Africa: From Natural Resources to Human Resources" (Washington, DC: Brookings Institution, July 13, 2016). Deborah Brautigam's *The Dragon's Gift: The Real Story of China in Africa* (New York: Oxford University Press, 2011) is another clear-eyed account of the pluses and minuses of China's engagement in Africa, and a good corrective to early hyperbolic accounts suggesting that China was simply a neocolonialist invader intent on extracting natural resources and propping up dictators.

On China's military capabilities and intentions, two level-headed studies are George J. Gilboy and Eric Heginbotham, *Chinese and Indian Strategic Behavior: Growing Power and Alarm* (Cambridge: Cambridge University Press, 2012) and M. Taylor Fravel, *Active Defense: China's Military Strategy Since 1949* (Princeton, NJ: Princeton University Press, 2019).

Finally, to navigate the swirling debate on the proper course for U.S.–China relations, an enduringly useful starting point is Aaron L. Friedberg, "The Future of US-China Relations: Is Conflict

Inevitable?" *International Security* 30, no. 2(Autumn 2005): 7–45, which lucidly lays out the key arguments and assumptions on all sides. Major statements of the need for a more adversarial U.S. policy toward China are Friedberg, *A Contest for Supremacy: China, America and the Struggle for Asia* (New York: W. W. Norton, 2011) and Robert Blackwill and Ashley Tellis, "Revising U.S. Grand Strategy Toward China," Council on Foreign Relations Special Report No. 72, March 2015. The case for a more restrained approach is made by Thomas Christensen, *The China Challenge: Shaping the Choices of a Rising Power* (New York: W. W. Norton, 2015); and Jeffrey A. Bader, "Changing China Policy: Are We in Search of Enemies?" (New York: Brookings Institution, June 2015). A pungent critique of both Xi Jinping's assertiveness and the United States' counterpunch is Susan Shirk, "Overreach and Overreaction: The Crisis In US-China Relations" (podcast; https://cscc.sas.upenn.edu/podcasts/2019/02/07/ep-9-overreach-and-overreaction-crisis-us-china-relations-susan-shirk), University of Pennsylvania Center for the Study of Contemporary China (February 7, 2019).

NOTES

Chapter 1

1. Foreign capital and technology were important, but foreign ideas and expertise were perhaps more so. For a vivid account of the influence of foreign institutions and economists in shaping much of the economic reform agenda of the 1980s and 1990s, see Julian Gewirtz, *Unlikely Partners: Chinese Reformers, Western Economists and the Making of Global China* (Cambridge, MA: Harvard University Press, 2017).

2. The phrase "crossing the river by feeling for the stones" was frequently used by both Deng and his rival Chen Yun, a more conservative official who essentially ran China's economic planning bureaucracy throughout the 1980s. In recent years, use of this phrase has lessened in favor of "top-level design," a slogan coined by Xi Jinping's top economic adviser, Liu He, to stress the need for greater central control. The Third Plenum Decision of 2013, Xi's first important economic strategy document, uses the odd phrase "strengthen the combination of top-level design with crossing the river by feeling for the stones" (*jiaqiang dingceng sheji he mozhe shitou guohe xiang jiehe*). This phrase nicely captures the tension between Chinese leaders' desire for all-encompassing plans and the messy, intractable reality that they must confront.

3. Alexander Gerschenkron, *Economic Backwardness in Historical Perspective* (Cambridge, MA: Belknap Press, 1962).

4. Paul Collier, *The Bottom Billion* (New York: Oxford University Press, 2008), points out that proximity to coasts with good ports and to other rich neighbors are virtually prerequisites for high-speed growth.

5. Elizabeth C. Economy, *The Third Revolution: Xi Jinping and the New Chinese State* (Oxford: Oxford University Press, 2018), 17.

Chapter 2

1. This includes twenty-two provinces, five "autonomous regions" that are ostensibly organized to permit some self-government for large ethnic minorities, and four independent municipalities, the largest of which, Chongqing, occupies an area the size of Austria. All these administrative units are at the same level in China's administrative hierarchy and will be referred to collectively as "provinces" in this book.

2. To be precise, 43 percent of China's land area lies east of the Hu Line and 57 percent to the west. An engaging illustration of the divisions implied by the Hu Line is "Hu Line: China's Forgotten Frontier," Sixth Tone, July 5, 2017. https://www.sixthtone.com/news/1000459/hu-line-chinas-forgotten-frontier.

3. For China's share of global GDP over the past 2,000 years, see Angus Maddison, *The World Economy: A Millennial Perspective* (Organization for Economic Cooperation and Development, 2006). For a still controversial view of China's position around 1800, see Kenneth J. Pomeranz, *The Great Divergence: China, Europe and the Making of the Modern World* (Princeton, NJ: Princeton University Press, 2001).

4. Seeking a commodity other than silver to balance its trade with China, Great Britain resorted to exports of opium grown in its Indian colonies. China prohibited imports of this drug, and its effort to enforce its ban led to the war. Britain won, and under the subsequent treaty it and other European powers gained greatly expanded trading rights within China. An authoritative history of the Opium War, its background and consequences, is Stephen R. Platt, *Imperial Twilight: The Opium War and the End of China's Last Golden Age* (New York: Alfred A. Knopf, 2018). Platt also wrote an excellent history of the Taiping Rebellion: *Autumn in the Heavenly Kingdom: China, the West and the Epic Story of the Taiping Rebellion* (New York: Alfred A. Knopf, 2012).

5. The best one-volume account of the Mao years is Andrew G. Walder, *China under Mao: A Revolution Derailed* (Cambridge, MA: Harvard University Press, 2015). An accessible account of the impact of China's nineteenth-century humiliations on its later politics is Orville Schell and John DeLury, *Wealth*

and Power: China's Long March to the Twenty-First Century
(New York: Random House, 2014).

Chapter 3

1. Technically, several other parties exist, but in practice they have no influence on government or the right to contest elections.

2. Richard McGregor, *The Party: The Secret Life of China's Communist Rulers* (Bristol, UK: Allen Lane, 2010), 72.

3. See Philip C. C. Huang et al., "Development 'Planning' in Present-Day China—Systems, Process and Mechanism," *Modern China* 20, no. 10 (2013): 1–78, for a detailed discussion from both Chinese and Western perspectives on the policy planning process.

4. All these generalizations are subject to the caveat that the party's internal workings are kept secret, so we don't know details about how power is exercised.

5. Strictly speaking, the power transitions are spread out over several months, with control of the party transferred at the Party Congress in the autumn and of the government and military at the National People's Congress session the following March. For the 1992 succession specifically, see Ezra Vogel, *Deng Xiaoping and the Transformation of China* (Cambridge, MA: Harvard University Press, 2012), 684–688.

6. Retirement rules were bent to enable Wang Qishan, a close confidant of Xi Jinping, to assume the new position of vice president after the 2017 Party Congress, when due to age he was forced to retire from the Politburo. But the fact that Wang observed the retirement rule and stayed on only by the creation of a special position suggests that the norms and institutions of the collective leadership system still have force, and Xi cannot simply do whatever he wants.

7. Actually, a misnomer, since numerous exceptions enabled many families to have more than one child. See Chapter 8 for details.

8. A good study of this paradox is Pierre Landry, *Decentralized Authoritarianism in China* (Cambridge: Cambridge University Press, 2008).

9. For instance, in 1979 Chinese central planners controlled the allocation of 600 commodities and the prices of a few thousand; Soviet central planners allocated 60,000 commodities and set millions of prices. The USSR had 40,000 state-run factories, many

of which were run directly from Moscow; China had 883,000,
of which 90 percent were run by city and country governments.
This decentralization partly resulted from China's geographical
size, population density and poor transport links, but was also
a deliberate strategy of Mao, who wanted industry dispersed
so that it would be less vulnerable to military attack. See Barry
Naughton, *Growing Out of the Plan: Chinese Economic Reform 1978–
1993* (Cambridge: Cambridge University Press, 1995), 40–50.

10. Varieties of this argument can be found in Susan Shirk,
China: Fragile Superpower (London: Oxford University Press,
2008); Minxin Pei, *China's Trapped Transition* (Cambridge,
MA: Harvard University Press, 2006); and Will Hutton, *The
Writing on the Wall* (New York: Free Press, 2006). A strong
counterargument, laying out the sources of the party's
durability and the logic of its governance system, is in
Frank N. Pieke, *Knowing China: A Twenty-First Century Guide*
(Cambridge: Cambridge University Press, 2016).

11. Vogel, *Deng Xiaoping and the Transformation of China*, 677.

12. Ibid., 677–681.

13. In Chinese, *fazhan cai shi ying daoli*. This phrase is often translated
as "Development is the only hard truth." I am grateful to Robert
Kapp for the suggestion that "iron law" better captures the
implication that development is a positive mandate imposed by
the party, rather than an unavoidable and perhaps unpleasant
necessity.

14. Vogel *Deng Xiaoping and the Transformation of China*, 423.

15. David Shambaugh, *China's Communist Party: Atrophy and
Adaptation* (Washington, DC: Woodrow Wilson Center,
2008), 60–81.

16. Survey data suggests that, so far, the Communist Party is
doing a good job of bolstering its legitimacy through provision
of public goods as well as income growth. And a surprising
number of urban Chinese seem to consider that China is already
"democratic" in some respects. See Bruce J. Dickson, *The
Dictator's Dilemma: The Chinese Communist Party's Strategy for
Survival* (New York: Oxford University Press, 2016).

17. Andrew Batson, "Is China Heading for the Middle-Income
Trap?" Gavekal Dragonomics research note, September 6, 2011.

18. The presentation of the East Asian development model from
which this section is mainly drawn is Joe Studwell, *How Asia*

Works (London: Profile Books, 2013). For more detail, see the sources listed in "For Further Reading." See also Arthur R. Kroeber, "Developmental Dreams: Policy and Reality in China's Economic Reforms," in Scott Kennedy, ed., *Beyond the Middle Kingdom: Comparative Perspectives on China's Capitalist Transformation* (Stanford, CA: Stanford University Press, 2011), 44–65.

19. List's importance of as the progenitor of the East Asian model is noted by Studwell (2013), as well as by James Fallows in his useful 1980s survey of the rising Asian economies, *Looking at the Sun* (Vintage, 1995).

20. See Yasheng Huang, *Capitalism with Chinese Characteristics* (Cambridge: Cambridge University Press, 2008).

21. A detailed analysis of the LSGs is Christopher K. Johnson, Scott Kennedy, and Mingda Qiu, "Xi's Signature Governance Innovation: The Rise of Leading Small Groups," Center for Strategic and International Studies, October 17, 2017 (https://www.csis.org/analysis/xis-signature-governance-innovation-rise-leading-small-groups).

Chapter 4

1. Wing Thye Woo, "The Art of Reforming Centrally-Planned Economies: Comparing China, Poland and Russia," *Journal of Comparative Economics* (June 1994): 276–308.

2. Concise descriptions of socialist-era agriculture and the early agricultural reforms are in Barry Naughton, *The Chinese Economy: Adaptation and Growth* (Cambridge, MA: MIT Press, 2018), 261–272, and in Nicholas Lardy, *Markets over Mao: The Rise of Private Business in China* (Washington, DC: Peterson Institute for International Economics, 2014), 60–62. For a more detailed overview of China's agricultural development, see Jikun Huang, Keijiro Otsuka, and Scott Rozelle, "Agriculture in 'China's Development: Past Disappointments, Recent Successes and Future Challenges,' in Loren Brandt and Thomas G. Rawski (eds.), *China's Great Economic Transformation* (Cambridge: Cambridge University Press, 2008), 467–505. A detailed discussion of Chinese agriculture up through 1982 is in Nicholas Lardy, *Agriculture in China's Modern Economic Development* (Cambridge: Cambridge University Press, 1983).

3. This data is from Naughton, *The Chinese Economy*, 268–269. Data on rural cash savings are from Jean Oi, *Rural China Takes Off* (Berkeley: University of California Press, 1999), 26.

4. Barry Naughton, *Growing of the Plan: Chinese Economic Reform 1978–93* (Cambridge: Cambridge University Press, 1995), 153.
5. Naughton, *The Chinese Economy*, 307–321. In 1995, total employment in China was 680 million, of which 120 million worked in rural enterprises (National Bureau of Statistics).
6. Chinese government data, sourced from the CEIC database. This is the ratio between urban per capita disposable income and rural per capita net income.
7. Gap between rural and urban incomes: World Bank/Democratic Republic of the Congo (DRC) 2013, 9; also see World Bank/DRC 2014, 105. Rural pension coverage: Thomas Gatley and Andrew Batson, "China's Welfare State: Mission Accomplished?" Gavekal Dragonomics research note, March 19, 2013. In 2014, the rural pension scheme was merged with the pension system for unemployed urban workers, making it difficult to tease out the number of rural people covered. By the end of 2018, the total number covered under this combined scheme, both urban and rural, was 943 million people.
8. The World Bank's definition of extreme poverty is daily expenditure of less than $1.90, in 2010 dollars adjusted for purchasing power parity (PPP). See http://povertydata. worldbank.org/poverty/country/CHN, which also enables one to display the reductions since 1990 in the number of people under other poverty thresholds. Even using a higher standard (daily expenditure of $3.20), the number of China's poor fell from one billion in 1990 to 95 million in 2015. By any measure, China's poverty-reduction efforts have been more successful than those of any other developing country.
9. The Landesa survey, its fifth in China, is "China's Farmers Benefiting from Land Tenure Reform," February 2011, http://www.landesa.org/where-we-work/china/research-report-2010-findings-17-province-china-survey. Specifically, Landesa found that 63 percent of farmers had land-right certificates and 53 percent had land-rights contracts, but only 44 percent had both as required by law. Landesa also found the persistence of many abuses, including inadequate compensation for land converted to urban use and forced leases to agribusinesses. See also Lardy, *Markets over Mao*, 61; and John Bruce, "China's Land System Reform: What Comes after the Third Plenum?" unpublished paper for World Bank Conference on Land Tenure, March 2015.

10. World Bank/DRC 2014, 17.

11. This arrangement may sound strange to Americans, who are used to freehold property rights, but it exists in other countries. Much of the real property in England is leasehold, as is all real property in Hong Kong, where the normal term of the leasehold is 99 years.

12. "Rural construction land" refers to rural land used for structures (mainly village housing, but also commercial and small-scale industrial buildings) rather than for cultivation.

13. This discussion largely follows Bruce, "China's Land System Reform." For a good discussion of the most recent developments in the land reform discussion, see Barry Naughton, "Is There A 'Xi Model' of Economic Reform? Acceleration of Economic Reform since Fall 2014," *China Leadership Monitor* 46 (Winter 2015), http://www.hoover.org/publications/china-leadership-monitor/spring-2015-issue-46.

14. A similar issue exists in regard to urban property, which has been overwhelmingly registered in men's names. See Leta Hong Fincher, *Leftover Women: The Resurgence of Gender Inequality in China* (London: Zed Books, 2014).

15. See Lester Brown, *Who Will Feed China?* (Washington, DC: Worldwatch Institute,1995) and *Full Planet, Empty Plates: The New Geopolitics of Food Scarcity* (New York: W. W. Norton, 2012).

16. Will Freeman, "How to Feed a Dragon," Gavekal Dragonomics research note, February 26, 2013.

17. A nice capsule summary of China's progress in expanding agricultural production, complete with interactive infographics, is "How Is China Feeding Its Population of 1.4 Billion?" Center for Security and International Studies, https://chinapower.csis.org/china-food-security/. For a discussion of how the focus of food security is also being broadened beyond the mere minimization of imports to include food safety, a rising concern among China's urban middle class, see Robert Ash, "A New Line on Food Security," *China Economic Quarterly* (September 2014): 45–48. Another good survey of food security issues is David Norse, Yuelai Lu, and Jikun Huang, "China's Food Security: Is It a National, Regional or Global Issue?" in Kerry Brown (ed.), *China and the EU in Context: Insights for Business and Investors* (London: Palgrave Macmillan, 2014).

Chapter 5

1. Trade data from World Trade Organization. Manufacturing data from the World Bank's World Development Indicators database. A good cross-country comparison is Daniel J. Meckstroth, "China Has a Dominant Share of World Manufacturing," Manufacturers Alliance for Productivity and Innovation, January 6, 2014, https://www.mapi.net/china-has-dominant-share-world-manufacturing.

2. Prasannan Parthasarathi, *Why Europe Grew Rich and Asia Did Not* (Cambridge: Cambridge University Press, 2011).

3. For a convincing discussion of the importance of Hong Kong's "soft" legal infrastructure to China's economic development in the 1980s and 1990s, see Yasheng Huang, *Capitalism with Chinese Characteristics* (Cambridge: Cambridge University Press, 2008), 1–10.

4. For price data, see Nicolas Lardy, *Markets over Mao: The Rise of Private Business in China* (Washington, DC: Peterson Institute for International Economics, 2014). For SOE market share data, see Loren Brandt, Thomas Rawski, and John Sutton, "China's Industrial Development," in Loren Brandt and Thomas G. Rawski, *China's Great Economic Transformation* (Cambridge: Cambridge University Press 2008), 572.

5. For an accessible explanation of this "golden age" of Chinese exports, see Alexandra Harney, *The China Price* (New York: Penguin Books, 2008).

6. The environmental scientist Vaclav Smil calculated that China used more cement in the 3 years 2011–2013 than the United States did during the entire twentieth century. This is a frightening statistic but skewed by the fact that in China virtually all housing and many rural roads are built with concrete, whereas in the United States wood-frame housing and asphalt paving are the norms. Measured on a per capita basis against other big Asian countries, China's consumption of steel and cement still looks high but not so outlandish. See http://www.independent.co.uk/news/world/asia/how-did-china-use-more-cement-between-2011-and-2013-than-the-us-used-in-the-entire-20th-century-10134079.html. For a good overview of the cement industry, see http://www.globalcement.com/magazine/articles/796-china-first-in-cement.

7. The term *indigenous innovation* was introduced in the "National Medium and Long-term Plan for Science and

Technology Development (2006–2020)" (summary English version here: https://www.itu.int/en/ITU-D/Cybersecurity/Documents/National_Strategies_Repository/China_2006.pdf).

8. Specifically, the Key Technologies R&D Program, focusing on industrial technology; the 863 Program (basic and applied research); the Torch Program (commercialization of high-tech projects); the 973 Program (cutting-edge projects); and the Spark Program (technology development in rural areas). A handy review is Joel R. Campbell, "Becoming a Techno-Industrial Power: Chinese Science and Technology Policy," *Brookings Issues in Technology Innovation* (Washington, DC: Brookings Institution, April 2013). https://www.brookings.edu/wp-content/uploads/2016/06/29-science-technology-policy-china-campbell.pdf

9. Technically, the "Decision of the CCP Central Committee Concerning Some Major Issues in Comprehensively Deepening Reform," passed at the Third Plenum of the 18th Central Committee of the CCP, November 12, 2013. The first plenary session (or "plenum") of the CCP Central Committee in each 5-year party congress session ratifies the selection of the new leadership team. The second plenum, held a few months later, conventionally deals with other personnel issues. The third plenum, usually held about a year after the first, is the traditional venue for the new leadership team to unveil its policy agenda. The first plenum under the Eighteenth Party Congress, in November 2012, named Xi Jinping CCP leader. The third plenum, in November 2013, issued the "Decision." The document is sometimes called "The Sixty Decisions," from the number of specific policy proposals. English translation: https://chinacopyrightandmedia.wordpress.com/2013/11/15/ccp-central-committee-resolution-concerning-some-major-issues-in-comprehensively-deepening-reform/. In Chinese: http://cpc.people.com.cn/n/2013/1115/c64094-23559163.html.

10. The original Made in China 2025 policy document (in Chinese) is at http://news.china.com/domestic/945/20150519/19710486_all.html. An excellent analysis of the strategy and its international implications is Jost Wuebbeke et al., "Made in China 2025: The Making of a High-Tech Superpower and Consequences for Industrial Companies," Mercator Institute for China Studies, December 2016, https://www.merics.org/en/papers-on-china/made-china-2025. A sector-by-sector breakdown of market-share

targets is in "Made In China 2025: Global Ambitions Built on Local Protections," U.S. Chamber of Commerce, March 2017, https://www.uschamber.com/report/made-china-2025-global-ambitions-built-local-protections-0. Chinese officials have consistently claimed that the market-share targets are not official policy, since they were in a think-tank report rather than in the main policy document.

11. Yoko Kubota, "China Sets Up New $29 Billion Semiconductor Fund," *Wall Street Journal*, October 25, 2019. https://www.wsj.com/articles/china-sets-up-new-29-billion-semiconductor-fund-11572034480

12. For details on guidance funds, see Lance Noble, "Paying for Industrial Policy," Gavekal Dragonomics, December 4, 2018.

13. For this comparison, see Arthur R. Kroeber, "Developmental Dreams: Policy and Reality in China's Economic Reforms," in Scott Kennedy, ed., *Beyond the Middle Kingdom: Comparative Perspectives on China's Capitalist Transformation* (Stanford, CA: Stanford University Press, 2011), 44–65.

14. Much investment by multinational companies in China is routed through Hong Kong subsidiaries.

15. Round-tripping is hard to measure, but analysts have long used the one-third figure as a rule of thumb.

16. For U.S. subsidies, see Lardy, *Markets over Mao*, 35–36.

17. See Tim Wu, "China's Online Censorship Stifles Trade, Too," *New York Times*, February 4, 2019. https://www.nytimes.com/2019/02/04/opinion/china-censorship-internet.html

18. Francis Cabot Lowell was unable to buy plans or drawings for the power looms that were essential for efficient production of modern textiles. So he talked his way into factories in Lancashire and made careful notes of the machinery so that he could replicate it back home in Lowell, Massachusetts. The role of textiles in the world economy of the 1820s was comparable to that of electronics today. What Lowell did then would now be considered industrial espionage.

19. Although it is a political document, the United States Trade Representative's (USTR) March 2018 investigation on China's trade practices contains a convincing catalogue of China's induced technology transfers and its persistent violation of commitments not to permit such transfers. See USTR, "Findings of the Investigation into China's Acts, Policies and Practices

Related to Technology Transfer, Intellectual Property, and Innovation" (March 27, 2018). https://ustr.gov/sites/default/files/Section%20301%20FINAL.PDF

20. See Brandt, Rawski, and Sutton, "China's Industrial Development," in Brandt and Rawski (ed.), *China's Great Economic Transformation* (2008).

21. See G. E. Anderson, *Designated Drivers: How China Plans to Dominate the Global Auto Industry* (Hoboken, NJ: John Wiley, 2012). For a condensed version, see G. E. Anderson, "Fat Profits, Fat Failures," *China Economic Quarterly* (June 2012): 43–47.

22. As the United States mounted a campaign to get its allies to ban the use of Huawei telecom equipment on security grounds, many countries pushed back, arguing that Huawei's equipment was the best available for 5G networks. See Stu Woo, "U.S. Push Against Huawei Gear Hits an Obstacle: Carriers That Love It," *Wall Street Journal*, February 14, 2019. https://www.wsj.com/articles/european-carriers-like-their-huawei-gear-despite-u-s-concerns-11550140200

23. For an excellent, readable, and nontechnical definition of innovation, see Amar Bhidé, *The Venturesome Economy* (Princeton, NJ: Princeton University Press, 2008).

24. Standard Chinese dictionaries translate *zizhu* as "independence, autonomy" (*Far East Chinese-English Dictionary* [Henrietta, NY: Far East Book Company, 1993]) or "to act on one's own, decide for oneself" (*Hanying Cidian* [Long Island, NY: Commercial Press, 1995]). It is clearly related to the term *zizhuquan*, which is one of the Chinese words for "sovereignty."

Chapter 6

1. For historical U.S. urban population data, see http://www.census.gov/population/www/censusdata/files/table-4.pdf. For South Korea, see the UN Population Division database, http://esa.un.org/unpd/wup. Combined size of New York and Philadelphia metro areas drawn from https://factfinder.census.gov/faces/tableservices/jsf/pages/productview.xhtml?src=bkmk. For international comparisons of urbanization rates, see World Bank/DRC 2014, 100–101.

2. Chinese officials and scholars have generally embraced the view that urbanization in and of itself is a driver of economic growth; this is one reason for ambitious urbanization targets. For a more

skeptical view, that urbanization itself is not a proven cause of economic growth, see World Bank/DRC 2014, Box 1.1, 85.

3. Brookings Institution, Global Metro Monitor, http://www.brookings.edu/research/reports2/2015/01/22-global-metro-monitor. The World Bank defines the three stages of urbanization's economic impact as agglomeration, specialization, and mobility; see World Bank/DRC 2014, 91ff.

4. Fang Cai and Dewen Wang, "The Sustainability of Economic Growth and the Labor Contribution," *Economic Research Journal* 10 (1999): 62–68.

5. World Bank/DRC 2014, 74 n. 1.

6. http://www.worldbank.org/en/news/press-release/2015/01/26/world-bank-report-provides-new-data-to-help-ensure-urban-growth-benefits-the-poor.

7. A good discussion of the problems of China's urban population data is OECD 2015, 31–37.

8. World Bank/DRC 2014, 5. An even more pessimistic view was that of the 670 million urban residents identified by the 2010 census, 314 million or 47 percent did not hold urban hukou. See World Bank/DRC 2014, 89.

9. See Tom Miller, *China's Urban Billion: The Story behind the Biggest Migration in Human History* (London: Asian Arguments, 2012), 33ff.

10. For the relative efficiency of larger and denser cities, see World Bank/DRC 2014, 7–8. An alternative view, which stresses that productivity benefits arise not because of sheer population density but by "the ease with which people can interact with large numbers of other people," is in *OECD Urban Policy Reviews: China 2015* (Paris: OECD Publishing, 2015), 44–47.

11. Relative Wages: World Bank/DRC, 180; on social mobility see World Bank/DRC, 179.

12. Rosealea Yao, "Housing and Construction Review," Gavekal Dragonomics research note, November 2014. The government's full urbanization strategy document, *Guojia xinxing chengzhenhua guihua* ("National New-Style Urbanization Program"), is available in Chinese at http://www.51baogao.cn/free/xinxingchengzhenhua_pdf.shtml. Since 2015, both Beijing and Shanghai have undertaken active policies to reduce their population, in part by forcing large numbers of unregistered people to leave.

13. For a comprehensive discussion of these issues, see World Bank/ DRC 2014, 186–195.

14. For the estimate of the value of the housing wealth transfer, see Arthur Kroeber, Rosealea Yao, and Pei Zhuan, "Housing: A Room of One's Own," *China Economic Quarterly* (December 2007): 53–58.

15. Work by my colleague Rosealea Yao suggests that 46 percent of all urban housing built in China from 2000 to 2012 satisfied upgrading demand, while only 36 percent reflected new demand from the increased urban population. The remaining 18 percent was replacement of demolished housing. See Yao, "Housing and Construction Review."

16. World Bank/DRC 2014, 21. Given that migrants make up about 40 percent of the urban population, this implies an overall urban home ownership ratio of around 50 percent. The U.S. home ownership rate is now 65 percent. The U.S. rates can be viewed on the handy website of the St. Louis Federal Reserve, http:// research.stlouisfed.org/fred2/series/USHOWN.

17. House price rises calculated from official data on the average cost of housing per square meter, NBS/CEIC. House prices in the most desirable neighborhoods, such as central Beijing and Shanghai, rose much more, sometimes by a factor of 8 or 10.

18. Yao, "Housing and Construction Review."

19. Comparisons with house price to income ratios in the United States are misleading. The United States is a relatively sparsely populated country where land is cheap, the government provides enormous support for home buyers, and investors have plenty of other places to store their wealth. In the two decades before the U.S. housing bubble of the early 2000s, the median U.S. house price was 2.6 times the median household income; figures for individual cities fluctuated between 2 and 5. In Asian countries like South Korea and Taiwan where population is dense and households see real estate as their primary store of wealth, house price to income ratios typically range between 6 and 9.

20. Down payments of 20 percent are permitted for small houses financed by loans from municipal housing provident funds. The high down-payment requirements for investment properties were relaxed in most cities in 2014 but have been reimposed in some places since then to curb speculation.

21. For a discussion of social housing programs, see World Bank/ DRC, 2014, 22–23.
22. Ports data courtesy of Charles de Trenck, a Hong Kong-based shipping analyst.
23. Infrastructure data from NBS/CEIC.
24. A detailed justification of the high-speed rail program is in Will Freeman, "High-Speed Rail: The Iron Rooster Spiffs Up," *China Economic Quarterly* (June 2010), 7–9.
25. A vivid account of the railway corruption scandal, and of the safety problems it caused, is in Evan Osnos, "Boss Rail," *The New Yorker*, October 22, 2012, http://www.newyorker.com/ magazine/2012/10/22/boss-rail. Hasty installation of signals on one high-speed rail route helped cause an infamous derailment in 2011 that killed forty passengers and led to national outrage when photos circulated on the Internet of local officials trying to bury the derailed train.

Chapter 7

1. The most forceful expression of the private-sector advance story is Nicholas Lardy, *Markets over Mao: The Rise of Private Business in China* (Washington, DC: Peterson Institute of International Economics, 2014). An important articulation of the state-sector dominance view is Yasheng Huang, *Capitalism with Chinese Characteristics: Entrepreneurship and the State* (Cambridge: Cambridge University Press, 2008); a similar view is advanced by Barry Naughton and Kellee S. Tsai (eds.), *State Capitalism, Institutional Adaptation, and the Chinese Miracle* (Cambridge: Cambridge University Press, 2015). Note that in his most recent book, *The State Strikes Back: The End of Economic Reform in China?* (Washington, DC: Peterson Institute of International Economics, 2019), Lardy observes that the trend toward private-sector advance has been arrested and that economic growth is being retarded by an army of loss-making and subsidized SOEs.
2. The best description of China's state-owned enterprise system is L.-W. Lin and C. J. Milhaupt, "We Are the (National) Champions: Understanding the Mechanisms of State Capitalism in China," *Stanford Law Review*, 65 (2013): 697–760. My account draws heavily on theirs. For a detailed understanding of SASAC and its role, the best source is a series of articles by Barry

Naughton for the Hoover Institution's *China Leadership Monitor* (http://www.hoover.org/publications/china-leadership-monitor), specifically: "The State Asset Commission: A Powerful New Government Body" (Issue 8, October 2003); "SASAC Rising" (Issue 14, April 2005); "Claiming Profit for the State: SASAC and the Capital Management Budget" (Issue 18, July 2006); "SASAC and Rising Corporate Power in China" (Issue 24, March 2008); and "Loans, Firms and Steel: Is the State Advancing at the Expense of the Private Sector?" (Issue 30, November 2009).

3. Lardy, *The State Strikes Back*, 83.

4. SASAC's control is contested. Other agencies, for instance, the Ministry of Industry and Information Technology, sometimes assert governance rights (Lin and Milhaupt, "We Are the (National) Champions," 726). Some SOEs enjoy the same ministry-level rank as SASAC and so take the view that they do not have to follow SASAC's orders (Lin and Milhaupt, 736). SASAC appoints only about half of top-level SOE management; the other half is appointed by the CCP Organization Department (Lin and Milhaupt, 738).

5. Lardy, *The State Strikes Back*, 87–88.

6. Again, these figures refer to individual SOE companies (layers 2 and 3 in the organizational structure we outlined above), not to the unlisted parent-group companies.

7. Also see Barry Naughton, "SOE Policy: Profiting the SASAC Way," *China Economic Quarterly* (June 2008: 19–26); and Andrew Batson, "Fixing China's State Sector," Paulson Institute Policy Memorandum, January 2014. Some analysts, notably the China Unirule Institute of Economics, argue that SOE profits in the 2000s were due entirely to preferential access to cheap land and capital. See Unirule Institute of Economics, "The Nature, Performance and Reform of the State-Owned Enterprises," April 12, 2011. This is implausible, since SOEs had just as much, if not more, access to cheap land and capital before 1998 and managed to rack up huge losses nonetheless. Hidden subsidies no doubt played a significant role in SOE profits, but they cannot explain the improvement in SOE financial performance between the 1990s and the 2000s.

8. See Barry Naughton, "Two Trains Running: Supply-Side Reform, SOE Reform and the Authoritative Personage," *China Leadership*

Monitor Issue 50, July 2016. https://www.hoover.org/research/two-trains-running-supply-side-reform-soe-reform-and-authoritative-personage.

9. Ministry of Finance, *Finance Yearbook 2016*.

10. See Przemyslaw Kowalski, Max Büge, Monika Sztajerowska, and Matias Egeland, "State-Owned Enterprises: Trade Effects and Policy Implications," OECD Trade Policy Papers No. 147 (2013), http://dx.doi.org/10.1787/5k4869ckqk7l-en. Technically, these data are expressed as a percentage of gross national income (GNI), which is GDP plus net income from abroad. In practice, the difference between GDP and GNI is small, so for simplicity I have used GDP rather than GNI.

11. This estimate comes from Zhang Bin of the Institute of World Politics and Economics at the Chinese Academy of Social Sciences, in a draft paper, *"Zhongguo jingji zengsu weihe fangman? Jingji jiansu, jinrong gao honggan yu zhengfu gaige de san nan xuanze"* (China's Trilemma: Economic Slowdown, Financial Leverage and Government Reform).

12. Lardy, *Markets over Mao*, 24–33.

13. For the lack of market exit, see Scott Kennedy, "Wanted: More Creative Destruction," Gavekal Dragonomics research note, February 10, 2014. On the antimonopoly law, see U.S. Chamber of Commerce, "Competing Interests in China's Competition Law Enforcement: China's Anti-Monopoly Law Application and the Role of Industrial Policy," September 2014, https://www.uschamber.com/report/competing-interests-chinas-competition-law-enforcement-chinas-anti-monopoly-law-application.

14. See Scott Kennedy, *The Business of Lobbying in China* (Cambridge, MA: Harvard University Press, 2008); and Erica Downs, "Business Interest Groups in Chinese Politics: The Case of the Oil Companies," in Cheng Li (ed.), *China's Changing Political Landscape* (Washington, DC: Brookings Institution, 2008).

15. Lin and Milhaupt, "We Are the (National) Champions," insightfully describe the relationship between SOEs and the state as one of "networked hierarchy."

16. For the number of Chinese and billionaires, see the Hurun Report, http://hurun.net/EN/Article/Details?num=E406EB5BC439.

17. Specifically, company registrations include many categories, such as collectives and joint-stock firms, which include both

private and state-owned firms. In some statistical series, private-sector activity is identified as such. In others (such as fixed-asset investment), it can only be estimated as a residual, "nonstate" activity, once the activity of explicitly identified state firms has been counted.

18. Sean Dougherty, Richard Herd, and Ping He, "Has a Private Sector Emerged in China's Industry? Evidence from a Quarter of a Million Chinese Firms," *China Economic Review* 18, no. 3 (2007): 309–334.

19. Lardy, *Markets over Mao*, 74.

20. Ibid., 81.

21. For a careful discussion of the *guojin mintui* phenomenon, see two articles by Scott Kennedy, "Private Firms: Pink Capitalists in Bloom," *China Economic Quarterly* (June 2012): 37–42, and "Wanted: More Creative Destruction," Gavekal Dragonomics research note, February 10, 2014.

22. Lardy, *The State Strikes Back*, 49–80, exhaustively documents the gap between SOE and private firm financial performance.

Chapter 8

1. See David Dollar and Bert Hofman, "Intergovernmental Fiscal Reforms, Expenditure Assignment, and Governance." In Lou Jiwei (ed.), *Public Finance in China: Reform and Growth for a Harmonious Society* (Washington, DC: World Bank, 2008), 40.

2. Ibid., 42.

3. High-profile corruption investigations are often politically motivated, with the aim of destroying local power fiefdoms. Prominent examples were the prosecutions of Beijing mayor Chen Xitong in 1995 and of Shanghai Party Secretary Chen Liangyu a decade later. Each case brought down an official with a strong local power base who was seen as a threat by the national leader. Other prominent anticorruption drives that targeted powerful local networks, though not competitors for the nation's top job, included the crackdown on smuggling in south China in the late 1990s, which basically gutted the city governments in several cities, including Xiamen and Shantou; and a sweep of gangster-run local governments in the northeast's Heilongjiang in the early 2000s.

4. A good comparison of governance in China and India is William Antholis, *Inside Out, India and China: Local Politics Go Global* (Washington, DC: Brookings Institution, 2013).

5. The lack of accountability of local governments should not be exaggerated. An argument can be made that unelected local governments in China have historically been more accountable to the needs of their constituents than are democratically elected local governments in India, whose mandate is not to maximize economic growth but to garner spoils for particular caste, language, or religious groups. See Antholis, *Inside Out*, 33, for a comparison; and Lily l. Tsai, *Accountability without Democracy* (Cambridge: Cambridge University Press, 2007) for a study of accountability mechanisms in Chinese local government. It is true, however, that Chinese citizens are generally less happy with the performance of local officials than of central officials. See Bruce J. Dickson, *The Dictator's Dilemma: The Chinese Communist Party's Strategy for Survival* (Oxford: Oxford University Press, 2016), 222.

6. Local governments are far less able to restrict trade and competition than in the 1980s and 1990s. See Barry Naughton, "How Much Can Regional Integration Do to Unify China's Markets," in Nicholas C. Hope et al. (eds.), *How Far across the River: Chinese Policy Reform at the Millennium* (Stanford, CA: Stanford University Press, 2003). But it is also clear that weak companies exit the market far more slowly in China than elsewhere—especially if they are state-owned—and this has largely to do with local support. (See Scott Kennedy, "Wanted: More Creative Destruction," Gavekal Dragonomics research note, February 10, 2014.) For a true market economy, both the entry of new players *and* the speedy exit of weak players are essential.

7. This is necessarily a simplified explanation; reality was not quite so centralized. In practice, localities controlled "extrabudgetary funds," which accounted for nearly a third of the finance for investment in the late 1970s (Naughton , 43).

8. It is not clear how much of the post-1996 increase in overall revenue was a real increase or just a better accounting of revenue that was there all along but hidden in various extrabudgetary funds. (Similarly, the apparent decline in revenue in the 1980s may have been due in part to revenues being squirreled away off-budget.) To this day, China's budgetary accounting is loose: a long-running effort to force each government agency to run all its revenues and expenses through a single account, visible to the Ministry of Finance, is far from complete.

9. For details see He Yuxin, "China Development Bank: The Best Bank in China?" Gavekal Dragonomics research note, July 1, 2010.

10. Only about 40 percent of local liabilities were local government financing vehicle loans; the remainder were a patchwork of other types of borrowing, as well as guarantees and contingent liabilities that local governments were not directly responsible for but could be forced to honor if economic conditions got worse. See National Audit Office, "Audit Results of Nationwide Governmental Debts," December 30, 2013, http://www.cnao. gov.cn/main/articleshow_ArtID_1335.htm.

11. IMF, Article IV Consultation, Staff Report (2019), https://www. imf.org/en/Publications/CR/Issues/2019/08/08/Peoples-Republic-of-China-2019-Article-IV-Consultation-Press-Release-Staff-Report-Staff-48576, 10, 16, 45, 50 and 54.

12. For an outline of the priorities that eventually found their way into the fiscal reform package, see Lou Jiwei's first budget report as finance minister, "Report on the Implementation of the Central and Local Budgets in 2013 and on the Draft Central and Local Budgets for 2014" (Ministry of Finance 2014). For a discussion of the impact of the revised budget law (in Chinese), see Lou's interview with the *People's Daily*, "*Xin yusuanfa: dajian xiandai caizheng zhidu kuangjia*" ("The New Budget Law: Framework for Building a Modern Fiscal System"), *People's Daily*, September 11, 2014, http://politics.people.com.cn/n/2014/0911/c1001-25637407.html.

13. Problems of the transfer system are detailed in Lou, *Public Finance in China*, especially David Dollar and Bert Hofman, "Intergovernmental Fiscal Reforms, Expenditure Assignment, and Governance" (39–52); and Anwar Shah and Chunli Shen, "Fine-Tuning the Intergovernmental Transfer System to Create a Harmonious Society and Level Playing Field for Regional Development (129–154). See also Xiao Wang and Richard Herd, "The System of Revenue Sharing and Fiscal Transfers in China," OECD Economics Department Working Papers, No. 1030 (Paris: OECD Publishing, 2013).

14. The reasons why the tax structure leads localities to overemphasize industry and infrastructure are complex and technical. For a good explanation, see World Bank/DRC 2014, 57; and Xinye Zheng and Li Zhang, "Fiscal Reform: A Better

Way to Tax and Spend," *China Economic Quarterly*, March 2013. A key factor is China's VAT system. In most countries, the VAT is effectively a consumption tax, since most of the net amount is paid by final goods consumers. China, however, has a "production VAT" in which much of the net receipts come from businesses, especially those investing heavily in capital equipment. Until 2016, unlike in most other countries, services were excluded from VAT, and service firms instead paid a "business tax" on their revenues (see Ehtisham Ahmad, "Taxation Reforms and the Sequencing of Intergovernmental Reforms in China: Preconditions for a *Xiaokang* Society," in Lou, *Public Finance in China*). This meant that service enterprises were heavily taxed, and users of these services cannot deduct their payments from their VAT obligations as they can for purchases of materials. This problem was solved in 2016 when the business tax was abolished and converted into a service-sector VAT. Another problem is that taxes shared by local and central governments, such as VAT and the corporate income tax, are shared based on the location of collection. So cities are extremely reluctant to permit enterprises to move to new locations or to be absorbed by another enterprise that pays tax in a different jurisdiction. In order to keep VAT payments flowing from a struggling enterprise, local governments will often give the firm some kind of benefit that does not impose an immediate budgetary impact, such as access to loans from a friendly local bank branch, cheaper electricity, or a discount on land.

15. Up through 2018, 44 percent of urban employed people paid personal income tax. A tax cut in early 2019 reduced that share to just 15 percent, which is the share of urban workers whose salary income is more than Rmb5,000 per month. See Ernan Cui, "The Large Print Giveth, the Small Print Taketh Away," Gavekal Dragonomics research note, January 31, 2019.

16. For a good discussion of the property tax and its problems, see World Bank/DRC 2014, 56 and 292–297.

17. For purposes of comparison, 47 percent of the U.S. Federal budget goes to entitlement programs such as Social Security and Medicare, 15 percent to national defense, and 9 percent to interest on the national debt (compared to 3 percent in China). The comparison is far from exact because the Chinese figures also include all spending by local governments. See "Monthly Budget

Review: Summary for Fiscal Year 2018," Congressional Budget Office, November 7, 2018. https://www.cbo.gov/system/files?file=2018-11/54647-MBR.pdf

18. In 2018, China's reported military expenditures ($168 billion) were about one-quarter those of the United States in absolute terms, about one-third of the U.S. level relative to GDP, and one-sixteenth of the U.S. level on a per capita basis. *The Military Balance 2019*, Institute of Strategic Studies, February 2019. https://www.iiss.org/publications/the-military-balance

Chapter 9

1. Much of the following discussion is drawn from Nicholas Lardy, *China's Unfinished Economic Revolution* (Washington, DC: Brookings Institution, 1998) and Nicholas Lardy, *Markets over Mao: The Rise of Private Business in China* (Washington, DC: Peterson Institute of International Economics, 2014).

2. Barry Naughton, *The Chinese Economy: Transitions and Growth* (Cambridge MA: MIT Press, 2007), 462.

3. Lardy, *China's Unfinished Economic Revolution*, 119.

4. The Agricultural Bank of China was the last of the Big Four to list, in 2010.

5. These are the China Development Bank (CDB), the Agricultural Development Bank of China, and the China Export-Import Bank. Of these three, the CDB (which from 1997 to 2013 was run skillfully by Chen Yuan, the son of Deng's old rival Chen Yun) became by far the most important. It financed a wide range of infrastructure projects, pioneered the land-based financing mechanism for local governments, and, beginning in the mid-2000s, became a major financier of China's global resource investments. See Erica S. Downs, "Inside China, Inc: China Development Bank's Cross-Border Energy Deals," Brookings Institution China Center Monograph, March 21, 2011; and Michael Forsythe and Henry Sanderson, *China's Superbank* (New York: Bloomberg Press, 2013).

6. Most analysts now group the original Big Four, along with the state-controlled Bank of Communications and Postal Savings Bank, into the "Big Six." The combined assets of the Big Six are still less than 40 percent of bank assets.

7. An insider's view of the improvement in Chinese bank practices is James Stent, *China's Banking Transformation: The Untold Story*

(New York: Oxford University Press, 2017). Stent, an American, served on the boards of two midsized Chinese banks for 13 years.

8. Lardy, *Markets over Mao*, 130.

9. In 1998, the banks got Rmb 270 billion in new capital by issuing special bonds that were purchased by MOF. But MOF did not actually have the money to pay for these bonds, so it gave the banks IOUs instead. Over the next several years, the banks earned high profits and paid a large chunk of those profits as dividends to MOF. MOF then recycled these proceeds back into the banks, paying down their IOUs. In other words, the "capital" used to recapitalize the banks did not actually exist in 1998 but was created later out of bank profits. This sleight-of-hand worked because (1) the banks were part of a unified, closed system entirely owned by the government, without external shareholders or auditors who could force the banks into bankruptcy; and (2) structural reforms created vast new profitable lending opportunities.

10. The term *shadow banking* seems to have been coined in 2007 by Paul McCulley, the respected chief economist at the investment firm PIMCO. My own view is that the term is not helpful since it bunches together many different kinds of financial activity of widely varying risk and unfairly implies that it is all potentially nefarious.

11. See Nicholas Borst, "Shadow Deposits as a Source of Financial Instability: Lessons from the American Experience for China" (Washington, DC: Peterson Institute for International Economics Policy Brief 13–14, May 2013), http://www.piie.com/publications/interstitial.cfm?ResearchID=2410.

12. The "Basel Standards" specify minimum capital standards and other regulatory guardrails for banks and have been widely adopted. They are developed by the Bank for International Settlements, a service provider for central banks and bank regulators, which is based in Basel, Switzerland. The basic Basel minimum capital standard is 8 percent (8 dollars of capital for each 100 dollars of risk-weighted assets). China's actual minimum capital requirement for its major banks is around 11 percent. Details on the Basel Standards are at https://www.bis.org/bcbs/index.htm.

13. The mechanics behind the rise of shadow banking and its relationship to financial deregulation are detailed in Chen Long,

"A Short History of Financial Deregulation," *China Economic Quarterly* (September 2017): 17–24, and Chen Long, "Three Sets Of Books," *China Economic Quarterly* (September 2017, 25): 36.

14. Nicholas Lardy, *The State Strikes Back: The End of Economic Reform in China?* (Washington, DC: Peterson Institute for International Economics, 2019), 105–106. In an earlier book, Lardy had noted the dramatic increase in private firms' share of corporate credit in the early 2010s. See Lardy, *Markets over Mao,* 99–111.

15. A detailed description of China's bond market is Alfred Schipke, Markus Rodlauer, and Zhang Longmei (eds.), *The Future of China's Bond Market* (Washington, DC: International Monetary Fund, 2019).

16. A comprehensive explanation of China's stock market today is Thomas Gatley, "A User's Guide to the Chinese Stock Market," Gavekal Dragonomics research note, April 2, 2019. For a colorful account of its origins and early development, see Carl E. Walter and Fraser Howie, *Privatizing China: The Stock Markets and Their Role in Corporate Reform* (New York: John Wiley, 2003).

17. There is a range of estimates for China's total debt, with some as high as 300 percent of GDP. Some of these higher estimates suffer from double-counting because of a failure to net out shadow-banking transactions. If Bank A lends to Trust Company B, which then lends the money to Company C, only one loan has really been made, not two. Another confusion in popular accounts arises from comparing China's *total* debt-to-GDP ratio with the ratio of *government debt* to GDP in other countries. The estimate used here comprises both government debt and lending to the private sector, which includes lending to all corporations (both state-owned and private) and to households. It is calculated by using the PBOC's broadest credit measure, aggregate financing to the real economy (AFRE, sometimes referred to as total social finance or TSF), subtracting equity issuance, and adding in some forms of shadow credit not captured by AFRE.

18. In China in 2018, there was almost one dollar of bank deposits for every dollar of credit to corporations and households (deposits of Rmb 176 trillion vs. Rmb 184 trillion in credit). The equivalent figure in the United States in 2008 was just 25 cents for every dollar of credit ($7 trillion in deposits vs. $24.4 trillion in credit). Data from the Bank for International Settlements and PBOC.

19. For a discussion of Japan's malaise, see Richard Koo, *The Holy Grail of Macroeconomics: Lessons from Japan's Great Recession* (Hoboken, NJ: John Wiley, 2009). There are some similarities between China today and Japan in the late 1980s but just as many differences. Japan's problems initially stemmed from a spectacular bubble in land and equity prices in the 1980s which popped in 1991, causing a collapse in asset prices from which the country in some ways has never recovered. Although land prices in China have risen steeply, they are nowhere as detached from underlying values as they were in late-1980s Japan. Moreover, Japanese policymakers throughout the 1990s stubbornly refused to admit that their banking system was effectively insolvent, and so they delayed dealing with the problem for many years. By contrast, Chinese regulators were quick to recognize the systemic banking problems during the nonperforming loan crisis of the 1990s and the shadow-banking explosion of the 2010s.

20. At the end of 1993, the official exchange rate was 5.8 to the dollar, and the market-based "swap rate," which traders used, was 8.7 to the dollar. In January 1994, the official exchange rate was set at 8.7 and allowed to float fairly freely, and so the separate swap rate was abolished.

21. Most financial news reports focus on the nominal rate of a currency against one other currency, usually the U.S. dollar. So the value of the renminbi might be reported as 6.9 against the dollar, the euro as 1.2 against the dollar, and so on. Economists prefer to look at effective exchange rates (EERs), which measure the value of a currency against numerous other currencies, weighted by the value of trade. So a country that did 50 percent of its trade with the United States, 30 percent with Europe, and 20 percent with China would have an effective exchange rate whose value was determined 50 percent by its currency's value against the dollar, 30 percent by the euro value, and 20 percent by the renminbi value. A nominal effective rate (NEER) is this simple trade-weighted average. A real effective rate (REER) also takes into account differences in inflation among the relevant countries.

22. Data on Rmb deposits and bond issuance from the Hong Kong Monetary Authority, http://www.hkma.gov.hk/eng/market-data-andstatistics/monthly-statistical-bulletin.

23. For foreign exchange trading data, see Bank for International Settlements, "Triennial Survey of Foreign Exchange and Derivatives Market Activity in 2019," September 2019, https:// www.bis.org/statistics/rpfx19.htm. For data on share of international reserves, see International Monetary Fund, Currency Composition of Official Foreign Exchange Reserves (COFER) database. For other indicators of the renminbi's international use, see Alicia Garcia Herrero and Jianwei Xu, "Natixis RMB Internationalization Monitor: Stagnation Continues," https://research.natixis.com/Site/en/publication/ tIFPfzJp3ALa8c13XWqMaw%3D%3D?from=share, Natixis Research, November 2019.

24. For a comprehensive discussion of the renminbi internationalization program and its relationship to economic reform, see Arthur Kroeber, "China's Global Currency: Lever for Financial Reform," Brookings Tsinghua Center for Public Policy, Monograph Series No. 3, April 2013, http://www. brookings. edu/research/papers/2013/04/china-global-currency-financial-reformkroeber; and Eswar Prasad and Lei Ye, "The Renminbi's Role in the Global Monetary System" (Washington, DC: Brookings Institution, February 2012, http://www.brookings.edu/research/reports/2012/02/ renminbi-monetary-system-prasad.

25. See, for instance, Arvind Subramanian, *Eclipse: Living in the Shadow of China's Economic Dominance* (Washington, DC: Peterson Institute for International Economics, 2011).

26. The IMF uses the SDR to denominate the loans it makes to member countries. Under the new formula approved by the IMF board on November 30, 2015, the renminbi has an 11 percent weight in the SDR, compared to 40 percent for the U.S. dollar, 32 percent for the euro, and 9 percent each for the yen and the pound sterling. This weight mainly reflects China's importance as a trading country. The renminbi's share of global reserve assets was then much lower, around 1 percent, and has barely risen since its SDR inclusion. The renminbi was not actually included in the SDR until a year after the initial announcement, in November 2016. See "China's Yuan in the SDR Basket," Bloomberg China Brief, November 30, 2015, http://newsletters. briefs.bloomberg.com/document/46z1i9i3mb3z15mu930/front.

27. An excellent account of the dollar's rise is Barry Eichengreen, *Exorbitant Privilege: The Rise and Fall of the Dollar and the Future of the International Monetary System* (Oxford: Oxford University Press, 2012).

28. See Chen Long and Arthur Kroeber, "Retreating from an International Renminbi," Gavekal Dragonomics research note, January 14, 2016.

Chapter 10

1. This calculation is based on energy consumption data from the *BP Statistical Review of World Energy 2019*, and GDP data (at current exchange rates) from the World Bank's World Development indicators. The BP review presents energy consumption data in million metric tons of oil equivalent (mtoe), which I have converted into barrels at the standard rate of 1 ton = 7.33 barrels. China's energy intensity relative to GDP would look less dire if we used a purchasing power parity (PPP) measure of GDP, which adjusts upward the value of China's nontradable goods and services. But since the vast majority of energy in China goes into the production of tradable goods whose prices are more or less at global levels, GDP at the current exchange rate seems to be the more appropriate denominator.

2. Specifically, a power plant must burn about 10,500 British thermal units (BTUs) of coal to generate 1 kilowatt hour of electricity; for natural gas, the figure is about 8,000 BTUs. See http://www.eia.gov/tools/faqs/faq.cfm?id=107&t=3. Coal shares in power generation from the *BP Statistical Review of World Energy 2019*.

3. *BP Statistical Review of World Energy, 2019*.

4. For the relative efficiency of U.S. and Chinese coal-fired power plants, see Melanie Hart, Luke Bassett, and Blaine Johnson, "Everything You Think You Know about Coal in China Is Wrong," Center for American Progress, May 15, 2017. Their study also found that every coal plant operating in the United States would fail to meet Chinese pollution standards. For Chinese vehicle fuel efficiency standards, see The International Council on Clean Transportation, https://theicct.org/chart-library-passenger-vehicle-fuel-economy. For background on the development of these standards, see Hongyan H. Oliver et al., "China's Fuel Economy Standards for Passenger Vehicles: Rationale, Policy Process and Impacts," Discussion

Paper 2009-03 (March 2009), Belfer Center for Science and International Affairs, Harvard Kennedy School.

5. For a detailed discussion of the major sources of inefficiencies and potential efficiency gains, see Nan Zhou et al., "China's Energy and Emissions Outlook to 2050: Perspectives from Bottom-Up Energy End-Use Model," Energy Policy 53 (February 2013): 14ff.

6. Figures on energy mix from BP Statistical Review 2019; fuel breakdown of China's power production from the National Bureau of Statistics (NBS). For projections of the energy mix in 2050, see Zhou et al., "China's Energy and Emissions Outlook to 2050."

7. China originally reported that coal use declined by 2.9 percent in 2014, but a comprehensive revision of historical energy statistics showed that total coal consumption was about 16 percent higher than previously estimated and that gross coal use in 2014 was essentially flat. On the other hand, the heat content of this previously hidden coal was very low, so the upward revisions to energy use and CO_2 emissions were smaller. A later revision pushed up total coal use but reaffirmed that use started to fall in 2014. See Rosealea Yao, "Finding the Missing Coal," Gavekal Dragonomics research note, December 3, 2015.

8. BP Statistical Review 2019.

9. However, as a result of the trade tensions with the United States since 2017, Chinese policymakers have become more concerned to ensure domestic self-reliance in as many key inputs as possible, including energy. The government is now putting pressure on the national oil companies to step up exploration and extraction of domestic oil and gas reserves. Erica Downs, "High Anxiety: The Trade War and China's Oil and Gas Supply Security," https://energypolicy.columbia.edu/research/commentary/high-anxiety-trade-war-and-china-s-oil-and-gas-supply-security, Columbia/SIPA Center on Global Energy Policy, November 12, 2019.

10. Data on greenhouse gas emissions from the Climate Action database. The six main greenhouse gases are CO_2, methane, nitrous oxide, and three fluorine-based gases. About three-quarters of global greenhouse gas emissions are CO_2, so China's emissions are more CO_2-heavy than the average. The CO_2 emissions of different fuels are at https://www.eia.gov/tools/faqs/faq.php?id=73&t=11.

11. Climate Action Tracker ranks China's climate policies as "highly insufficient" (consistent with a global temperature rise of 3–4 degrees Celsius). This puts China between the EU ("insufficient") and the United States ("critically insufficient"). See https:// climateactiontracker.org/countries/china.

12. On "Airpocalypse" and the general question of air pollution from PM2.5 small particulates, note that while China's average PM2.5 level (as high as 90 micrograms per cubic meter (μ/m3) in the early 2010s; now around 50) is often compared with the World Health Organization's (WHO) "safe" standard of 25 μ/m3. The WHO in fact has a graded set of recommended levels (70, 50, and 30 μ/m3), recognizing that developing countries are likely to have higher emissions in the early stages of industrialization. See WHO, http://whqlibdoc.who.int/hq/2006/ WHO_SDE_PHE_OEH_ 06.02_eng.pdf, 12. For a dense but useful technical discussion of China's air pollution problems, progress, and policy prescriptions, see Chris P. Nielsen and Mun S. Ho (eds.), *Clearing the Air* (Cambridge, MA: MIT Press, 2007); and Chris P. Nielsen and Mun S. Ho, *Clearer Skies over China* (Cambridge, MA: MIT Press, 2013).

13. For discussion of the Great Smog and a comparable disaster in Donora, Pennsylvania in 1948, see Stephen Mihm, http://www.bloombergview.com/articles/2013-11-06/ londons-great-smog-provides-lessons-for-china.

14. The technical term for this relationship between income and environmental protection is the Environmental Kuznets Curve (EKC), so named because of the analogy with Simon Kuznets's theory that income inequality rises in the early stages of development but abates as a country grows richer (see Chapter 13 for a discussion of inequality and the classic Kuznets curve). Like the traditional Kuznets curve for inequality, the EKC has been criticized on empirical grounds. See David I. Stern, "The Rise and Fall of the Environmental Kuznets Curve," *World Development* 32, no. 8 (2004): 1419–1439, which argues that many developing countries are tackling environmental problems earlier than the classic EKC would predict. Nonetheless, the data presented here suggests that there is a good correlation between per capita income and environmental action.

15. For details on the issues and data discussed in this section, see Angel Hsu, The Environmental Horizon: Still Murky," *China Economic Quarterly* (December 2017), 55–60; Calvin Quek,

"Bringing Back the Blue Sky Days," *China Economic Quarterly* (September 2014) 18–25; Angel Hsu, "A Real War, More Ammo Required," *China Economic Quarterly* (September 2014) 10–17; and Michal Meidan and Rosealea Yao, "King Coal's Long, Slow Decline," *China Economic Quarterly* (March 2015) 28–34. On the primacy of coal in emissions, the Beijing office of Greenpeace estimates that coal combustion accounts for 45 to 50 percent of PM2.5 emissions, while transport accounts for 15 to 20 percent (Quek, "Bringing Back the Blue Sky Days"). Nielsen and Ho, *Clearing the Air*, 57, find that a quarter of the health damage from air pollution came from the electricity sector and that another quarter cane from cement, chemicals, and steel. In their later work, they found that the cement, brick, and glass industries account for 54 percent of total particulate pollution, with electricity generation and metals smelting contributing another 14 percent. For sulfur dioxide emissions, power generation (51 percent) is the main culprit, with cement, brick, glass, and metals accounting for another 11 percent.

16. A good assessment of the industrial energy campaign is Jing Ke et al., "China's Industrial Energy Consumption Trends and Impacts of the Top 1000 Enterprises Energy-Saving Program and the Ten Key Energy-Saving Projects," *Energy Policy* 50 (November 2012): 562–569.

17. For energy price data, see *China Energy Databook 9* (Lawrence Berkeley National Laboratory China Energy Group, 2016), https://china.lbl.gov/china-energy-databook.

18. "China's War on Particulate Air Pollution Is Causing More Severe Ozone Pollution," Harvard John A. Paulson School of Engineering and Applied Science, December 31, 2018. PM2.5 data from the World Bank, World Development Indicators, and the National Bureau of Statistics.

19. Ke Li et al., "Anthropogenic Drivers of 2013–2017 Trends in Summer Surface Ozone in China," *Proceedings of the National Academy of Sciences* 116, no. 2 (January 8, 2019): 422–427, https://www.pnas.org/content/116/2/422.

Chapter 11

1. Yang Jisheng, *Tombstone: The Untold Story of Mao's Great Famine* (London: Allen Lane, 2012); and Judith Banister, *China's Changing Population* (Stanford, CA: Stanford University Press, 1987).

2. Guo Zhigang, "Family Planning Policy: Too Few by Far," *China Economic Quarterly* (June 2012): 22–26.

3. In 2018, China's labor force was 776 million people, while that of the United States was 162 million. Figures from the CEIC database for China and from the Bureau of Labor Statistics for the United States. See http://data.bls.gov.

4. Wang Feng, "Demographic Transition: Racing towards the Precipice," *China Economic Quarterly* (June 2012): 17–21; and Judith Banister, "Labor Force: No Need to Panic," *China Economic Quarterly* (June 2012): 27–30.

5. Guo, "Family Planning Policy."

6. Fertility data from the World Bank's World Development Indicators, http://data.worldbank.org. A comprehensive and scathing analysis of the one-child policy is Martin King Whyte, Wang Feng, and Yong Cai, "Challenging Myths about China's One-Child Policy," *China Journal* 74 (2015): 144–159.

7. Guo, "Family Planning Policy 2012."

8. Nicholas Lardy, *Moon over Mao: The Rise of Private Business in China* (Washington, DC: Peterson Institute of International Economics, 2014), 214–215.

9. Fang Cai, Albert Park, and Yaohui Zhao, "The Chinese Labor Market in the Reform Era," in Loren Brandt and Thomas G. Rawski (eds.), *China's Great Economic Transformation* (Cambridge: Cambridge University Press, 2008), 171.

10. Jean C. Oi, *Rural China Takes Off: Institutional Foundations of Economic Reform* (Stanford, CA: Stanford University Press, 1999), 62–66. The term *collective* generally implies that an enterprise is controlled by a state entity at lower than the city level.

11. Cai et al., "The Chinese Labor Market in the Reform Era," 176–177.

12. U.S. nonfarm employment fell from a peak of 138.4 million in January 2008 to a trough of 129.7 million in December 2010. U.S. manufacturing employment peaked at 19.5 million in 1979 and fell to 11.5 million in 2009. Data from the Bureau of Labor Statistics.

13. The official "registered urban unemployment" statistic, which has remained virtually static at just over 4 percent for many years, is widely considered useless because it excludes migrant workers and people who do not register for unemployment benefits. Since 2015, the government has published surveys of

urban employment that show more variability and a slightly higher rate (5.2 percent for most of 2019), but these do not cover all economic sectors. Studies by government think-tanks and independent scholars have estimated unemployment rates of anywhere from 6 percent to 10 percent for various periods. For a careful scholarly estimate of unemployment up to 2009, see Shuaizheng Feng, Yingyao Hu, and Robert Moffit, "Long Run Trends in Unemployment and Labor Force Participation in China," *Journal of Comparative Economics*, 45, no. 2 (2017): 304–324. For later figures, see Yang Liu, "The Chinese Labour Market: High Unemployment Coexisting with a Labour Shortage," July 19, 2014, http:// www.voxeu.org/article/ china-s-unemployment-and-labour-shortage.

14. For the rise in the working-age population, see World Bank/DRC 2013, 277, fig. 4.5. For relative Chinese and Thai wage levels, see World Bank/DRC 2013, 349, fig. 5.12. The fall in the labor income share is from the flow of funds data in the national accounts. Two Chinese scholars, Bai Chong'en and Qian Zhenjie, found that the household share of national income (which includes financial income as well as wage income) fell from 67 percent in 1996 to 54 percent in 2005. See Bai and Qian, "Who Is the Predator, Who the Prey: An Analysis of Changes in the State of China's National Income Distribution," *Social Sciences in China* 30, no. 4 (November 2009): 179–205. Varying estimates of China's Gini coefficient are examined in more detail in Chapter 13; all estimates agree that China's Gini rose substantially from 1995 to 2010. The figures cited here are from World Bank/DRC 2013, 275 and the National Bureau of Statistics.

15. The relevance of Lewis's work to China was first highlighted by an important Chinese labor economist, Cai Fang, in a 2008 book which was originally treated skeptically by government officials, who assumed that China's overabundant labor supply was a permanent condition. Cai's views have since become widely accepted. For a summary in English, see Cai Fang, "Approaching a Triumphal Span: How Far Is China towards Its Lewisian Turning Point?" UNU-WIDER Research Paper No. 2008/2009, February 2008, http://iple.cass.cn/upload/2012/06/ d20120606103343081.pdf.

16. W. Arthur Lewis, "Economic Development with Unlimited Supplies of Labour," *Manchester School of Economic and*

Social Studies 22 (1954): 139–191. Available at http://www.
globelicsacademy.net/2008/2008_lectures/lewis%20
unlimited%20 labor%20supply%201954.pdf. A brief summary
and explanation of its relevance to China are in World Bank/
DRC 2014, 89. Lewis's detailed views are subject to various
objections: in particular, some developing countries such as
China have seen strong growth in nominal and real wages
during the "unlimited labor" phase. But as a stylistic depiction
of the dynamics of growth in a developing economy and how
they differ from those of rich countries, the Lewis model remains
illuminating.

17. Specifically, from 230 million in 2010 to 150 million in
2023, a 35 percent decline. See Arthur Kroeber, "Economic
Rebalancing: The End of Surplus Labor," *China Economic
Quarterly*(March 2010): 35–46.

18. World Bank/DRC 2014, 180, shows migrant wages rose from
52 percent of urban hukou in 2007 to 65 percent in 2012, and the
wage gap for comparable work has vanished.

19. A good discussion of how Chinese firms are successfully
adapting to higher wage costs is "China's Next Leap In
Manufacturing," Boston Consulting Group, December 13, 2018,
https://www.bcg.com/en-us/publications/2018/china-next-
leap-in-manufacturing.aspx.

20. For total migrant numbers, see Lardy, *Markets over Mao*, 17. For
the breakdown of migrant origins and destinations, see World
Bank/DRC 2014, 98, Table 1.4 and Figure 1.11.

21. For estimates of rural surplus labor, see World Bank/DRC 2014,
100. For estimates of total migrant flows and ultimate urban
population, see World Bank/DRC 2014, 114. For the slowdown
in migrant flows since 2010, see Ernan Cui, "How Demographics
Are Changing China's Future," Gavekal Dragonomics research
note, October 2018.

22. Child labor was legal in the United States until 1938, when the
United States was by some measures more prosperous than
China today. Federal restrictions on child labor still do not apply
to agriculture.

23. A carefully reported and sensitive account of the lives and
struggles of Chinese migrant workers is Leslie Chang, *Factory
Girls: From Village to City in a Changing China* (New York: Spiegel
& Grau, 2008). For a well-informed view of China's many

labor problems, see *China Labor Bulletin*, www.clb.org.hk. An interesting perspective on Chinese and American approaches to labor relations is in *American Factory*, a 2019 documentary film directed by Julia Reichert and Stephen Bognart, which chronicles the takeover of an Ohio factory by Fuyao Glass, a world-leading Chinese automotive glass maker. The Chinese workers who are brought over to teach their American colleagues glass-making skills work extraordinarily long hours. They are also highly skilled and proud of their work, and unsympathetic to efforts by their American coworkers to unionize the plant.

Chapter 12

1. In the "expenditure" breakdown, GDP is made up of gross capital formation (investment), consumer spending, government spending, and net exports. There are two other ways to break down GDP. First, the production approach measures the economy as the sum of value added in agriculture, industry, construction, and services. Second, the income approach divides it into wages, corporate profits, and government tax revenue. The expenditure approach is the one most commonly used by economists and government statisticians. China is unusual in that it mainly reports GDP in production terms, publishing expenditure data in much less detail.

2. The remaining 19 percent of GDP is made up of government spending, exports, and inventories, which are sometimes counted as part of investment. Here I use the narrower measure of investment, excluding inventory accumulation. This is because from 1980 to 1996 inventories were an unusually large share of the economy (7 percent on average), thanks to the huge number of inefficient state-owned factories producing goods no one wanted to buy. These inventories were liquidated under the SOE reforms of 1995–2005; since the year 2000, inventories have averaged around 2 percent of GDP. Including inventories substantially overstates the level of productive investment in the 1980s and obscures the underlying trend of a steady increase in productive investment in the first two decades of reform. Including inventories, China's investment-to-GDP ratio peaked at 48 percent in 2011 and drifted down to 45 percent by 2018.

3. For this comparison, see Arthur Kroeber, "China's Consumption Paradox: Causes and Consequences," *Eurasian Geography and*

Economics 52, no. 3 (2011): 330–346. Japan's consumption rate fell by 14 percentage points (pp) (66 percent to 52 percent) between 1955 and 1970; Taiwan's by 9 pp (62 percent to 53 percent) between 1974 and 1986; and South Korea's by an astonishing 30 pp (80 percent to 50 percent) between 1967 and 1988. In this context, China's 15 pp decline (51 percent to 36 percent) between 1989 and 2010 seems far from extraordinary.

4. That is, $10,000 of per capita GDP times 50 percent (the household income share of GDP) times 67 percent (the share of household income that is spent rather than saved).

5. Car data from NBS/CEIC. Tourism data everywhere are troublesome because it is often hard to separate personal from business travel and because tracking spending is tricky. China's official figure on outbound tourist trips, cited here, seems more accurate than the much higher numbers of the World Tourism Organization, which evidently include business and official travel. China's balance-of-payments statisticians have revised their approach to tourism spending several times, and the current figure seems reasonably reliable. See Ernan Cui, "What Is Happening with the Tourism Numbers?" Gavekal Dragonomics research note, April 13, 2017.

6. The U.S. consumption ratio, at 68 percent, is unusually high. This is important to note, since U.S.-centric economists often present the American economic structure as "normal," even though it is in fact abnormal. The global average figure is 58 percent. The most relevant comparisons for China are its East Asian neighbors South Korea, Taiwan, and Japan, which have household consumption ratios of 48 percent, 54 percent, and 56 percent, respectively. (Data from World Bank, World Development Indicators https://databank.worldbank.org; Taiwan data from CEIC.)

7. "Housing services" in economic jargon means the part of housing expenditure that represents consumption of the "service" of having a place to live, as opposed to investment in real estate. For renters, this is simply the amount of the rent they pay. For homeowners the calculation is more complicated since their mortgage payments include both the implicit purchase of housing services and the purchase of an asset. Statisticians usually compute the services part by assigning an "imputed rent" to owner-occupied housing, based on average rental prices.

In a country like China with a relatively small rental market for
which data is poor, this is hard to do.

8. Nicholas Lardy *Sustaining China's Economic Growth after the
    Global Financial Crisis* (Washington, DC: Peterson Institute of
    International Economics, 2012), Appendix A, suggests that
    a proper accounting for housing services would add 3 to
    4 percentage points to the consumption ratio. Thomas Gatley
    ("China's Missing Consumption," Gavekal Dragonomics
    research note, July 2013) argues that the official data undercounts
    not only housing services but also other household services and,
    surprisingly, purchases of cars and cell phones. Two Shanghai
    scholars, Zhu Tian and Zhang Jun, estimate that the consumption
    ratio should be adjusted upward by 10 to 15 percentage points,
    thanks to unrecorded spending on these items and health
    and education; see Stephen Green, "China Is Not Really That
    Imbalanced," Standard Chartered Bank research note, September
    24, 2013.

9. See, for instance. Dominc Barton, Yougang Shen, and Amy Jin,
    "Mapping China's Middle Class," *McKinsey Quarterly* (June
    2013); Michael Silverstein et al., *The $10 Trillion Prize: Captivating
    the Newly Affluent in China and India* (Cambridge, MA: Harvard
    Business Review Press, 2012). A good summary of different
    estimates is "How Well-off Is China's Middle Class?" China
    Power Project, Center for Strategic and International Studies,
    https://chinapower.csis.org/china-middle-class. A careful
    academic treatment that breaks down patterns of urban and
    rural income growth and reaches conclusions similar to those
    presented in this chapter is Bjorn Gustaffson, Terry Sicular, and
    Xiuna Wang, "China's Emerging Global Middle Class," *Centre
    for Human Capital and Productivity Working Paper Series* 2017-14,
    August 2017.

10. World Bank/DRC 2014, 104–105. The World Bank's income
    thresholds are in 2005 dollars at purchasing power parity (PPP).
    It found that about 20 percent of urban dwellers, but only
    3 percent of rural residents, qualified as middle class.

11. These thresholds are adapted from Michael Silverstein, Abheek
    Singhi, Carol Liao, David Michael, and Simon Targett, *The $10
    Trillion Prize: Captivating the Newly Affluent in China and India*
    (Cambridge, MA: Harvard Business Review Press, 2012), using
    the procedure followed by Thomas Gatley, "Accelerating into

Affluence," *China Economic Quarterly* (March 2013). The $33,000 threshold for "upper affluent" is based on McKinsey research on high-income consumers. The average household size in China is three people, so to convert these figures into per capita numbers one must divide by three. A household with annual income of $13,000 equates to three people, each with a per capita income of $4,333.

12. One issue affecting passenger car sales is that an increasing number of cities are following the lead of Beijing and Shanghai and are tightly restricting the number of license plates they issue in order to curb traffic and air pollution.

13. There are, unfortunately, two very different series for China's household savings rate. The one quoted here comes from the government's quarterly survey of household income and expenditure. The second is in the "flow of funds" statistics, which measure financial movements between economic sectors as part of GDP calculations. This generally shows a savings rate that is about 10 pp higher than the household survey figure, but the trends are roughly the same. On flow of funds data, household savings rose from 27 percent of disposable income in 2002 to 39 percent in 2010 and then drifted down to 36 percent by 2016. Both series have their pluses and minuses. They agree on two key points, however: (1) household saving rose sharply until about 2010 and have very gradually declined since then; and (2) China's household savings are very high by international standards. Most OECD countries have household saving rates of 0–10 percent, and even the high-savings outliers have rates below 20 percent. See Kate Stratford and Arianna Cowling, "Chinese Household Income and Savings," *Reserve Bank of Australia Bulletin* (September 2016): 31–40. For a comparison of Chinese versus OECD household saving rates, see https://data.oecd.org/hha/household-savings.htm.

14. These figures are the 5-year compound average growth rate for real per capita consumer spending in constant dollars, using the World Bank data that generated Figure 12.2.

15. Chong-en Bai and Zhenjie Qian, "Who is the Predator, Who the Prey: An Analysis of Changes in the State of China's National Income Distribution," *Social Sciences in China* 30, no. 4 (November 2009): 179–205.

16. See World Bank/DRC 2014, 198–214, for an excellent discussion of social welfare issues; also Thomas Gatley and Andrew Batson, "China's Welfare State: Mission Accomplished?" Gavekal

Dragonomics research note, March 19, 2013. If one includes the vague category of "urban and rural affairs," total social spending in 2018 was 47 percent of the budget and over 11 percent of GDP. This category includes housing and other subsidies, as well as some infrastructure-related development spending, so it is not really comparable to "social welfare spending" in other countries.

Chapter 13

1. See https://data.oecd.org/inequality/income-inequality.htm.
2. Gini index estimates vary because to calculate income inequality precisely would require knowing the exact income of every person in the country. In practice, Ginis are estimated using income surveys. For a good roundup of private Gini estimates for China, see Yu Xie and Xiang Zhou, "Income Inequality in Today's China," *Proceedings of the National Academy of Sciences*, February 20, 2014, www.pnas.org/cgi/doi/10.1073/pnas.1403158111. For the comparison between China's high inequality and the relatively low inequality of other East Asian countries, see Martin King Whyte, "Soaring Income Gaps: China in Comparative Perspective," *Daedalus* 143, no. 2 (Spring 2014): 39–52. For a critique of the Gini and other measures of inequality, such as the Theil index, see Thomas Piketty, *Capital in the Twenty-First Century* (Cambridge, MA: Harvard University Press, 2014), 266–269.
3. The data in Figures 13.1 and 13.2 come from the Standardized World Income Inequality Database (SWIID), version 8.1, https://dataverse.harvard.edu/dataset.xhtml?persistentId=doi:10.7910/DVN/LM4OWF. Note that China's official Gini coefficient data correspond to the higher, pretransfer figures in the SWIID database. This is an important distortion, since in most other countries Gini coefficients are reported on a post-tax and transfer basis. An earlier effort to look systematically at trends in global income inequality over time is Christoph Lakner and Branko Milanovic, "Global Income Distribution: From the Fall of the Berlin Wall to the Great Recession," World Bank Policy Research Working Paper 6719, December 2013.
4. World Bank/DRC 2014, 16. In 2019, the top 10 percent of the U.S. population controlled 64 percent of the nation's wealth. See Alexandre Tanzi and Michael Sasso, "Richest 1 percent of Americans Close to Surpassing Wealth of Middle Class," *Bloomberg News*, November 9, 2019.

5. Simon Kuznets, "Economic Growth and Income Inequality," *American Economic Review* 45, no. 1 (1955): 1–28, available at https://www.aeaweb.org/aer/top20/45.1.1-28.pdf. Many researchers dispute Kuznets's hypothesis, noting that, over time, survey-based studies of income inequality in many countries fail to support it. Whyte, in "Soaring Income Gaps," exemplifies the skeptics. A detailed defense of Kuznets's basic insight, which I find persuasive, is James K. Galbraith, *Inequality and Instability: A Study of the World Economy Just before the Great Crisis* (Oxford: Oxford University Press, 2012).

6. Andrew Batson and Thomas Gatley, "Inequality Is Improving, Discontent Is Not," Gavekal Dragonomics research note, November 4, 2013.

7. See World Bank/DRC 2014, 105.

8. Andrew Batson, "The Rise of the Middling," Gavekal Dragonomics research note, October 10, 2012.

9. Andrew Batson, "The Equality Engine Is Stalling," Gavekal Dragonomics research note, October 13, 2016.

10. See Barry Naughton, *The Chinese Economy: Adaptation and Growth* (Cambridge, MA: MIT Press, 2007), 384–385.

11. For a vivid picture of official corruption in China's railway industry, see Evan Osnos, "Boss Rail," *The New Yorker*, October 22, 2012, http://www.newyorker.com/magazine/2012/10/22/boss-rail.

12. A well-documented example is the 2007 IPO of Ping An Insurance, which proved immensely profitable to relatives of Premier Wen Jiabao. See David Barboza, "Lobbying, a Windfall, and a Leader's Family," *New York Times*, November 25, 2012. https://www.nytimes.com/2012/11/25/business/chinese-insurers-regulatory-win-benefits-a-leaders-family.html

13. For the China rich list, see http://www.hurun.net/EN/Home/Index. For Wen Jiabao's family wealth, see David Barboza, "Billions Amassed in the Shadows by the Family of China's Premier," *New York Times*, October 26, 2012. For the wealth of Xi Jinping's family and other top leaders, see "Xi Jinping Millionaire Relations Reveal Fortunes of Elite," Bloomberg News, June 29, 2012; and "Heirs of Mao's Comrades Rise as New Capitalist Nobility," Bloomberg News, December 27, 2012. On Zhou Yongkang's wealth, there is no independent confirmation of the vast sums supposedly confiscated by police, and there is an

ancient tradition in China of lurid and probably exaggerated accounts of the financial and sexual misdeeds of disgraced officials. When Zhou was actually tried, he was charged with accepting a mere $118,000 in bribes, and prosecutors alleged his family accumulated assets of $300 million. See http://www.wsj.com/articles/chinas-former-security-chief-zhou-yongkang-sentenced-to-life-in-prison-1434018450.

14. The best expression of this view is Minxin Pei, *China's Crony Capitalism: The Dynamics of Regime Decay* (Cambridge, MA: Harvard University Press, 2016), which expands the argument of his earlier *China's Trapped Transition: The Limits of Developmental Autocracy* (Cambridge, MA: Harvard University Press, 2006).

15. For a colorful account of this scandal, see Oliver August, *Inside the Red Mansion: On the Trail of China's Most Wanted Man* (New York: Houghton Mifflin Harcourt, 2007).

16. A superb discussion of corruption in the reform era, on which I have drawn heavily, is Andrew Wedeman, *Double Paradox: Rapid Growth and Rising Corruption in China* (Ithaca, NY: Cornell University Press, 2012).

17. See Yuen Yuen Ang, "China's Corrupt Meritocracy," Project Syndicate, October 4, 2019, https://www.project-syndicate.org/commentary/china-corrupt-meritocracy-by-yuen-yuen-ang-2019-10.

18. "In order to promote the nation's governance system and modernize governance capacity, achieve the targets of the 'two one-hundred-year' struggles: a "moderately prosperous society" by 2021, the 100th anniversary of the founding of the Chinese Communist Party; and completing China's development as a strong, democratic, civilized, harmonious modern socialist state by 2049, the 100th anniversary of the founding of the People's Republic] and the great rejuvenation of the Chinese people and the China Dream . . . it is necessary to persevere in having the party manage the party strictly, and to deepen the struggle for clean governance and anti-corruption." From "The 2013–2017 Work Plan to Establish a Robust System for Punishing and Preventing Corruption," http://news.xinhuanet.com/politics/2013-12/25/c_118708522.htm (in Chinese). The obscurity of this turgid prose is a good reminder of why deciphering the intentions of the Communist Party leadership remains such a specialized skill, even among Chinese people.

19. Yanmei Xie, "Beyond Anti-Corruption," Gavekal Dragonomics research note, March 20, 2018.

20. Wide discussion of "mass incidents" began in 2006 with the publication data from the Public Security Ministry, which indicated that mass incidents rose from under 20,000 a year in the late 1990s to 87,000 in 2005. Since then, the government has published no systematic data, nor has it offered definitions or breakdowns that would enable analysis of the existing data. For a good review of the problems, see Austin Strange, "Mass Incidents in Central China: Causes, Historical Factors and Implications for the PAP," *The Monitor* 17, no. 2 (Summer 2012), http://web.wm.edu/so/monitor/issues/17-2/3-strange.pdf. A good recent assessment of the issue is "Why Protests Are So Common In China," *The Economist*, October 4, 2018, https://www.economist.com/china/2018/10/04/why-protests-are-so-common-in-china.

21. Martin Whyte and Dong-Kyun Im, "Is the Social Volcano Still Dormant? Trends in Chinese Attitudes toward Inequality," *Social Science Research* 48 (2014): 62–76, http://scholar.harvard.edu/files/martinwhyte/files/pdf_0.pdf. Also, Martin Whyte, *Myth of the Social Volcano* (Stanford, CA: Stanford University Press, 2010). For Pew data, see http://www.pewglobal.org/database. The Pew survey data are actually compiled by Horizon Research, the leading independent polling firm in China.

22. Lakner and Milanovic, "Global Income Distribution."

23. China scores reasonably well on the Asian Development Bank's social protection indicator (SPI), an effort to summarize all spending on social insurance and social welfare in a single index. The two SPI surveys, for 2012 and 2015, both found that China's spending on social protection was higher, relative to GDP, than that in any South or Southeast Asian country, and not far behind that of South Korea, which is a much richer country. It is also worth noting that ADB's estimate for China's total social protection spending in 2015 was $835 billion, several times more than the amount spent on domestic security enforcement. *The Social Protection Indicator: Assessing Results for Asia* (Asian Development Bank, 2016) and *The Social Protection Indicator for Asia: Assessing Progress* (Asian Development Bank, July 2019).

24. Since 2010, China's annual budgeted spending on domestic security at all levels of government has exceeded budgeted

military expenditure. In recent years, the gap has widened, in part because of the intense security crackdown in Xinjiang that culminated in 2018–2019 with the detention of as many as a million ethnic Uighurs in internment camps. In 2018, spending on domestic security was Rmb 1.38 trillion, 22 percent more than official defense spending of Rmb 1.12 trillion. As in the United States, China's total military spending almost certainly exceeds the official military budget by a large margin, so it may not be the case (as some journalistic accounts allege) that domestic security spending exceeds the true national defense budget. See Josh Chin, "China Spends More on Domestic Security as Xi's Powers Grow," *Wall Street Journal*, March 6, 2018. Note that as we showed in Chapter 8, total government spending on "social management," which includes social welfare schemes and local development projects, is about five times the spending on domestic security.

25. Bruce J. Dickson, *The Dictator's Dilemma: The Chinese Communist Party's Strategy for Survival* (New York: Oxford University Press, 2016). Chapters 4–6 contain a wealth of fascinating survey data, including the surprising result that a majority of urban Chinese believe that the country already enjoys a high level of democracy.

Chapter 14

1. There are various estimates for China's capital stock, which can be tricky to calculate given data gaps. The capital stock figures presented in Figure 14.1 come from the IMF Investment and Capital Stock Dataset (www.imf.org/external/np/fad/publicinvestment/data/data122216.xlsx), which has the advantage of presenting internationally comparable capital stock figures over a long time span.

2. This larger estimate of the stimulus is drawn from Victor Shih, "Local Government Debt: Big Rock Candy Mountain," *China Economic Quarterly* (June 2010): 26–32. It represents the total increase in credit over a hypothetical "business-as-usual" scenario. Rmb 11 trillion was about 15 percent of combined 2009–2010 GDP.

3. OECD, *Economic Survey of China 2015*, 26, fig. 12. For the 2017 incremental capital-output ratio, see OECD, *Economic Survey of China, 2019*, 44, fig. 19c. Although the generalization that the productivity of capital in China has declined since the global

crisis is supported by a wealth of evidence, there is substantial disagreement about the severity of the decline and the present level of returns to capital. Given that many private-sector firms in China, both domestic and foreign, continue to generate large profits, a good argument can be made that, despite many problems, return on capital in China is still fairly high. For a more optimistic view, see Ya Tang, Jianguo Xu, and Xun Zhang, "China's Investment and Rate of Return on Capital Revisited," *Journal of Asian Economics* 49 (2017): 12–25.

4. OECD, *Economic Survey of China 2015*, 26, fig. 12.

5. Some commentators in the United States claim that before Xi, China was "converging" (albeit slowly) with Western norms and market practices, and that the distinctive feature of policy under Xi is to shift China to a "nonconvergent" direction. I believe that this exaggerates the extent to which China was "converging" before Xi and does not accurately describe the policy shifts under Xi. See Daniel H. Rosen, "A Post-Engagement US-China Relationship?" https://rhg.com/research/post-engagement-us-china-relationship/ Rhodium Group, January 19, 2018.

6. By party protocol, the first plenary session or plenum of each 5-year party congress session elects the new leadership team. The second, held a few months later, deals with other personnel issues. The third, held about a year after the first, is the traditional venue for the new leadership team to unveil its policy agenda.

7. The name of the program caused some confusion among foreign analysts, since "supply-side reform" was the label applied to the market-friendly, deregulatory policies of Ronald Reagan and Margaret Thatcher in the United States and UK, respectively, in the early 1980s. China's "supply-side" reform had nothing to do with deregulation and marketization. Instead, it was a heavy-handed move by the government to intervene in the market and correct excesses—a state capitalist rather than a market capitalist policy.

8. For a detailed account of the specifics of the supply-side structural reform campaign and of the difficulties and confusions of implementation, see these three articles from Barry Naughton: "Supply-Side Structural Reform: Policy-makers Look for a Way Out," *China Leadership Monitor 49* (Winter 2016); "Two Trains Running: Supply-Side Reform, SOE Reform and the Authoritative Personage," *China Leadership Monitor 50*

(Summer 2016); and "Supply-Side Structural Reform at Mid-year: Compliance, Initiative, and Unintended Consequences," *China Leadership Monitor 51* (Fall 2016).

9. China's credit statistics are messy, and there is no good single public indicator of credit growth. The PBOC series "aggregate financing to the real economy," sometimes referred to as "total social finance" is problematic because it includes equity finance from stock market listings, which is not credit, and misses some shadow credit. The figures here are from the broadest credit measure used by my colleagues at Gavekal Dragonomics, which includes all loans to companies and households (including shadow finance) and local government bond issuance. The growth rates are the year-on-year increase in the total stock of outstanding credit.

10. Examples include Minxin Pei, *China's Trapped Transition* (Cambridge, MA: Harvard University Press, 2006) and Will Hutton, *The Writing on the Wall* (Washington, DC: Free Press, 2006).

11. According to the World Bank's World Development Indicators database, the world average GNI in 2018 was $11,100. At $9,470, China's GNI was still below the world average but will probably exceed it in a few years. Russia's GNI was $10,230.

Chapter 15

1. See U.S. Department of Defense, Base Structure Report, Fiscal Year 2018 Baseline, https://www.acq.osd.mil/eie/Downloads/BSI/Base%20Structure%20Report%20FY18.pdf.

2. In other words, as long as it is properly managed, the large national debt of the United States is a strength, not a weakness. Alexander Hamilton recognized this over two centuries ago when he advocated the creation of a permanent debt in his First Report on the Public Credit in 1790, http://www.milestonedocuments.com/documents/view/alexander-hamiltons-first-report-on-publiccredit/. The unique position of the U.S. dollar was decried by Valéry Giscard d'Estaing, Charles De Gaulle's finance minister, as an "exorbitant privilege." John Connally, President Nixon's treasury secretary, boasted of this privilege when he told his European counterparts that the dollar "is our currency and your problem." For a full explanation of the dollar's role as the global reserve currency, see Barry

Eichengreen, *Exorbitant Privilege: The Rise and Fall of the Dollar and the Future of the International Monetary System* (New York: Oxford University Press, 2011). For a brief summary, see Arthur Kroeber, "Debt, Innovation and the Durable Dollar," *China Economic Quarterly* (December 2008): 50–55.

3. Strictly speaking, the European Union is the world's biggest economic unit. But this technical fact is not of much relevance in discussions of global political and economic power. Economically, despite its formal freedom of flows of labor and capital, the EU remains fragmented among its twenty-eight member economies, which maintain separate governance structures, separate fiscal and financial systems, and, in some cases, currencies other than the euro (not to mention different languages). Politically and militarily, European force projection capacity is severely undermined by this fragmentation, and the geopolitical influence of "Europe" as a whole is arguably less significant than that of its most powerful member state, Germany.

4. In 2014, headline writers jumped on a study by the World Bank reckoning that, adjusting for purchasing power parity (PPP), China's economy was already the biggest in the world. This conclusion ought not to be taken seriously. PPP is a technical tool economists use to account for the different prices of nontradable goods in countries with different labor costs. The classic example is a haircut, which might cost $5 in Shanghai and $30 in New York because labor in China is so much cheaper. Therefore, a Shanghainese with $5 has the same purchasing power, in regard to haircuts, as a New Yorker with $30 (assuming the quality of the two haircut experiences is identical, which can be doubtful). PPP is useful for comparing average living standards across countries with different wage rates. It is useless for comparing the size of whole economies, whose relative importance is determined by their international, not their domestic, purchasing power. Obviously, the Shanghainese who moves to New York with $5 will purchase far fewer haircuts than the New Yorker who moves to Shanghai with $30. For similar reasons, efforts by defense analysts to inflate China's military spending using PPP adjustments are bogus: all these estimates tell you is how much China would spend on its military if it paid its soldiers and officers as much as the U.S. military does. See George J. Gilboy and Eric Heginbotham,

Chinese and Indian Strategic Behavior: Growing Power and Alarm (Cambridge: Cambridge University Press, 2012).

5. For a pessimistic view of China's long-run growth prospects, see Lant Pritchett and Lawrence H. Summers, "Asiaphoria Meets Regression to the Mean," NBER Working Paper 20573, October 2014 (http://www.nber.org/papers/w20573). For a more optimistic prognosis, see Dwight H. Perkins and Thomas G. Rawski, "Forecasting China's Economic Growth to 2025," in Loren Brandt and Thomas G. Rawski (eds.), *China's Great Economic Transformation* (Cambridge: Cambridge University Press, 2008): 829–886; and Dwight Perkins, "Understanding the Slowing Growth Rate of the People's Republic of China," *Asian Development Review* 32, no. 1 (2015): 1–30.

6. The exact connotation of this phrase is subject to dispute. In ordinary use, it can imply either biding one's time or simply taking time to recuperate from a setback. Western defense analysts often assume the former connotation; Chinese scholars generally assign the latter meaning. Given that Deng popularized the phrase at a time when China was poor, weak, and diplomatically isolated, the Chinese interpretation seems more plausible. Zha Daojiong, a professor of international relations at Peking University, says that the phrase means that "a person with a weakened physical situation should not take that as cause for despair." (Personal communication.)

7. "Direct investment" comprises both corporate investments in subsidiaries, infrastructure investment, and so on, and financial investments accounting for at least 10 percent of the target company. "Portfolio investment" refers to holdings of stocks and bonds, below the 10 percent ownership threshold. China's outward direct investments surged in 2015 and 2016 as companies and individuals scrambled to move money offshore ahead of a currency devaluation. Since then, stricter capital controls have made it much harder to move money out of China, even for legitimate purposes. Chinese regulations have long tightly limited the amount of portfolio outflows, a practice that is unlikely to change any time soon. See Rose Cunningham, Eden Hatzvi, and Kun Mo, "The Size and Destination of China's Portfolio Flows," Bank of Canada Discussion Paper 2018-11 (2018).

8. One prominent example was sanctions on South Korean firms in retaliation for Seoul's decision to install a U.S.-supplied

missile defense system in 2017. See Celine Ge, "China's Online Boycott Puts Lotte in Cross Hairs Amid THAAD Row," *South China Morning Post*, March 6, 2017. Sanctions on Lotte were lifted 2 years later. In this case, it is not clear what China gained from this pressure campaign, but it is possible that future South Korean governments will be more reluctant to take actions that offend Beijing. Fear of losing the benefits of the economic relationship with China probably also played a role in Philippines president Rodrigo Duterte's decision in 2016 to ignore an international arbitration panel's finding against China's territorial claims in the South China Sea.

9. See Brad Setser, "President Xi, Still the Deglobalizer in Chief," Council on Foreign Relations, https://www.cfr.org/blog/president-xi-still-deglobalizer-chief, June 25, 2019.

10. "Macroeonomic Developments and Prospects in Low-Income Developing Countries—2018, "IMF policy paper, February 15, 2018, Table 4 (p. 51).

11. Sebastian Horn, Carmen Reinhart, and Christoph Trebesch, "China's Overseas Lending," Kiel Institute for the World Economy Working Paper 2132 (June 2019).

12. The most famous example of this supposed deliberate debt trap was the China-funded Hambantota port in Sri Lanka; see Maria Abi-Habib, "How China Got Sri Lanka to Cough Up a Port," *New York Times*, June 25, 2018. The claim has been debunked by research showing that the Sri Lanka case had more to do with corruption and mismanagement by the Sri Lankan government and that China's normal procedure in cases of defaults is to reschedule the loans, not seize the assets. See Umesh Moramudali, "Is Sri Lanka Really a Victim of China's 'Debt Trap'?" *The Diplomat*, May 14, 2019; Agatha Kratz, Allen Feng, and Logan Wright, "New Data on the 'Debt Trap' Question," Rhodium Group, https://rhg.com/research/new-data-on-the-debt-trap-question/, April 29, 2019; and Roland Rajah, Alexandre Dayant, and Jonathan Prkye, "Ocean of Debt: Belt and Road and Debt Diplomacy in the Pacific," Lowy Institute, October 21, 2019.

13. An egregious example was an offer to bail out a scandal-plagued development fund in Malaysia, 1MDB, in return for lucrative railway and pipeline concessions. Tom Wright and Bradley Hope, "China Offered to Bail Out Troubled Malaysian Fund in Return for Deals," *Wall Street Journal*, January 7, 2019.

14. A detailed analysis of the military–civil fusion program is "Open Arms: Evaluating Global Exposure to China's Defense-Industrial Base," C4ADS.org, October 18, 2019. See also Elsa Kania, "In Military–Civil Fusion, China Is Learning Lessons from the United States and Starting to Innovate," https://thestrategybridge.org/the-bridge/2019/8/27/in-military-civil-fusion-china-is-learning-lessons-from-the-united-states-and-starting-to-innovate, *The Strategy Bridge*, August 27, 2019.

15. See Damien Cave, "Australia's China Challenge," *New York Times*, May 20, 2019.

16. Details of the comparison between China's pre–1980 and post–1980 record, and between China and India, can be found in Gilboy and Heginbotham, *Chinese and Indian Strategic Behavior*. The authors find that total military spending in China (including items outside the formal defense budget) has consistently been lower, as a share of both the government budget and of GDP, than in India (117–119), and that the frequency of use of force in international affairs has been identical for the two countries since 1980 (76–79). Obviously, since China's economy is much larger than India's, its spending is larger in absolute terms. But the claim that China devotes an unusually large proportion of government spending to the military is not borne out by the facts.

17. Lindsey A. O'Rourke, "The U.S. Tried to Change Other Countries' Governments 72 Times during the Cold War," *Washington Post*, December 23, 2016.

18. A landmark was a 2005 speech by then Deputy Secretary of State Robert Zoellick suggesting that China should become a "responsible stakeholder" in the global order: http://www.ncuscr.org/files/2005Gala_RobertZoellick_Whither_China1.pdf.

19. A helpful introduction to China's ambitions in Asia, and the role of infrastructure diplomacy, is Tom Miller, *China's Asian Dream: Empire Building along the New Silk Road* (London: Zed Books, 2017). Details on the lending capacity of the AIIB, New Development Bank, and Silk Road Fund are in Arthur Kroeber, "Financing China's Global Dreams," *China Economic Quarterly* (November 2015): 27–36. Constantly updated information and useful analysis are available via Berlin's Mercator Institute for China Studies, "MERICS Belt and Road Tracker," https://www.merics.org/en/bri-tracker.

20. See Tom Miller, "The Belt and Road Slims Down," Gavekal Dragonomics research note, October 8, 2019.

21. See https://www.statista.com/statistics/780367/global-mobile-handset-profit-share-by-vendor

22. Yuqing Xing, "How the iPhone Widens the US Trade Deficit with China: The Case of the iPhone X," GRIPS Discussion Paper 19–21 (October 2019), National Graduate Institute for Policy Studies, Tokyo. Available at https://voxeu.org/article/how-iphone-widens-us-trade-deficit-china-0.

23. Jonathan Woetzel et al., *China and the World: Inside the Dynamics of a Changing Relationship*, McKinsey Global Institute (July 2019), Exhibit E5, p 11.

24. Scott Kennedy, *The Fat Tech Dragon: Benchmarking China's Innovation Drive*, Center for Strategic and International Studies, August 2017.

25. This point is made forcefully by Kai-fu Lee, *AI Superpowers: China, Silicon Valley and the New World Order* (New York: Houghton Mifflin, 2018). Lee offers a somewhat overoptimistic assessment of China's capabilities in artificial intelligence, but his observations on China's innovation ecosystem and how it compares to that of Silicon Valley deserve to be taken seriously.

26. Woetzel et al., *China and the World*, p. 12.

27. Most favored nation (MFN) status is a somewhat confusing term. It seems to imply the granting of special privileges, but in reality it describes equal treatment for all countries. Under the WTO and its predecessor, the General Agreement on Tariffs and Trade, MFN means that a member country that grants a trade preference (such as a lower tariff) to one country must give the same preference to all other members. Thus, each country in the agreement gets the same treatment as the "most favored nation"—that is, all countries are treated equally. When China was outside the WTO, its ability to continue trading with the United States on normal (MFN) terms was contingent on an annual human rights certification. To clarify that MFN referred to normal trade relations rather than the granting of special favors, the term was dropped in the political debate in favor of "permanent normal trade relations" or PNTR. Once China joined the WTO, it automatically gained reciprocal MFN status with all other member nations. See https://www.investopedia.com/terms/m/mostfavorednation.asp.

28. There is a voluminous debate about whether the constructive
engagement policy "failed," based on the false premise
that it was designed to encourage China's democratization.
The opening salvo was James Mann, *The China Fantasy*
(New York: Viking, 2007), which was prescient in raising the
question of how the West would respond to a China that was
economically much more powerful *and* much more authoritarian.
But like most later critics, Mann vastly oversimplified the aims
of the policy. Two good scholarly treatments of this question
are Alastair Iain Johnston, "The Failures of the 'Failure of
Engagement' with China," *The Washington Quarterly* 42,
no. 2 (Summer 2019): 99–114, and Harry Harding, "Has U.S.
China Policy Failed?" *The Washington Quarterly* 38, no. 3 (Fall
2015): 95–122.

29. Some variant of the "strategic competitor" label was used in
three important strategy documents published in late 2017 and
early 2018: the National Security Strategy (National Security
Council, December 2017, https://www.whitehouse.gov/wp-
content/uploads/2017/12/NSS-Final-12-18-2017-0905.pdf);
the 2018 National Defense Strategy: Sharpening the Military's
Competitive Edge (Department of Defense, January 2018,
https://dod.defense.gov/Portals/1/Documents/pubs/2018-
National-Defense-Strategy-Summary.pdf); and the 2018 Trade
Policy Agenda (United States Trade Representative, January
2018, https://ustr.gov/about-us/policy-offices/press-office/
reports-and-publications/2018/2018-trade-policy-agenda-and-
2017). Note that the general idea was not new: the incoming
George W. Bush administration in 2001 toyed with labeling
China a strategic competitor, only to drop the notion after the
September 11 attacks, when China's cooperation in the "War on
Terror" was considered essential.

30. For the impact of Chinese imports on U.S. manufacturing
production and employment, see David H. Autor, David Dorn,
and Gordon H. Hanson, "The China Syndrome: Local Labor
Market Effects of Import Competition in the United States,"
American Economic Review 103, no. 6 (2013): 2121–2168; as well
as Autor, Dorn and Hanson, "The China Shock: Learning from
Labor Market Adjustment to Large Changes in Trade," NBER
Working Paper 21906 (January 2016); and David H. Autor, "Trade
and Labor Markets: Lessons from China's Rise," IZA World of

Labor (February 2018). For the labor income share, see Michael
W. L. Elsby, Bart Hobin, and Aysegul Sahin, "The Decline of the
U.S. Labor Share," Brookings Papers on Economic Activity, Fall
2013. See also Avraham Ebenstein, Ann Harrison, and Margaret
McMillan, "Why Are American Workers Getting Poorer? China,
Trade and Offshoring," NBER Working Paper 21027, March 2015
(http://www.nber.org/papers/w21027). A careful treatment
of the problems China poses for the WTO is Mark Wu, "The
'China Inc.' Challenge to Global Trade Governance," *Harvard
International Law Journal* (Spring 2016), 57: 261–324.

31. Data from the U.S. Department of Commerce's Bureau of
    Economic Analysis, https://www.bea.gov/data/intl-trade-
    investment/activities-us-multinational-enterprises-mnes.

32. The claim that China's increasingly bellicose attitude requires
    the United States to respond with a modified strategy of
    containment, analogous to its Cold War policy against the
    Soviet Union, is advanced by Robert Blackwill and Ashley
    Tellis, "Revising U.S. Grand Strategy Toward China," Council
    on Foreign Relations Special Report No. 72, March 2015.
    A convincing rebuttal is Jeffrey A. Bader, "Changing China
    Policy: Are We in Search of Enemies?" Brookings Institution, June
    2015. More elaborate statements of these broad positions are,
    respectively, Aaron L. Friedberg, *A Contest for Supremacy: China,
    America and the Struggle for Mastery in Asia* (New York: W.
    W. Norton, 2011); and Thomas J. Christensen, *The China
    Challenge: Shaping the Choices of a Rising Power* (New York: W.
    W. Norton, 2015). A crisp deflation of the argument for a
    new Cold War against China is Fareed Zakaria, "The New
    China Scare: Why America Shouldn't Panic about Its Latest
    Challenger," https://www.foreignaffairs.com/articles/china/
    2019-12-06/new-china-scare?utm_campaign=special-preview-
    120519-china-zakaria-actives&utm_content=20191206&utm_
    medium=promo_email&utm_source=special_send&utm_
    term=all-actives, *Foreign Affairs*, December 6, 2019.

33. See, for instance, Gideon Rachman, *Easternization: Asia's
    Rise and America's Decline from Obama to Trump and Beyond*
    (New York: Other Press, 2017). The most theatrical statement of
    the risk of U.S.–China great power conflict is Graham Allison,
    Destined For War: Can America and China Escape Thucydides's Trap?
    (New York: Houghton Mifflin Harcourt, 2017).

34. Pew Global Attitudes and Trends Survey (2017), https://www.
pewresearch.org/global/2017/07/13/more-name-u-s-than-
china-as-worlds-leading-economic-power. Also Pew (2020),
https://www.pewresearch.org/global/2020/04/21/u-s-views-
of-china-increasingly-negative-amid-coronavirus-outbreak/

35. Helene Cooper, "U.S. Defense Secretary Supports Trade Deal
With Asia," *New York Times*, April 6, 2015.

36. See Austin Ramzy and Chris Buckley, " 'Absolutely No
Mercy': Leaked FilesExpose How China Organized Mass
Detentions of Muslims" *New York Times*, November 16, 2019.

37. See Martin Purbrick, "A Report of the 2019 Hong Kong Protests,"
Asian Affairs, 50, no. 4 (2019): 465–487.

38. The most important of these concerns is the perception that
China is engaged in a large-scale effort to influence public
discourse (both political and academic) in Western nations
through "coercive, covert and corrupt" means. For the most
expansive indictment of Chinese practices in this area, see
*Chinese Influence and American Interests: Promoting Constructive
Vigilance* (Stanford, CA: Hoover Institution, 2018). Note, however,
that this report has been criticized (including a dissent by one of
the report's working group participants, respected China scholar
Susan Shirk) for inflating the actual threat that these influence
activities represent. Shirk, who served in the State Department
in the Clinton White House, offers a useful critique of both Xi
Jinping's more aggressive foreign policy and the U.S. response
to it in "Overreach and Overreaction: The Crisis in US-China
Relations" (podcast; https://cscc.sas.upenn.edu/podcasts/2019/
02/07/ep-9-overreach-and-overreaction-crisis-us-china-relations-
susan-shirk), University of Pennsylvania Center for the Study of
Contemporary China, February 7, 2019.

INDEX

Tables and figures are indicated by *t* and *f* following the page number

For the benefit of digital users, indexed terms that span two pages (e.g., 52–53) may, on occasion, appear on only one of those pages.